Lecture Notes in Computer Science 6537

Commenced Publication in 1973
Founding and Former Series Editors:
Gerhard Goos, Juris Hartmanis, and Jan van Leeuwen

Xiangfeng Luo Yiwei Cao Bo Yang
Jianxun Liu Feiyue Ye (Eds.)

New Horizons in Web-Based Learning - ICWL 2010 Workshops

ICWL 2010 Workshops: STEG, CICW, WGLBWS, and IWKDEWL
Shanghai, China, December 7-11, 2010
Revised Selected Papers

Springer

Volume Editors

Xiangfeng Luo
Shanghai University, E-mail: luoxf@shu.edu.cn

Yiwei Cao
RWTH Aachen University, E-mail:cao@dbis.rwth-aachen.de

Bo Yang
University of Electronic Science and Technology of China, Chengdu
E-mail:boyang.uestc@gmail.com

Jianxun Liu
Hunan University of Science and Technology, E-mail: ljx529@gmail.com

Feiyue Ye
Shanghai University, E-mail: yefy@shu.edu.cn

ISSN 0302-9743 e-ISSN 1611-3349
ISBN 978-3-642-20538-5 ISBN 978-3-642-20539-2 (eBook)
DOI 10.1007/978-3-642-20539-2
Springer Heidelberg Dordrecht London New York

Library of Congress Control Number: 2011925160

CR Subject Classification (1998): H.4, H.3, I.2.6, H.5, K.3, D.2, I.2

LNCS Sublibrary: SL 3 – Information Systems and Application, incl. Internet/Web and HCI

Typesetting: Camera-ready by author, data conversion by Scientific Publishing Services, Chennai, India

Printed on acid-free paper

Springer is part of Springer Science+Business Media (www.springer.com)

Workshop Editors

STEG 2010

Yiwei Cao
RWTH Aachen University, Germany
Ahornstr. 55, 52056, Aachen, Germany
E-mail: cao@dbis.rwth-aachen.de

Dominik Renzel
RWTH Aachen University, Germany
Ahornstr. 55, 52056, Aachen, Germany
E-mail: renzel@dbis.rwth-aachen.de

David Farrell
Glasgow Caledonian University, UK
Cowcaddens Road, Glasgow, G4 0BA, Scotland, UK
E-mail: david.farrell@gcu.ac.uk

Stephan Lukosch
Delft University of Technology, Netherlands
Jaffalaan 5, 2628BX, NL-2600GA, Delft, The Netherlands
E-mail: S.G.Lukosch@tudelft.nl

Emmanuel Stefanakis
Harokopio University of Athens, Greece
70, El.Venizelou Ave, Athens, 17671, Greece
E-mail: estef@hua.gr

CICW 2010

Xiangfeng Luo
Shanghai University, School of Computer Engineering and Science
Xingjian Building, No. 149Yanchang Road, Shanghai 200072, China
E-mail: luoxf@shu.edu.cn

Yingxu Wang
University of Calgary, Schulich School of Engineering
2500 University Drive N.W. Calgary, Alberta Canada T2N 1N4
E-mail: yingxu@ucalgary.ca

Xiao Wei
Shanghai University, School of Computer Engineering and Science
Xingjian Building, No. 149Yanchang Road, Shanghai 200072, China
E-mail: xwei@shu.edu.cn

WGLBWS 2010

Jianxun Liu
Hunan University of Science and Technology, Knowledge Grid Lab
Xiangtan, Hunan 411201, China
E-mail: ljx529@gmail.com

IWKDEWL 2010

Bo Yang
University of Electronic Science and Technology of China, School of Computer Science and Engineering
No. 2006 Xiyuan Avenue, High-Tech Zone (West), Chengdu 611731, China
E-mail: boyang.uestc@gmail.com

Lixin Jia
Xi'an Jiaotong University, School of Electrical Engineering
No.28 Xian Ning West Road, Xi'an Shaanxi 710049, China
E-mail: lxjia@mail.xjtu.edu.cn

Xinzheng Niu
University of Electronic Science and Technology of China, School of Computer Science and Engineering
No. 2006 Xiyuan Avenue, High-Tech Zone (West), Chengdu 611731, China
E-mail: xinzhengniu@126.com

Tao Li
Florida International University, USA
ECS 318, 11200 SW 8th Street, Miami, FL 33199, U.S.A.
E-mail: taoli@cs.fiu.edu

Preface to ICWL 2010 Workshops

Welcome to the proceedings of the workshops associated with ICWL 2010. ICWL is an annual international conference series on Web-based learning that has so far been held in Asia, Europe and Australia. As always, the aim of the workshops was to give researchers and participants a forum to discuss cutting-edge research in Web-based learning and to examine some of the challenges that arise when applying Web-based learning in less traditional areas. The workshops provided an intensive collaborative forum for exchanging late-breaking ideas and theories in an evolutionary stage.

This year, STEG, CICW, WGLBWS, and IWKDEWL were selected competitively from a call for workshop proposals. STEG is the international workshop on Story-Telling and Educational Games, CICW is the international workshop on Cognitive-Based Interactive Computing and Web Wisdom, WGLBWS is the international workshop on WebGIS and Location-Based Web Service, and IWKDEWL is the international workshop on Knowledge and Data Engineering in Web-Based Learning.

We would like to thank the Workshop Chairs and their Program Committees for their diligence in selecting the papers in this volume. We would also like to thank the main ICWL 2010 conference committees, particularly the Conference Co-chairs, Qing Li, Wolfgang Nejdl and Wu Zhang, the conference Program Co-chairs, Marc Spaniol and Lizhe Wang, the Webmaster, Haoran Xie, the Finance Co-chairs, Howard Leung, Shunxiang Zhang, and the Registration Co-chairs, Jiying Wang, Xiaobo Yin, for their support in putting the program and proceedings together.

December 2010

Xiangfeng Luo
Yiwei Cao
Bo Yang
Jianxun Liu
Feiyue Ye

ICWL 2010 Workshops Organization

General Co-chairs

Xiangfeng Luo	Shanghai University, China
Yiwei Cao	RWTH Aachen University, Germany
Bo Yang	University of Electronic Science and Technology of China, China
Jianxun Liu	Hunan University of Science and Technology, China
Feiyue Ye	Shanghai University, China

STEG 2010 Workshop Chairs

Yiwei Cao	RWTH Aachen University, Germany
Dominik Renzel	RWTH Aachen University, Germany
David Farrell	Glasgow Caledonian University, UK
Stephan Lukosch	Delft University of Technology, The Netherlands
Emmanuel Stefanakis	Harokopio University of Athens, Greece

STEG 2010 Program Committee

Alev Elci	Eastern Mediterranean University, Magusa, North Cyprus
Amanda Gower	British Telecommunications plc, UK
Anna Hannemann	RWTH Aachen University, Germany
Bailing Zhang	Victoria University, Australia
Baltasar Fernández Manjón	Complutense University of Madrid, Spain
Carlos Delgado Kloos	Carlos III University, Spain
Carsten Ullrich	Shanghai Jiaotong University, China
Christian Guetl	IICM, Graz University of Technology, Austria
Cord Hockemeyer	University of Graz, Austria
Eeva Nygren	University of Eastern Finland, Finland
Georg Thallinger	Joanneum Research, Graz, Austria
Harald Kosch	University of Passau, Germany
Helen Ashman	University of South Australia, Australia
Jose Luis Sierra	Complutense University of Madrid, Spain
Manuel Fradinho	Cyntelix, Ireland
Marc Spaniol	MPI, Saarbruecken, Germany
Mathias Lux	Klagenfurt University, Austria

Michael Granitzer	Know Center, Graz, Austria
Michael Hausenblas	DERI, National University of Ireland, Ireland
Michael D. Kickmeier-Rust	University of Graz, Austria
Nalin Sharda	Victoria University, Australia
Pablo Moreno-Ger	Complutense University of Madrid, Spain
Ralf Klamma	RWTH Aachen University, Germany
Romulus Grigoras	ENSEEIHT, France
Ronan Champagnat	La Rochelle University, France
Stamatia Dasiopoulou	ITI Thessaloniki, Greece
Stefan Göbel	TU Darmstadt, Germany
Vincent Charvillat	ENSEEIHT, France
Werner Bailer	Joanneum Research, Graz, Austria
Wolfgang Gräther	Fraunhofer FIT, St. Augustin, Germany

CICW 2010 Workshop Chairs

Xiangfeng Luo	Shanghai University, China
Yingxu Wang	University of Calgary, Canada
Xiao Wei	Shanghai University, China

CICW 2010 Program Committee

Farhad Arbab	Leiden University, The Netherlands
Feiyue Ye	Shanghai University, China
Jan van Leeuwen	Universiteit Utrecht, The Netherlands
Lizhe Wang	Indiana University, USA
Ronald R. Yager	Iona College, USA
Stephane Bressan	National University of Singapore, Singapore
Styliani K. Loizo	University of Leeds, UK
Wanchun Dou	Nanjing University, China
Wolfgang Nejdl	University of Hannover, Germany
Wu Zhang	Shanghai University, China
Xiangfeng Luo	Shanghai University, China
Xiao Wei	Shanghai University, China
Yingxu Wang	University of Calgary, Canada
Yiwei Cao	RWTH Aachen University, Germany

WGLBWS 2010 Workshop Chair

Jianxun Liu	Hunan University of Science and Technology, China

WGLBWS 2010 Program Committee

Shah Asaduzzaman	Carleton University, Canada
Jian Cao	Shanghai Jiao Tong University, China
Tao Hu	Hainan University, China
Jin Liu	Wuhan University, China
Jian Lin	Hunan University of Science and Technology, China
Tianming Liu	Georgia University, USA
Xitong Li	Massachusetts Institute of Technology, USA
Xiangfeng Luo	Shanghai University, China
Chunjie Zhou	Ren Ming University of China, China

IWKDEWL 2010 Workshop Chairs

Bo Yang	University of Electronic Science and Technology of China, China
Lixin Jia	Xi'an Jiaotong University, China
Xinzheng Niu	University of Electronic Science and Technology of China, China
Tao Li	Florida International University, USA

IWKDEWL 2010 General Chair

Bo Yang	University of Electronic Science and Technology of China, China

IWKDEWL 2010 Program Chairs

Lixin Jia	Xi'an Jiaotong University, China
Xinzheng Niu	University of Electronic Science and Technology of China, China
Tao Li	Florida International University, USA

IWKDEWL 2010 Program Vice Chairs

Bo Xu	University of Illinois at Chicago, USA
Reynold C.K. Cheng	The University of Hong Kong, China
Jin Liu	Wuhan University, China

IWKDEWL 2010 Steering Chairs

Philip S. Yu	University of Illinois at Chicago, USA
Peter Scheuermann	Northwestern University, USA
Ling Feng	Tsinghua University, China

IWKDEWL 2010 Program Committee

Gansen Zhao	South China Normal University, China
Gangquan Si	Xi'an Jiaotong University, China
Hui Cao	Xi'an Jiaotong University, China
Jing Zhou	Communication University of China, China
Liang Chang	Guilin University of Electronic Technology, China
Mingsheng Shang	University of Electronic Science and Technology of China, China
Ouri Wolfson	University of Illinois at Chicago, USA
Puwei Wang	Renmin University of China, China
Qingpei Hu	Chinese Academy of Sciences, China
Xiaojun Wu	Northwestern Polytechnical University, China
Yutao Ma	Wuhan University, China
Yunchuan Sun	Beijing Normal University, China
Zheng Wang	Southwestern University of Finance and Economics, China

STEG 2010 Workshop Chair's Message

The Third International Workshop on Story-Telling and Educational Games (STEG 2010) comprised a series of workshops to extend new horizons for Web-based and technology-enhanced learning. Since the first STEG workshop in 2008, this series of workshops have raised great interest of researcher communities with two workshop proceedings of STEG'08 and STEG'09.

Stories and story-telling are cultural achievements of significant relevance even in modern times. Nowadays, story-telling is being enhanced with the convergence of sociology, pedagogy, and technology. Computer gaming is also deployed for educational purposes and has proved to be an effective approach to mental stimulation and intelligence development. Many conceptual similarities and some procedural correlations exist between story-telling and educational gaming. Stories cover the instructional part of an educational game, while the game adds the motivation and engagement part. Therefore, these two areas can be clubbed for research on technology-enhanced learning (TEL). Many facets of story-telling and educational gaming emulate real-life processes.

STEG 2010 aimed at bringing together researchers, experts and practitioners from the domains of non-linear digital interactive story-telling and educational gaming to share ideas and knowledge. The celebration of this workshop allowed the participants to discover and leverage potential synergies and explore new research challenges.

We would like to thank to all STEG Program Committee members especially those who were involved in the paper reviewing to guarantee a high scientific quality of the workshop papers. They are Werner Bailer, Michael D. Kickmeier-Rust, Carlos Delgado Kloos, Baltasar Fernandez-Manjon, Wolfgang Graether, Christian Guetl, Stefan Goebel, Harald Kosch, Mark Kroell, Mathias Lux, Pablo Moreno-Ger, Eeva Nygren, Marc Spaniol, and Carsten Ullrich. Special thanks also go to Ralf Klamma, who came up with this idea firstly and initiated this series of workshops.

December 2010

Yiwei Cao
Dominik Renzel
David Farrell
Stephan Lukosch
Emmanuel Stefanakis

CICW 2010 Workshop Chair's Message

CICW 2010 was the First International Workshop on Cognitive-Based Interactive Computing and Web Wisdom. Recently, many new theories and technologies for Web wisdom have made the Web much wiser. Among these technologies, cognitive-based interactive computing is one of the newest directions of Web wisdom and should be paid more attention to. Interaction is more effective than algorithms in dealing with the mass Web resources and providing better services, because interactive computing (IC) promotes the understanding and knowledge fusion between humans and the Web. Cognitive informatics (CI) is an emerging discipline that studies the natural intelligence and internal information-processing mechanisms of the brain, as well as the processes involved in perception and cognition. Thus, cognitive-based interactive computing takes advantage of interactive theory and cognitive theory and promotes WI to a great extent.

CICW 2010 was held in conjunction with the 9th International Conference on Web-Based Learning (ICWL 2010) in Shanghai in December 2010. The conference attracted 31 submissions from eight countries and regions and each submission was reviewed by three reviewers rigorously. Taking into consideration the review scores and comments, the Organizing Committee selected 11 papers out of 31 papers to be presented at CICW 2010. After the conference, the authors were asked to revise their paper according to the discussions.

We would like to thank the members of the Organizing Committee and all reviewers for their hard work. Finally, we would like to thank all the authors who submitted their research work to this workshop. We also look forward to seeing you at CICW 2011.

December 2010

Xiangfeng Luo
Yingxu Wang
Xiao Wei

WGLBWS 2010 Workshop Chair's Message

WGLBWS is the International Workshop on WebGIS and Location-Based Web Service. With the development of the Internet and mobile communication, WebGIS and location based service (LBS) have become a vibrant and rapidly evolving application area. Location-based services are often used via Web browsers and are in this case considered as a particular type of Web services. WebGIS can also be constructed via Web services. These represent a novel challenge for WebGIS and LBS.

This year, WGLBWS 2010 provided a forum for researchers, practitioners and developers from different background areas such as service computing, cloud computing and GIS to exchange their latest experiences, research ideas and synergic research and development on fundamental issues and applications on WebGIS and LBS in service and cloud computing environments. The workshop solicited high-quality research results in all related areas.

WGLBWS 2010 was held in conjunction with the 9th International Conference on Web-Based Learning (ICWL 2010) in Shanghai in December 2010. We would like to thank the members of the WGLBWS 2010 Organizing Committee and all reviewers for their hard work. Finally, we would like to thank all the authors who submitted their research work to this workshop.

December 2010 Jianxun Liu

IWKDEWL 2010 Workshop Chair's Message

Welcome to the proceedings of the 2010 International Workshop on Knowledge and Data Engineering in Web-Based Learning (IWKDEWL 2010). As computer systems become increasingly large and complex, we are seeing more sophisticated techniques being developed to support e-learning especially in the area of knowledge and data engineering. The rapid development of Web-based learning and new concepts such as virtual classrooms, virtual laboratories and virtual universities introduces many new challenging issues to be addressed. This conference aims at providing an in-depth study of the technical, pedagogical as well as management issues of Web-based learning. On the technical side, we need to develop effective e-technologies for supporting distance education. On the learning and management side, we need to consider issues such as new styles of learning and different system set-up requirements. Finally, the issue of standardization of e-learning systems should also be considered.

Held jointly with ICWL 2010, in Shanghai, China, this workshop attracted submission from the entire world. Although the total number is small, a rigorous review process included an average three reviews per paper. Taking into consideration the review scores and reviewer comments, the Organizing Committee selected 10 out of many papers to appear at IWKDEWL 2010. Authors of accepted papers are from China, USA, Italy, Korea, among other areas.

We thank the members of the IWKDEWL 2010 Organizing Committee, the Steering Committee and all reviewers for their hard work. Without it, this workshop would not be possible. Finally, we would like to thank all the authors who submitted their research work to this workshop.

December 2010

Bo Yang
Lixin Jia
Xinzheng Niu
Tao Li

Table of Contents

2010 International Workshop on Story-Telling and Educational Games

2010 International Workshop on Cognitive-Based Interactive Computing and Web Wisdom

2010 International Workshop on WebGIS and Location Based Web Service

2010 International Workshop on Knowledge and Data Engineering in Web-Based Learning

Educational Game Design for Teaching Chinese as a Foreign Language by Effective Learning Environment, Flow, Motivation

Yi Zhang, Liming Shan, and Shixiang Li

Department of Information Technology,
Huazhong Normal University, Wuhan, China
zhangyi@mail.ccnu.edu.cn,
shanliming29@126.com

Abstract. With the rapid development of the online games, the educational game has been demonstrated as a potential learning tool which can enhance learning motives [1]. Now the educational game represents a new interesting development in the field of education. In this paper, we first introduce the effective learning environment, flow, motivation (EFM) model which is a user-centered game design model, and then design the educational game for teaching Chinese as a foreign language based the EFM model's idea. This educational game creates engaging and immersive learning experience for delivering learning outcomes, it attempts to provide a new study way and new study experience to the foreigners.

Keywords: effective learning environment, flow, motivation, educational game, design.

1 Introduction

Educational game in China started comparatively late compared to foreign counties. Since 1990s, with the rapid development of computer technology, the theory and practice also advances quickly. Now most of the educational games which only add educational contents to the games can't improve the learners' interest and help learner's learning outcomes, because the educational games can't combine interesting and educational reasonably.

As China's global influence expanded, more and more people are learning Chinese, so there is unfolding a vigorous mass campaign for learning Chinese. However, according to the articles and teachers, the traditional teaching pattern and teaching resources didn't unable to satisfy with the growing trend of learning Chinese. In order to solve the difficulties of studying Chinese and to provide new teaching resources, the author conducted a survey in the foreigners who are studying Chinese in International Cultural Exchange School of Huazhong Normal University. Based on the result of the survey and the EFM model, we designed this educational game for teaching Chinese as a foreign language.

X. Luo et al. (Eds.): ICWL 2010 Workshops, LNCS 6537, pp. 1–10, 2011.

2 EFM: A Model for Educational Game Design

EFM stands for an effective learning environment, flow and motivation, EFM educational game design model as shown in Fig. 1.

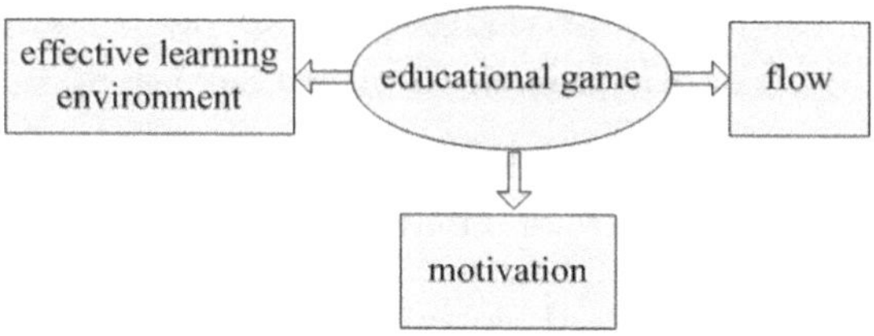

Fig. 1. EFM model

2.1 Correlation Theory of EFM

EFM educational game design model has the following three related theories [2].

Supporting conditions which can promote the learners' development integrates learning environment [3]. Learning environment creates the appropriate situation which propose is to promote learner's learning and self-competence for the learners. Norman identifies seven basic requirements of a learning environment [4]. An effective learning environment has seven prerequisites, as follows: (1) provide highly interaction and feedback; (2) with a specific goal and scheduled program; (3) has incentive mechanism; (4) provide continuous challenges; (5) provide direct participation;(6) provide appropriate tools for users; (7) not destruct subjective experience.

Psychologist Mihaly Csikszentmihalyi's (1990) famous investigation of 'optimal experience' has revealed that what makes an experience genuinely satisfying is a state of consciousness called **flow** [5]. Flow Theory describes a state where the subject experiences a perfect balance between challenge and ability. During flow, people typically experience deep enjoyment, creativity, and a total involvement with life. Producing flow experience need nine conditions:(1) clear objectives; (2) instant feedback to action; (3) balance of skills and challenges; (4) combine action and consciousness; (5) concentrate what you are doing; (6) not worry about failure; (7) self-consciousness evaporates; (8) distort the sense of time; (9) experience.

In traditional instructional design practice, motivation is often considered as a preliminary step in the instructional process (Chan & Ahern, 1999). Learning motivation is the internal cause which can promote students' learning activities and is also a driving force that can stimulate and guide students. Learning motivation can maintain learning activities and help the students achieve the learning objectives finally. John Keller synthesized existing research on psychological motivation and created the ARCS model of Motivational Design [6]. The ARCS Model identifies four components for motivating instruction: attention strategies, relevance strategies, confidence strategies, and satisfaction strategies (Keller, 1983).

2.2 Analyze EFM Model

Educational game has been recognized as an engaging and effective pedagogical tool and represent an interesting development in the field of education [5], it can provide game environment with learning content for the player. Players participate in the educational game's action and then get feedback from the interaction. Under the incentive mechanism, players create the motivation to continue to play the game. Clear objectives and tasks, the appropriate challenges, then high interaction and feedback are the usual elements in an effective learning environment. These elements are just consistent with the factors that produced by the flow. The effective learning environment is the foundation of flow, only in an effective learning environment, players can produce flow experience.

The four basic elements of ARCS relate to the target, challenge, feedback and interest. However, flow state includes the four basic elements of learning motivation. When players reached the flow experience, they can study in the game process driven by the internal motivation. After all, flow experience may help the players to improve the game motivation. Improving the game motivation allows the players to immerse in learning environment which provided by educational game, finally, it can improve their study efficiency through educational games.

In conclusion, we explained the relationship between EFM model theory and educational game as Fig. 2. .

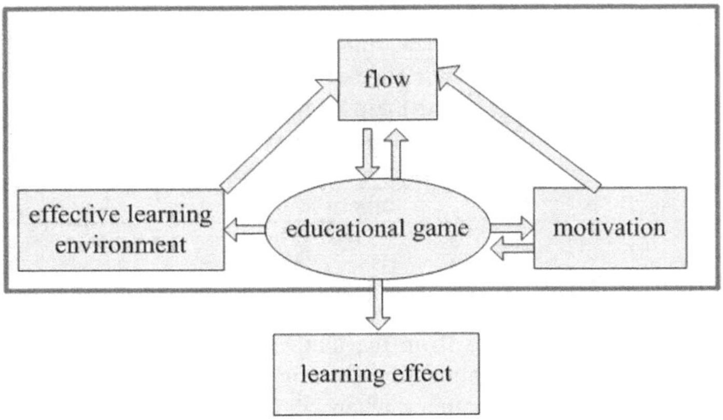

Fig. 2. EFM model and learning effect

3 Design Educational Game for Teaching Chinese as a Foreign Language

Based on the result of the survey, and by using EFM game design model, the author designed and developed the educational game for teaching Chinese as a foreign language from the game environment, game tasks and game motivation. This educational game designed by foreigners' cognitive styles and learning styles, the players said the educational game made them feel the profound traditional Chinese culture and experience China's increasingly powerful cultural strength.

3.1 Design an Effective Learning Environment

The educational game reflects its effective game environment through its realistic game scenarios, moving story and appropriate sound effects. According to the results of the sample survey, as table 1 shows, finding the option that natural sceneries and historical relics as game scenes owing on the ratio has accounted for over 27%, the option that use a certain identity of tourists visiting the places of interest in China as the main line has a high proportion. Therefore, the author chose Beijing's traditional culture as the game theme and Alice who was an American girl hunted for treasures as the game plot to develop the educational game.

Table 1. The results of sample surrey on the game scenario and game plot

Title	Option	Percent
game scene	to show an intense flavor of traditional Chinese culture with ancient Chinese society in the background	21.7
	to show China's modern charm with modern Chinese society in the background	18.5
	natural sceneries and historical relics as game scenarios	27.2
	the daily life of the Chinese people as background	19.6
	others	5.4
game plot	the life experience of a historical figure as the main line	20.7
	a certain identity of a tourist to visit the places of interest in China as the main line	28.3
	a Chinese lovers' experience of the daily life in China as the main line	25.0
	a certain identity of a researcher to study Chinese civilization as the main line	13.0
	others	4.3

3.1.1 Design Game Scene

Scene is the place where the player can reach in the game, and can support flow and enable learning [7]. Game scenes form the clothes of the game environments which have great potential to support immersive learning experiences. A scene in the game can show the place and environment where the player is at, market the player's geographical location, and can also create an appropriate atmosphere.

This educational game chose Beijing's traditional culture as a subject, so the game scenes fully reflect Beijing's cultural characteristics. There are some aerial views of traditional architecture, game scene walking scene different. The distance, size, density and movement of the object are properly handled in the game scene. Magnificent buildings and tiny little things are natural and harmonious, such as the majestic ancient tower and the letters of the shops' banner. Realistic game scenes vividly demonstrate the Chinese glorious culture and folk culture.

In the scene, players can see the traditional wine shops and teahouses, traditional folk houses and markets (Fig. 3.) which full of past breath of life. In the game, players can enjoy Beijing snacks, visit the streets and housing which full with traditional

Fig. 3. A street market

Fig. 4. The living room

cultural flavor. For example, players can see light blue tiles, grey walls, green plants and a red gate, which are typical images of a Beijing quadrangle. In the living room (Fig. 4.), there were dark red carpets, Chinese calligraphy and paintings.

3.1.2 Design Game Plot

This educational game is a RPG game which biggest feature is to have an attractive story. Moving story is one of the main reasons to attract players to play the game, it can stimulate the player's imagination and natural curiosity. According to questionnaires and interviews, the author designed an interesting story. In order to satisfy dying grandmother's wish, Alice alone took the jade to come to China looking for the ancestral Dragon-shaped box. Unfortunately, Alice encountered a bandit who wanted to rob the money. At this moment, Zixuan who is a Chinese student helped Alice get rid of the bandits and they became friends. Then, Zixuan assisted Alice to find the clue of the jade in Beijing Hutongs. During hunting treasure, they travelled to places of historic interest and felt the profound Chinese traditional culture. In the end, they overcame the difficulties and succeeded in finding the ancestral Dragon-shaped box.

3.1.3 Design Sound Effects

The game scene and sound are the external manifestations of the game design, just as the clothes of a game. As a successful game, the reasonable sound is a crucial factor. To make players more prone to immersion, the author changed the sound timely according to the specific circumstances and the course of the story. Therefore, the music and the story are tightly together with player's psychology. In that playing environment, learners can be fully immersed in the game.

* **background music**

This educational game aims at helping foreigners with Chinese, the story takes place in Beijing, so the background music uses the sound of traditional Chinese zither and clarinet which have bright and cheerful tone; In the appropriate scene, there will appear the crisp sound of birds. The beautiful tone with the ancient Chinese traditional architecture brings the visual and auditory pleasure feeling to players.

In the fight scenes, we use the sound of knives and swords which can give a real fight scene feel. When the players hear the sound, they create a feel that they are in the fight scenes. For example, when Zixuan were fighting with the robbers there were true voice of the knives and swords. Moreover, the sound is short and sharp which can bring players a tense atmosphere.

In the end of the game, when Alice left China, she was reluctant to say goodbye to Zixuan. At that moment, a sad music which increases the sorrow atmosphere sounded. The background music only consistent with the story brings the player immersion that is the experience of becoming engaged in the game-playing.

* **dubbing**

Richard E. Mayer proposed the principles of multimedia design including personalization principle and voice principle. In his opinion, students may learn better when the language present as a dialogue style and standard accent of the people rather then informal reading style and machines' voice. According to Mayer's principles, taking into account the game's dubbing to meet the roles' characteristic, we recorded different voices for the roles and then used the software Audition edited, so it could make easy for players to immerse in the game.

For example, when the dying grandmother asked Alice to accomplish her last wishes, firstly appeared a hasty cough, then the grandmother's faint voice; When Alice encountered the robbers on the road, the robber's voice is fierce and cruel; In Quanjude Roast Duck Restaurant, the waiter's voice was humorous and cheerful; In the part of learning knowledge, we used the standard Putonghua which could help the players learn Chinese more easier.

3.2 Design Game Task

Both effective learning environment and the flow experience included the clear objectives, namely learning task. In educational game, game tasks mostly reflect the learning tasks. Therefore, in order to make the player immerse in the game and generate flow experience, we must set clear game tasks.

Designing the learning tasks in educational game is the core factor of the RPG game design, because it reflects the game's learning goals and carries the learning content. When players play games, they must constantly finish the task on time and upgrade their equipment. After that they can grow and become strong. The process of completing the task is also a process of acquiring knowledge, a process to reach the intended teaching goal. In that process, players get both situational and emotional experience.

3.2.1 Difficulty Levels of the Game Task

Designing game task is the soul of the educational game. Defining the difficulty levels of the game task is a very difficult problem. This is because a game with challenge and competition among the gamers can motivate and involve them in playing games. If the game task is too simple, the players will be lack of challenges, and it will reduce the players' interest; If too difficult, it will let players lose confidence and hope. Therefore, the author considered the players' characteristics, then according to Lev Vygotsky's zone of proximal development, designed the game tasks. We designed different levels of game tasks for players, the challenges in the game is slightly higher than the players' skill levels, so the player can make an effort to complete the game tasks. We arrange the game tasks form easy to hard, and this is compatible with cognitive learning theory. The simple game tasks examine players' common sense, such as China's four great inventions, four Treasures of the study; the difficult game tasks are asked the player to distinguish the meaning of the words.

3.2.2 Types of the Game Task

According to the teaching objectives and teaching contents, we set the game tasks in detail. The game tasks are divided into two types, one is answering questions, the other is finishing tasks provided by the game system.

* **The game tasks of answering questions**

In the game, we set up different issues according to the game story and scenes. These issues with related to knowledge are asked the learners to master. For example, we set two levels of problems in Quanjude Roast Duck Restaurant.

Q1: Is Quanjude Roast Duck Restaurant the most famous duck restaurant?

A: Yes, it is.   B: No, it isn't.

Q2: deposit & accumulate

The classical fragrant and elegance raise its remote taste in the () of culture.

The purpose of education is not just () information.

A: deposition, accumulating   B: accumulating, deposition

The first question is simple, but the second one is a little difficult. The second question may help the player distinguish the words between deposit and accumulate.

* **The tasks provided by the game system**

In the course of the game, the system provided appropriate tasks for the players on the basis of the game progresses. For instance, in a restaurant, the boss would ask the player to serve his guest because of so many guests. The player could choose to send food to the guest or not send. When the player passed the school, the teacher would ask him to buy the four treasures of study. If the player accepted the challenge, he could go to Beijing Liulichang Culture Street which is a traditional Chinese street to buy the things. In Beijing Liulichang Culture Street, the player could experience the traditional atmosphere and understand the history of the four treasures of study.

3.3 Design Game Motivation

In the EFM model, learning motivation and an effective learning environment are closely related to flow experience. Learning motivation directly impacts on the production of flow experience. Conversely, the flow experience also affects the player's learning motivation and learning effect. To improve the player's motivation on the game, the author takes the following measures according to Keller's ARCS model.

3.3.1 Attract the Attention of the Player and Inspire the Player's the Game Motivation

In order to attract the attention of the player, the game has realistic game scenes. For example, in Beijing Liulichang Culture Street, the player can see the typical Beijing quadrangle, the tailor shop, the old pawnshop, and the teahouse and so on. In the traditional house, there are Chinese traditional lanterns hanging on the eaves and the Chinese knot on the wall; In the market, there are all kinds of Beijing snacks and a fortuneteller and oil-paper umbrellas; In the shop door, the banner is flying in the wind; In the tailor shop, there is the Chinese dress which is a typical example of Chinese costume culture and an exotic flower of world costume industry. Such vivid and ultra-realistic scenes are very easy to attract the player's attention and stimulate his game motivation. It is easy for the player to understand the profound Chinese culture and help the player construct knowledge. This educational game creates real learning situations for the player which is consistent with constructive teaching.

3.3.2 Make Connections and Enhance the Player's Game Interest

In the game design, we should make connections between knowledge and task, with the purpose of attracting the player's attention. In this game, the task which the player should complete is closely related to the story plot and the learning content, and is also related to the game scenes. If the game task is not relevant to the story and the learning content, it will reduce the player's game interest and motivation. For example, when the player goes through the school, the teacher would ask him to buy the four treasures of study not to send food to the guest.

Game task related to the teaching objective can strength the game interest and motivation, and player can immerse in the game environment which is closer to real life and deal with life-like role.

3.3.3 Timely Feedback and Appropriate Incentive

Timely feedback is one of the vital conditions that produced flow. The player can immediately know his learning effect through the timely feedback of game system. Using the formative evaluation can keep the player have a deep interest in studying Chinese. The player can know which knowledge he didn't master through the feedback, but also see his success which can enhance the confidence to keep playing game. There is a positive feedback and negative feedback in the game. The positive feedback is given reward to the player when he correctly answered the question or finished the task; the negative feedback is given the prompt and encouragement, sometimes punishment. In our game, in order to enhance the player's game motivation, the negative feedback does not provide punishment just gives prompts to help the player complete the task; the system will give timely feedback according to the player's answer and action. If the player answered the question correctly, the game system will tell him 'Congratulations, your answer is correct! ', then he will get the money, goods and experience as a reward (Fig. 5.). If the player gave the wrong answer, then he will get the prompt that 'Sorry, your answer is not correct! ', sometimes will get the right answer. For example, about usual food serving order, the player should answer when to serve soup. If the player chose soup first, he will get the prompt (Fig. 6.).

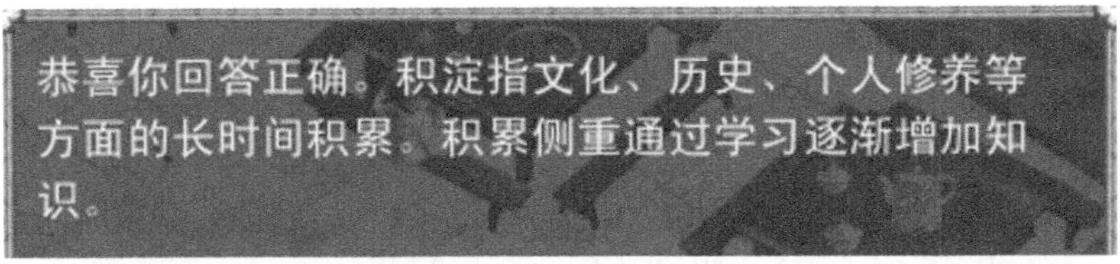

Fig. 5. The positive feedback

Fig. 6. The prompt about the wrong answer

Getting a reward makes the player feel good and can stimulate his motivation to keep playing games and immersing in the game. In summary, the player completes the learning task in an effective environment and then gets a reward which can enhance the learning motivation; Enhancing learning motivation makes the player easy to immerse in the game.

4 Conclusions

Based on Edgar Dale's Cone of Experience, teaching should be started with concrete experience then gradually transform to abstract experience [8]. In the educational game teaching Chinese as a foreign language, there are vivid scenes which help the player construct knowledge. The realistic scenes create an effective learning environment where the player can feel the profound Beijing traditional culture which may let the player immerse in the game; Immersing in the game can stimulate and enhance the player's learning motivation, finally can facilitate the learning in a degree.

Now this educational game has been developed, then we will modify it based on the trial using. We hope it can be used as a Chinese learning tool effectively.

Acknowledgement

This paper is one research result of the research project ***Educational Game Design and Development for Teaching Chinese as a Foreign Language by EDR*** (Project Number 09YJA740043) which conducted by the Ministry of Education in China, is also one of the research results of the research project ***Educational Game Software about Politics and Theory Course in Universities Research and Application by EDR*** (Project Number CCNU09A04020) that conducted by Independence Research Project of Huazhong Normal University .

References

1. Ke, F.: A qualitative meta-analysis of computer games as learning tools. In: Ferdig, R.E. (ed.) Handbook of Research on Effective Electronic Gaming in Education, vol. 1. Information Science Reference, Hershey (2009)
2. Song, M., Zhang, S.: EFM: A Model for Educational Game Design. In: Proceedings of the 3rd international Conference on Technologies for E-learning and Digital Enterainment (2008)
3. Bransford, J., Brown, A., Cocking, R. (eds.): How people learn: Brain, mind, experience, and school, Washington, DC (2000)
4. Houser, R., Deloach, S.: Learning from Games Seven principles of Effective Design. Technical Communication 45(3), 319–329 (1998)
5. Csikszenmaihalyi, M.: CREATIVITY.: Flow and the psychology of discovery and invention. Harperennial, New York (1997)
6. The ARCS model, `http://www.e-learningguru.com/articles/art3_5.htm`
7. Paras, B.S., Bizzocchi, J.: Game, Motivation, and Effective Learning: An Integrated Model for Educational Game Design. In: DiGRA 2005 Conference: Changing Views–Worlds in Play (2005)
8. The Cone of Experience, `http://web.utk.edu/~mccay/apdm/selusing/selusing_d.htm`

A Narrative Architecture for Story-Driven Location-Based Mobile Games

Katsiaryna Naliuka, Tara Carrigy, Natasa Paterson, and Mads Haahr

School of Computer Science and Statistics,
Trinity College Dublin, Ireland

Abstract. Dramatic improvements in smartphones over the last few years have positioned them as a major platform for interactive media content. In addition to being much more portable than laptop computers, smartphones also support a sophisticated combination of GPS, sensors and communications interfaces that allow extracting context information related to their environment, such as location, orientation and weather data. This combination of mobility and context-sensitivity opens up interesting possibilities in relation to interactive narrative, and for example allows audience immersion into an interactive story to be improved by placing the content in physical locations that are of direct relevance to the story. In this paper, we present a general-purpose narrative architecture that allows a considerable range of story-based game and guide content to be expressed in location-aware manner. We also present a case study of an actual location-aware augmented reality game, which demonstrates the architecture in a commercial setting and shows that it is sufficiently lightweight to run on the current generation of smartphones.

Keywords: Narrative Architecture, Mobile Gaming and Storytelling.

1 Introduction

Smartphones are emerging as a personal computational platform of significant popularity. The latest generation of handsets are equipped with a sophisticated combination of camera, GPS, orientation sensors and excellent data transmission capabilities. For the purposes of games, these features allow a much greater degree of sophistication than past generations of mobile games. In particular, they facilitate creation of a new genre: location-based mobile games (LBMGs).

One of the advantages of location-awareness is that it lends itself well to presenting the historical information by placing the player in a relevant context. This is why location-aware games have significant educational potential and can be used as interactive mobile guides. However, a significant challenge remains with regard to structuring the story content in a fashion that allows it to be presented adaptively in response to changes in user location and other types of context. To address this challenge, we have developed a flexible narrative architecture that allows non-linear stories with multiple branches to be delivered in a location-aware manner. In addition, the architecture supports efficient resource management, which is critical for mobile applications.

X. Luo et al. (Eds.): ICWL 2010 Workshops, LNCS 6537, pp. 11–20, 2011.

In this paper we present the architecture and discuss our preliminary experiences with it in the context of Viking Ghost Hunt (VGH), a location-based, story-driven, augmented reality game that runs on Android smartphones. The game is a hybrid of a mystery game and Gothic ghost story that incorporates historical information about the Viking presence in Dublin (800–1169 AD). The locations, in which the game is played, are selected because of the association with the Irish Viking history and are of direct historical significance to the story.

The rest of the paper is structured as follows. In Sec. 2 we briefly review the related work. Sec. 3 describes Viking Ghost Hunt and the requirements it sets for the narrative architecture. Sec. 4 presents the architecture to support interactive context-dependent narrative, which is the main contribution of the paper. In Sec. 5 we describe how the architecture is applied in VGH. Sec. 6 contains discussion of the approach. Concluding remarks in Sec. 7 end the paper.

2 Related Work

The capabilities of GPS enabled devices have motivated the development of numerous applications that use the information about the physical location of the user. Location-based mobile games (LBMGs) and tourist guides are popular applications for such location-aware technology. During the last few years a broad range of such applications was developed, ranging from virtual tourist guides [17] to location-aware multimedia storytelling [15]. The settings, in which location-aware applications are employed, range from the user strolling freely in the urban or countryside environment [16] to the user being a passenger on a journey, upon which he or she exercises no control [5].

Generally speaking location-aware applications can be more or less interactive, ranging from more traditional mobile guides with limited user interaction, such as the Lancaster *GUIDE* project [6] to, at the other extreme, highly interactive LBMGs [3]. Many of the latter operate in an open-ended game world with set up rules but with no underlying narrative, such as the *Can you see me now?* game where physical players chase the online users through the city streets. More sophisticated game world is created in the *Pirates!* [4] game, where players can undertake predefined missions, however the core of the game is interaction with other players and with NPCs.

The interaction in the game does not need to be limited to the explicit actions of the player. The player's behavior, such as walking in a particular direction or staying for some time in the particular place, can also be used to affect narrative. For instance, in the *Geist* project [12] the player walks through a historical site and is presented with location related stories. However, in contrast with conventional mobile guides where the user is always presented with the same content at the same location, in *Geist* the story is automatically adapted to the user experience. The player gets a different story depending on the order in which the locations are visited and on the amount of time spent in each location. Yet the application aims to bind these stories together in a consistent experience. It is worth noting that the boundary between LBMGs and interactive guides seems to be blurring, since factually correct information is incorporated in some games, and mobile guides aim to present the historical information to the user in more entertaining way. For example, the *Who Killed Hanne Holmgaard?* project [16] engages the player in a detective game, while at the same time familiarizing him or her with the history of Denmark under the Nazi occupation. From the other hand, in the *Voices of Oakland* project [7] the guided tour is shaped as engaging encounters with ghosts. In the classification of interactive mobile guides by Kjeldskov and Paay [10] LBMGs are included in this definition.

In our research we were concerned with developing an architecture for handling narrative suitable for a wide range of location-based and, more broadly, context-aware games. The *beat sequencer* from *Façade* is the closest example of similar architecture [13]. In *Façade* the story is told through *beats*, i.e., pieces of narrative united by a common topic. Beats are sequenced in response to player interaction. When one beat is over, the beat sequencer is responsible for selecting the next. The choice is guided by metadata associated with the beats, and each beat is characterized by its set of preconditions, priority and story effects. The goal of the beat sequencer is to select an available beat with the story tension effects matching an author-specified story tension arc.

3 Viking Ghost Hunt

The game that we constructed, Viking Ghost Hunt (VGH), is a location-based adventure game, driven by a Gothic ghost story set in Viking Dublin (800–1169 A.D.). In this game the player assumes the role of a paranormal investigator and moves around the city hunting for ghosts, collecting evidence and solving the mysteries of haunted Viking Dublin. The game is narrative-driven in the sense that, in order to progress the game, the player must unlock a sequence of distributed, location-specific, narrative fragments, which together make up a meaningful story arc. Hence, the VGH narrative, which is mapped onto actions and space, is revealed through the players' activities as they move through the locations and, in order to preserve the aesthetics of the role-play, these activities are presented in the context of paranormal investigation. In this form of storytelling, the player is not an external observer, but becomes an active player, who advances in the game and progresses the story by interacting with narrative elements, such as location, character and plotline.

As is typical of the quest structure, and common in the adventure game genre, the player's actions are crucial to accessing the narrative and the challenges faced by the player integrate the story elements into the game play [1,8,9]. The purpose of the quest, therefore, is two-fold; it is both symbolic and structural. By linking the narrative to the player's activities, the quest provides the player with meaningful goals while simultaneously functioning as a structure for achieving these goals through specific activities [19]. The quest provides a bridge between the game fiction and game rules and for this reason it is a useful technique for creating the illusion of agency, which Janet Murray describes as "the satisfying power to take meaningful action and see the results of our decisions and choices" [14, p.126]. Supported by storytelling it can be a powerful medium to convey the historical information to the player in entertaining form.

The characteristic of the quest structure that contributes most significantly to the player's sense of agency is the balance between embedded and emergent narrative [11,18]. Embedded narrative is pre-generated prior to player's interaction and tends to be more linear in nature. It contains the over-arching story arc and gives structure to the order in which the narrative is conveyed, thus preserving a coherent expression of the plotline. Emergent narrative is more open-ended and less predictable but is more responsive to the player's interaction and therefore facilitates a greater sense of agency. While a linear narrative structure fits easily with the classic Hollywood 3-act structure, which is popular for building dramatic tension and emotional impact, a non-linear, branching structure affords the player increased agency and the potential of re-playing the game.

With these considerations in mind, we were motivated to create a quest structure that could balance both embedded and emergent narrative. Multiple branching options were introduced at key points of an essentially linear structure, thus forming parallel story paths. In order to contain the potential unwieldiness of these optional branches, a set of inevitable event points to which all player must return, was introduced. This fold back structure [2], is especially useful in narrative-driven location-based gaming where game designers may also want to guide people through both essential narrative plot-points and specific locations.

The main success criteria for the architecture to support the described type of narrative can therefore be summarized as follows:

- it should be capable of supporting location-specific narrative;
- it should have ability to handle non-linear branching stories;
- as smartphones remain a resource-constrained platform it should facilitate efficient resource management.

4 Narrative Architecture

The main concept of our infrastructure is the concept of the *challenge*. Challenge refers to an atomic part of the story, i.e, to the task that the player needs to accomplish to advance the game. The challenge is responsible for manipulating (creating, destroying or changing) the *passive entities*, through which the narrative is delivered to the player. In VGH, these entities include map overlays, ghosts (which are defined by their video and/or audio manifestations) and atmospheric background sound effects.

The lifecycle of the challenge is regulated by a set of *controlling conditions*, which consists of the *precondition*, the *abort condition* and the *completion condition*. Initially, each challenge is in the *passive* state. The passive challenge can never be completed unless it becomes *active*. A challenge is activated when its precondition is satisfied. An active challenge may become completed if a new event satisfies its completion condition. If the abort condition is satisfied it becomes passive again (see the state diagram in Fig. 1(a)). A challenge might change between active and passive states an arbitrary number of times, but it can only be completed once. A completed challenge can still be activated and deactivated and can manipulate its passive entities. This can be useful if the challenge controls a permanent part of the game world. In this case, completion of the challenge triggers the progress in the game but passive entities controlled by the challenge remain in the game and can enhance the further game experience.

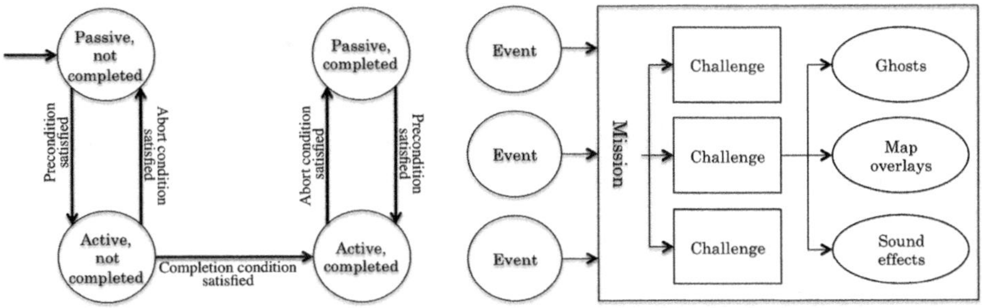

(a) Challenge state diagram (b) Mission infrastructure

Fig. 1. Main components of the narrative architecture

Each change in the state of the challenge triggers the corresponding action. When the challenge is activated, its *start* action is triggered, deactivation triggers the *stop* action and completion triggers *complete*. These actions can be specified for each challenge separately and allow the challenge to adopt to its new state, for instance, by manipulating the managed passive entities. The change in the internal state of the challenge is not perceivable to the player but the change in passive entities can be perceived through the corresponding UI elements.

The challenges are notified about changes in the game state through *events*. Events are small objects that encapsulate relevant information about changes. Examples of events include receiving a new update about the relevant context changes (e.g., change of the location of the player), seeing or hearing the ghost manifestation or the completion of one of the challenges. This last type of events makes it possible to build a hierarchy of challenges by using completion of one of the challenges in the controlling conditions of another. For instance, in this way it is possible to chain the challenges, activating the next when the previous is completed. Another way to create a more complex structure is to define a master challenge that manages several smaller challenges and is completed when a certain number of these "child" challenges is completed. Some examples of such composite challenges are described in Section 5.

To bind all challenges together and to ensure delivery of events to each of them the challenges are encapsulated inside the *mission* component. This component handles all challenges that relate to the particular story. It is responsible for accumulating game events and delivering them to the challenges according to their internal state. When a new event is received the mission checks preconditions of passive challenges and activates those for which preconditions are satisfied.

For active challenges the mission checks abort and completion conditions and changes the state of the challenges accordingly. Figure 1(b) shows the overall picture of the mission infrastructure. The arrows show how events are propagated through the mission to challenges, and how the challenges in response modify passive entities managed by mission.

In practice, there is no need to load all possible challenges into the infrastructure from the very start of the game. Instead we allow challenges to instantiate other challenges at the appropriate times. Therefore only a limited set of the initial challenges is instantiated first. Challenges are also allowed to unload themselves from the mission. After unloading they will no longer be notified about the new events, and the resources that they hold at this point can be deallocated. This strategy is particularly advantageous in the resource-constrained environment of the mobile device.

5 Case Study

The mission that we used as a proof-of-concept for our narrative architecture is set in the surroundings of the medieval church of St. Audoen. The church lies within the old Viking city walls in Dublin and is surrounded by public parkland. There is a number of local stories associated with the place. In particular, the church has in its keeping the so-called 'Lucky Stone', a medieval tombstone, which is believed to possess magical qualities. Several ghosts from different times are believed to haunt the area including the Green Lady doomed to look eternally for her lost baby and the local gang member murdered in vicious street fights during the 18th century. Including these ghosts in the game allowed us to expand the focus of the mission from the Dublin Viking history to other parts of the city's past without breaking consistency of the story.

The mission unfolds as follows. When players launch the game, the icon on the map notifies them that the surroundings of St. Audoen's church are haunted. Once the player reaches the site they begin undertaking an investigation by searching for and locating evidence of paranormal activity. In this part of the game, spots of paranormal activity are randomly located around the site. The evidence that the player gathers at this point include pictures of Viking artifacts and 'ghostly' sounds. This gives the player a chance to get used to the game interfaces while at the same time getting immersed in the atmosphere of historical/paranormal investigation. Once the player gathers enough evidence of paranormal activity the new ghost appears. This is Olaf, a trapped Viking ghost who solicits the player to help him escape and thus provides the player with a motivating goal for the rest of the mission. At this point, Olaf also delivers the player's first explicit challenge commanding him to find the Lucky Stone. After finding the ghostly remnant of the Stone at the spot where it was originally located the player returns to Olaf to receive further instructions.

At this point the player is confronted with a narrative fork that contains a dramatic choice. By way of completing the final challenge, the player must choose between two routes and two approaches: take the easiest and quickest

Southern route but at great risk to Olaf or take the longer and more dangerous Northern route and face impending doom. On both routes the player encounters other St. Audoen's ghosts, and Olaf tells their stories to the player. Both routes eventually lead the player to the same target: the garden where Olaf wants to return. Once the player reaches the garden he or she receives Olaf's thanks as well as a medieval coin as a token of Olaf's appreciation.

We implemented the described mission using the narrative architecture presented in Sec. 4. To capture the story we use 30 instances of 11 different challenges. Most of these challenges havea fairly simple structure. For example, there is a challenge "Play narrative once near ghost", which is activated when the player sees the visible ghost. The challenge then starts playing an audio file associated with that ghost and is complete when the playback is finished. Seven instances of this challenge are used in the game, each one parametrized with the particular ghost and the audio file. Two more interesting challenges, which we would like to draw attention to, are the transition between the atomic challenges part and the encounter with Olaf, and the branching point in the mission.

The activation condition for the ghost of Olaf is that the player found 3 out of 10 pieces of evidence of paranormal activity located in the region. Finding each piece of evidence constitutes a simple atomic challenge: its precondition is that the player is in the region and the completion condition is that the player captures the corresponding piece of evidence. In order to keep track of how many atomic challenges have been accomplished, a more complex challenge is created (see Fig. 2(a)). This challenge maintains an internal counter, which is increased each time when one of the atomic challenges is completed. The completion condition for this challenge is that this internal counter reaches the number of 3. When the challenge is complete it activates the new 'find Olaf' challenge. Also, the completion of this challenge is a signal for remaining atomic challenges to abort and to release their resources.

A more complicated challenge is used to manage the two branches of the game. The principal scheme of this challenge is presented in Fig. 2(b). Subchallenges that are managed by this challenge are represented as rectangular shapes while

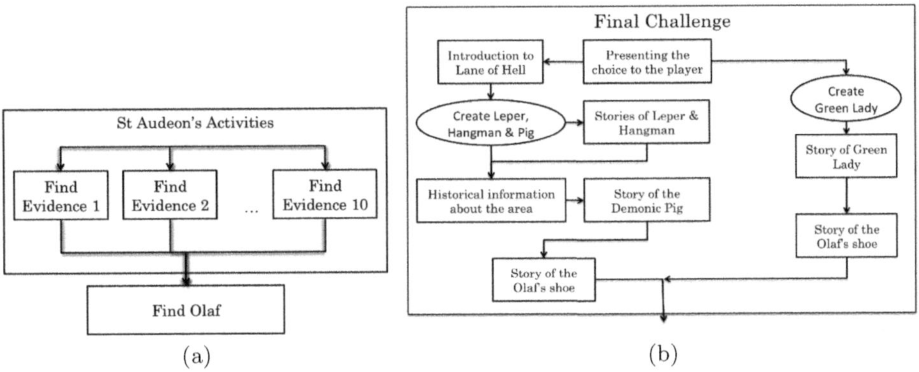

Fig. 2. Structure of some sample challenges

oval shapes mark the actions by which the superchallenge reacts in response to completion of the subchallenges. Subchallenges in this case are responsible for triggering pieces of narrative either at certain locations or when the player sees the visible ghost.

At the branching point the progression of the game is determined by which of the two challenges gets completed first. If the player follows the Northern route they will first encounter the Lane of Hell while on the Southern route the Green Lady will be met. Depending on which of the two the player reaches first, the remaining challenges of the Northern or the Southern route are activated while the challenge associated with the alternative branch is removed. Some challenges placed on the Northern route are optional. For example, passing the Lane of Hell the player can encounter some of the ghosts haunting the lane (the Leper and the Hangman) and learn their stories. However, if the player does not find them it is still possible to proceed to the subsequent parts of the game. Other pieces of narrative are critical for the consistence of the story and therefore mandatory.

6 Discussion

In Sec. 3 we stated the key requirements for the narrative supporting architecture for *Viking Ghost Hunt*. In this section we review our proposed architecture to determine the extent to which it meets these requirements.

Delivering location-specific (and, generally, context-specific) narrative is ensured by the ability of challenges to react to changes in the context through events. As challenges are capable of changing their state in response to the events, the delivered narrative can be context-specific. Non-linearity of the story is achieved by the fact that multiple challenges are allowed to be active simultaneously. In this case, the player's actions define which of the challenges will be accomplished and therefore which branches of the story will be unlocked next. The resource management is simplified by the fact that the resources are managed by each challenge autonomously. Together with "on-demand" loading of challenges, this ensures that only the necessary resources are allocated, and that the resources are deallocated as soon as they are no longer required.

It is not an easy task to evaluate the architecture in isolation from the game it was used in. To illustrate its applicability for a broader range of LBMGs, we examine how it can be used for supporting the five types of LBMGs identified in the survey undertaken by Kjeldskov and Paay [10]. The first type of games they mention is *treasure hunt* games with linear story. They can be represented as a sequence of challenges creating and loading the next one when completed. *Jigsaw puzzles* is the type of the games to which *Viking Ghost Hunt* most closely relates. Its defining characteristic is that the player collects seemingly random fragments of the narrative, which gradually combine into the bigger story. This type of narrative can be modeled by creating "branches" of challenges that all ultimately meet at one final point. As challenges from different branches are active simultaneously the user will always have the possibility to give up a certain branch to follow the other one (possibly even without noticing the fact).

Fig. 3. Playing Viking Ghost Hunt: the ghost is seen on the screen

Domino games are similar to *treasure hunt* games except that the context in which the current narrative fragment is delivered suggests which of the several possible next fragments should be selected. This type of story can be supported by our framework since active challenges are notified about all relevant changes in the context. The context information will determine, which challenge is to be created and loaded next. *Scrabble* games offer to the player a highly interactive experience adopting the story to many events that are happening around the player. The example the authors give uses information from the Bluetooth profiles of the surrounding phones to modify the story. To create this kind of game with our framework it is necessary to introduce new types of game events to capture relevant information from the surroundings. Once this is accomplished it becomes possible to adapt the behavior of the challenges to the contextual information.In *collecting butterflies* type of games unrelated self-contained stories are linked to the locations. To support this type of games multiple challenges can be created, each using the player location in its controlling conditions.

7 Conclusion

In this paper we have presented an architecture to support location-based and, more broadly, context-sensitive interactive narrative. The architecture has been successfully applied in practice to develop a location-aware mobile game *Viking Ghost Hunt* for Android handsets. We have also discussed the capability of the architecture to support a wide range of LBMGs and interactive mobile guides.

The architecture is specifically designed to meet the requirements of the resource-constrained environment of the smartphone and can be applied to simplify the development of future mobile applications. More extensive evaluation including field user trials is reserved for future work.

Acknowledgements

We are grateful to the National Digital Research Center (NDRC) for funding the work described in this paper.

References

1. Aarseth, E.: Quest games as post-narrative discourse. In: Narrative across Media: The Languages of Storytelling, pp. 361–376. U. of Nebraska Press (2004)
2. Adams, E., Rollings, A.: Fundamentals of Game Design. Prentice Hall, Upper Saddle River (2006)
3. Benford, S., Crabtree, A., Flintham, M., Drozd, A., Anastasi, R., Paxton, M., Tandavanitj, N., Adams, M., Row-Farr, J.: Can you see me now? ACM Trans. Comput.-Hum. Interact. 13(1), 100–133 (2006)
4. Björk, S., Falk, J., Hansson, R., Ljungstr, P.: Pirates! Using the physical world as a game board. In: Interact 2001: 8th IFIP TC.13 Conf. on HCI, pp. 9–13 (2001)
5. Brunnberg, L., Juhlin, O., Gustafsson, A.: Games for passengers: accounting for motion in location-based applications. In: FDG 2009: Proc. of the 4th Int. Conf. on Foundations of Digital Games, pp. 26–33 (2009)
6. Cheverst, K., Davies, N., Mitchell, K., Friday, A., Efstratiou, C.: Developing a context-aware electronic tourist guide: some issues and experiences. In: CHI 2000: Proc. of the SIGCHI Conf. on Human Factors in Comp. Systems, pp. 17–24. ACM, New York (2000)
7. Dow, S., Lee, J., Oezbek, C., MacIntyre, B., Bolter, J.D., Gandy, M.: Exploring spatial narratives and mixed reality experiences in Oakland Cemetery. In: Advances in Computer Entertainment Technology, pp. 51–60. ACM, New York (2005)
8. Howard, J.: Quests: Design, theory, and history in games and narratives. A.K. Peters, Wellesley (2008)
9. Juul, J.: Half-Real: Video Games Between Real Rules and Fictional Worlds. MIT Press, Cambridge (2005)
10. Kjeldskov, J., Paay, J.: Augmenting the city with fiction: Fictional requirements for mobile guides. In: Mobile Interaction with the Real World 2007/5th Workshop on HCI in Mobile Guides Singapore, pp. 41–45 (2007)
11. LeBlanc, M.: Feedback systems and the dramatic structure of competition. In: Game Developers Conference (1999)
12. Malaka, R., Schneider, K., Kretschmer, U.: Stage-based augmented edutainment. In: Butz, A., Krüger, A., Olivier, P. (eds.) SG 2004. LNCS, vol. 3031, pp. 54–65. Springer, Heidelberg (2004)
13. Mateas, M., Stern, A.: Structuring content in the facade interactive drama architecture. In: Proc. of the 1st Art. Intelligence and Interact. Dig. Entertainment Conf., pp. 93–98 (2005)
14. Murray, J.H.: Hamlet on the holodeck: The future of narrative in cyberspace. Free Press, New York (1997)
15. Nisi, V., Oakley, I., Haahr, M.: Location-aware multimedia stories: Bringing together real and virtual spaces. In: ARTECH Conf. on Dig. Arts., pp. 72–81 (2008)
16. Paay, J., Kjeldskov, J., Christensen, A., Ibsen, A., Jensen, D., Nielsen, G., Vutborg, R.: Location-based storytelling in the urban environment. In: OZCHI 2008: Proc. of the 20th Australasian Conf. on CHI, pp. 122–129. ACM, New York (2008)
17. Roberts, D.L., Cantino, A.S., Isbell Jr., C.L.: Player autonomy versus designer intent: A case study of interactive tour guides. In: AIIDE, pp. 95–97 (2007)
18. Salen, K., Zimmerman, E.: Rules of play: game design fundamentals. MIT Press, Cambridge (2004)
19. Tosca, S.: The quest problem in computer games. In: Proc. of The Technologies for Interact. Dig. Storytelling and Entertainment Conf. (TIDSE), Darmstadt (2003)

A Story on Internet Safety: Experiences from Developing a VR Gaming Environment

Maria Fountana, Dimitris Kalaitzis, Eftychios Valeontis, and Vasilis Delis

Research Academic Computer Technology Institute, Patras, Greece

Abstract. This work presents the authors' on-going experience in implementing an online VR platform targeted to young pupils with the aim to achieve an in-depth understanding regarding Internet safety risks, protective measures and actions, primarily within the school and family environment. We a) outline design and technical considerations with respect to 'SimSafety' development, b) present technical prospects and limitations related to the provision of conceptually 'rich' activities to support our educational goals and c) briefly discuss SimSafety's pilot application so far, under the "story telling" paradigm.

1 Introduction

Internet provides significant opportunities as a means for information sharing, communication and learning. Still, Internet has dark sides that present risks and concerns for the well-being of non-adult users. The recognition that the boundaries between offline and online social presence of kids are particularly elusive (often dissolving) raises the need for sophisticated mechanisms and frameworks for effectively negotiating cyberspace and avoiding risks and areas of concern [10]. Most of the initiatives and actions taken so far include awareness campaigns for safer Internet, the establishment of awareness Nodes and Hotlines in many counties as well as filtering and rating systems[1].

Learning through game playing is hardly a new concept. Its positive impact as a methodological approach in teaching and learning is well known to scholars [5,7,8]. Good entertainment games provide problem solving spaces which are expected to involve content, skills, values and conceptual understandings we believe are important [2]. Virtual worlds, perceived as environments that stimulate immersive learning, have received much attention lately and are increasingly being examined under the experiential learning paradigm (based on the work of Dewey, Lewin and Piaget [6]). Relevant research argues that people primarily think and learn through experiences and not merely through abstract calculations and generalisations [1,3]. Through virtual reality games users develop an intimate involvement with the virtual world as an extension of their physical presence. Eventually, the experiences and learning gains associated with the virtual world would transfer to the real world as long as they are structured by specific goals set along with enjoyment [2]. To add a teachers' viewpoint within

[1] The interested reader can refer to `http://www.saferinternet.org`

X. Luo et al. (Eds.): ICWL 2010 Workshops, LNCS 6537, pp. 21–27, 2011.

the context of an in-class application of such virtual environments, combining gaming and learning is a rather labored task. It demands not only the ability to properly moderate and debrief students' experiences, but also the construction of an adequate pedagogic framework.

SimSafety (acronym for "Flight Simulator for Internet Safety"[2]) is an ongoing project that aspires to develop a comprehensive virtual environment which would engage kids, parents and teachers into a shared experience that provides information, social activities and fun and ultimately raises kids' awareness on Internet risks. Our target group consists of kids 9-11 years old as well as of parents and teachers. Although immersive learning environments, like Second Life, have been studied as adult training spaces with promising results [4], few studies involving children are so far available. The innovation of this project lies both in the theme (protecting young kids against Internet related risks) as well as in the technical approach: the development of a custom 3D space that provides a broad range of activities -some of them simulating real-life Internet activities- as well as risks and pitfalls, under a "safe" (controlled) mode. Our finished work so far involves the implementation of the environment and scenarios of in-class pilot application in approximately 10 EU countries, while a thorough evaluation of our approach and results is under preparation in order to conclude the project.

The structure of the rest of the paper is as follows: Section 2 outlines the design and contents of the SimSafety environment, laying emphasis on the implementation of conceptually rich activities related to the use of Internet and on-line communication in general. In Section 3 we briefly present our methodology for implementing in-class scenarios, discuss means of exploitation under the story-telling paradigm and highlight recent experiences from sessions in schools.

2 The SimSafety Park

2.1 Customising OpenSimulator

With enjoyment being at the heart of digital gaming, the search for the appropriate platform to meet our needs (catchy 3D graphics, school-lab compliant installation, community support, flexibility, etc.) was of utmost importance. Through an extensive market analysis we finally adopted OpenSimulator[3] as the hosting platform. OpenSimulator is an open-source application server, able to host massive multiplayer on-line 3D environments. The platform bears many similarities to the popular Second Life environment, since it is actually the result of reverse-engineering Second Life and deploying its functionality under open-source terms.

Among the most difficult challenges we faced during the development of the virtual environment was the need for conceptually rich activities and scenarios. OpenSimulator and all similar platforms are mainly intended to function as fancy, 3D-boosted chat environments where advanced graphics and artifacts

[2] `http://www.simsafety.eu`
[3] `http://opensimulator.org`

are provided to primarily enhance the social/chat experience. Therefore, concepts that would familiarise kids with Internet-related activities and eventually transfer the virtually gained experience to real life, such as friendship tracking, cyber-bullying simulation, tracking spatial and/or temporal proximity of events, reporting to a helpline and in general monitoring a user's (re)actions were particularly difficult (if possible at all) to track and further process. Guided by the conceptual game framework described in the project report on game specification[4], the development team devised advanced programming techniques and mechanisms to enhance existing OpenSimulator's functionality. A custom database was created, working side by side with the original OpenSimulator database, in order to accommodate several game-related data (such as scoring, user log data, several game parameters such as cyber-bullying frequency and content, quiz data, dynamic content, etc.). A www tool was developed allowing for the administration of various game and session parameters, account approvals, user rights, scores, dynamic content,etc. OpenSimulator's platform functionality has been extended through the use of modules, which are programmed using a native API (Application Programming Interface) that allows programmers to access and alter core functions and variables of the simulator. Non playing characters (NPCs) were employed in order to simulate internet dangers but also to provide guidance to the players. Once logged in, a player may become victim of a cyber-bulling NPC, receive spam or turn to another for help.

2.2 SimSafety Park Components

SimSafety aspires to serve as a comprehensive park. Its users are presented with a broad range of activities, including leisure (such as gardens, a lake in which you can chat while sailing, etc), stand-alone activities (like quizzes, information spots, free expression areas, gadgets or avatar customisation areas), group activities (e.g. video or www presentation areas, role-playing games, simulated cyber-bullying, friendship establishment), etc. In this section we briefly present the main virtual spaces comprising the "SimSafety Park" along with their indented functionality.

Welcome area. It is a pleasant area that accommodates newcomers, also including basic navigation instructions and game controls.

Avatar Customisation area. The avatar customisation simulates a clothing store. Players have a wide range of jackets, trousers, shirts, etc. to choose from and create their unique outfit.

Information Center. A modern building providing Internet Safety material in the form of posters was among the first to be "built" in the SimSafety Park. This building was designed in a museum-like fashion, so that a classroom could make a visit and learn about current issues concerning Internet dangers and threats. Additionally, there is a special multi-language room where posters

[4] D2.1(b): Report on Game Specification (final release). Deliverable co-authored by all project partners of the SimSafety Project. Available at: `http://www.simsafety.eu`, June 2010.

hosted can be translated into several languages. Current posters contain information available at Safer Internet nodes.

Mini Games Zones. The mini-game zone provides the setting for multi-user role-playing games. These activities are little theatrical acts based on a real-life incident (see Section 3 for more information).

Quiz and puzzles. "Quiz boxes" and puzzles are scattered throughout the world in various locations frequently visited by the players. For the latter, trying to solve the puzzle (e.g. image sorting) subliminally conveys the appropriate message.

Cyber-bullying. Being one of the major Internet threats, particularly among young kids, cyber-bullying is extensively modeled and treated in SimSafety. Several NPCs randomly bullying the players while they walk around are implemented. The NPCs communicate through the players' native language and the user is judged (gets a score) according to his/her reaction to bullying. The recommended action is to visit the "report center" and file a report.

Free expression areas. Such areas are meant to foster the children's creativity by allowing them to freely free construct 3D artifacts, or create wall graffiti.

Gadgets. Several gadgets (like a credit card, a mobile phone, etc) are scattered throughout the SimSafety park, which provide some typical functionality upon discovery by a user (e.g. to withdraw money from an ATM, or to be delivered to the Lost & Found department of the Report Centre). The way a user handles a gadget can be penalised or credited, accordingly.

Scoring. SimSafety supports a scoring system, combining points that a user may get or loose from almost any kind of activity (quizzes, mini games, visits to the info center, response to bullying and friendship invitations, gadget handling, etc.). A Hall of Fame is provided to reward the "good" players, based on overall performance.

3 SimSafety and Story-Telling

Taking into consideration that good judgment often comes from experience while, on the other hand, experience might also come from bad judgment [1,3], we aimed at raising awareness of Internet dangers by investigating appropriate approaches in order to guide pupils in (a) understanding and contextualise the risks, (b) taking proactive measures, (c) handling possible incidents.

In our case, maybe direct exposure to safety pitfalls could be a harmful approach and therefore chose to focus on presenting danger through simulation by a combination of role playing, storytelling and game-playing activities.

Storytelling was considered a powerful way of organizing information, a means of transmitting concepts, experiences, perceptions but also a way to convey ideas and emotions as well as to build communities. What is more, learners tend to find stories intrinsically motivating while the storylistening experience is also an effective tool for parents wishing to communicate important values to their children [9].

In SimSafety, young players come across objects and agents with a particular functionality/role, e.g. a credit card which the player may choose to insert to an ATM, an agent insulting players who can be either ignored or reported. Storytelling comes to practice through the mini games, similar to short theatrical plays where players are given specific roles and are invited to improvise.

Table 1. An example of the roles automatically appointed to game players in one of the mini games in SimSafety

Role	*Description*
Barbara	You find out that private pictures of Annabelle have been published on the web. You go and see the pictures, you spread rumor to some of your co-players.
George	You find out that private pictures of Annabelle have been published on the web. You decide to access the pictures but you tell nobody about it. You do nothing about it.
John	You find out that private pictures of Annabelle have been published on the web. You decide not to access the pictures and you try to convince your other co-players to notify your teacher.
Emilia	You find out that private pictures of Annabelle have been published on the web. You do not access the pictures and you believe that the message should be deleted and you try to convince your other co-players to do the same.
Fiona	You are the teacher and you do not know anything about the private photos of Annabelle. You ask your co-players what is going on. You think they look nervous.

An example of such an activity would be the following: pupils, in groups of five, are invited to investigate the risk of uploading photos on the web. The teacher informs the game players about the scenario of the mini game. The players are active in their roles for 20–25 minutes and they vote whether each game character dealt with the given dilemma in the appropriate way. After the end of each mini game, players are required to narrate to the rest of their classmates their experience, in the form of a story. As it can be inferred, storytelling is triggered twice in SimSafety. First, through a set of activities, in the form of role game playing scenarios. Secondly in its most conventional interpretation, storytelling takes place inside the classroom, as part of the activities designed to be implemented with the guidance of the teacher (or indeed at home with the support of a parent), in which case the pupils are invited to narrate their story in the classroom, discuss the different arguments raised, the scores gained and other aspects of their experience.

4 Pilot Implementation Results

Pilot implementation has provided interesting and fruitful feedback. Questionnaires were handed out to the nearly one thousand participants, through which we tried to assess the impact this project had on them. The first finding of this process was that children enjoyed activities that were designed in a playful manner.

Storytelling has also proved to be a powerful tool in increasing the communicative ability of learners as well as their improvisation and imagination. Players are encouraged to play and communicate while any learning and awareness gained are transferred subliminally.

Teachers supervising the implementation reported that their students were eventually aware and sensitive on dangers they had not experienced before. Most of the students were able to identify several risks presented in the game and stated that they intended to revisit the environment, provided that it would be enhanced with new features and activities.

Moreover, the issue that received much attention is privacy and the availability of sensitive private information on the web. Since the majority of young pupils make extensive use of social networks, the idea of being "watched' without one's consent was at the center of long discussions and controversy in most of the sessions. In such cases the teachers' interventions and guidance with respect to good social network practices and "netiquette" were reassuring. In several other cases piracy and free data exchange on the web, which was a common (not questioned) practice for some of the participants, have arisen in the context of several mini games and activities.

Finally, kids reflecting on in-class experiences realised the importance of crossing the established boundaries between school and domestic environment and having their parents involved in their virtual activities. As suspected right from the beginning of the project, parents' involvement is a key factor for shaping a kids' attitude towards the use of Internet. In fact, it seems that it was the attitude and misconceptions of the parents that were changed in favor of a more realistic type of guidance on Internet use as opposed to narrow-minded denial and eventual abandonment.

5 Conclusion

In this work we briefly present our experiences from the development of SimSafety, a virtual world targeted to young kids (as well as parents and teachers), combining enjoyment and educational activities in order to raise kids' awareness on Internet risks. As part of an on-going project, we a) first set out the scope and purpose, then b) briefly presented the main components of our virtual world as well as some design considerations and c) finally discussing our application methodology and pilot implementation of real-class scenarios.

Pilot implementation so far has been embraced by teachers and pupils and provides strong indication that this idea may be at the right track towards offering a fresh and up-to-date approach to an equally new and up-to-date problem.

Future efforts of the project team will include further development of educational activities in SimSafety and laying emphasis on the involvement of parents in supporting their children deal with Internet risks through SimSafety.

Regarding current technical limitations, mainstreaming of the application to multiple school labs both in terms of server performance as well as typical system requirements is among the most important ones. The need to provide conceptually rich activities will always remain a challenge for the designers and the developers of SimSafety. To this extent, future enhancements of the platform indicatively include more sophisticated use of audio for the deployment of educational activities, enhancing AI aspects of NCP behavior and experimenting with newer OpeSimulator versions and features.

Acknowledgements

This work us supported by funding under the Lifelong Learning Program of EU, Transversal Programme/Key Activity 3: ICT, Contract Ref. 143689- GR-2008-KA3-KA3MP.

References

1. Barsalou, L.W.: Perpetual Symbol Systems. Behavioural and Brain Sciences 22, 577–660 (1999)
2. Gee, J.P.: Deep Learning Properties of Good Digital Games. In: Ritterfeld, U., Cody, M., Vorderef, P. (eds.) Serious Games, Mechanisms and Effects. Taylor & Francis Group, Routledge (2009)
3. Hawkins, J.: On Intelligence. Henry Holt, New York (2005)
4. Jarmon, L., Traphagan, T., Mayrath, M., Trivedi, A.: Virtual world teaching, experiential learning and assessment: An interdisciplinary communication course in Second Life. Computers and Education 53, 169–192 (2009)
5. Klopfer, E., Osterweil, S., Salen, K.: Moving Learning Games Forward: Obstacles, Opportunities, and Openness, The Education Arcade, Massachusetts Institute of Technology (2009)
6. Kolb, D.A., Boyatzis, R.E., Mainemelis, R.: Experiential on cognitive, learning, and thinking styles. In: Sternberg, R.J., Zhang, L.F. (eds.) Perspectives Learning Theory: Previous Research and New Directions, pp. 227–248. Lawrence Erlbaum, Mahwah (2002)
7. Ritterfeld, U., Cody, M., Vorderef, P.: Serious Games, Mechanisms and Effects. Taylor & Francis Group, Routledge (2009)
8. Royle, K.: Computer games and realising their learning potential: Crossing Borders, Blurring Boundaries and Taking Action, Gamebasedlearning.org.uk (2009)
9. Sturm, B.: Storytelling theory and practice. Information in Life Digital Video Series. Henry Holt, New York (2007)
10. Willard, N.E.: Cyber-Safe Kids, Cyber-Savvy Teens. John Wiley & Sons, Chichester (2007)

Story Telling for Cultural Knowledge Sharing

Cat Kutay and Peter Ho

Computer Science and Engineering,
The University of New South Wales
{ckutay,peterh}@cse.unsw.edu.au
http://www.cse.unsw.edu.au/~ckutay,
http://www.cse.unsw.edu.au/~peterh

Abstract. We present the development of learning resources using multiple contributors. The resources are to assist learning a specific set of cultures, those of the Aboriginal and Torres Strait Islander communities in Australia, using stories uploaded onto a web site. The work is aimed at cultural preservation through non-linear digital stories, and re-presenting it in educational settings.

By enabling the community contributors to tag their artefacts according to themes, relationships, location and language we can provide a way for the learner-user to select relevant stories to their learning experience. The three learning environment interfaces, combined with the contributor's tagging of their story, provides the interconnection between stories and the learning path for the users.

1 Introduction

To teach cultural understanding, the optimal conditions are for immersion within the culture. Adult learners are highly motivated when re-living real life scenarios [1]. However this process is not feasible for the many people in Australia who with to broaden their understanding of the local Indigenous cultures. However, providing material online is contentious as members of the Indigenous community are wary of their knowledge and stories being used or analysed out of context, and without acknowledgment. Given the vast difference in culture and learning processes between the Indigenous and non-Indigenous communities in Australia, we need creative means to assist novice computer users to construct useful learning material that retains their cultural values and intent.

This work deals with a similar scenario to that considered in the Virtual Campfire cultural archive developed by Klamma et al. [2] with Web 2.0 features for user-generated content. The present system is aimed at more collaboration features, similar to the proprietary software VoiceThread [3] for collaboration around multimedia artefacts.

We are dealing with novice users as contributors and users, who are highly mobile and often not confident to express themselves in written English. Hence the system is required to support multimedia sharing of knowledge, utilising audio, video and image artefacts, and mobile access. We are using MPEG-7

X. Luo et al. (Eds.): ICWL 2010 Workshops, LNCS 6537, pp. 28–34, 2011.

format on images to enable linking to items within images and MPEG-21 [4] for setting rights of access. Also we are implementing the free and open-source server Annodex [5] for video/audio time-coding designed to chop continuous streams and local caching to reduce download, and adapting this annotation system for HTML5 [6]. Given the contributors come from a mobile population, the trend away from Flash for products such as iPad and iPhone supports this approach.

For Aboriginal and Torres Strait Islander people, story telling is the main mode of knowledge sharing and this requires much repetition for the learner to hear various version from different story tellers in order to understand all the different nuances. While the specific needs addressed in this work apply to the Indigenous people of Australia, there are similar modes of knowledge sharing in other Indigenous cultures.

The learning contexts are non-technical areas of training, where the knowledge experts are not confident with computers, and the community nature of the story makes it hard to develop complex story telling designs, so evaluation of the work has to date been focused around the level of participation in the development of the sites and feedback from workshops. We are interested in using gaming tools to enhance learning but this has been limited to using a simple selection of pathways through collaborative contributions. When the teaching mode is better understood we hope to use other techniques from similar systems to combine multimedia resources into training sessions (Spaniol et al. [1]).

2 Research into Indigenous Knowledge

This work is motivated by an interest in the wealth of knowledge that exists as oral memory within an Indigenous culture, and in particular how this knowledge may be learnt by those modern cultures who have lost their location in time and space, their link to a specific area of land, and the type of environmental and social knowledge that is embodied in such a lifestyle.

While much Indigenous knowledge has been brushed aside as irrelevant to modern society, there is now growing interest in re-gaining access to this knowledge. The main areas of interest are: knowledge about the local environment, its historical changes, and how to reduce the effect of modern societies demands on the environment; and how we relate to each other in a communal sharing society, rather than an individualistic one.

Accessing this knowledge must be done in a manner in which the ownership rests with the community. This provides some apparently conflict between individual contributors and the community authority to share knowledge. For instance these is often a notion that individual stories may conflict around a theme. However the stories are based on personal experience, and the language reflects an understanding of this context. The authority to tell a story is embodied in the knowledge sharing protocols that is understood and generally adhered to by individuals in the community [7] and [8]. Also oral mechanisms exist for the community to verify that the protocol is being followed and this is linked to the development of the web sites through community consultation and involvement in the design.

In this model, a story is developed by members of a community or group creating the story from individual parts, without external expert direction, or any overarching editorial or coordination control (cf. [9]). The process of combining the parts must be under some control by the contributors, who can edit previous artefacts, subject to restrictions, link their material to other items and add their own artefacts. Hence in this domain we focus on two evaluative forms. Firstly the trust of the community to place knowledge in the environment, and secondly the ability of the system to provide a coherent collection of stories as response to a learner-user's search.

3 Learning from Context

To assist the contributors to combine stories into a learning environment, we are designing interfaces that focus cultural learning on the three areas of: kinship, location and language. Both the contributors and the learner-user view through the same interface, so that contributors understand where their story will be viewed when they have uploaded an artefact. This assists with tagging their stories to fit within an interface and reassures the contributors on how their stories will be viewed. Figure 1 shows the mashup of functionality used for different multimedia.

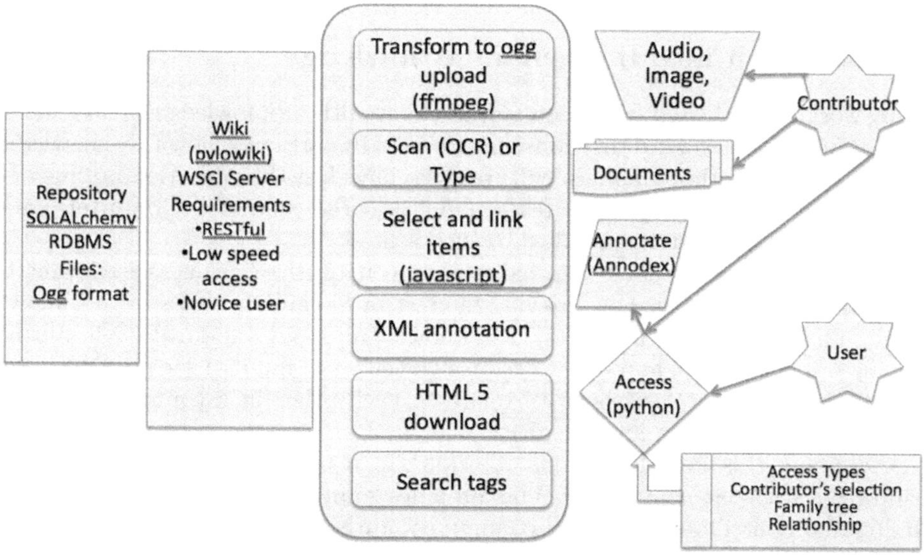

Fig. 1. Interfaces for linking artefacts with contributors' annotation

3.1 Kinship

Knowledge in Indigenous societies is generally specific to the kinship relation you hold to the knowledge teller. The aim of this interface is to enable the learner-user to understand the effect of this cultural aspect on people's experience within mainstream society. The interface enacts the rules of this kinship through the learning paths available. For instance, once you have selected a kinship role, you have open access to information from your sibling and cousins. You have some responsibility for the information of your spouse and their cousins. You may have no access to the information of your in-laws.

Much of the knowledge explains how to relate to people in these relationship roles. These are the rules and regulations of a trading culture, which are relevant in this day of rapid team turnover in employment areas [8], frequent transfer of dwelling and the influx of refugees in many countries.

3.2 Location

Knowledge in Indigenous stories as told in Australia are usually presented through location. A story is a collection of items, usually on one theme, that is recounted in sequence according to the track or storyline followed through the landscape. The time location is less significant than the theme and location of the event. This interface is used to emulate the environmental story telling process in communities, where stories are an explanation of the environment and people's relationship to this and each other within the environment.

The knowledge tagged by location in the repository also includes thematic sorting, to enable learner-users to focus on themes in their learning, and for contributors to select the thematic context of their own story. For instance we use the workplace of the user as one theme, as people may wish to know more about working with Indigenous Australians. The Indigenous historical experience of law courts will colour their actions in such an environment. Law enforcement officers and lawyers could be better equipped and less prejudiced if they are aware of some of the oral history their clients are bringing with them.

3.3 Language

Many recordings of language are held in archives, but are not accessible, or even known by the community. To place these on the web is not always appropriate. However those that are allowed to be published can then be used as the framework for other speakers (and linguists) to put up additional information. Each segmentation of a resource to link to a specific topic, enhances the use of these resources for hearing the language as spoken, and in context.

As many languages are endangered, the language context is for Indigenous people to reclaim their language. Existing resources need to tagged with relevant sections and annotated with their learning context (e.g. part of speech or complexity of grammar). The learning process one of incrementally adding complexity to the language examples and extending the themes discussed.

4 Story Collections

We are collecting and displaying oral stories, untranscribed, in a web interface. Initially the material was collected under a flat content management system generally used for museum style presentations. The first repository was language resources for learning. The second was stories of the Stolen Generations, those children forcibly removed from families. The third was stories collected about the day to day experience of cultural conflict, which were often related to the differing rules of kinship obligations.

We have two concerns as feedback. Firstly as a trust issue, we need to permanently tagging artefacts with author information. Secondly for learning we need to provide a way to link different contributors' stories.

Therefore we are enhancing these flat systems with XML wrapping of content for tagging with contributor information and thematic information. These artefacts are then viewed with HTML5 (see Figure 2). The first metadata added is the authorship and participation information which, together with the story, forms the artefact for upload. Subsequent annotation is used to enable segmentation of video and audio items and the highlighting of features in images. The interface is designed around contributors providing links to related artefacts, to assist in combining many different sources, or 'voices'. This process enhances the community nature of the knowledge, rather than presenting the story as a single isolated viewpoint (see [10]). To provide some cohesion between the stories being presented, we provide interfaces that contain implicit paths through the related themes, and allow users to become immersed in the material that is selected by the repository search engine as relevant to that interface, and their own selection.

While much of the data relevant to each interface may differ, this approach is a generic method to allow learner-users to focus their viewing on items relevant to them. Also within each context we designed a visual interface that provides a framework for the storyline, or a learning path. Also the user-learner's choice of what they listen to effects the next options that are shown, through linked material or user learning progression. This learning path is based on progress along a travel along a map route, or graded language learning. For the kinship learning context, the path is initially set by providing a theoretical introduction with examples. The next stage is to provide editors to enable the contributors to provide more elaborate links to other artefacts so that they too can generate learning paths.

	Initial	Build trust	Interface	User	Contributor	Maintain
Web2.0	Repository of audio, images, video material	Establish access privileges to each item	Provide learning context for immersion	Search items according to themes and links in story	View others contributions - form sequence or grouping	Update tags and story path
XHTML5	Login based on family connections	Metadata package- author and participant details	Provide paths through interface to guide learning	Implement Annotea and MPEG-7/21 annotation	Enhance XML editor to link to segmentation	Access privilege database

Fig. 2. Stages of story annotation

5 Search Mechanisms

Within the learning interface, the learner-user can select options to describe what sort of knowledge they seek, their kinship relationship to the authors, or their language level. For such users selections there will not always be specifically relevant stories. However we do need to keep the story flowing. If there is no story tagged exactly to that selection, or no further links from their previous selection, we allow the search mechanism to select the most relevant story that exists in the repository, where feasible.

Also where there are multiple stories offered to the user, we want the user to hear all of these if relevant, in a coherent form. For this we have developed an outline of each storyline or learning process which we ask the contributors to use to order their artefacts. We are also trying to re-use stories in different contexts by allowing multi-tagging of stories.

The interface grows as the repository grows. As tags are added to the database by the contributors creating new tags, under the separate categories, these new tags or options can then be offered to the user when they move around the learning environment. Also contributors are able to view the existing resources under each category. Initially this is in a simple table interface, for quicker access to the different link options. With the next version we are improving the interface to allow XML annotation of items and time-coding linkage.

6 Retaining Context

The problem remains that as oral or video records, the stories cannot be dissected as is done by text searches, hence we rely on manual annotation. Also artefacts cannot be broken down, but must often be stored in their entirety out of respect for the contributor. While we are enabling the downloading of segments, these must always be presented as being part of the fuller material.

We are also aware that users may not listen to each story to their completion. We are encouraging contributors to split each long piece into segments, and tag, so that these annotations can be used to focus stories more to the user. The users are also made aware that they are viewing a segment, and can select the whole story from that person.

The main concern, after specifying the access privileges to any story, is to ensure that both the story retains the contributor's information, and the context it applies to, as well as any updated information relating to respect for those who have recently passed away. Using metadata for encoding the media, the server can ensure this encoding remains with any copying of the media, rather than relying on a central repository of XML data on each artefact. However there remain limitations, as we cannot avoid users making local recordings or screen capture of images.

7 Conclusion and Further Work

Providing the medium for Indigenous users to educate and share knowledge poses many issues. The main concern it to retain as much of the original cultural approach to story telling and knowledge sharing as possible in the new environment. With recent developments of HTML5 and time-coded streaming, we can make this repository of stories into a useful learning interface through allowing the contributor-instructors to categorise and link their stories, with other audio, video and image artefacts.

This paper deals with the development of the initial repository and the issues that have led to the next design and development stage using XML tagging and HTML5 technology. Focusing on open-source systems we hope to engage the broader software community in this project, while trying to retain an interface that is user friendly to novice users.

References

1. Spaniol, M., Cao, Y., Klamma, R., Moreno-Ger, P., Manjón, B., Sierra, J., Toubekis, G.: From story-telling to educational gaming: The bamiyan valley case. In: Li, F., Zhao, J., Shih, T., Lau, R., Li, Q., McLeod, D. (eds.) ICWL 2008. LNCS, vol. 5145, pp. 253–264. Springer, Heidelberg (2008)
2. Klamma, R., Toubekis, G., Cao, Y., Renzel, D., Jarke, M., Jansen, M.: Virtual Campfire - Cultural Heritage Management and Presentation on Mobile Devices based on Interoperable Cross-Platform MPEG-7 Multimedia Web Services. In: Proceedings of the 22nd CIPA Symposium - Digital Documentation, Interpretation & Presentation of Cultural Heritage, Kyoto (2009)
3. VoiceThread, `http://voicethread.com/`
4. Hunter, J.: Rights Markup Extensions for the Protection of Indigenous Knowledge. In: The 11th International World Wide Web Conference - Global Community Track, Honolulu (2002)
5. Pfeiffer, S., Parker, C., Schremmer, C.: Annodex: A Simple Architecture to Enable Hyperlinking, Search, and Retrieval of Time- Continuous Data on the Web. In: Proc. 5th ACM SIGMM Int'l. Workshop Multimedia Information Retrieval, pp. 87–93. ACM Press, New York (2003)
6. Schroeter, R., Thieberger, N.: Sustainable Data from Digital Fieldwork. In: Proceedings of the Conference Held at the University of Sydney (2006), `http://hdl.handle.net/2123/1297`
7. Nakata, M., Nakata, V., Byrne, A., McKeough, J., Gardiner, G., Gibson, J.: Australian Indigenous Digital Collections: First generation issues (2008), `http://hdl.handle.net/2100/631`
8. Kutay, C., Ho, P.: Australian Aboriginal Protocol for Modelling Knowledge Sharing. In: Proceedings of IADIS International Conference on Applied Computing, Rome, Italy (2009)
9. Valle, C., Raybourn, E., Prinz, W., Borges, M.: Group Storytelling to Support Tacit Knowledge Externalization. In: Stephanidis, C. (ed.) Universal Access in HCI: Inclusive Design for the Information Society, pp. 1218–1222. Lawrence Erlbaum Associates, Mahwah (2003)
10. Minoru, H.: Reading oral histories from the pastoral frontier: A critical revision. Journal of Australian Studies 26(72), 21–28 (2002)

Digital Storytelling for Competence Development

Edgar Santos[1], Claudia Ribeiro[1], Manuel Fradinho[2], and João Pereira[1]

[1] INESC-ID, Rua Alves Redol, Lisboa, Portugal
[2] Cyntelix, Business Inovation Center, Upper Newcastle Road, Galway, Irland
{edgar.santos,claudia.sofia.ribeiro}@ist.utl.pt,
mfradinho@cyntelix.com, jap@inesc.pt

Abstract. The acquisition of complex knowledge and competences raises difficult challenges for the supporting tools within the corporate environment, which digital storytelling presents a potential solution. Traditionally, a driving goal of digital storytelling is the generation of dramatic stories with human significance, but for learning purposes, the need for drama is complemented by the requirement of achieving particular learning outcomes. This paper presents a narrative engine that supports emergent storytelling to support the development of complex competences in the learning domains of project management and innovation. The approach is based on the adaptation on the Fabula model combined with cases representing situated contexts associated to particular competences. These cases are then triggered to influence the unfolding of the story such that a learner encounters dramatic points in the narrative where the associated competences need to be used. In addition to the description of the approach and corresponding narrative engine, an illustration is presented of how the competence "conflict management" influences a story.

Keywords: Emergent Narrative, Story Creation, Digital Storytelling.

1 Introduction

Technology has fostered the collapse of the world into a small village, where businesses have become globally driven at an exceedingly fast pace to outperform their competitors to secure a share in a finite market. Human capital is recognized as key asset in an organization to achieve its goals, but the business, technology and societal pressures make corporate training a major concern where rapid competence development is the new mantra driving competitive advantage. However, the increase of complexity of knowledge and the constraint of acquiring it in shorter time frames imposes hard challenges to the competence development within the corporate environment. This is the case of soft skills, even more so when considering the richness of situations where one encounters multiple cultures. In addition, the digital native generation [1] has different expectations and learning patterns that compound the challenges of traditional approaches to corporate training.

The advent of serious games has given rise to the possibility of enhancing learning [2] with an increasing number of advocates promoting the use of serious games as a delivery platform[3,4] for education and competence development. The benefits of

X. Luo et al. (Eds.): ICWL 2010 Workshops, LNCS 6537, pp. 35–44, 2011.

serious games over more traditional learning methods and on-the-job training include the increase of learner motivation, ego gratification, fostering of creativity, socialization and above all making the experience fun. Although the body of evidence remains scarce, there is a growing evidence for the efficacy of serious games as educational tools with a growing number of research studies finding improved rates of learning and retention over more traditional learning methods [24,25].

Since people are social beings that communicate and socialize with one another, the use of storytelling has played a crucial role in exchanging and transferring complex knowledge and foster understanding [5]. Therefore, it has been recognized that narratives are a valid support for learning because it helps make sense of experience and organize knowledge, in addition to increasing motivation [23]. Therefore, it would beneficial to combine storytelling with serious games, but considering that a story implies the reflection of past events that unfolded with a particular order and that one of the strengths of serious games is the sense of agency of the learner[6], this raises a challenge known as Narrative Paradox [12]. A possible approach to address this paradox is by allowing for "emergent narrative" [26], where the story emerges from characters' local interactions. Louchart et al.[7] researched how an emergent narrative can be authored since it reflects the obvious paradox of the narrative being "authored" at run-time as it emerges from the characters' interactions. It usually implies an iterative process where the characters are modeled carefully, requiring several iterations are made to assure that the desired stories emerge and undesired stories are kept from happening. As stated by Crawford:

"while architectural valid stories can be created by algorithm, humanly interesting stories can be created only by artists"

Therefore, the authoring process can be costly and impose constraints on creation of viable stories that address desired learning outcomes. This paper presents an innovative approach to storytelling for the purpose of development of complex competences within the context of the TARGET project, which aims to support rapid competence development in project management and innovation. Consequently, the focus of the paper is the component – the Narrative Engine - responsible for the unfolding of an interactive story taking into account the learning outcomes in developing a particular set of competences along the lines of "sense-making", "conflict management", "time management".

2 Challenge

To better understand the challenge tackled by the TARGET project, one might begin by understanding the complexity of emergent storytelling. For such, one may consider the use of the story landscape [7] to demonstrate the space of possible story outcomes that can emerge from the underlying narrative engine. As the story unfolds, a plot across the landscape is made, which takes into consideration the surrounding hills and valleys. An elevation in the landscape represent potential dramatic points in the story, which the narrative engine (or drama manager) will influence the story for a user to experience whilst a valley represents situations where a user is faced with multiple paths, but once climbing a hill, the dramatic context intensifies and moves in the particular direction of the elevation peak.

3 Our Approach

In the context of TARGET, the aim is not only to create engaging stories with emergent storytelling, but to promote particular learning outcomes, which leads to reshaping the landscape as the points are influenced not only by the dramatic element of a particular situation, but also its relevance to the learning plan of an individual. This requires runtime analysis of the story unfolding based on a formal representation.

3.1 Fabula Model

From a Narratology perspective, a distinction is often made between the *fabula* of the story and the *story*. *Fabula* is a series of causally and chronologically related events that are caused or experienced by characters in a story world. *Story* is a *fabula* that is looked at from a particular viewpoint. Considering these definitions, the Narrative Engine should document the sequence of events through a fabula, since it reflects an omniscient form of the narrative. Swartjes used such a representation in "The Virtual Storyteller"[10] and named it "Fabula Model" [11]. The expressive power of the model is not solely due to the different causality elements (**E**vent, **P**erception, **I**nternal **E**lement, **G**oal, **A**ction and **O**utcome), which are causally connected, but also because of the causal connections that have semantic meaning (ϕ – physical; ψ: psychological; *e*: enablement; *m*: motivational). These are necessary taking into account the goal of the project in which they were used. In the Virtual Storyteller, a Plot Agent component uses this model, instantiates it with the events of the world simulation and a Narrator component can translate them to natural language.

3.2 Fabula Model Adaptation

According to the original model, "enablement" is the weakest form of causality. It represents the fact that "if a fabula element A enables another fabula element B, then B is possible because of A and no more than that"[11]. In practice it means that effects of A satisfy preconditions of B. Since TARGET shows the stories visually rather than use natural language to tell a story, "the enablement" element was discarded. Consequently, in TARGET, the fabula elements are causally connected but it is not necessary to make explicit the fact that those connections can be semantically different.

Another major difference is the fact that TARGET supports interactive stories, meaning that some characters can be played by a human user. This raises a challenge concerning how to document the user's character Internal Elements, Goals, Outcomes and event Perceptions. A character controlled by a player is what we call "viewpoint character" (VC) and we only represent its' actions in the emerging fabula. The VC is a character through which a player "percepts" the emerging events into a story in a process called "storification"[12]. Notice that causality between VC's actions and their consequences still remains. What we don't represent is what caused a given VC's action. This is not a limitation at all since we don't want to control player's actions and we assume that the player will act "in-character" interpreting a given role as in the premises of Barros et al [13]. The resulting modifications to the Fabula model are captured in Figure 1.

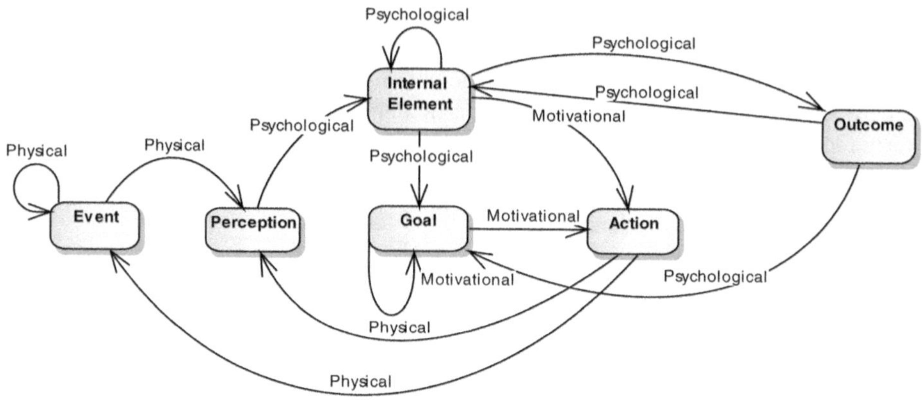

Fig. 1. TARGET's Fabula Model

3.3 Cases

The use of the TARGET Fabula model enables the system to recognize where in the story landscape a VC is navigating. The shaping of the story is done by both dramatic and learning outcomes, which is achieved by the use of Cases.

A Case represents part of a fabula that implicitly reflects an authorial vision of an interesting sequence of events and is used in the process of "narrative inspiration"[14]. It also serves the purpose of identify points in the emerging fabula where the author viewpoint might be imposed. According to [15] the following constraints should hold:

1) A Case captures a narrative concept, which could for instance be 'hiding from a threat' or 'flying over an area to search for something'. Therefore a case has the representation of the story elements corresponding to a problem and the associated solution, which means that for each narrative concept, there may be multiple cases.
2) A Case must be context complete with regards to the associated narrative concept, which implies the existence of all the elements necessary for the case to be regarded as believable by the author of the case. Therefore, not all elements within a case are instantiated if they don't contribute for the expression of the narrative concept.

However, in TARGET, one needs to consider not only the *storyness*, but also *learning outcomes*. Consequently, a case corresponds to a situated context where a leaner needs to use a particular competence. This implies that for each competence, there are one or more cases associated to it and these are used to "inspire" story direction.

3.4 Case Retrieval

The case selection mechanism used in TARGET is captured in the block diagram of figure 2.

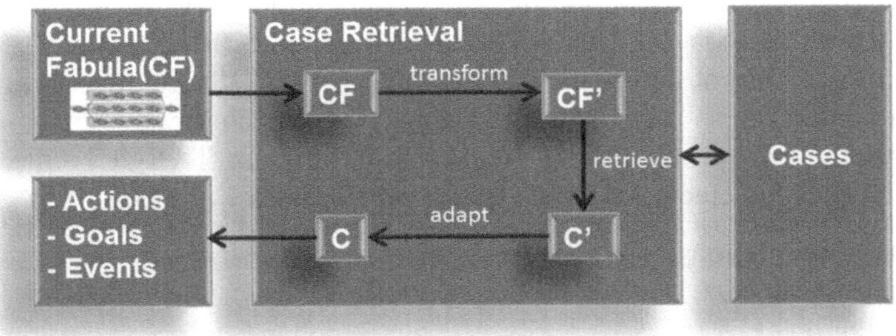

Fig. 2. Case selection overview

The process starts with the transformation of the current fabula to expand the space of possible applicable cases. This analysis is done with some abstraction so generalization transformations are used based on the knowledge representation of the world domain (e.g. "Talk with a person" can be generalized to "Communicate with a person"). Once a Case is retrieved, it is necessary to apply the inverse transformations previously made to adapt the case to the current context. Finally, suggested characters' actions, characters' goals or simulation events are returned based on the retrieved case.

This process identifies in the current emerging fabula, situations similar to the ones represented in the cases. When at least one Case is retrieved, the TARGET Narrative Engine has the opportunity to intervene in the story and direct it. This "direction" relates to the process of "Narrative Control" and a number of issues arise when it is used with emergent narrative. Naturally, any form of control embodies the challenges associated to Narrative Paradox. Consequently, the TARGET Narrative Engine adopts some intervention guidelines that aim to shape the story without compromising its believability. These guidelines are based on the "Drama Management properties" identified by Swartjes [16]:

1) If autonomous characters are used, drama management is incremental.
2) If autonomous characters are used, drama management must be opportune.
3) If autonomous characters are used, story-level goals must be optional.

These properties reflect the facts of building on what has already emerged instead of taking the future into account (1), pursue story-level goals when opportunities occur to achieve them instead of coerce the event sequence (2) and since guidance is unreliable, abandoning story-level goals does not make the simulation fail (3). In practice, (1) is satisfied because we retrieve narrative cases based on the fabula built with the events so far, (2) is satisfied by the fact of waiting for events to occur until a case is applicable and (3) is satisfied simply because the simulation will not fail when a story-level goal is not achieved.

To achieve a story goal, characters have to be influenced by the "Drama Manager" to do the "interesting" thing given certain situations. However, characters should also stay in character (IC) in order to maintain their believability. Directing autonomous characters is a research topic addressed in a number of works as referenced in [17, 18, 19]. According to Blumberg et al., we can see external control of characters as "weighted preferences or suggestions" that are in favor or against behaviors or actions. Swartjes argued that this form of control is ultimately "unreliable" as agents may or may not follow the suggestions but concluded that "It is, however, the price to pay for trying to control autonomous believable agents". Szilas investigation points towards the use of this "unreliable" guidance of believable autonomous characters through the use of a "negotiation" mechanism [20]. In TARGET, the Narrative Engine influences the emerging fabula in three different ways:

1) Character's actions;
2) Character's goals;
3) Simulation events;

The first one is strongly influenced by Szilas work on combining plot direction with character believability. The second and third also work with a mechanism of negotiation to maintain consistent character personalities (2) and realistic simulation (3). The next section describes the Narrative Engine module and how the cases are used to guide the emergent narrative.

4 TARGET's Narrative Engine

The Narrative Engine (NE) is the module that supports the generation and control of interesting stories. The high level overview of how the NE integrates with the TARGET Platform is captured in Figure 3.

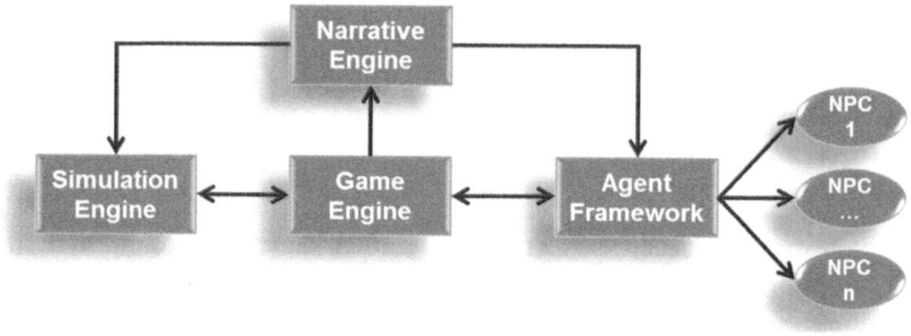

Fig. 3. Narrative Engine in relation to other components in TARGET platform

The Game Engine is responsible for rendering the story in 3D and it is through this component that the learner interacts with the story. The NPCs (Non-Player Characters) are managed and controlled by an Agent Framework and the simulation processes are handled by a Simulation Engine, which defines the reality. The conceptual architecture of the Narrative Engine is captured by Figure 4.

A Story has several associated elements: *Competences* denote the learning goals the player wants to achieve through storytelling. To each learning goal, we associate a set of cases. This process corresponds to the instantiation of the Cases sub-module. *Roles* refer to characters' behavior as believable autonomous agents within the world simulation. Roles are used to instantiate the AF which will manage each character. *Processes* and *Rules* are the elements that represent what simulation processes will be

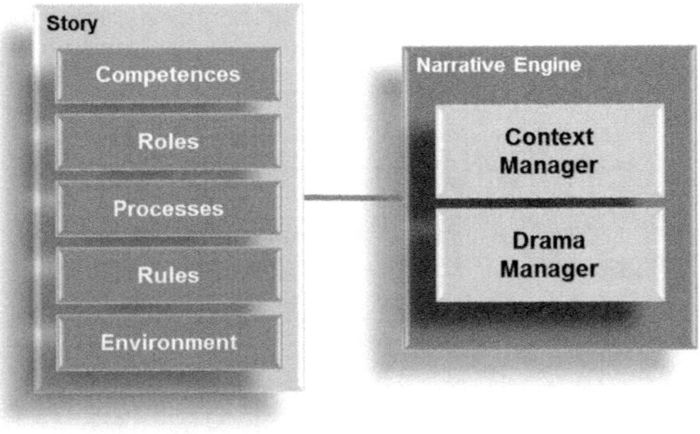

Fig. 4. Narrative Engine conceptual architecture

used and the rules to which they must obey. These elements are used to instantiate the Simulation Engine. *Environment* describes the space in which the story will take place. These elements are used to instantiate the Game Engine. After the explained instantiations, the *Drama Manager* will start listening to events generated by the story world and starts building the emerging fabula. Whenever the *Content Manager* detects an opportunity to apply a Case (or a set of Cases) that can be applied to the current context, *narrative control* is enabled.

4.1 Narrative Control

Injecting narrative control according to the underling cases can be done either by triggering simulation events or suggesting new goals and actions to characters without compromising simulation realism or character's believability. Therefore, in order to manage this tradeoff a negotiation mechanism between the Narrative Engine and the Agent Framework/Simulation Engine was used.

When the Drama Manager triggers an event, the Simulation Engine may or may not accept that request depending on if the current simulation rules will hold or not. Changing a character's goal requires the representation of Personal Values of the character, which then permit it to decide whether to adopt (or not) the suggested goals. Notice that influencing a character goal or a character's actions has substantial different effects on believability. A goal is a general behavior while actions depend on the character's personality. The negotiation mechanism involving simulation events and agent goals is illustrated in figure 5.

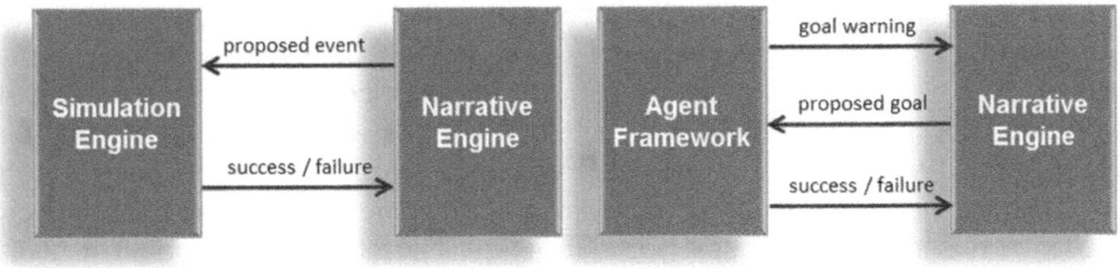

Fig. 5. Negotiation mechanisms (left: events, right: goals)

The negotiation mechanism that involves influencing characters actions is illustrated in figure 6.

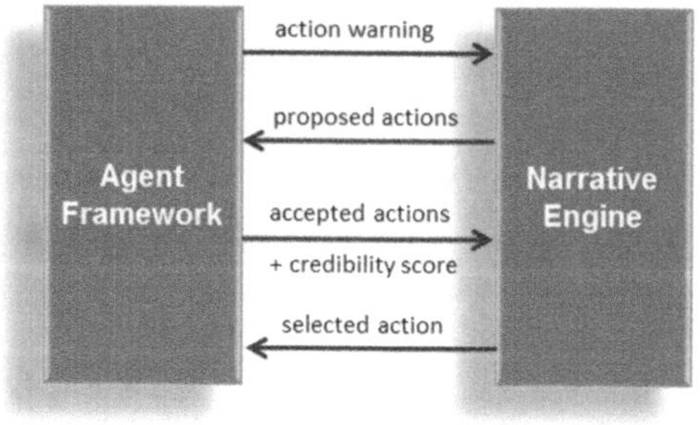

Fig. 6. Action selection negotiation

This mechanism was strongly influenced by Szilas work on Drama Manager and Intelligent Agent's (IA's) cooperation [20]. When the Narrative Engine is warned by the Agent Framework regarding an incoming character's action, it suggests a set of meaningful actions to the Agent Framework. These actions have a correspondent narrative interest score that is calculated according to the level of resemblance between the current situation and the Cases. These set of actions are then classified by the Agent Framework according to its credibility, which reflects each action's believability. The Narrative Engine then confronts this information with the level of narrative interest and chooses the most appropriate action. The process of confronting believability and narrative interest is based on balanced combination of a set of thresholds.

Finally the action is sent to the Agent Framework and played by the character. Note that the set of proposed actions may not contain any "acceptable action". In that case, the character will not be influenced by the Narrative Engine.

4.2 Example

A very simplified example is presented using the current implementation of the approach proposed in this paper. In Figure 7 is a *representation* of an authored case about "conflict seeding", applicable when teaching the "conflict management" competence. The character "Adam" is the protagonist and the character "Bob" is the antagonist. This case represents a story where Adam is a project manager that requires a resource (Herb) who belongs to another project manager – Bob. Adam has setup a meeting with Bob to discuss the temporary ownership transfer of the said resource from Bob to Adam. The associated competence to this story is leadership, and one of the associated cases is the management of resources that belong to another project manager. So even if Bob is unhappy with the request, conceding to the request will lead the story to the desired situated context where the learner (in the role of Adam) needs to demonstrate leadership towards Herb since he doesn't have formal authority.

Let's consider that the emerged fabula context matches the case when Bob decides to do an action the Agent Framework warns the Narrative Engine about it and the "Accept Adam's Request" action (or an adaptation of it) will be suggested. If the

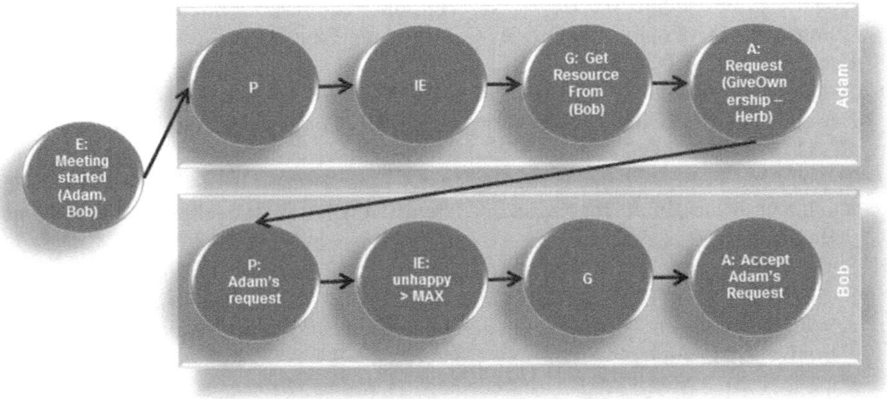

Fig. 7. Graphical representation of an example case

Agent Framework complies with this suggestion, Bob will concede the resource leading to the desired situated context. Note that the case can be transformed and adapted to match different similar contexts, for instance, characters can have other name and the protagonist can perform other actions instead of "GiveOwnership".

5 Conclusions

In this paper, we presented a narrative engine that supports emergent storytelling for the development of complex competences. Towards this purpose, the Fabula model was extended to support interactive storytelling with learning outcomes shaping the story in addition to the dramatic content. The underlying framework has been developed with some examples and current work involves the creation of more elaborate contexts.

References

1. Bennett, S., Maton, K., Kervin, L.: The 'Digital Natives' Debate: A Critical Review of the Evidence. British Journal of Educational Technology 39(5), 775–786
2. de Freitas, S.: Using Games and Simulations for Supporting Learning. Learning, Media and Technology 31, 343–358 (2006)
3. Prensky, M.: Don't Bother Me Mom I'm Learning. St. Paul, MN
4. Aldrich, C.: Learning by Doing: A Comprehensive Guide to Simulations. In: Computer Games, and Pedagogy in E-learning and other Educational Experiences. Pfeiffer, San Francisco
5. Papadimitriou, C.H.: MythematiCS: In Praise of Storytelling in the Teaching of Computer Science and Math. SIGCSE Bull. 35, 7–9
6. Murray, J.H.: Hamlet on the Holodeck: the Future of Narrative in Cyberspace. MIT Press, Boston
7. Louchart, S., Swartjes, I., Kriegel, M., Aylett, R.: Purposeful authoring for emergent narrative. In: Spierling, U., Szilas, N. (eds.) ICIDS 2008. LNCS, vol. 5334, pp. 273–284. Springer, Heidelberg (2008)

8. Hulpus, I., Fradinho, M., Hayes, C., Hokstad, L., Seager, W., Flanagan, M.: Rapid Competence Development in Serious Games: using Case-Based Reasoning and Threshold Concepts. In: CSEDU (2010)
9. Aylett, R., Louchart, S., Dias, J., Paiva, A., Vala, M., Woods, S., Hall, L.: Unscripted Narrative for Affectively Driven Characters. IEEE Computer Graphics and Applications, 42–52 (May/June 2006)
10. Theune, M., Faas, S., Nijholt, A., Heylen, D.: The Virtual Storyteller: Story creation by intelligent agents. In: Technologies for Interactive Digital Storytelling and Entertainment (TIDSE), pp. 204–215 (2003)
11. Swartjes, I., Theune, M.: A fabula model for emergent narrative. In: Göbel, S., Malkewitz, R., Iurgel, I. (eds.) TIDSE 2006. LNCS, vol. 4326, pp. 49–60. Springer, Heidelberg (2006)
12. Aylett, R.: Emergent Narrative, Social Immersion and "Storification". In: Proceedings Narrative and Learning Environments Conference NILE 2000, Edinburgh, Scotland (2000)
13. Barros, L.M., Musse, S.R.: Introducing Narrative Principles into Planning-based Interactive Storytelling. In: Proc. of ACM SIGCHI Intl. Conference on Advances in Computer Entertainment Technology (ACE 2005), pp. 35–42 (2005)
14. Swartjes, I.: Using narrative cases to author interactive story content. In: Ma, L., Rauterberg, M., Nakatsu, R. (eds.) ICEC 2007. LNCS, vol. 4740, pp. 205–210. Springer, Heidelberg (2007)
15. Swartjes, I., Vromen, J., Bloom, N.: Narrative Inspiration: Using Case Based Problem Solving to Support Emergent Story Generation. In: Proceedings of the International Joint Workshop on Computational Creativity, Goldsmiths, University of London, June 17-19 (2007)
16. Swartjes, I.: Whose Story is it Anyway: How Improv Informs Agency and Authorship of Emergent Narrative (2010), `http://www.vf.utwente.nl/~swartjes/dissertation/`
17. Riedl, M.O., Stern, A.: Believable Agents and Intelligent Story Adaptation for Interactive Storytelling. In: Göbel, S., Malkewitz, R., Iurgel, I. (eds.) TIDSE 2006. LNCS, vol. 4326, pp. 1–12. Springer, Heidelberg (2006)
18. Riedl, M.O., Stern, A.: Failing Believably: Toward Drama Management with Autonomous Actors in Interactive Narratives. In: Göbel, S., Malkewitz, R., Iurgel, I. (eds.) TIDSE 2006. LNCS, vol. 4326, pp. 195–206. Springer, Heidelberg (2006)
19. Figueiredo, R., Brisson, A., Aylett, R., Paiva, A.: Emergent stories facilitated. In: Spierling, U., Szilas, N. (eds.) ICIDS 2008. LNCS, vol. 5334, pp. 218–229. Springer, Heidelberg (2008)
20. Szilas, N.: The Future of Interactive Drama. ACM International Conference Proceeding Series, vol. 123, pp. 193–199. Creativity & Cognition Studios Press, Sydney (2005)
21. Szilas, N., Axelrad, M.: To Be or Not to Be: Towards Stateless Interactive Drama. LNCS, pp. 280–291. Springer, Heidelberg (2009)
22. Figueiredo, R., Brisson, A., Aylett, R., Paiva, A.: Emergent stories facilitated. In: Spierling, U., Szilas, N. (eds.) ICIDS 2008. LNCS, vol. 5334, pp. 218–229. Springer, Heidelberg (2008)
23. Dettori, G., Paiva, A.: Narrative Learning in Technology-Enhanced Learning. In: Balacheff, N., Ludvigsen, S., Jong, T., Lazonder, A., Barnes, S. (eds.) Narrative, pp. 55–69 (2009)
24. Druckman, D., Bjork, R.A.: In the Mind"s Eye: Enhancing Human Performance. The National Academies Press, Washington (1991)
25. Charles, D., McAlister, M.: Integrating ideas about invisible playgrounds from play theory into online educational digital games. In: Rauterberg, M. (ed.) ICEC 2004. LNCS, vol. 3166, pp. 598–601. Springer, Heidelberg (2004)
26. Ayllet, R.: Narrative in Virtual Environments towards Emergent Narrative. In: Proceedings AAAI Symposium on Narrative Intelligence (1999)

Community Adaptive Educational Games

Clement Leung[1], Yuanxi Li[1], Jiming Liu[1], and Alfredo Milani[1,2]

[1] Department of Computer Science
Hong Kong Baptist University, Hong Kong, China
{clement,yxli,jiming}@comp.hkbu.edu.hk
[2] Department of Mathematics and Computer Science
University of Perugia, Italy
milani@unipg.it

Abstract. This paper presents an adaptive architecture for educational games which are evolved and optimized in order to fulfill the educational goals while reflecting the specific requirements and features of the user community. The approach is based on an online genetic framework where typical genetic operators like crossover and mutation are designed to evolve a population of games, and the online fitness driving the evolution is given by a metric of user behavior/performance, evaluated on the actual community of users. The evolutionary structure adapt can also be applied for continuous game adaptation in dynamical domains where the user community and/or the educational goals are changing over the time.

Keywords: community adaptive games, educational game, genetic algorithms.

1 Introduction

A major problem in Educational Games (EGs) design is to generate games which represent an effective match between the user characteristics and the educational goals which are expected to be obtained through the practice of the EG. The user interactive behavior and the effectiveness of reinforcement learning process activated by EG, largely depends on social, cultural, and individual factors which cannot be easily foreseen, or even known, by the EG designer [1]. EG design is then essentially an experimental activity where designers use their knowledge of users in a design and experiment cycle similar to classical software development models. Techniques of automatic game synthesis [2] has been introduced to enhance the design phase, and *adaptive educational games(AEGs)* [3], [4], [5] have been proposed in order to adapt the games in real time to the characteristics of the *individual* players, some major drawback has to be considered: sometime AEGs require a knowledge of the user characteristics which is not available in advance [3]; some user/system precious times is "wasted" in the adaptive process; adaptation is usually made on an individual basis [6] and similar individuals cannot benefit from the previous adaptation process. A user community, for instance, often share general features (age group, social level etc.) and common behaviors should be embedded in the design of EGs for that community [7].

X. Luo et al. (Eds.): ICWL 2010 Workshops, LNCS 6537, pp. 45–54, 2011.

The increasing number of online games [8], [9], either educational or not, with a potentially huge number of users, which are shared in the framework of user social networks and communities [10], [11] poses the question if it is possible to automate the process EG design/testing, such that the EGs can be adapted to the user community while maintaining their specific educational purposes.

In this paper we propose an architecture for adaptive educational games, where EGs are evolved and optimized in order to fulfill the educational goals while reflecting the specific requirements and features of the user community. The approach is based on a promising online Genetic Algorithms (GA) [12] framework which has been applied to online multimedia retrieval [13] and content generation [14], [15]. In the proposed framework, typical GA [16] operators like crossover and mutation evolve a population of games, the online fitness driving the evolution is given by a metric of user performance.

In this architecture the role of the *educational game designer* consists in defining the constraints of the game domain, i.e. space of possible games, and in providing an appropriate fitness metric which embeds the educational goals. The GA "survival of the fittest" heuristics will explore the game domains by generating new games instances which are evaluated on the actual community of users, and which eventually converges toward a population of games which reflect the learning features of the users.

Although a simple *Treasure* game is used as reference example, the proposed evolutionary architecture is quite general and can be applied to games with more complex structures and using more complex metrics to evaluate the achievement of the educational goals.

```
CURR_GAMES := Initialize()     //a random population of games
while (Termination_condition() or #iterations < max) do
      NEXT_GAMES :=Elitism(CURR_GAMES)
      repeat
          g1 ← Selection(CURR_GAMES) // Selection
          if (rand( pcross ))        //Crossover with probability pcross
                                     g2 ← Selection(CURR_GAMES)
                                     (gnext1, gnext2) ← Crossover(g1 , g2)//
          else gnext ←g1
          if (rand( pmut ))          //Mutation with probability pmut
                                     gnext← Mutation(gnext)
          NEXT_GAMES ← NEXT_GAMES ∪ gnext
      until (sizeof(NEXT_GAMES) = pop_size )
      CURR_GAMES ← NEXT_GAMES
      Deploy(CURR_GAMES)
      Evaluate_fitness(CURR_GAMES)
      #iteration ← #iteration + 1
wend
```

Fig. 1. The Adaptive Genetic Algorithm for EG

In Section 2 the Evolutionary Adaptive architecture for EGs is introduced together with the *Treasure* game and the user metric used as reference. The issues of adapting the genetic operator and representation to the EG context are discussed in the Section 3. Future work is discussed and conclusions are drawn in Section 4.

2 An Evolutionary Architecture for Educational Games

Genetic algorithms are popular heuristics [17] inspired by the natural evolution principle of survival of the fittest which have been successfully applied to many different optimization problems [18]. Although most GAs carry out offline optimizations, i.e. the fitness function can be computed by the algorithm, online genetic algorithms [12] have been proposed for optimization problems where the fitness is represented by some online function external to the algorithm. A typical example is [14] where an online GA is used to manage an *online newspaper*; in this case the fitness is represented by the user's satisfaction, and it cannot be known until the users actually read the newspaper. In [13] the online user feedback has been integrated in the evolutionary process to drive image retrieval.

The online genetic algorithm scheme proposed for evolving educational games is shown in fig.1. The algorithm starts with a current initial population of games, and then it iterates until certain termination conditions are met, for instance the maximum number of iterations or a given fitness level are reached.

At each iteration, the algorithm loops through a sequence of phases of *selection*, *crossover*, and *mutation* in order to build a new population of improved games for the next iteration. Once the next generation of games has been produced, the games are *deployed* to the user community which actually plays them. The *assessment* phase consists in measuring the achievement of the educational goals by analyzing different aspects of the game played by the users, such as performance, behavior, acquired skills and abilities etc. This measure is then used as *fitness* to guide the evolution of the next iteration. The *elitism* phase consists in passing a subset the best game instances to the next generation.

In the following we will analyze the main issues in designing a genetic algorithm for evolving and optimizing Educational Games. In general the representation techniques and the genetic operators can greatly differ depending on the given game.

Without lost of generality we will consider a sample "Treasure" game which has features which can be found in many classes of games.

2.1 The Sample Treasure Game Domain

The sample game, *Treasure*, is a simple path based game where the user has to reach the *treasure box* in room R_N, starting from room R_1 while traversing a series of non linearly interconnected *rooms/scenarios*. The user has no initial knowledge of the game map.

In each room the user can find a different set of challenges represented by *animated characters agents* [19] $C_i \in C$ to be defeated in order to pass to one of the next available scenarios. Associated with the animated characters C_i there are some abilities required by the user in order to successfully interact with the character. For instance an animated character can assess *knowledge on a scientific subject*, e.g. a character C_1 asks questions of chemistry, characters C_2 and C_3 ask questions of math and physics respectively, other characters can assess *coordination ability*, (e.g. C_4 requires to fight with a sword, and C_5 is a snake whose bite has to be avoided) finally other characters can assess *visual ability*, e.g. the user has to recognize figures painted by character C_6.

The purpose of a scenario is also providing an environment which contains *learning elements* helping the user to learn knowledge on given subjects (e.g. by observing experiments or reading books), or to learn abilities by practice (e.g. by repeatedly fighting against character C_4, or by exercising the figure recognition skills with characters C_6. The learning elements of a room cannot be modified while the characters contained in a room can vary.

Moreover it is assumed that in each game instance the number of available rooms $R_1,\ldots R_N$ is fixed, and each room has 4 doors which can directly lead to any other room depending on the game map. For the sake of simplicity, we assume that *valid maps* are in the shape of 3-ary trees, where room R_1 is the root and R_N is reachable by one or more leaf nodes. Not all the scenarios R_2 ,..., R_{N-1} are necessarily present in all valid maps. The doors can be concealed behind objects or other elements of the scenario. Once the player have found a door, it can appear safeguarded by one animated agent which has to be defeated in order to open the door for discovering if there is a dead end behind, or it leads to some other room or possibly to the *treasure box*.

Given the previous description, the *domain G* of possible games which can be generated is represented by all the possible 3-nary trees which can be obtained by combining the *N-1* scenarios, in all the $/C/^4$ variations possible for each scenarios by placing (or not) an animated character to guard a door, and the possible ways of assigning the treasure room R_N to the leaves of each tree.

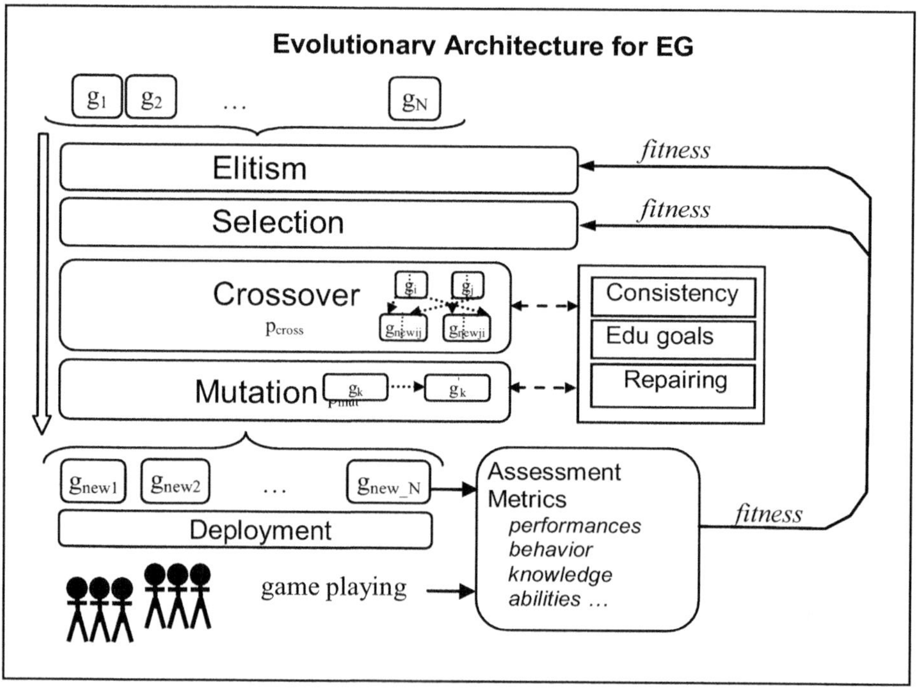

Fig. 2. The Adaptive Evolutionary Architecture for EG

2.2 A Sample Metric for the Treasure Game

An appropriate metric which can be used as a GA fitness should measure the achievement of the educational goals by the user who has played the game and the achievement of other goals such as elapsed time, quality of the game experience etc.

Let us assume for example that the educational goals of the *Treasure* game are to develop the user ability in the three aforementioned categories *knowledge*, *coordination* and *visual* skills; moreover, playing the game should take the shortest possible time. A possible *metric of user u performance on an instance* $g \in G$ of the sample game can then be defined by

$$m_{u,g} = w_1 * (min(c_1 + c_2 + c_3, max_1) + w_2 * (min(c_4 + c_5, max_2)) + \\ + w_3 * (min(c_6 , max_3) - w_4 * t$$

where w_1, w_2, w_3 and w_4 are respectively the weighted scientific *knowledge*, *coordination* ability, *visual* ability, and playing *time* and the values c_i represent the number of defeated characters for each category as a result by user *u* playing the instance *g*, i.e. we assume that defeating an animated character is a way of assessing the user's respective ability [20], [21]. The operator *min* has the purpose of cutting at max_i the values in each category thus avoiding bargaining, for instance, *knowledge* for *visual ability*.

Definition. The Community EG Optimization Problem can be defined as the problem of finding the best game configuration instance *g* in a game domain *G* which optimizes (maximizes) the metric $m_{u,g}$ on a community *U* of users.

In other words the Community EG Optimization problem consists in finding $g \in G$ such that

$$\Sigma_{(u \in U)}\, m_{u,g} = max_{g' \in G} \left(\Sigma_{(u \in U)}\, m_{u,g'} \right)$$

It is apparent that although both the game structure and the metric are intentionally simplified for the sake of exposition clarity, the same general definition and scheme holds for more complex metrics and game structures, whenever the goal is optimizing the overall performance of the user community.

3 Genetic Operators for Educational Games

3.1 Hybrid EG Chromosomes

A basic issue in evolutionary algorithm is to design a suitable representation for the chromosomes, i.e. the population of the individuals representing the objects to be evolved. Classic GA uses a straightforward binary representation for numerical optimization problems, where each individual chromosome is a sequence of bits and each gene is represented by a single bit, while in *genetic programming* evolutionary operators are applied to complex structures such as syntactic trees or networks.

In the case of EGs the most suitable solution is to use a hybrid representation: the chromosome genes are partitioned in different classes in order to reflect the features of the different component of the games, where different classes of genes will undergo different genetic operators. In the case of the sample Treasure game, we can identify two main different classes of genes: *combinatorial genes* and *structured genes*, the first class represents assignments of animated characters to the room's doors, the second describes the 3-ary tree structure D_{tree}.

A possible representation for a game instance g in the population is then a tuple

$$g \equiv (D_1 ,\ldots, D_{N-1} , D_{tree})$$

where each $D_i=(d_{i,1}, d_{i,2}, d_{i,3}, d_{i,4})$ represents the assignments of guardians to the 4 doors for each room R_i , and each $d_{i,j}$ varies in the domain {C ∪ null}, *null* represents no guardians at a door.

3.2 Selection and Elitism for EG

Selection is the phase of the GA scheme where the best individuals are selected in order to form the next generation. Selection is based on random methods, such as the "roulette-wheel" which assigns each individual a sector of the "wheel" proportional to its fitness and uses a uniformly distributed random variable.

In the case of EG the natural solution is to give a game g chances proportional to the value of metric $m_{u,g}$ which the game g has previously obtained by the users who have played it.

It is worth noting that in order to give a reliable evaluation of the fitness each instance of game g should be experimented by an appropriate number of users U_{size} and the fitness should be taken as the averaged fitness on those users.

The purpose of the randomization is to avoid premature convergence of the population and maintaining genetic variety by giving some non null chances of survival to individuals with low fitness since their evolution can lead to improvement in the current results. On the other hand randomization can sometimes delete the best performing individuals from the next generation. In order to avoid this problem, the *elitism* mechanism selects a set of k individuals to pass unchanged to next generation, thus preserving the best so far chromosomes. The size of k should be lower in the first iterations in order to privilege exploration capabilities while it should increase in the last iterations to facilitate convergence.

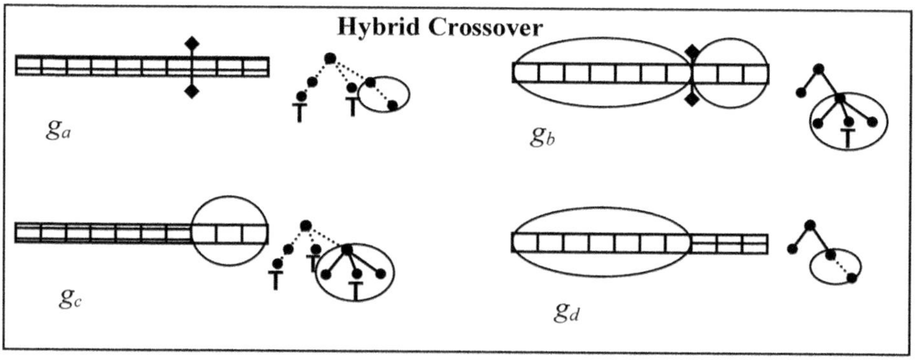

Fig. 3. Hybrid Crossover for EG

3.3 Crossover for EG

The purpose of the crossover phase is to generate new games by combining the best games selected in the current population. The underlying idea is that the best features of both *parents* games can be transmitted to their outbreed. Crossover is regulated by a probability parameter p_{cross}. A great variety of crossover operators exists in the literature, they are designed to guarantee the exploration of the search space and to maintain in the descendants some features of the parents. A typical property of the crossover operator is the fixed point property *g=Crossover(g,g)*, i.e. an individual which is mated with itself should produce the same individual unchanged.

In the case of the hybrid chromosome representation for EGs, different crossover operators are applied to different classes of genes. In the case of the *Treasure* game given the chromosomes of the two games g_a and g_b

where $g_a \equiv (D_{1a}, \ldots, D_{N\text{-}1a}, D_{tree,a})$ and $g_b \equiv (D_{1b}, \ldots, D_{N\text{-}1b}, D_{tree,b})$ their crossover is defined by

$$(g_c,g_d) \leftarrow Crossover(g_a , g_b)=Crossover((D_{1a},\ldots,D_{N\text{-}1a},D_{tree,a}),(D_{1b},\ldots,D_{N\text{-}1b},D_{tree,b}))$$

Crossover function acts separately on the *combinatorial* and the *structured* genes by the two operators $Cross_1$ and $Cross_2$ the results are then passed to the *repair* function which checks and possibly re-establishes the consistency of the generated games.

Crossover operator $Cross_1$ is a single point crossover operator acting on the vectors of the rooms configuration: a room index *k* in [1,N-1] is randomly selected and then the first *[1,k]* (*[k+1, N-1]*) room configurations of g_a (g_b) are joined with the *[k+1, N-1]* (*[1,k]*) rooms of g_b (g_a) to form the *[1,N-1]* room vector of g_c (g_d).

$$((D_{1c}, \ldots, D_{N\text{-}1c}), (D_{1d}, \ldots, D_{N\text{-}1d})) \leftarrow Cross_1((D_{1a}, \ldots, D_{N\text{-}1a}),(D_{1b}, \ldots, D_{N\text{-}1b}))$$

The crossover operator $Cross_2$ is a tree cross over operator typical of genetic programming techniques: a node k_a in $D_{tree,a}$ is randomly selected, the *corresponding node*[1] k_b in $D_{tree,b}$ is also selected, then the two subtrees rooted in k_a and k_b *are* exchanged, generating the two new trees $D_{tree,c}$ and $D_{tree,d}$.

$$(D_{tree,c} , D_{tree,d}) \leftarrow Cross_2(D_{tree,a} , D_{tree,b})$$

The role of *repair* operator will be explained in the following paragraph. The results g_c and g_d of applying *crossover* to g_a and g_b are depicted in figure 3. Note that $Cross_1$ and $Cross_2$ both verify the fixed point property for crossover.

3.4 EG Consistency and Repairing

The application of genetic operators can lead to inconsistent chromosomes, i.e. individuals which do not correspond to valid games; in this case a repairing phase is necessary to ensure that games g_c and g_d are consistent:

$$g_c \leftarrow \text{repair}(D_{1c}, \ldots, D_{N\text{-}1c} , D_{tree,c}) \quad g_d \leftarrow \text{repair}(D_{1d},\ldots, D_{N\text{-}1d} , D_{tree,d})$$

---

[1] Given a node k_a in a tree $D_{tree,a}$ its *corresponding node* k_b in tree $D_{tree,b}$ is defined as the node in $D_{tree,b}$ which is reached by a path from the root which descends the same arcs in the same order, if a corresponding node does not exist then the most distant node along the path is selected as k_b.

The inconsistency can be a *logical inconsistency*; for instance in certain conditions $Cross_2$ can generate a tree where no path to the treasure room exists (see for example the tree structure of g_d in fig.3 which has no treasure node), or where some rooms are doubled then violating the constraint on the rooms' topology. While the first kind of inconsistency can be easily re-established by selecting one or more leaf to be connected to R_N, the other could require a deep rearrangement of the tree's nodes. On the other hand we can also have *educational inconsistencies*; for instance $Cross_1$ can generate a room configuration vector where no animated characters of type C_4 and C_5 exists. This means that *educational goals* are not reachable since the user coordination ability, assessed by these characters, is impossible to verify in that game instance. In this latter case consistency can be re-established by adding appropriate characters to reachable rooms or by connecting to the tree rooms which contain the needed animated characters. In general a consistency check and repairing module should be taken into account of violation of logical consistency determined by games rules as well as of violation of educational goals.

3.5 Mutation in EG

The mutation operators guarantee genetic variation and avoid that the population of the GA stucks in local maxima. Their application is regulated by a probabilistic parameter p_{mut} . Different mutation operators mut_1 and mut_2 are defined for the different classes of genes.

Mutation mut_1 operates on the room configuration vector by randomly selecting: a *room* and a *door* to mutate and a *new value* for the chosen door in the characters domain {C ∪ `null`}.

Operator mut_2 mutates the game *path tree structure* by using genetic programming techniques as described by $mut_{2.1}, mut_{2.2}$ .and $mut_{2.3}$, they randomly select a tree node and:

- $mut_{2.1}$ delete one of its arcs;
- $mut_{2.2}$ add one arc toward another randomly selected node;
- $mut_{2.3}$ substituted it with another unused node randomly chosen

It is also worth noting that the *mutation* operators can lead to inconsistencies of either types which have to be checked and removed by the *repair* operator.

3.6 Initialization, Termination and Continuous Evolution of EG

The idea underlying online Educational Games evolution is that the user community can shape the form of the game with respect to its requirements, abilities and idiosyncrasies. For instance a community of users which is very good in *manual coordination* will not require many animated characters to test their specific ability, while a less expert community could require more characters, and a longer path to the '*treasure*' in order to be trained and reach a good performance at the end of the game.

Usually genetic algorithms randomly choose the initial population, in the case of EGs it is reasonable to expect that an initial population of games given by the *game designer* will produce a faster and more effective evolution.

A relevant difference between static GA and online GA is that in certain domains it is possible and likely to avoid the termination condition. For instance, in a user community, it is reasonable to continuously evolve the best so far population of *educational games,* instead of selecting a *final optimal game*. The reason is that the user community features dynamically change over the time: new/old members enter/leave the community; the users themselves are changed by the act of playing the game by improving their abilities or by preferring new characters and scenarios. The self-adaptive genetic mechanism is then expected to follow the community trend.

Elitism is also particularly important with continuous community optimization since we are interested not only in finding the final optimal game, but also in optimizing the overall performance during the iterations.

4 Conclusion

In this paper we have introduced an evolutionary framework for Community Adaptive Educational Games, where instances of games in an educational game domain are optimized by online user assessment, with respect to the educational goals and to the features of the user community. Specific issues concerning GA operators and their definitions in the EG context have been presented and discussed. The proposed method is self-adaptive in the sense that different user communities can produce different game evolution with the same educational goals[21][22]. Moreover, the GA proposed approach is also suitable for managing continuous evolution in dynamic domains where the features of the user community or the educational goals change/evolve over time.

We devise a future where educational games can be evolved by different community of users; in this view the role of the *educational game designer* can be rather redefined as a designer of *educational game domains,* which define the *space* of possible games where the user driven evolution can take place. The designer should primarily identify the game components their compositional structure and their role in the educational process, and focus on definition of fitness metrics which guide the GA evolution by assessing the achievement of educational goals thru the analysis of user performances and interaction.

Further research will regard the extension of the GA framework to other classes of game domains, the evaluation of the performances in a simulated user environments and the experimentation in a real user community.

References

1. de Freitas, S., Oliver, M.: How can exploratory learning with games and simulations within the curriculum be most effectively evaluated? Computer & Education 46, 249–264 (2006)
2. Bieliková, M., Divéky, M., Jurnečka, P., Kajan, R., Omelina, L.: Automatic generation of adaptive, educational and multimedia computer games. Signal, Image and Video Processing 2(4), 371–384, doi:10.1007/s11760-008-0086-z
3. Peirce, N., Conlan, O., Wade, V.: Adaptive Educational Games: Providing Non-invasive Personalised Learning Experiences. In: DIGITEL 2008: Proc.of IEEE Int. Conf. on Digital Game and Intelligent Toy Enhanced Learning, pp. 28–35. IEEE Press, Los Alamitos (2008)

4. Torrente, J., Moreno-Ger, P., Fernández-Manjón, B., del Blanco, Á.: Game-Like Simulations for Online Adaptive Learning: A Case Study. In: Chang, M., Kuo, R., Kinshuk, Chen, G.-D., Hirose, M. (eds.) Learning by Playing. LNCS, vol. 5670, pp. 162–173. Springer, Heidelberg (2009)
5. Champagnat, R., Prigent, A., Estraillier, P.: Scenario building based on formal methods and adaptative execution. In: Proceedings of ISAGA, Atlanta, USA (2005)
6. Conati, C., Manske, M.: Evaluating adaptive feedback in an educational computer game. In: Ruttkay, Z., Kipp, M., Nijholt, A., Vilhjálmsson, H.H. (eds.) IVA 2009. LNCS, vol. 5773, pp. 146–158. Springer, Heidelberg (2009)
7. Liu, F., Zhang, N., Cao, S., Lu, R.: An Approach of User Community Preference Discovery Applied in IPTV Personalized Interactive Services. In: MASS 2009, Int. Conf. on Management and Service Science, September 20-22, pp. 1–4 (2009)
8. Harger, B., Jimison, D., Myers, E., Smith, B., Tellerman, S.: Emergent Stories in Massively Multiplayer Online Games: Using Improvisational Techniques to Design for Emotional Impact. In: Rauterberg, M. (ed.) ICEC 2004. LNCS, vol. 3166, pp. 359–362. Springer, Heidelberg (2004)
9. Chambers, C., Feng, W.-c., Sahu, S., Saha, D., Brandt, D.: Characterizing Online Games. IEEE/ACM Transactions on Networking 18(3), 899–910 (2010)
10. `http://www.facebook.com`
11. `http://www.myspace.com`
12. Milani, A.: Online genetic Algorithms. International Journal of Information Theories and Applications (2004) ISSN 1310-0513
13. Chan, A., Leung, C., Milani, A.: Community Adaptive Search Engines. International Journal of Advanced Intelligence Paradigms (IJAIP) 1(4), 432–443 (2009), Inderscience, ISSN 1755-0386, doi:10.1504/IJAIP.2009.026763
14. Falcinelli, E., Marcugini, S., Milani, A.: An Architecture for Dynamical News Providers. In: IEEE/WIC/ACM International Conference on Web Intelligence and Intelligent Agent Technology (WI-IATW 2006), pp. 200–203. IEEE Press, Los Alamitos (2006)
15. Leung, C., Milani, A., Santucci, V.: Optimizing Web Content Presentation: A Online PSO Approach. In: Wi-iat, vol. 3, pp. 26–29. IEEE Press, Los Alamitos (2009) ISBN: 978-0-7695-3801-3
16. Fogel, D.B., Ghozeil, A.: A note on representations and variation operators. IEEE Transactions on Evolutionary Computation 1(2), 159–161 (1997)
17. Holland, J.H.: Adaptation in Natural and Artificial Systems. Univ. Michigan Press, Ann Arbor (1975)
18. Goldberg, D.E.: Genetic Algorithms in Search Optimization and Machine Learning, p. 41. Addison Wesley, Reading (1989)
19. Cavazza, M., Charles, F., Mead, S.J.: Character-Based Interactive Storytelling. IEEE Intelligent Systems 17(4), 17–24 (2002)
20. Delmas, G., Champagnat, R.: Augeraud, Plot monitoring for interactive narrative games. In: Proc.of Int.Conf. on Advances in Computer Entertainment Technology, Salzburg, Austria (2007)
21. Young, R.M., Riedl, M., Branly, M., Martin, R.J., Saretto, C.J.: An architecture for integrating plan-based behavior generation with interactive game environments. Journal of Game Development 1, 51–70 (2004)
22. Young, R.M.: Notes on the Use of Plan Structures in the Creation of Interactive Plot. In: Amer. Assoc. Artificial Intelligence Fall Symp. Narrative Intelligence. AAAI Press, Menlo Park (1999)

Hybrid Filtering-Based Personalized Recommender System for Revitalization of Jeju Water Industry

Jungwon Cho[1], Eui-young Kang[1], Hanil Kim[1], Hyungchul Kim[1], Youngseok Lee[2], and Seungdo Jeong[3]

[1] Dept. of Computer Education, Jeju National University,
66 Jeju-daehaklo, Jeju-si, Jeju-do, 690-756 S. Korea
euiyoung1@hanmail.net, k2youngc@naver.com
{jwcho,hikim}@jejunu.ac.kr

[2] Dept. of of Electronics Computer Engineering, Hanyang University,
17 Haengdang-dong, Seongdong-gu, Seoul, 133-791 S. Korea
yslee38@hanyang.ac.kr

[3] Dept. of Information & Communication Engineering, Hanyang Cyber University,
17 Haengdang-dong, Seongdong-gu, Seoul, 133-791 S. Korea
sdjeong@hycu.ac.kr

Abstract. Information filtering is one of the core technologies in a recommender system for personalized services. Each filtering technology has such shortcomings as new user problems and sparsity. Moreover, a recommender system dependent on items decreases reusability. In order to solve these problems, we developed a personalized recommender framework with hybrid filtering. This framework consists of reusable and flexible modules for recommended items. Further, this framework improves the productivity of programming. As an application of this framework, we implemented a personalized tourist recommender system and analyzed it. Also, we applied the system to Jeju beer recommender system. The results show the performance of the framework proposed in this paper.

Keywords: Jeju Water Industry, personalization, hybrid filtering, recommender framework, recommender system, tourist recommender, Jeju beer recommender.

1 Introduction

Personalization helps users find desired information effectively in a flood of information. A personalized recommender system provides information in tune with the needs, purpose, knowledge, interests or other characteristics of a user [1]. Recommendation filtering is one of the core technologies for a recommender system. However, every filtering technology has such shortcomings as new user problems and sparsity [2]. Furthermore, recommendation service providers ineffectively repeat the same efforts according to the changes in items to recommend because a recommender system dependent of items has low reusability. Therefore, service providers invest much time and effort to develop an efficient system. This study used hybrid filtering

X. Luo et al. (Eds.): ICWL 2010 Workshops, LNCS 6537, pp. 55–65, 2011.

to solve the shortcomings of single filtering. Thus, we can provide reusable, personalized services independent of application items.

For this purpose, we propose a framework for a personalized recommender system based on hybrid filtering (hereinafter called the "framework"). This framework has structured item properties and presents personalized information according to the preferences of the user. In Chapter 2 of this paper, we survey related studies, while the proposed framework is described in detail in Chapter 3. In Chapter 4, we apply the proposed framework to a tourist recommender system. Chapter 5 describes the performance of the framework. Lastly, In Chapter 6, we conclude 1this study and describes our planned directions for future study.

2 Related Work

2.1 Recommender Filtering

A personalized service recommends information appropriate for each user. To recommend specific information to each user, this service requires a process to filter variable, bulky data. This is called "information filtering" [3].

There are many filtering techniques. Based on the recommendation access method, they can be divided into content-based filtering [4], collaborative filtering [5], rule-based filtering, demographic filtering, and case-based inference [6]. As each filtering technique has its own strengths and weaknesses, usually two or more filtering techniques are used together rather than any one filtering technique [7, 8]. There are three types of hybrid methods. The first is to perform each filtering and then mix the filtering results. The second is to mix the characteristics of one filtering technique with another filtering technique. The third is to mix the characteristics of all filtering techniques and build a completely integrated model. The hybrid filtering recommended in this paper is similar to the first type. Consequently, it overcomes the limitations of single filtering, and its modification and expansion is easy because each filtering technique is applied separately.

2.2 Framework for Personalized Service

A framework is a reusable, semi-complete application which can be used for the production of a specific application [9]. The studies related to a personalized framework are summarized below. [10] suggests a CXMS (Context Management Framework) management tool. CXMS provides useful information to the user through a context-awareness which manages and analyzes contexts. This system provides personalized services with four layers: sensor layer, semantic layer, control layer, and director/actor layer. CXMS has a meaningful structure and role for each layer, but is based on the regular flow of personal behavior and situations. Moreover, its target items are in the domain of digital documents. Therefore, its limitation is that it is inappropriate to cope with the change of items.

3 Framework Architecture

This study attempted to develop a framework which overcomes the shortcomings of single filtering and has modules independent of a change of target items. To achieve this goal, we focused on the following three points:

First, we separated the structure of data properties from the modules for recommendation. As a result, there are two objects: "Item" and "People". "Item" is an object that represents all items (e.g., Web contents, books, music CD, places of interest), and "People" is an object that indicates the characteristics of a user. Furthermore, the framework manages all items and user information with hash tables. Each item has its own properties and offers a method of reflecting the characteristics of each item and user through inheritance of object behavior. In the processing modules, only these objects ("Item" and "Person") are used for recommendation. Therefore, the recommendation is carried out independently of any items with specific characteristics.

Second, the framework must be able to accept new modules to expand the recommendation techniques. In this study, the filtering techniques are mixed in the system. The framework provides basic filtering in a module unit. If additional modules are necessary, they can be added to the framework by modifying the control module.

Third, a method of controlling recommendations according to the item type must be considered. The framework does not only present one flow but has another flow through an extended module of our study. In other words, the application of filtering is determined by the module that controls flow, and the priority and weight are modified in accordance with the target item. Ultimately, we can implement this system just by defining data properties and modifying the recommendation control module.

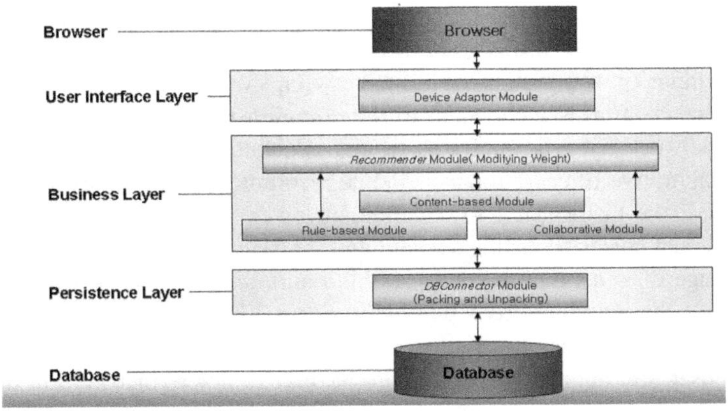

Fig. 1. Layer Structure of the Hybrid Filtering Framework

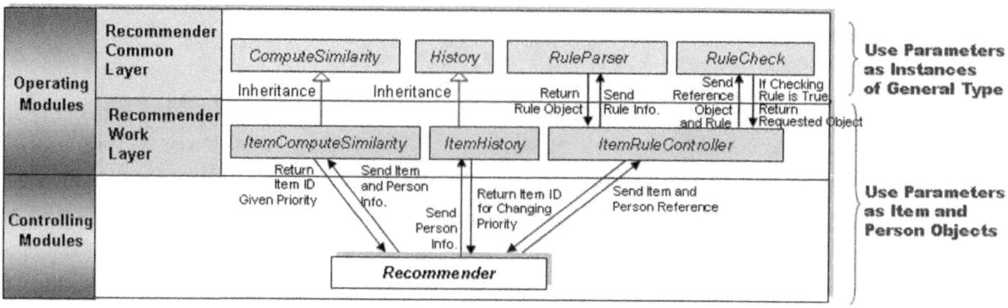

Fig. 2. Business Layer

The proposed framework largely consists of three layers Fig.1. The Persistence Layer plays the role of packing and unpacking to enable the use of data in the database. The three key roles of this layer are the database connection setting, data management of stored items, and user profile data management.

The Business Layer is the most important layer of the framework which operates the direct recommendation and has the structure in Fig.2. This layer uses three types of filtering: content-based filtering, collaborative filtering, and rule-based filtering. In this layer, *Recommender* plays the role of controller (here, classes are expressed in italics). Further, the weight and priority for the filtering application are modified in this class. This layer is divided into two sub-layers, common and work layers, to process data properties independent of item type. The common layer is composed of parent modules used to filter items. The work layer is composed of modules which inherit properties from the common layer or which create and use objects such as item and person. As these layers exist, developers only need to create child modules of *Recommender* with the existing or added data properties.

Filtering with the keywords of an item is one of the content-based filtering techniques. However, it is impossible to recommend without the same keywords or without connection between items and user preferences. Therefore, we use similarity instead of keywords to filter the information for a user. The basic formula for calculation of similarity in this framework is vector similarity. The vector similarity measures similarity with the cosine value between two vectors. The work layer sends data extracted from a user and item to the common layer. Then, the common layer returns to the work layer the similarity results calculated between a user and item.

The collaborative filtering-related module recommends new items to an individual user by using the history of items recommended to the individual and other users. This module calculates the same set rate and the sequence rate. The same set rate is the percentage of items recommended to both an individual user and another user in the items that the individual user purchased or used before. The sequence rate is the percentage of items that were purchased or used in the same sequence by an individual user and another user. The similar user is determined on the basis of the same set rate and the sequence rate over the critical values. These critical values can be changed in the child module of *Recommender*. In the hierarchy of collaborative filtering, the work layer extracts the details of the items and preferences of individual or other users and transmits them to the common layer. Then, the common layer determines similar users based on the same set rate and the sequence rate of individual and other users, and returns their identifiers to the work layer.

Moreover, this framework can recommend using specific rules between user and items. The priorities of recommended items are changed by the predefined rules. This framework uses the following rule syntax:

Class1:Field1='value1' AND *Class2:Field2*='value2' THEN *Class:Field*

The meaning of this statement is that if the value of *Field1* of *Class1* is 'value1' and the value of *Field2* of *Class2* is 'value2', and then the value of *Field* of *Class* is returned in object type. This framework includes a module to parse and check the rules to analyze them. A rule consists of a conditional part and a result part, as well as logical operators such as AND and OR used in the conditional part. The operator between filed and value is '=', '!=', '<', or '>', which means 'equal', 'not equal', 'small' and 'big'.

In addition, there is the User Interface layer, which transmits information to individual users. This layer can adapt an interface to the terminal device of user.

4 Example Application

This chapter describes the design and implementation of a recommender system using the proposed framework. As application items, the places of interest in Jeju Island in Korea were selected. The main programming language is Java, which is device independent and highly scalable. Moreover, this system was implemented as a Web application to provide personalized services on the Web.

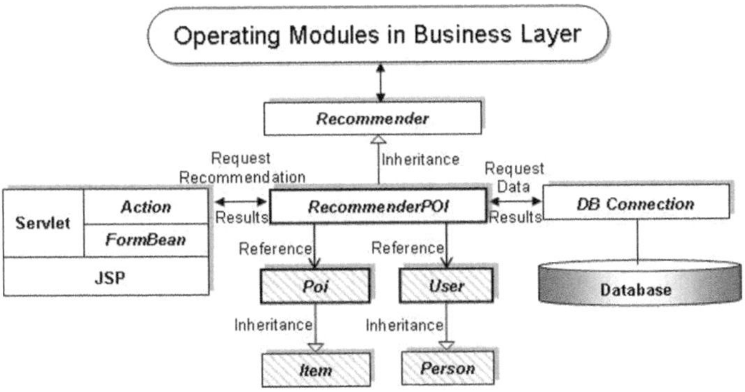

Fig. 3. Personalized Tourist Recommender System

Fig. 3 shows the structure of this personalized tourist recommender system. The information on places of interest for this system are focused on objective properties, which means information on places of interest that can attain general agreement, such as geographical location [11]. The information on places of interest consists of geographical position, local position, themes, activities, and the characteristics of high-demand season. Fig. 4 shows the class fields of *Poi* and *User*. The main modules of the business layer perform operations using objects created by *Poi* and *User*. An example of applying place of interest recommendation to the three types of filtering of the framework is described below.

User Class Fields

```
private int id;
private String login_id;
private String name;
private String email;
private String gender;
private String birth;
private String zipcode;
private String addr1;
private String addr2;
private int geo[];
private int local[];
private int theme[];
private int act[];
private int season[];
private int history[];

//Traveling companion
private String friends;
```

Poi Class Fields

```
//Tourist Point
private String name;
//Tourist Point Id
private int id;

//Geographic
private int geo;
//Location
private int local;
//Theme
private int theme;
//Activity
private int act;
//Season
private int season;
```

Fig. 4. User and Poi Class Fields

First, the content-based filtering-related module calculates the similarity using the vector similarity between user preferences and the properties of places of interest. Second, there are users who go to the place of interest through a similar path. For example, one individual user visits places of interest A, B, and C in this sequence. And another user visits places of interest A, B, C and D in this sequence. In fact, this means that they have similar tour paths. Therefore, the module can discover similar paths by comparing the histories of different users. Then, the system recommends the place of interest D, which the user has not visited yet but other users have visited. Third, examples of rule-based filtering are as follows:

(a) User:friends='family_children' AND Poi:theme='amusement park'
THEN Poi:id
(b) Weather:temp>'23' AND Weather:wind<'5' AND
Weather:rain<'5' AND Poi:act='water sport' THEN Poi:id

Rule (a) gives a high priority to amusement park as a destination to visit with children. Rule (b) recommends water sports if the average daily temperature is over 23 degrees, the wind velocity is less than 5 m/s, and the rainfall is less than 5 mm. As shown by these examples, this system can recommend places of interest according to specific rules.

5 Performance

5.1 Evaluating the Tourist Recommender System

We evaluated the proposed system with 96 places of interest and 47 tourists on the basis of the tourist destinations and swimming beaches registered with the Jeju-do Tourist Association, Republic of Korea. We compared the hit ratios between the proposed system and a recommender system based on the number of visitors. The equation for hit ratio is as shown in (1) below:

$$Hit-ratio = \frac{Number\ of\ Hits}{Number\ of\ Events} \quad (1)$$

The results are shown in Fig. 5 and Table 1. Here, Top-N indicates that among the recommended items, those from the top to the Nth priority were chosen. The result shows that the proposed system has higher hit ratios in general regardless of Top-N. Specifically, our system had a higher hit ratio by 7% on average than the recommender system based on the number of visitors. This proves the high performance of our proposed system in recommending places of interest.

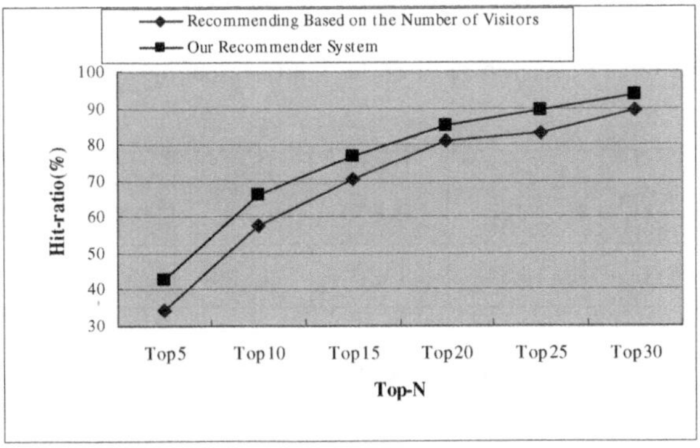

Fig. 5. Performance of the Tourist Recommender System

Table 1. Hit-ratio(%) of the Tourist Recommender System

Top-N	Top5	Top10	Top15	Top20	Top25	Top35
Recommending Based on the Number of Visitors	34.0	57.4	70.2	80.9	83.0	89.4
Our Recommender System	42.6	66.0	76.6	85.1	89.4	93.6

Other indicators of the performance of the recommender system besides hit ratio are recall ratio and precision ratio. Although recall ratio and precision ratio are often used in information retrieval (IR), recently, they have also been used in recommender systems. The recall ratio is the percentage of hit items recommended by the recommender system against the target items searched by user. This equation is expressed as (2) below. The precision ratio is the percentage of the number of hit items in the target items against the items recommended by the recommender system. This equation is expressed as (3) below.

$$Recall-ratio = \frac{Number\ of\ Hit\_Items}{Number\ of\ Target\_Items} \quad (2)$$

$$Precision-ratio = \frac{Number\ of\ Hit\_Items}{Number\ of\ Recommended\_Items} \quad (3)$$

For example, if the target items are {a, b, c, d}, and the recommended items are {a, c, e, f, g}, the recall ratio is 50% and the precision ratio is 40%.

Table 2. Recall-ratio of the Tourist Recommender System

Recall-ratio, %

Top-N	Top5	Top10	Top15	Top20	Top25	Top35
Recommending base on the Number of Visitors	8.5	15.36	27.88	40.10	40.87	45.39
Our Recommender System	14.9	27.53	34.93	41.02	45.77	52.38

Table 3. Precision-ratio of the Tourist Recommender System

Precision-ratio, %

Top-N	Top5	Top10	Top15	Top20	Top25	Top35
Recommending base on the Number of Visitors	9.09	8.63	10	10.79	8.9	8.33
Our Recommender System	14.54	13.63	11.96	11.96	9.54	9.16

Tables 2 and 3 show the average recall ratio and the average precision ratio of the tourist recommender system. Because the number of target items is 5 on average, which is smaller than the number of recommended items, the hit ratio of target items is lower than the increase rate of N in Top-N. Consequently, as shown in Table 3, the precision ratio decreases as more items are recommended. Because the number of target items is smaller than N, we cannot achieve a 100% precision ratio by calculation even with the best hit ratio. Therefore, it is beyond the scope of this model to achieve precision by absolute value. Thus, we understand precision relatively in relation to other systems. From this viewpoint, the measurements of our system showed excellent performance in both the recall ratio and precision ratio. However, the precision ratio of the recommender system based on the number of visitors increased from top-10 to top 20 in Table 3. As shown in Table 2, the cause of this is that the recall ratio increases more rapidly in this section than other sections. In other words, this is a transient phenomenon that occurred because the system suddenly discovered many recommended items in the target items. Nevertheless, our system maintains higher values in all sections.

5.2 Framework Productivity

We have implemented a framework for a personalized recommender system and applied the proposed framework to the tourist recommender system. Then, we measured hit ratios with the recommendation results. As a result, we showed that our system has a higher hit ratio than another system. General frameworks are typically evaluated by productivity and quality. They must be evaluated by many developers over a long period. However, it is difficult to do this for short-term, small-scale projects such as this study. Therefore, studies on small-scale frameworks usually analyze them through the evaluation of internal modules and applications. In addition to this, this study analyzed the number of coding lines and modules to measure the quantitative productivity of frameworks. For this evaluation, we compared the following two systems: System A is a tourist recommender system customized to tourism only [12]. And system B is a tourist recommender system to which the proposed framework is applied. The modules with the coding lines included in the measurement are the core modules of our system, which are related to tour item object, user object, and recommendation strategies. Table 4 shows the number of coding lines and modules of the two systems.

Table 4. The Program Coding Productivity

SYSTEM	A System	B System
The Number of Lines (Conding Lines / Total Lines)	2,117(100%)	854(34.16%)
The Number of Modules (Coding Module / Total Modules)	16/16(100)%	4/20(25%)

These two systems have similar hit ratios and algorithms. However, the productivity of system B is higher than that of system A by approximately 66%. This is because while the developer must write 100% of the core modules of system A, the developer only has to write approximately 34% of the total coding lines and approximately 25% of the modules of system B due to its hierarchical structure and minimization of redundancies. Therefore, the proposed framework can improve productivity by saving code development costs and time when it is used to develop a recommender system.

6 Novel Recommender Application to Jeju Beer

Fig. 6 shows the interface for Jeju beer recommendation. Top 3 beers which are recommended by our system are placed in top-left of the interface with tap control. Each tap has information about respective beer in terms of taste, color, flavor, career groups of consumers, ages, and sex. Evaluation for recommendation also performed by user selecting "Good" or "Bad" in bottom-right side. We expect to elevate customer's satisfaction applying the proposed system to Jeju water industry.

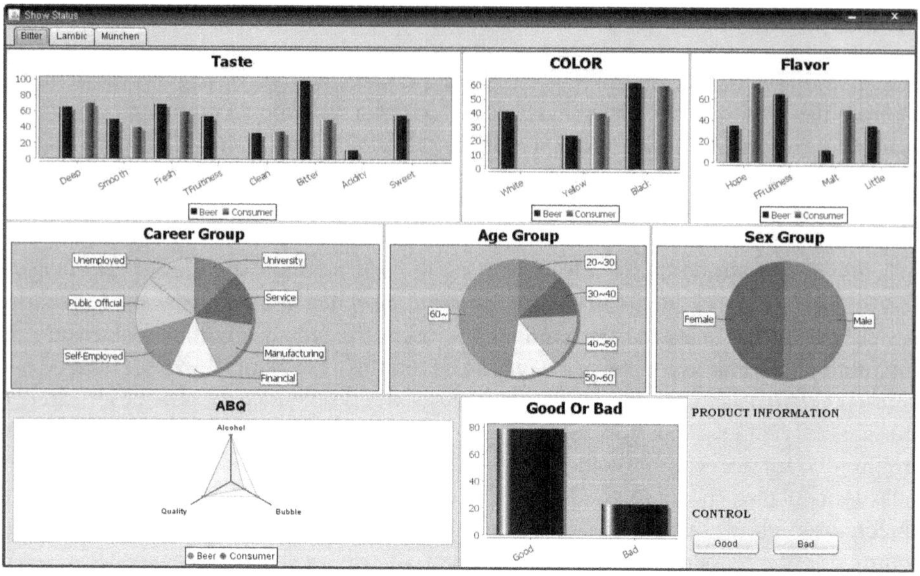

Fig. 6. User interface of the Jeju beer recommender system

7 Conclusions

This paper proposed a personalized recommender system based on hybrid filtering. The conclusions of our study are summarized as follows:

First, we developed a framework for personalized services to which filtering techniques were applied. Second, we configured data properties and implemented an actual recommender system to which this framework was applied. Third, we evaluated the proposed framework and proved its excellent performance.

This study designed a framework using hybrid filtering techniques, and implemented a recommender system just by adding control modules and data objects to the framework. Furthermore, the implemented system showed a higher hit ratio than another system. This means that the proposed framework provides an environment for the development of effective, useful recommender systems in various areas.

In the future, this framework needs to complement the user interfaces to adapt to various types of devices. Besides, more research into intelligent inference to improve rule-based filtering is required. Further discussions are also required on methods to quickly and easily implement data properties while sufficiently reflecting the item characteristics.

Acknowledgement

This work is the results of a study on the "Human Resource Development Center for Economic Region Leading Industry" Project, supported by the Ministry of Education, Science & Technology(MEST) and the National Research Foundation of Korea(NRF).

References

1. Park, S.P., Kim, J., Kim, Y.K.: A Personalized Service System based on Vector Model in Distributed Heterogeneous Internet Shopping Mall Environment. The Korea Information Science Society 8(2), 206–218 (2002)
2. Kim, H.I., Kim, J.T.: Data Blurring Method for Solving Sparseness Problem in Collaborative Filtering. The Korea Information Science Society 32(6), 542–553 (2005)
3. Kim, B.M., Li, Q., Kim, S.G., Lim, E.K., Kim, J.Y.: A New Approach Combining Content-based Filtering and Collaborative Filtering for Recommender Systems. The Korea Information Science Society 31(3), 332–342 (2004)
4. Basilico, J., Hofmann, T.: Unifying Collaborative and Content-Based Filtering. In: Proceedings of the 21st International Conference on Machine Learning, vol. 69. ACM Press, New York (2004)
5. Miller, B.N., Albert, I., Lam, S.K., Konstan, J.A., Riedl, J.: MovieLens Unplugged: Experiences with an Occasionally Connected Recommender System. In: Proceedings of the ACM 2003 International Conference on Intelligent User Interfaces, pp. 263–266. ACM Press, New York (2003)
6. Kim, Y.J., Mun, H.J., Ok, S.H., Woo, Y.T.: Design and Implementation of Personalized Recommendation System using Case-based Reasoning Technique. The Korea Information Processing Society 9-D(6), 1009–1016 (2002)
7. Ko, S.J.: Extracting Typical Group Preferences through User-Item Optimization and User Profiles in Collaborative Filtering System. The Korea Information Science Society 32(7), 581–591 (2005)
8. Adomavicius, G., Tuzhilin, A.: Toward the Next Generation of Recommender Systems: A Survey of the State-of-the-Art and Possible Extensions. IEEE Transactions on Knowledge and Data Engineering 17(6), 734–749 (2005)
9. Husted, T., Dumoulin, C., Franciscus, G., Winterfeldt, D.: Struts in Action: Building Web Applications with the Leading Java Framework. Manning Publications (2002)
10. Zimmermann, A., Specht, M., Lorenz, A.: Personalization and Context Management. User Modeling and User-Adapted Interaction 15(3-4), 275–302 (2005)
11. Kang, E.Y., Kim, H., Cho, J.: Personalization method for tourist point of interest (POI) recommendation. In: Gabrys, B., Howlett, R.J., Jain, L.C. (eds.) KES 2006. LNCS (LNAI), vol. 4251, pp. 392–400. Springer, Heidelberg (2006)

Modelling Text File Evaluation Processes

José Paulo Leal[1] and Ricardo Queirós[2]

[1] CRACS & INESC-Porto LA, Faculty of Sciences, University of Porto,
Rua do Campo Alegre, 1021 4169-007 Porto Portugal
zp@dcc.fc.up.pt
[2] CRACS & INESC-Porto LA, Faculty of Sciences, University of Porto,
Rua do Campo Alegre, 1021 4169-007 Porto Portugal
ricardo.queiros@eu.ipp.pt

Abstract. Text file evaluation is an emergent topic in e-learning that responds to the shortcomings of the assessment based on questions with predefined answers. Questions with predefined answers are formalized in languages such as IMS Question & Test Interoperability Specification (QTI) and supported by many e-learning systems. Complex evaluation domains justify the development of specialized evaluators that participate in several business processes. The goal of this paper is to formalize the concept of a text file evaluation in the scope of the E-Framework – a service oriented framework for development of e-learning systems maintained by a community of practice. The contribution includes an abstract service type and a service usage model. The former describes the generic capabilities of a text file evaluation service. The later is a business process involving a set of services such as repositories of learning objects and learning management systems.

Keywords: e-learning, SOA, interoperability.

1 Introduction

The majority of e-learning systems include the automatic evaluation of quizzes as a feature. Quizzes have the advantage of being generic and usable in any learning domain. However, the most effective types of exercises in any learning domain, both for knowledge acquisition and for student grading, are seldom quizzes. For instance, it is hard to imagine learning computer programming without actually programming. An attempt to solve a programming exercise is written in a specific language (a programming language) that cannot be evaluated simply by comparing it with predefined answers, as in quiz evaluation.

Text file automatic evaluation differs significantly from quiz evaluation based on the IMS Question & Test Interoperability (QTI) specification. QTI describes a data model for questions and test data and, since version 2.0, extends the IEEE Learning Object Metadata (LOM) standard with its own meta-data vocabulary. QTI was designed for questions with a set of pre-defined answers, such as multiple choice, multiple response, fill-in-the-blanks and short text questions. It supports also long text answers but the specification of their evaluation is outside the scope of the QTI. In

X. Luo et al. (Eds.): ICWL 2010 Workshops, LNCS 6537, pp. 66–74, 2011.

fact, the evaluation of text files requires extra resources and specialized metadata. For this reason the authors consider that QTI is not adequate for text file automatic evaluation, as would be expected since it was not designed for this purpose. Extensions to learning object specification have to be developed to support text file evaluation [4]. Unlike text file evaluation, QTI quiz evaluation is integrated in many e-learning systems, especially in Learning Management Systems (LMS). On one hand text file evaluation is too specialized to justify its integration in a general LMS. On the other hand, provided as a service it can used by many kinds of systems. For instance, a programming evaluation service may have as clients programming assignment managers, self-evaluation tools and contest management systems. Its services can also be used by plug-ins of extensible systems, such as LMS or Integrated Development Environments (IDE).

The motivation for this research comes from the experience of the authors with systems such as Mooshak [5] and EduJudge [3]. The former is a contest management system for ICPC contests that is being used since 2002 also as an e-Learning tool in computer programming courses. The later is a system developed for enabling the access of LMS to the collection of programming exercises of the UVA on-line judge. Both systems include automatic evaluation components that if recast as services could provide their functions to different types of e-Learning systems.

The goal of this paper is to formalize services and processes involving text file evaluation in the scope of an e-learning framework. The purpose of an *e-learning framework* is to support the integration of systems within educational institutions using a Service Oriented Architecture (SOA) [1]. In this paper the authors report on the contribution to a particular e-learning framework – the e-Framework. This framework was selected based on a previous survey [2] since it has an active community of practice and accepts abstract definitions of services as contributions.

The contribution described in this paper includes an abstract definition of a type of service and a description of a business process model. The service modelled by the proposed definition receives a text file with an attempt to solve an exercise and produces an evaluation report. The exercise is referenced as a learning object (LO) available on an interoperable repository [3] supporting extended definitions of learning objects [4]. The business process model relates several abstract services definitions from the e-Framework, including the proposed service.

Examples of the applicability of this service usage model can be drawn from different areas, although the authors are particularly interested in the automatic evaluation of programming exercises. A program evaluation service compiles a program source code, executes it with test data and compares obtained and expected outputs contained in a learning object. Other examples of evaluator services process different types of text files: an electronic circuit evaluator receive a description of a circuit, injects input signals, simulates the circuit and compares output signals; a diagram evaluator receives a description of a diagram (e.g. UML) – a typed graph – and tries to create a graph homomorphism with a solution. In all cases the service receives both a text file attempting to solve an exercise and a reference to an exercise specified as a learning object, containing other files with special roles in the evaluation process, and produces a detailed evaluation report.

The remainder of this paper is organized as follows. Section 2 details the evolution towards the e-learning frameworks and introduces the e-Framework. Section 3 proposes a new abstract service type for text file evaluation and section 4 builds a service usage model using this abstract type. As a validation of these proposals, section 5 presents the definition of a concrete service based on the text file evaluation genre and a concrete service usage model for evaluation of programming exercises. Finally, a summary of the major contributions of this paper and a prospect of future work are presented.

2 Evolution towards E-Learning Frameworks

The architectures of e-learning platforms had a considerable evolution in the last two decades. Starting with the early monolithic systems developed for specific learning domain to domain-independent systems featuring reusable tools that can be used virtually in any e-learning course [6]. These last systems follow a component oriented architecture in order to facilitate tool integration. Integrated environments have been successfully used to leverage the advantages of ICTs, but have also been target of criticism. These systems, based on pluggable and interchangeable components, led to oversized systems that are difficult to reconvert to changing roles and new demands such as the integration of heterogeneous services based on semantic information and the automatic adaptation of services to users (both learners and teachers).

These issues triggered a new generation of e-learning platforms based on services that can be integrated in different scenarios. This new approach provides the basis for SOA. In the last few years there have been initiatives [2] to adapt SOA to e-learning [7]. These initiatives, commonly named e-learning frameworks, had the same goal: to provide flexible learning environments for learners worldwide. Usually they are characterized by providing a set of open interfaces to numerous reusable services organized in genres or layers and combined in service usage models. These initiatives use intensively the standards [8, 9, 10] for e-learning content sharing and interoperability developed in the last years by several organizations (e.g. ADL, IMS GLC, IEEE). Based on a previous survey [2], the authors conclude that E-Framework (E-F) [11,12] and Schools Interoperability Framework (SIF) [13] to be the most promising e-learning frameworks since they are the most active projects, both with a large number of implementations worldwide.

In the E-F, the on-line community is the corner stone of the contribution process [14]. The technical model of the E-F structures the contributions as service genres, expressions and usage models. A *service genre* is an abstract definition of a type of service. A *service expression* is the formalization of the implementation approaches of a specialization of a service genre. A *service usage* model describes the requirements and processes within a particular domain relating them to a collection of service genres or expressions.

On SIF it's impossible to make this type of contribution to the abstract framework. However, developers are encouraged to contribute with new agents, such as learning objects repositories.

3 Text File Evaluation Service Genre

In the e-Framework a *service genre* describes generic capabilities of a specific service expressed in terms of their behaviours, without prescribing how to make them operational.

In this section a text file evaluation service genre is proposed to the E-Framework. A service of this genre is responsible for the assessment of a text file with an attempt to solve an exercise described by a LO. It supports three functions:

- `ListCapabilities:` provides the requester with a list of all the capabilities supported by a specific evaluator;
- `EvaluateSubmission:` performs the evaluation of a submission to a given exercise, using some of the available capabilities;
- `GetReport:` accesses a detailed report of a previous evaluation.

In the following sub-subsection the three service internal functions are detailed.

3.1 The ListCapabilities Function

The **ListCapabilities function** informs the client systems of the capabilities of a particular evaluator. Capabilities depend strongly on the evaluation domain. For instance, in a computer programming evaluator the capabilities are related with the programming language compiler or interpreter. Each capability has a number of features to describe it and for a programming language they may be the language name (e.g. Java) its version (e.g. 1.5) and vendor (e.g. JDK). On an electronic circuit simulator a capability may be a collection of gates that are allowed on a circuit and features may be the names of individual gates.

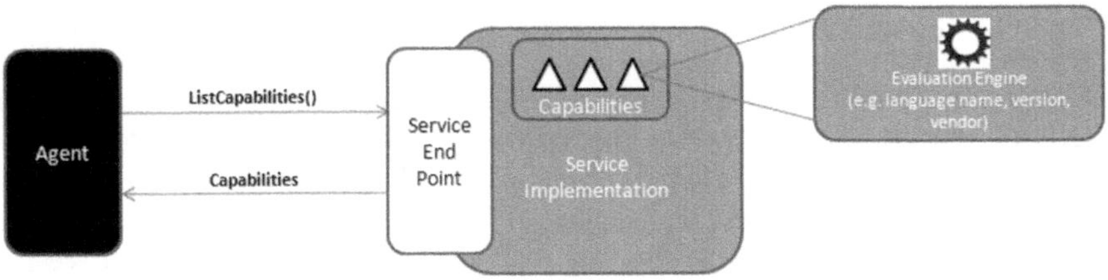

Fig. 1. The ListCapabilities function

In this function, the request doesn't accept any parameter and the response returns a list of all capabilities of the evaluator. Each capability is described by a list of features, with a name and a value.

3.2 The EvaluateSubmission Function

The **EvaluateSubmission** function allows the request of an evaluation for a specific exercise. The request includes an exercise or a reference to an exercise represented as a learning object held in a repository and a single attempt to solve a particular exercise. The request may include a specific evaluator capability necessary for a proper evaluation of the attempt. The response returns a ticket for a later report request and may return also a circumstantial report about the respective evaluation of the requester attempt.

A schematic of this function is shown in Figure 2. The service endpoint provides the interfaces for the requests and responses for the evaluation functionality. Internally the service implementation may include several features (indexing, queuing, transforming, flow control, etc.) needed to provide the defined functionality and a connection with a remote data source holding the objects such as a LOR.

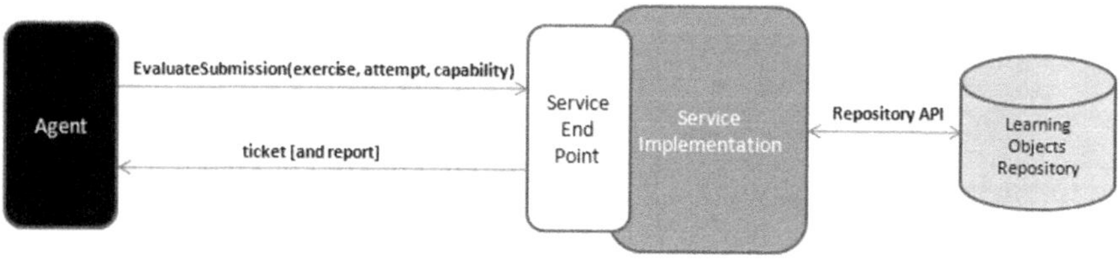

Fig. 2. The EvaluateSubmission function

The evaluator returns a report on the evaluation, if it is completed within a predefined time frame. The report must contain information about the assessment of the attempt but should not reach to any conclusion. The raw data sent to the client can be used as input for other systems (e.g. classification systems, feedback systems).

In any case the response will include a ticket to recover the report on a later date. Requesting a report using a ticket is supported through another function called GetReport detailed in the next sub-subsection.

3.3 The GetReport Function

The **GetReport function** allows a requester to get a report for a specific evaluation. The report included in this response may be transformed in the client side based on a XML stylesheet. This way the client will be able to filter out parts of the report and to calculate a classification based on its data. The request of this function includes a ticket sent previously by the service in response to an evaluation. The response returns a report about an evaluation.

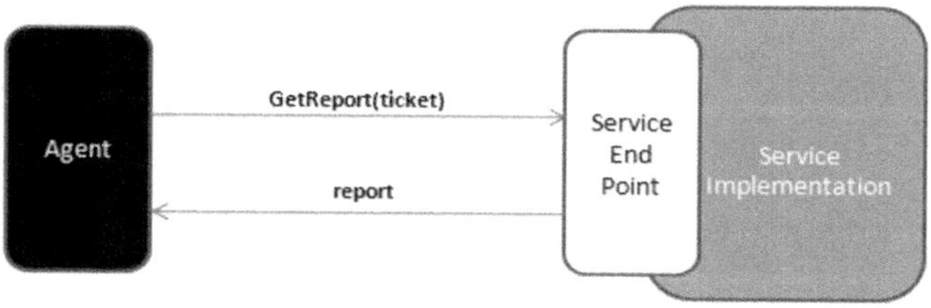

Fig. 3. The GetReport function

4 Text File Evaluation Service Usage Model

In the E-Framework, a Service Usage Model (SUM) describes the needs, requirements, workflows, management policies and processes within a domain. A SUM is composed of either Service Genres or Service Expressions, but not a mixture. In this section the SUM for the text file evaluation of learning objects is detailed. The E-Framework has 22 distinct elements to describe a SUM, 12 are required elements and the rest is either recommended or optional. For the sake of terseness just a subset of the SUM content based on the templates provided by the E-Framework is detailed. In concrete is described the SUM diagram, the technical functionality, the structure and arrangement of the functions and the data sources and services used.

The **SUM Diagram element**, depicted in Figure 4, defines a visual representation of the SUM for presentation purposes. This type of diagram is suggested by the E-F templates [12]. It organizes business processes in columns. For each business process the summary and name are highlighted in square rectangles in the top and the services genres it includes as ovals. Data sources are represented in the footer of the diagram.

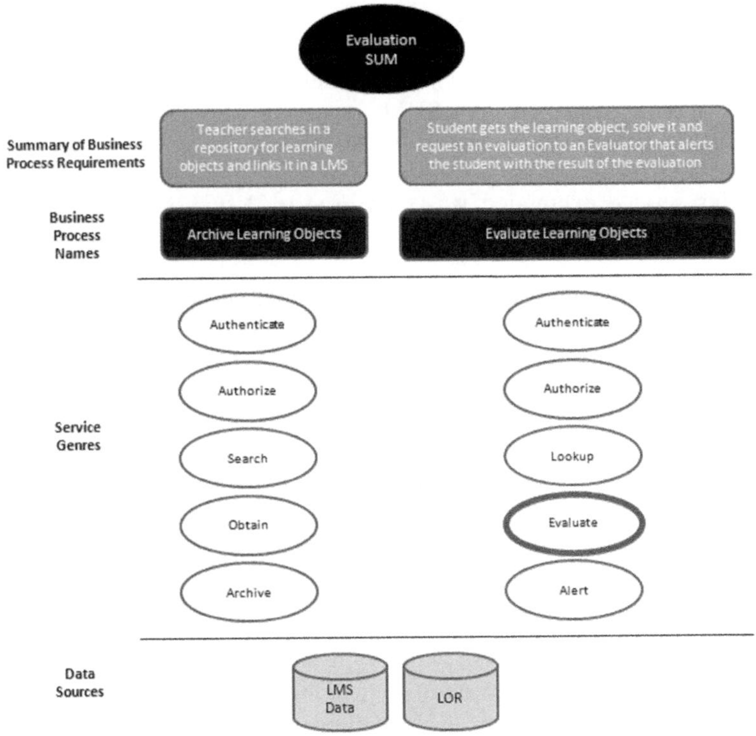

Fig. 4. The SUM diagram

In the first business process called Archive Learning Objects, the teacher searches in a repository for learning objects. Then, it selects the most appropriate and archives it, for instance, in a LMS for future use.

The Evaluate Learning Objects business process details the attempt of the student to solve a particular learning object and the request for its evaluation. In this business process the Evaluation Service Genre, detailed in the previous subsection, was used. This service includes the EvaluateSubmission function that returns ticket for a later report request and may also return an evaluation report. The report could be sent to both student and teacher or be transformed for a personalized notification about the evaluation of the students' attempt.

The **Functionality element** categorizes the functions supported by the SUM from a system viewpoint. The functions used in this SUM are organized as follows: common functions (Authenticate and Authorize), repository functions (Search, Obtain, Archive, Lookup and Alert) and evaluation functions (Evaluate).

The **Structure & Arrangement element** illustrates how a SUM is used in a particular business process by identifying the services used, data sources and their interactions within the SUM. An apt illustration of the use of this SUM is the pedagogical learning process involving the evaluation of programming exercises, presented in the following section.

5 Validation

The contribution of this paper is twofold and includes the abstract definition of a text evaluation service genre and a SUM involving this genre. To evaluate the practicability of these abstracts definitions we made a concrete definition of a service expression based on the proposed service genre, a programming exercise evaluation service. This service expression was then used to define a concrete service usage model for solving programming exercises in the context of computer programming course.

The definition of the programming exercise evaluation service was also done in the context of the e-Framework. The new service expression specializes the proposed service genre by refining its behaviours and requests, and by specifying implementation approaches such as applicable standards and interface definitions. Details of this specialization process can be found elsewhere [15].

We are currently developing an evaluation engine based on this service expression. The implementation is based on Virtual Machines (VM) to execute the programs on a safe and controlled environment and is divided into five components, two controlling the evaluation service and other three supporting the execution of the programs on the VM. The five independent components give the evaluation engine a higher scalability. The use of VM allows us to manage a high number of capabilities such as languages and programming environments from different operating systems, including obsolete versions.

A text evaluation service with the features outline in the previous paragraphs was designed for a SUM involving the evaluation of programming exercises. At the heart of this SUM resides an evaluation engine – a service of the text file evaluation genre – supplying its services to several e-learning systems such as LMS, LOR or experimentation environments. An example of an experimentation environment would be an IDE such as Eclipse, with plug-ins to interoperate with other services, where students would solve their programming exercises. Figure 5 shows a concrete business process model based on the proposed SUM.

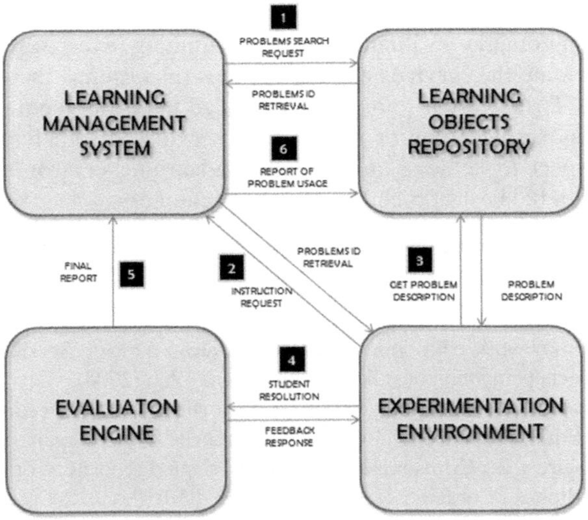

Fig. 5. Service integration in a pedagogical e-Learning process

The teacher 1) searches for relevant exercises in the repository. Then the learner 2) gets the exercises from the LMS. The Experimentation Environment 3) recovers the exercises descriptions from the repository and shows it to the learner. After coding the program the learner send an attempt 4) to the Evaluation Engine. The learner may submit repeatedly, integrating the feedback received from the Evaluation Engine. In the end, the Evaluation Engine 5) sends a grade to the LMS that records it and reports 6) the LO usage data back to the repository. This last task will provide data for future adaptability services that will adjust the presentation order in accordance with the effective difficulty of programming exercises (not the difficulty stated on the LO) and the needs of a particular student.

6 Conclusion and Future Work

In the research presented in this paper the authors modelled text file evaluation services and detailed a contribution to the E-Framework, consisting of a new Service Genre and a new Service Usage Model. In the Service Genre the authors made an abstract description of the behaviours expected from a text file evaluation service. In the Service Usage Model the relationships between services through business processes and the usage scenario based on a particular domain - the automatic evaluation of programming exercises – were presented.

To validate the proposed model the authors presented a concrete service expression consisting of a programming exercise evaluation service, and a concrete usage model based on this service expression.

In the continuation of this line of work these contributions to the e-Framework will be used to design actual implementations of text file evaluation services, not only of programming exercises and also for other domains, such as UML diagrams.

The proposed service usage model will be used to implement an e-learning process centred in the automatic evaluation of programming exercises. This e-Learning process will integrate the services exposed by several systems, including an LMS, an IDE and a LOR. These systems are being extended to enable them to expose some of their functions as services and/or to consume services of other systems. With this approach we expect to achieve an integrated e-learning environment for computer programming with the best of bread tools in each category.

References

1. Girardi, R.: Framework para coordenação e mediação de Web Services modelados como Learning Objects para ambientes de aprendizado na Web (2004)
2. Leal, J.P., Queirós, R.: eLearning Frameworks: a survey. In: Proceedings of International Technology, Education and Development Conference 2010, Valencia, Spain (2010)
3. Leal, J.P., Queirós, R.: CrimsonHex: A service oriented repository of specialised learning objects. In: Filipe, J., Cordeiro, J. (eds.) EIS 2009. LNBIP, vol. 24, pp. 102–113. Springer, Heidelberg (2009)
4. Leal, J.P., Queirós, R.: Defining Programming Problems as Learning Objects. World Academy of Science, Engineering and Technology 58, 1033–1040 (2009)
5. Leal, J.P., Silva, F.: Mooshak: a Web-based multi-site programming contest system Software. Practice & Experience 33(6), 567–581 (2003) ISSN:0038-0644
6. Dagger, D., O'Connor, A., Lawless, S., Walsh, E., Wade, V.: Service Oriented eLearning Platforms: From Monolithic Systems to Flexible Services (2007)
7. Wilson. S, Blinco, K. Rehak, D: Service-Oriented Frameworks: Modelling the infrastructure for the next generation of e-learning systems (2004)
8. IMS CC Specification, Version 1.0 Final Specification, `http://www.imsglobal.org/cc/index.html`
9. Bohl, O., Scheuhase, J., Sengler, R., Winand, U.: The shareable content object reference model (SCORM)-a critical review. In: Proceedings of the International Conference on Computers in Education, pp. 950–951 (2002)
10. Hatala, M., Richards, G., Eap, T., Willms, J.: The interoperability of learning object repositories and services: standards, implementations and lessons learned. In: Proceedings of the 13th International World Wide Web Conference on Alternate Track Papers & Posters. ACM, New York (2004)
11. Wilson, S., Blinco, K., Rehak, D.: An e-Learning Framework. Paper prepared on behalf of DEST (Australia), JISC-CETIS (UK), and Industry Canada (2004)
12. e-Framework Technical Walk-through, `http://www.e-framework.org/Portals/9/docs/e-Framework%20technical%20walk-through%20v1.1.pdf`
13. Collins, L.: Schools Interoperability Framework White Paper. Schools Interoperability Framework Association, Washington DC (2005)
14. Stock, K., Butchart, B., Higgins, C., Chen, Y.: From Here to Eternity: An Experiment Applying the e-Framework Infrastructure for Education and Research and the SUMO Ontology to Standards-based Geospatial Web Services. International Journal of Spatial Data Infrastructures Research 5, 1–57 (2010)
15. Leal, J.P., Queirós, R., Ferreira, D.: Specifying a programming exercises evaluation service on the e-framework. In: Luo, X., Spaniol, M., Wang, L., Li, Q., Nejdl, W., Zhang, W. (eds.) ICWL 2010. LNCS, vol. 6483, pp. 141–150. Springer, Heidelberg (2010)

Duplicate Page Detection Algorithm Based on the Field Characteristic Clustering

Feiyue Ye, Junlei Liu, Bing Liu, and Kun Chai

Dept. of Computer Engineering and Science, Shanghai University
Shanghai, China
{yefy,meteorsbelief,liubing1985324,chaikun1985}@shu.edu.cn

Abstract. The speed and accuracy for the cognitive based interactive-computing is crucial in an information retrieval system of web wisdom. In this page, we propose a new duplicate detection algorithm based on the field characteristic clustering after the analysis of the common duplicate detection algorithm and finding their existing drawbacks. By using the field knowledge to build the characteristic string and taking advantage of the improved k-means clustering algorithm, we shorten the time in the comparison process for the duplicate detection. Finally, through the experiment to compare the performance of the traditional SCAM, DSC with this algorithm on the time consumption, the rate of accuracy and the recalling rate quality. The result shows this algorithm overcome the time and storage consumption when compared with the traditional SCAM algorithm. On comparison with another DSC algorithm, it improves the drawback of the inaccuracy brought by the use of shingles to representing a page in the duplicate detection process. We conclude the duplicate detection algorithm based on the field characteristic clustering raise its precision and recall rate in the field of web duplicate page detection and will improve the speed and accuracy in an information retrieval system of web wisdom.

Keywords: web wisdom, cognitive based, interactive computing, duplicate detection, field knowledge, characteristic string, field characteristic clustering.

1 Introduction

With the rapid development of internet technology, the internet has become the largest and most widespread information library from where we can get extensive information. Recent years, the exceptional increasing and the easily replicable information on the internet added massive duplicate message and brought tremendous difficulties for the cognitive-based interactive computing on the web pages. The key to this problem is the massive duplicated web page detection [1].

The duplicate web page detection is one of the important parts for the cognitive-based interactive computing. The eliminating of the duplicated web pages can not only guarantee the information interacting between the user and computer with less redundancy, so as to make the cognitive-based interactive computing more accurate and faster. But also, in the information retrieval, it can reduce the waste of storage and faster

X. Luo et al. (Eds.): ICWL 2010 Workshops, LNCS 6537, pp. 75–84, 2011.

the retrieval efficiency. Elimination of duplicated web pages detection technology is to quickly remove the massive duplicate pages on the internet, to facilitate the interactive computing and improve the efficiency of the retrieval system. So the detection and eliminating work of duplicated web pages have significant meaning.

This research originates from the Shengli Oil Company's project "oil knowledge-based data mining in vertical search engine"; it's an information retrieval system of the web wisdom. In this vertical search engine project, the performance of duplicate page detection in the oil field has great influence on the retrieval effect. the application of oil field special knowledge has great impact on the better analysis of oil related web pages, further to influence on the result of the duplicate detection. In this project, we take advantage of the duplicate page detection algorithm based on the filed characteristic clustering (FCC), and achieve good results on its application on the duplicate page detection of the oil related web pages.

2 Regular Duplicate Page Detection Algorithm Analysis

2.1 Duplicate Page Detection

The duplicate page detection technology is the elimination of duplicate web content by recognition and combination the similar pages, thus saves the storage space and shortens the operation time consumed on the web page [2].

The judgment on the webpage duplication differs as their different duplicate reason, but almost all duplicate detection algorithm are based on such basic idea [3]: calculate a group of fingerprints according to certain algorithm for each documents, if the two documents have the certain amount identical fingerprint, then these two documents content overlapping is high, namely the two are the duplicate ones.

In view of the web page with relatively similar content, current most successful search engine system is based on the key words match or the vector space model to deal with the task of duplicate page detection. The Google and the Tianwang system [4] are the representative of such typical system. Usually, the main duplicate detection process of these system is that, to preprocess and do the page clean work of the web pages crawled by the spider, then extract the subject and subject related content which includes web page logo, page type, content category, title, keyword, abstract, text, links and other information, finally to judge the similarity of the two web pages according to the characteristics extract by these information.

To ensure that the reproduction of your illustrations is of a reasonable quality, we advise against the use of shading. The contrast should be as pronounced as possible.

2.2 Regular Duplicate Page Detection Algorithm

The duplicate detection algorithm aboard was initially targeted at large file systems, and later was extended to the digital library project and the search engine system. The common algorithms are SCAM [5], DSC and its improved algorithm [6], [7] and so on. The SCAM (Stanford Copy Analysis Mechanism) algorithm, detects duplicate document based on comparing the word frequency occurrences of the new document against the exist ones by calculating the distance of the two vectors. DSC (digital syntactic clustering) algorithm represents a document by shingles. The document is first separated into several shingles composed of certain words, and then according some certain filter rules to filter out the shingles to participate in the duplicate detection comparison.

Some well-known domestic university also has their own research on duplicate detection algorithm. The Tianwang system of Peking University [8] extract and record the keywords while collects and analyses a webpage, then give each keyword a weight according to certain formula. The weight of these key words forming a vector space can be used to represent the page. The way to extract keywords and represent document of the Tsinghua University is to extract two characters in front of and behind each comma and full stop, thus to form the characteristic string. Harbin Institute of Technology extracts the keyword from certain position of the each paragraph in the document [9]. Although there is some difference in the extraction process of Chinese characters, they both take punctuation as the extraction mark and thus raise the algorithm efficiency. Because the extraction string of character is linear time, they simply the $O(n^2)$ time complexity's question to the O (n) .

2.3 The Limitation of the Exists Duplicate Detection Algorithm

The main duplicate page detection algorithms in this article still exists some limitations. The SCAM algorithm's efficiency is not very high, and the storage space it request is huge; The DSC algorithm do not need a large storage space, but with the increase of the times to compare, its efficiency reduced gradually, and the accuracy of this algorithm, largely depend on the chosen of the characteristic string, sometimes is not quite ideal. Several domestic algorithms mostly take the similar thoughts of the foreign methods, and have a variety of similar problems on efficiency, accuracy, and the time consumption.

3 Duplicate Page Detection Algorithm Based on the Field Characteristic Clustering

3.1 The Basic Thoughts of the Duplicate Page Detection Algorithm Based on the Field Characteristic Clustering

According to the problem met in the oil search engine development, the spider could not automatically abandon the duplicate pages that exists in the huge amount of web pages, and these duplicate pages aggravate the query process time consume and bring very low quality results to the user. Generally, the duplicate pages exist on the internet are divided into two kinds, one is the exact same page content, which usually appears in the different sub domains of the same main domain, another kind is the theme with the same content but slightly modified reproduced pages, which exist in many different domain pages. In this article, after analyze the feature of the oil industry web pages and establish a specialized vocabulary of the oil field, we firstly fast removed the duplicate pages under the same domain based on the method of oil domain clustering, then used the improved k-means clustering algorithm, supplemented by existing words frequency statistical information and the classification knowledge of the oil field, to do the clustering work based on the calculating the distance of the two characteristic string before the duplicate page detection, finally make these clustered class center characteristic string as the standard to make the comparison. Under this circumstance, as the comparison is within the divided class, the process of the duplicate page detection speeds up. This thought is simultaneously take the utilization of the word frequency statistics of the SCAM and the thought of DSC based on building block features in the characteristic string forming and distance calculating process. On this basis, we take the use of oil specialized vocabulary, domain of the oil field pages and the improved k-means algorithm, building up a new field characteristic clustering algorithm(FCC), to deal with the mass oil field web pages' similarity recognition, thus to realize the automatic duplicate detection effect.

3.2 The System Flow of Similarity Processing Model

Fig. 1 gives a processing flow chart based on the field characteristic clustering algorithm for elimination duplicate web page. The process includes the following parts: the cache, page preprocess, specialized vocabulary, characteristic extraction phrase, field characteristics clustering, duplicate detection based on domain cluster, based on field characteristic cluster, the original word frequency statistics, the improved k-means clustering algorithm with defined initial class center and the final index file which has eliminated the duplicate pages. Preliminary work needs to be done is to collect the cache containing the duplicate page, build the specialized vocabulary on the professional field knowledge. In this processing flow, the main task is to analyze the cache page crawled by the spider and to construct the characteristic string through the assistance of the specialized vocabulary. Finally, take advantage of the characteristic string to cluster and detect duplicate page.

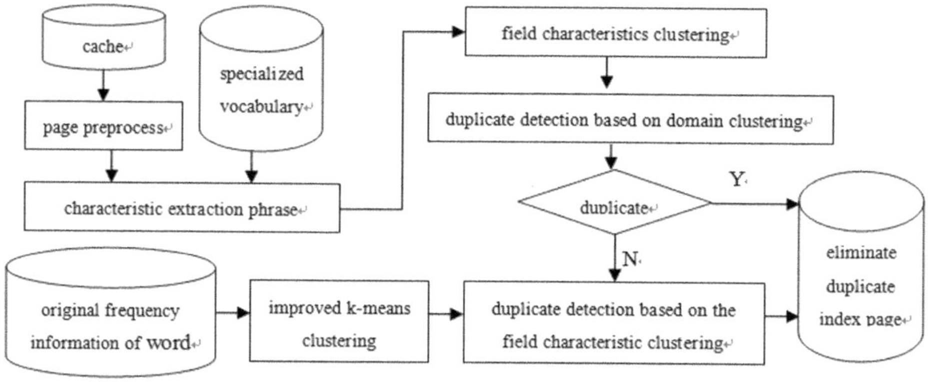

Fig. 1. Processing Flow of the Algorithm

3.3 Algorithm Description

3.3.1 Field Characteristic String Establishment

Through page preprocess and specialized vocabulary database, we extract the characteristic words both exist in the page and the database, count these words frequency, and then range these words in a descending sequence, separated them by comma between each two word, and add the number N representing the character number of the page at the end of the string. At last, we constitute the field characteristic string $C=\{c_1, c_2, ... c_n, N\}$. In the comparison process, we considerate two page to be the duplicate page when the field characteristic string is similar to another string in the same class after the field characteristic clustering. Each filed characteristic string of the same class is stored line by line in a text divided by classes.

3.3.2 The Improved K-means Clustering Algorithm

The k-means algorithm can be described as follows: to a certain dataset n with an input number k, the n data objects will be divided into k clusters, each object of the same cluster assumed to be highly resemble and the similarity of these objects in different cluster is smaller. Cluster similarity is calculated by the using of a "central object" which is obtained from the average value or commonly appearance item of the objects in each cluster.

The traditional K-means algorithm is sensitive to the initial cluster centers, so the result of clustering is volatility with different initial input. In order to eliminate this sensitivity, we improved the K-means algorithm in the clustering process. According to the concept of different subject in oil field [10], we provide some guidance in the selection of the initial cluster center. For this purpose, the concept of oil field was divided into ten categories as follows: geological-geophysical, drilling and completion, logging technology, oil and gas, reservoir engineering, well stimulation, storage, transportation and refining, petroleum machinery, and geochemistry. This approach improves the k-means clustering algorithm by lowering the dependence on initial value, at the same time enhances the stability of clustering results, thus able to achieve better distinguish between the various categories as well as more desirable results of duplicate detection.

3.3.3 Algorithm Realization

In the duplicate detection procedure, after the establishment of field characteristic string, we first divided the web page by their domain, as there are some duplicate pages in the same domain. Once we cluster the pages into the difference class by their domain, we can realize the rapid identification of the duplicate pages by use the redundant criterion of the characteristic string.

Take use of the filed characteristic generated by the original word frequency statistics, to cluster the field characteristic string by the improved k-means algorithm. Use the cosine function as the standard evaluation function, and set the 0.2 as the ending threshold for the distance between each center of the classes which was initialized into the ten classes by the oil field knowledge. After the field characteristic clustering process, we gain the 10 classes of field characteristic string collection B and the centers of the classes C.

Once a new page after the domain cluster comparison and is not a duplicate page, the field characteristic string of this page is calculate with the 10 class center C using cosine function.

Then select the maximum correlation result as its most relevant class, and to make string comparison with the field characteristic string in this class. And if there is a class that takes over more than 30% of the total page number, we recall k-means to separate this class into two.

The specific algorithm steps description is as follows:

1) Initially, using the improved k-means algorithm to cluster the cache A into ten classes, the class collection $B\{B_1...B_2, B_{10}\}$ and the field characteristic string center collection $C\ \{C_1...C_2, C_{10}\}$ is generated.

2) When a new page arrival, get its domain D_k by preprocess analyze. Find the same domain in the domain classes, if not exists the current domain D_k,suppose there already had D_n domain items, then use the new page domain name to create the new domain class D_{n+1}, and save the field characteristic string C_k into domain D_{n+1} class.

3) If the domain D_k exists, then compare the field characteristic string C_k with the field characteristic $C_1...C_n$ with in the domain class. If there exists a $C_j\ (1<j<n)$ and its field characteristic string is same as the C_k. Then we recognize the coming page as a duplicate one.

4) If the coming page is a duplicate one, its field characteristic string will not be saved and simultaneously deletes the corresponding preserved page content in the search engine. To compare the next page, repeat step 2).

5) If the coming page is not a duplicate one, write this field characteristic string C_k into the last line of the domain class D_k, and carry on the following comparison.

6) Using the cosine function to calculate the correlation between the page field characteristic string C_k and the ten field characteristic center string collection C which is clustered by the field characteristic algorithm, and get the result $V_1,\ V_2...V_{10}$.

7) To select the class B_k according to the most related result V_k, and then compare the field characteristic string C_k with the field characteristic $C_1...C_n$ with in the B_k class. If there exists a $C_j\ (1<j<n)$ and its field characteristic string is same as the C_k. Then we recognize the coming page as a duplicate one.

8) If the coming page is a duplicate one, its field characteristic string will not be saved and simultaneously deletes the corresponding preserved page content in the search engine.

9) If the coming page is not a duplicate one, write this field characteristic string C_k into the last line of the center class B_k,

10) Carry on the following comparison, repeat step 2).

Fig. 2 is the pseudo code for the algorithm implementation. The function CreatNewDomainCluster() is to create the new domain name cluster which is correspond to the step 2) mentioned above, FeatureStrExistInDomain() carries out the duplicate detection based on the domain cluster, the step 3) is related to it. They are both used in the domain cluster duplicate detection. The step 6) and 7) is correspond to the CaculateSimilarityWithAllCenter() and SelectTheRelatestCenter() functions. The CaculateSimilarityWithAllCenter() is used to calculate the Vi among the collection B classes while the SelectTheRelatestCenter() is to choose the most related Vi and its center class Bi. The final steps 8) and 9) is in corresponds with the FeatureStrExistInCenter() function. When the duplicate page is detected, we will delete it by the operation of files[0].delete().

```
public static void main(String[] args) {
    //pseudo-code realization
    String inputDir="d://cache";
    File filesDir = new File(inputDir);
    File[] files = filesDir.listFiles();
    while(files.length>0){
         preprocess();
         String FeatureStr=ExtractFeatureString();
        if(DomainExist(GetDomain(files[0])))
             {
                  CompareInDomain(FeatureStr);
                      if(FeatureStrExistInDomain())
                        {
                         files[0].delete();
                         continue;
                         }
             }
        else{
                   CreatNewDomainCluster();
                   WriteFeatureStrInNewDomain();
             }
        CaculateSimilarityWithAllCenter();
        SelectTheRelatestCenter();
        CompareInCenter();
             if(FeatureStrExistInCenter())
                  {
                   files[0].delete();
                   continue;
                  }
             else{
                   WriteFeatureStrInCenter();
                  }
      files = filesDir.listFiles();
     }
}
```

Fig. 2. Pseudo Code for the Algorithm implementation

Fig. 3 shows the file architecture of the domain cluster and field characteristic cluster. The 'I' is the domain clustering files expression while the 'II' indicates the field characteristic classes clustered by the improved k-means algorithm.

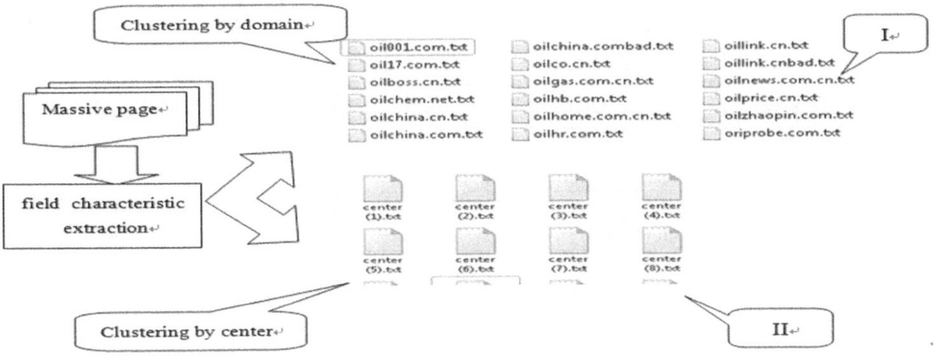

Fig. 3. File Architecture

4 Experimental Results and Analysis

4.1 Experimental Methods

The experiment use two types of web page together as the basic experimental data: one is randomly crawled by the professional search engine in oil field, the other one is the 1187 duplicate pages with different URLs which collected by artificial methods. We made experimental simulation for the duplicate detection algorithm based on SCAM and DSC then compared these two traditional algorithms with the new algorithm's performance in pretreatment and time consumption to verify the effectiveness of the proposed algorithm. Through recording the time consume of dealing with the same number of pages, the amount number of pages to be eliminate and the number of pages to be eliminate correctly, we compare these data to get the three algorithms in terms of performance, precision rate and recall rate. The three algorithms are carried out under the same experimental environment, dealing with the same number of the same cache. Test procedures are developed using java language and run in win7 operation system.

4.2 Analysis of Experimental Results

We designed three indicators to evaluate the algorithm, including complexity of the algorithm, recall ratio and precision rate. The recall ratio refers to the percentage of duplicate pages found by the duplicate detection algorithm among the total pages, and precision rate reflects the number of these duplicate pages which is in the real repetition.

Through experiments and a comparison of the duplicate detection algorithm based on SCAM, DSC and the duplicate detection algorithm based on field characteristic clustering, the feasibility of the method proposed in this paper was further illustrated.

By analyzing the two parameters: precision and recall, the experiments made a duplicate analysis on 4078 crawled pages (which contain 1187 duplicate pages) and the experiment results are compared. The statistical results are showed in Table 1.

Table 1

Duplicate Detection Algorithms:	SCAM-based	DSC-based	FCC-based
Amount pages to deal with (piece):	4078	4078	4078
Actual duplicate pages T(piece):	1187	1187	1187
duplicate detection(ms):	472916	262795	367927
page preprocess (ms):	4407520	1566400	1713406
pages been eliminated A(piece):	1240	1291	1315
Correctly eliminated D(piece):	985	898	1020
Precision rate(P)%:	83.0%	75.7%	90.1%
Recall rate(R)%:	79.4%	70.1%	82.1%

Precision rate (P) = number of pages to be eliminated correctly (D) / number of pages to be eliminated (A);

Recall rate (R) = number of pages to be eliminated correctly (D) / number of actual duplicate pages (T);

On the analysis of 4,078 crawled pages, we see by Fig. 4, three algorithms almost have the same time consumption in the duplicate detection process. However, on considering the algorithm performance, compared with the two traditional methods, the overall time consumption of page preprocess and duplicate detection of the field characteristic clustering algorithm, although a little longer than the DSC algorithm, is far below the SCAM algorithm, as it omitted the complicated vector calculation process. On the other hand, in the effectiveness of the algorithms, seen from Fig. 5, compared with the two traditional methods, there is certain improvement of precision and recall rate of the duplicate pages about oil fields got by the method proposed in this paper.

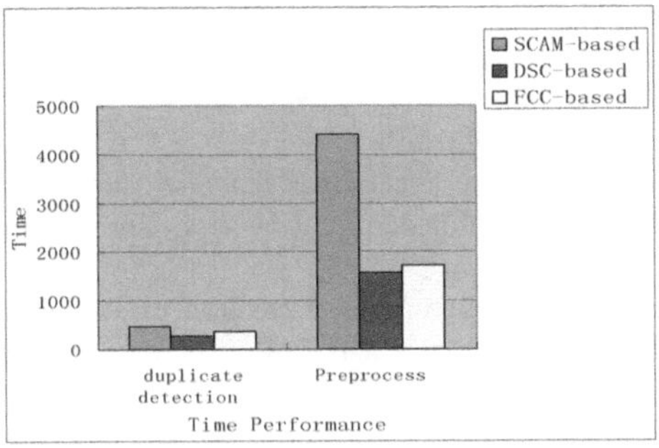

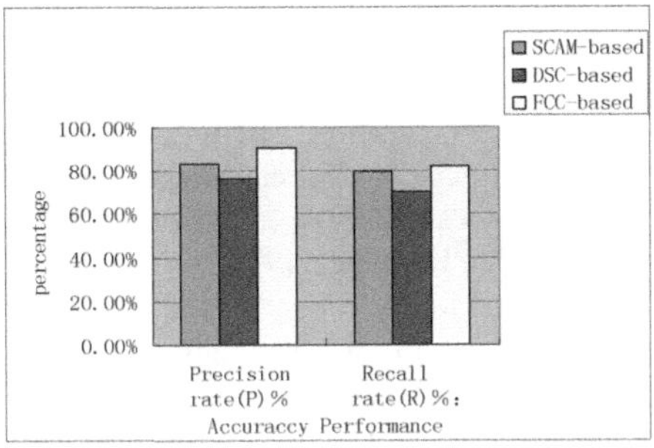

Fig. 4. Duplicate Detection and Time Consumption **Fig. 5.** Precision and Recall Rate

5 Conclusion

The web duplicate detection is very important for the information retrieval of web wisdom; it decides the accuracy of cognitive study and the speed of the interactive computing. And for the search engine within an information retrieval system, the web duplicate detection decides the index quality. In this article, we propose the duplicate detection algorithm based on field characteristic clustering. This algorithm overcome the time and storage consumption when use the traditional SCAM algorithm. And when compared with another DSC algorithm, it improves the drawback of the inaccuracy brought by the use of shingles to representing a page and comparing in the duplicate detection process. The duplicate detection algorithm based on the field characteristic clustering raise its precision and recall rate in field web page duplicate page detection.

We also believe that our techniques can generalize to other similar problem domains. Given any technique that extracts a set of characteristic from an object, we can measure the similarity of any two objects or cluster the sets of similar objects from a large number of objects.

However, this algorithm do have a high requirement for the building of the specialize vocabulary database, and need to have a pre-clustering job with the k-means algorithm which need to consume some time and its pre-cluster results will influence on the final duplicate detection outcome. In the future research, we need to continuously improve and update the specialize vocabulary and to add on more professional words, so as to build a better field characteristic string and thus carry out more accurate duplicate detection algorithm.

References

1. Bai, G.: Research and Application on Automatic Detect Duplication Technology in Internet. Chinese Academy of Science graduate school (2006)
2. Li, X., Yan, H., Wang, W.: The principle, technology and system of the Search engine. Science Press, Beijing (2005)
3. Xie, H., Qin, J.: Study on the Duplicated Web Pages Detection Algorithm with Meta Search Engine. Computer System and Application 17(8) (2005)
4. Yao, M.: Research on Duplicate Page Detection Technology in Internet Based on Document Clustering. Beijing Jiaotong University (2008)
5. Shivakumar, N., Garcia-Molina, H.: SCAM: A Copy Detection Mechanism for Digital Documents. In: Proceedings of the Second Annual Conference on the Theory and Practice of Digital Libraries (1995)
6. Elhadi, M., Al-Tobi, A.: Use of Text Syntactical Structures in Detection of Document Duplicates. In: 3rd International Conference on Digital Information Management, ICDIM 2008, pp. 520–525 (2008)
7. Broder, A.Z., Classman, S.C., Manasse, M.S.: Syntactic Clustering of the Web. In: Proceedings of the 6th International Web Conference (1997)
8. Zhang, Z., Chen, J., Li, X.: An Approach to Reduce Noise in HTML Pages. Journal of the China Society for Scientific and Technical Information 23(004), 387–393 (2004)
9. Xin, C., Wang, X.: Method of Parallel Removing Duplicates in Large Scale Chinese Web Pages Based on Feature Code. Harbin Institute of Technology (2008)
10. Zhang, C., Xia, S.: K-means Clustering Algorithm with Improved Initial Center. In: Secend International Workshop on Knowledge Discovery and Data Mining, WKKD (2009)

A Load-Balance Based Resource-Scheduling Algorithm under Cloud Computing Environment

Haihua Chang and Xinhuai Tang

School of software, Shanghai Jiao Tong University, NO. 800, Dongchuan Road, Shanghai, 200240, China
pangpangcs@gmail.com, tang-xh@cs.sjtu.edu.cn

Abstract. The algorithm for scheduling resources under clouding computing environment is different from that under traditional distributed computing environment because of the high scalability and heterogeneity of computing resources in cloud computing environment. In this paper, a resource-scheduling algorithm based on dynamic load balance is presented. The different data-processing power of nodes in cloud is considered in this algorithm, as well as different data-transferring power and transfer delay between nodes in cloud. The algorithm selects the "best" node to fulfill the task in order to improve the efficiency of cloud computing and minimize the average response time of tasks. And the simulation results show that the algorithm distinctly reduces the average response time of tasks.

Keywords: Cloud Computing, Load Balance, Cluster, Task-Scheduling.

1 Introduction

Cloud computing is a fully new distributed computing mode. It puts computing task in a resource pool which is made up of large number of computers which are also called "computing nodes" or "nodes", and this support different applications in the "cloud" to get specified computing power, storing spaces and information services that they need [1]. Computing task is finally fulfilled by computing nodes in resource pool; and they accomplish computing task through collaborative work.

Nodes in resource pool have different computing power and the networks between nodes are also heterogeneous, so we need an effective resource-scheduling algorithm to select the most appropriate node to finish one computing task, which can reduce the average response time of tasks and improve efficiency of cloud computing. In order to do this, the resource-scheduling algorithm should consider the computing power of nodes, the current load state of nodes and the estimated time for nodes to use to finish current task.

The resources in resource pool include storage resource, computing resource, network resource, basic establishment resource and other resources, such as accounts of clients, processes and so on [2]. We mainly focus on computing resource in this paper.

On the aspect of constructing the cloud storing architecture, we use the anisomerous architecture which is called LCA [3]; LCA is short for "Low Composed Anisomerous";

X. Luo et al. (Eds.): ICWL 2010 Workshops, LNCS 6537, pp. 85–90, 2011.

under this architecture, all resources is scheduled by one center scheduling program, which runs on one special machine, where all available resources' information is stored. Above is the cloud computing environment that this paper is based on.

There are 2 objectives for the algorithm brought up in this paper. The first is to improve resource utilization ratio and the second is to reduce the average response time of tasks. Those require that the algorithm can dynamically get the load states of computing nodes so that tasks can be assigned to computing nodes which are free currently or have light load; also for computing nodes that have stronger computing power, they should get more tasks. The simulation results show that the algorithm reaches its objectives: it remarkably reduces the average response time of tasks and improves utilization ratio of resources in the "cloud".

2 System Model

Next I will firstly illustrate the resource-allocating process under cloud computing environment, then introduce the load balance model, and finally give the resource-scheduling algorithm.

2.1 Process for Allocating Computing Resource

According to the frame and structure brought up by Map/Reduce [4,5] for cloud computing, one cell in cloud computing environment is composed of one master job tracker and several slave task trackers; while each slave task tracker is managed by the master job tracker. In the following part of this paper, we also called the master job tracker "master node" and called the slave task tracker "slave node". The master job tracker does the job of scheduling tasks which form an entire job, also it observes and confirms the execution of tasks, reschedules the tasks which are not successfully executed. When the master job tracker schedules tasks, it selects the most appropriate slave task tracker to fulfill the task. The slave task tracker executes the task assigned by the master job tracker; when receiving a task, it starts to fulfill it; whether finish it successfully or not, it should return result to the master job tracker.

How can the master job tracker select the most appropriate slave task tracker to fulfill the task? There are several factors to consider: computing power, current load, network station and so on. This paper presents an algorithm for the master job tracker to assign task to the slave task tracker, and the algorithm is based on dynamic load balance. And next we will show details about such a load balance model.

2.2 Load Balance Model

The load balance model in this paper is referenced to literature [6]: When node "Ni" in nodes' cluster is firstly used in a computing system, the system manager(in cloud computing environment, it refers to the master job tracker or the master node) gives it an initial weight value: DW(Ni), which is determined by the node's hardware configuration – The higher the hardware configuration is, the larger DW(Ni) is. The system manager uses DW(Ni) and the run-time information to calculate the dynamic weight value of the node.

The dynamic weight value is calculated through several parameters about the run-time information of the node. And we select the most important ones: CPU resource, memory resource, current count of processes and average response time of tasks. We get the new weight value according to such information and the old weight value. The dynamic weight value should reflect current load state of node in order to forecast the future load state.

For different kinds of applications, the importance of those parameters is not same. As to the web application, available memory and average response time of tasks are more important than CPU resource and count of processes; but for the database transaction, CPU resource and memory available are more important. In order to facilitate changing the proportion of each parameter for different applications, we set for each parameter a constant coefficient: Ri, which is used to represent the importance of the various load parameters, while Σ Ri = 1. Therefore, the weight value of Ni can be described as next formula:

$$\text{LOAD(Ni)} = \text{R1} * \text{Lcpu(Ni)} + \text{R2} * \text{Lmemory(Ni)} + \text{R3} * \text{Lio(Ni)} + \text{R4} * \text{Lprocess(Ni)} + \text{R5} * \text{Lresponse(Ni)} \quad (1)$$

While LOAD(Ni) expresses current load value of node Ni, Lcpu(Ni) expresses current CPU usage of node Ni, Lmemory(Ni) expresses current memory usage of node Ni, Lio(Ni) expresses current disk I/O access rate of node Ni, Lprocess(Ni) expresses current total of processes of node Ni and Lresponse(Ni) expresses Ni's average response time of tasks.

For example, as to web application, we use coefficient list {0.1,0.4,0.1,0.1,0.3} to initialize R1~R5; here we think the memory and average response time of tasks are more important. If current coefficient Ri can not reflect the importance of resources for current application, system manager should modify Ri continuously until it is right or closely right; here "right" means Ri can well reflect the importance of resources.

In addition, about periodically collecting the parameters of run-time information("Lxxx(Ni)" in the formula); although collecting information in a very short cycle can more accurately reflect current load state of each node, frequent collection (such as one time per second or many times per second) will bring burden to nodes, and it may increase network load unnecessarily. Also, under this condition, the experimental results show that the curve for load information of nodes was severe jitter, the system manager can not accurately capture the real changing trend for the nodes' load.

To solve these problems, on one hand we should adjust the frequency of collecting the run-time information of nodes: through a large number of trials, we recorded the nodes' load parameters periodically with different collecting rates, then calculated LOAD(Ni) and recorded it in plane coordinate system graphs, then analyzed those graphs, we got that collecting the run-time information of nodes generally every 5 to 10 seconds per time can better reflect the real changing trend for the node's load; on the other hand, we use moving averages [7] or sliding window [8] to avoid jitter, making the curve for the parameters' value be smooth, so that the effect of negative feedback will be better.

The system manager collects the dynamic weight value periodically: it traverses every node, tries to get its run-time information, and calculates the dynamic weight value LOAD(Ni). With the initial weight value of node "DW(Ni)" and the calculated weight value LOAD(Ni), we get the final new dynamic weight value of node "Wi", which can be expressed by the other 2 values through the formula below:

$$Wi = A * DW(Ni) + B * (LOAD(Ni) - DW(Ni)) / 3 \quad (2)$$

In the formula above, if the newly generated "Wi" equals the initial DW(Ni), it indicates that the node's load condition just achieve the desired condition. If Wi is larger than the initial DW(Ni), it indicates the node's load is light, the system manager will increase the allocation of tasks to the node. If Wi is smaller than the initial DW(Ni), it indicates that the node's load is in heavy condition, the system manager will reduce the allocation of tasks to this node. In actual use, if all the weights of nodes are smaller than their initial DW(Ni), it indicates the current nodes' cluster is overloaded.

2.3 Resource-Scheduling Algorithm

First, find nodes which are light loaded(Wi>DW(Ni)), and calculate "T_trans" of such nodes, "T_trans" is the time used for transferring data about one task:

$$T\_trans = t\_delay + Z / BWj \quad (3)$$

While t_delay is time delayed for transferring data from the master node to the slave node, which includes start-up costs and time used for competition on the transmitting medium; Z is the total bytes of the task, BWj is the data transmission rate between the slave node and the master node. Both t_delay and BWj could be dynamically predicted through "The Network Weather Service" [9].

Also there are methods to predict time used for the computing node to finish one task [10], and we defined this time T_do; then we defined another time T_all, while T_all = T_trans + T_do. Among the light-loaded slave nodes, find the one which has the minimum T_all and assign task to it. If this node fails to finish the task, then find the slave node which has the second minimum T_all and assign task to it.

If there is no light-loaded node or we can not find the appropriate computing node, then the master node transfers the computing task to another nodes' cluster, which is also made up of one master node and many slave nodes.

3 Simulation

Under the cloud computing environment which is composed of heterogeneous computing nodes(To build a simple cloud computing environment, we use the open source tool: hadoop, hbase, php with API enclosed, and then prepare 3 computers, which are all assembled with 2 G memory and 2.10GHz CPU, deploy those tools on these 3 computers and configure them; we simulate 3 computing nodes' clusters: each cluster has 9 computing nodes, one is master, others are slave), we use the algorithm that this article presented to do experiment. In the experiment, the main input parameter is the average system load. And we use the quotient of the average task reaching rate and the average task finishing rate to express it. Generally, the average system load = the average task reaching rate / the average task finishing rate; of course, we do some

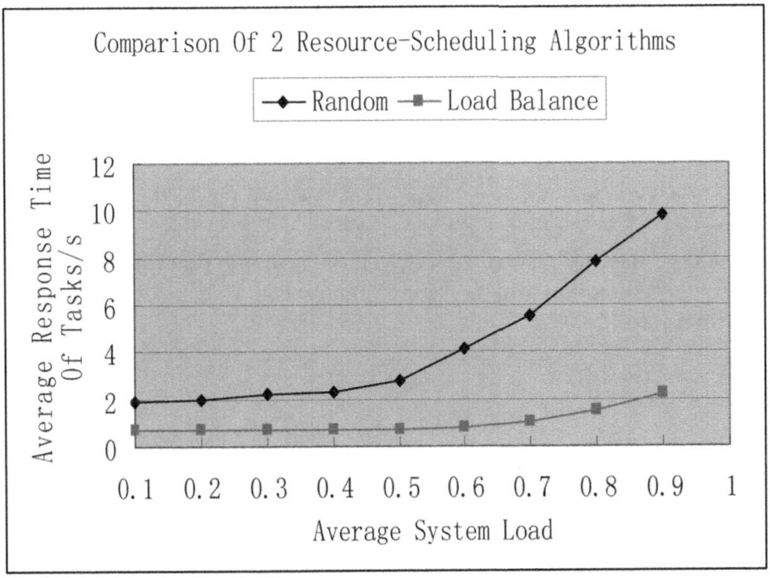

Fig. 1. Comparison Of 2 Resource-Scheduling Algorithms

processing to the quotient to make it above 0 and below 1. To get different system load, we change the task-generating frequency, thus we can get different task reaching rate and then get different system load; the emulating result is shown as follows:

In Fig. 1 above, "Random" refers to under the random resource-scheduling algorithm environment; when task arrives, the master node randomly selects one slave node to finish the task. While "Load Balance" refers to under the environment using load-balance-based algorithm presented in this paper. Through analyzing the chart above, we can get that: for both algorithms, when system load is below 50%, the average task response time does not become longer obviously as the system load gets heavier; and our algorithm based on load balance does not show its advantage except that the average task response time is a little shorter; but when the system load is above 50%, as the system load is becoming heavier, the average task response time becomes longer sharply under the random resource-scheduling algorithm environment, but it is only a little longer than before under the algorithm environment based on load balance.

To summarize, the algorithm brought up in this paper reduces the average task response time, increases the throughput of the whole system and improves the efficiency of cloud computing.

4 Summary

As a new distributed computing mode, cloud computing is different from the traditional distributed computing: loose organization, high scalability, heterogeneity, and so on. And all these make the resource-scheduling algorithm under the cloud computing environment different from that under the traditional distributed computing environment. This article showed a resource-scheduling algorithm which could be used under cloud computing environment; the algorithm is based on load balance theory [11] and the theory that the time used for node to finish task can be predicted. The simulation results show that the algorithm reaches its objectives: compared with the random resource-scheduling algorithm, it deeply reduces the average response time of tasks, increases the throughput of the whole system and improves the efficiency of cloud computing.

The inadequacy of this paper is: when making simulation, the parameters used in experiment were some realistic and we did not consider the dynamic extension of computing nodes; also our research is base on the research that time for nodes to finish one task can be predicted; while this research now is not very deep and people should put more efforts into it.

References

1. China cloud computing website. Definition and traits of cloud computing [EB/OL] (February 15, 2009), `http://www.chinacloud.cn/show.aspx?id=741&cid=17`
2. Li, T., Li, X.: Research on resource management of cloud computing. Computer & Telecommunication 01(1), 62 (2010)
3. Storage of cloud computing. LCA of cloud storage [EB/OL] (August 11, 2010), `http://tech.watchstor.com/cloud-storage-126949.htm`
4. Yang, H.-c., Dasdan, A., Hsiao, R.-L., et al.: Map-reduce-merge, simplified relational data processing on large clusters. In: International Conference on Management of Data. ACM SIGMOD, CA (2007)
5. Ghemawat, S., Gobioff, H., Leung, S.-T.: The google file system. In: 19th ACM Symposium on Operating System. Association For Computing Machinery, New York (2009)
6. Zhang, W.: Load balancing algorithm based on dynamic feedback [EB/OL], `http://zh.linuxvirtualserver.org/node/44`
7. 360 doc website. Moving average and its application [EB/OL] (August 4, 2009), `http://www.360doc.com/content/09/0804/07/180530_4654593.shtml`
8. Baidu encyclopedia. Data stream and sliding window model [EB/OL], `http://baike.baidu.com/view/166248.htm`
9. Wolski, R., Spring, N.T., Hayes, J.: The network weather service: A distributed resource performance forecasting service for metacomputing. Journal Future Generation Computing Systems 15(5,6), 757–768 (1999)
10. Hua, X., Zheng, J., Hu, W.: Ant colony optimization algorithm for allocating resources under cloud computing environment. Journal of East China Normal University (Natural Science) 01(1), 128–130 (2010)
11. Heirich, A., Taylor, S.: A parabolic load balancing method. In: Proceedings of the 24th International Conference on Parallel Processing, August 1995, vol. III, pp. 192–202. CRC Press, Urbana-Champaign (1995)

Research on Semantic Web Reasoning Based on Event Ontology

Wenjie Xu[1,2], Wei Liu[1,2], Jianfeng Fu[1], and Zongtian Liu[1]

[1] School of Computer Engineering and Science, Shanghai University
Shanghai 200072, China
[2] Research Center for Urban Public Safety Information Services, Shanghai University
Shanghai 200072, China
{jiex,liuw,ztliu}@shu.edu.cn, fujianfeng2000@gmail.com

Abstract. Ontology is one of the key technologies in Semantic Web. And the traditional ontology is only used to describe the concepts and the relations between them which neglected to describe dynamic knowledge. However, the Semantic Web offers services, which allow their users to effect changes in the world. In this paper, the dynamic knowledge in Semantic Web is described by a 3-tuple formal definition of action with temporal information which defined in event. And an Action-TBox and an Action-ABox are also proposed at the background of event ontology. Based on this formalism, several inference services of dynamic knowledge are discussed.

Keywords: Semantic Web, Event, Event Ontology, Action, Description Logic.

1 Introduction

The Semantic Web [1] is the emerging landscape of new web technologies aiming at web-based information and service that would be understandable, reusable and reasonable by both humans and machines [2]. Ontology, the major technology of the Semantic Web, is defined as a formal representation of the knowledge of a particular domain, and has attracted wide attention. However, the representation and reasoning about knowledge in Semantic Web is a very difficult problem, especially dynamic knowledge. Current formalisms about the dynamic knowledge appear to various kinds of representation methods which are often depicted by action [3-7]. But they all neglect that temporal information of action will change the representation and reasoning process of action. In real world, behavior (movement, change) can be described by "*event*". And events are specific facts which change over time. There are inherent relations between events. So to describe history is to describe a series of events and relations between them. In this paper, the dynamic knowledge in Semantic Web is depicted by action and time based on event ontology. We aim at the representation and reasoning of actions at the background of event extracted from text.

In our recent paper [8], event is defined as the basic unit of human knowledge comprised of action, objects, time, environment, assertions and language expressions. And an event ontology model was proposed in [9]. In comparison with traditional ontology, event ontology integrates dynamic action and temporal information with

X. Luo et al. (Eds.): ICWL 2010 Workshops, LNCS 6537, pp. 91–101, 2011.

static concepts, which challenge current action formalisms and action inference mechanisms. Especially, we believe that time information will impact the reasoning process of action and should not be neglected that did in most action formalisms. Because of description logic (DL)'s advantages in semantical representation and decidability, it is reasonable to extend DL to represent and reason about action. In this paper, a formal definition of action as a 3-tuples based on event ontology is proposed, which combined with a temporal dimension. The elements in 3-tuples are pre-conditions set, intermediate processes set and post-conditions set. With this definition, the representation of action is more accurate and complete. It does not only describe the states changing and the procedure but also indicate explicit temporal information of action. For the representation of time, we define some necessary constructors. These constructors can be used to represent time instant and time interval. And there is a duration time of a time interval which can do some logical and arithmetical operation on time. Especially, the principle of minimal change of action is adopted to constrain the *Pre* and *Post* sets. Several problems about DL-based action reasoning in event ontology, including satisfiability, instance checking, and possible effects of action are studied. As well, a transfer chain of the non-taxonomic relations of events that support the association problem among events is discussed in this paper. The rest of the paper is organized as follows: Section 2 proposes some definitions related to event and action. Section 3 discusses the inference services about actions in event. Section 4 provides an overview of related works in dynamic knowledge representation and reasoning in Semantic Web. In section 5, conclusions are drawn.

2 Related Definitions about Event and Action

Definition 1 (*Event*). We define event as a thing happens in a certain time and environment, which some actors take part in and show some action features. Event *e* can be defined as a 6-tuple formally:

$$e ::=_{def} (A, O, T, V, P, L)$$

We call elements in 6-tuple as event factors, including action, objects, time, environment, assertions, and language expressions. A detailed description of event factors can be seen in [9].

Definition 2 (*Action*). The definition of action involved in event is the form as:

$$A(x_1, \ldots, x_n, T) \equiv (Pre, Mid, Post)$$

Where,

(1) *A* is the action name.

(2) $x_1, \ldots, x_n$ are individual variables that denote the objects the action operate on.

(3) *T* is a predicate denotes the execute time of action.

(4) *Pre* is a finite set of preconditions, called pre-conditions, it specify under which conditions the action will be executed.

(5) *Mid* is a finite set of intermediate processes of composite actions, which describes a sequence of atomic actions and relations between atomic actions in a certain period *T*. It designs to represent the processes of composite actions. A *Mid* set of atomic action can be represented as an empty set $\{ \varnothing \}$.

(6) *Post* is a finite set of results, called post-conditions. It describes all possible effects after an action executed.

In comparison with the definition of action in [4], a predicate T is added at the left of equation to express the temporal information of action (both a time instant and a time interval). And a tuple *Mid* set is introduced to this formalism to represent the procedure of states changing for composite actions. By this definition, actions can be described more detailed and accurate.

Definition 3 (*Non-taxonomic Relations of Events*). According to the features of event, we define four kinds of non-taxonomic relations of events: (1) *composite relation*. Suppose an event e can be decomposed to several events $e_i(i>0)$ with smaller granularity. If all the smaller events e_i have been finished means e is finished, then there exists composite relation between e and e_i, denoted as $e \nless e_i$. (2) *causal relation*. If an event e_1 happens, an event e_2 is more likely to happen above a specified probability threshold, there is a causal relation between e_1 and e_2, denoted as $e_1 \rightarrow e_2$. (3) *follow relation*. If in a certain length of time, an event e_2 follows an event e_1 above a specified probability threshold, there is a follow relation between e_1 and e_2, denoted as $e_1 \rhd e_3$. (4) *accompany relation*. If an event e_1 concurs with an event e_2 in a certain period of time, and the occurrence probability is above a specified threshold, there is an accompany relation between e_1 and e_2, denoted as $e_1 \| e_2$. These four kinds of non-taxonomic relations of events can be also used to represent non-taxonomic relations of actions.

Definition 4 (*Transfer Chain of Non-taxonomic Relations of Events*). If an event e_1 and an event e_2 have a non-taxonomic relation R_1, and an event e_2 and an event e_3 have a non-taxonomic relation R_2, we can obtain a transfer chain formed by these events. The relation R_1 can be same with R_2, or different with R_2. For example, "*collision*→ (*injured* ‖ *death*)⊳ *send_to_hospital*", There is a transfer chain of non-taxonomic relations exist among these events. We can describe an event with big granularity or a topic through this transfer chain. And we can also describe a passage through one or more transfer chains.

The non-taxonomic relation R doesn't have the mathematical transitivity. But in the event ontology, the transitivity of the non-taxonomic relations is reflected by semantical interpretation and time information of actions. So, the transitivity of R can be regarded as succession in semantics and time. The transfer chain is a kind of deep reasoning in event ontology which acts as association in brain. It could associate the events which are not related. And it is also widely used in event ontology applications. For example, we can determine which topic a text belongs to through this transfer chain. As well, it can be used to text understanding, information query, automatic question answering and information mining.

Definition 5 (*Action Time*). In order to express temporal information of action, a set of time constructors are introduced. It can be expressed as: (*at* | *before* | *after*) T, T can be described as a ordered pair $<t_1, t_2>$ formally, and t_1=*start*(T), t_2=*end*(T). So, T can be expressed as a time instant or a time interval. e.g.<14:00, 16:00>, *at*<12:00, 12:00>. When T is a time instant, the start time of T is equal to the end time of time T which can be denoted as *start*(T)=*end*(T).

Definition 6 (*Time* |*T*|). Time |*T*| is a duration time of *T*, and it can be used in arithmetical operation. For example, |<14:00, 16:00>|=2 hours.

3 Inference Services of Action in Event Ontology

According the definition of action above and the architecture of description logic, we proposed an extended Action-TBox and an extended Action-ABox based on general TBox and ABox which describe the concepts, roles and individuals in *Pre* and *Post* sets of action in dynamic knowledge base.

3.1 An Extended Description Logic for Action

The architecture of traditional description logic contains a knowledge base and inference services based on it [11]. A DL knowledge base is made up of two parts, a terminology part (called the TBox) and an assertion part (called the ABox). TBox is a finite set of the form $C \equiv D$ ($R \equiv S$) and $C \sqsubseteq D$ ($R \sqsubseteq S$), where *C*, *D* are concepts, and *R*, *S* are roles. The inference services in TBox are satisfiability and subsumption of concepts and roles. ABox is a finite set of instances of the form *C*(*a*) and *R*(*a*, *b*), where *C* is concept, *R* is role, and *a*, *b* are individuals. The inference services in ABox are instance checking and consistence of knowledge base. In this paper, we expand DL knowledge base with a terminology part (called Action-TBox) and an assertion part (called Action-ABox), each part consists of a set of formula about actions.

Definition 7 (*Action-TBox*). Action-TBox is a finite set of general action definitions and the relations of actions in which the participants are individual variables. The structures of the relations are of form as $A_1 \sqsubseteq A_2$, $A_1 \rightarrow A_2$, $A_1 \rhd A_2$, $A_1 \| A_2$, $A_1 \not< A_2$. In the definition of action, *Pre* is a set of which conditions that action will be executed. *Post* is the set of all possible effects after an action executed. Two of them are of the form $C(x_i)$ or $R(x_i, x_j)(i, j{=}1, 2,\ldots n)$, where *C* is a concept, and *R* is a role name, x_i and x_j are individual variables. *Mid* set is represented as a set of a sequence of atomic-actions. For example, an atomic action "*eat*" is described as follows:

$$eat(x, y, at\ t) \equiv (\{human(x), food(y), hungry(x)\}, \{\varnothing\}, \{\neg hungry(x), \neg food(y)\}) \quad (1)$$

In instance (1), it indicates that someone *x* eat food *y* at *t*, and then he or she is not hungry, and food *y* has been eaten. From (1), we can see that there are static concepts "*human*", "*food*", "*hungry*" in *Pre* and *Post* sets which have been defined in general TBox. The *Post* set of "*eat*" is the only results after it executed. But, for some other atomic actions, there may have a variety of different kinds of results after they executed according to specific environment. For example, an atomic action "*collision*" can be described as follows:

$$collision\ (x, y, at\ t) \equiv (\{vehicle(x), vehicle(y), driving(a, x), driving(b, y), at\_place(x, place_1), at\_place(y, place_1)\}, \{\varnothing\}, \{damaged(x), damaged(y), died(a), died(b), injured(a), injured(b)\}) \quad (2)$$

In instance (2), it indicates that vehicle *x* and *y* collide at *t*. And *x* and *y* may be damaged. The person *a* who is the driver of *x* may be died or injured. The person *b* who is the driver of *y* also may be died or injured. The concepts and roles in *Pre* and *Post* sets such as "*vehicle*", "*driving*", "*damaged*" are defined in general TBox. According to some facts that different vehicles or degree of collision, the actual results may be one of them, or some of them. Probably, there exist some other results that not described in *Post* set. So, the *Post* set may be of very large size. Therefore, this paper provides a principle of minimal change of action to constrain the *Post* set.

Definition 8 (*The Principle of Minimal Change of Action*). The principle of minimal change of action is that all the changes of action must be minimized [12]. The principle describes that the set of *Pre* and *Post* sets must be the sets which are of minimal change. That is to say, the set of *Pre* meet all the conditions which led to action execute. The other conditions are not needed if they are not described in *Pre* set in spite of they are needed in some situations. And so does the set of *Post*. The set of *Post* is all the possible effects after an action executed. There are also some results that not described in *Post* set in spite of they are true in some situations.

There are three typical problems (the frame problem, the qualification problem, and the ramification problem) in action reasoning. The frame problem describes that it is hard to give a proper description about what properties have no change after an action executed. The qualification problem describes that it is hard to give a proper description about what are the pre-conditions that an action will be executed. The ramification problem describes that it is hard to give a proper description about what the results after an action executed [12]. In fact, the qualification problem is to be occurred while describing the *Pre* set. And the ramification problem is to be occurred while describing the *Post* set. These three problems can be settled through the principle of minimal change. In order to simplify the representation and inference of action, we assume that the sets of *Pre* and *Post* satisfy this principle. Following are examples for these problems.

As to the qualification problem in *Pre* set in (1), the *Pre* set of "*eat*" which we described as $\{human(x), food(y), hungry(x)\}$. Obviously, these predicates are not all the necessary conditions. Some predicates such as $exist(y)$, $near(y, x)$ and $enough(y)$ may be also the pre-conditions of "*eat*", whereas it is not necessary to describe all the conditions. In fact, it is also impossible to do it. The principle used in *Pre* set of "*eat*" is to avoid describing too many pre-conditions, and just consider the three necessary conditions in *Pre* set.

As to the ramification problem in *Post* set in (2), the *Post* set of "*collision*" may exists other results, such as $\exists c.(passenger(c) \cap (injured(c) \cup died(c))$. The principle used in *Post* set of "*collision*" is to avoid considering too many post-conditions. These result predicates can be added to a certain specific action as constraint conditions.

In Action-TBox, there are also definitions of composite actions. Fox example, a composite action "*go_to_work*" in Action-TBox can be described as follows:

$$go\_to\_work(x,\ loc_1,\ loc_2,\ am\ T) \equiv (\{human(x),\ home(loc_1),\ work\_place(loc_2),\ at\_palce(x,\ loc_1)\},\ \{walk(loc_1,\ place_1,\ am\ T_1) \rhd train(place_1,\ place_2,\ am\ T_2) \rhd walk(place_2,\ loc_2,\ am\ T_3)\},\ \{at\_place(x,\ loc_2)\}) \quad (3)$$

In instance (3), it describes that there are three small atomic-actions in action "*go_to_work*": *walk*, *train*, and *walk*. It makes the action "*go_to_work*" more materialization. In other dynamic knowledge representation system, a composite action can only be described with a set of start states and a set of end states, the intermediate processes are neglected.

Definition 9 (*Action-ABox*). Action-ABox is a finite set of action instances and relation instances of actions. That is to say, the individual variables x_1, $x_{2,\ldots,}$ x_n and time T in actions are instanced.

If T_1 is the time of action A_1, T_2 is the time of action A_2, and there is a relation which is of *composite*, *causal*, *follow*, or *accompany* between A_1 and A_2, then *start*(T_1) is before *start*(T_2). Thus, the composite action "*go_to_work*" can be instanced as follows:

$$go\_to\_work(Fred,\ A,\ B,\ am\ T) \equiv (\{human\ (Fred),\ home\ (A),\ work\_place(B),\ at\_place(Fred,\ A)\},\{(walk(A,\ C,\ am\ T_1) \rhd (train(C,\ D,\ am\ T_2) \rhd (walk(D,\ B,\ am\ T_3)\},\{at\_place(Fred,\ B)\}) \quad (3')$$

T=(8:00, 9:00) $|T|$=1 hour T_1=(8:00, 8:10) $|T_1|$=10 minutes
T_2=(8:10, 8:50) $|T_2|$=40 minutes T_3=(8:50, 9:00) $|T_3|$=10 minutes

In instance (3'), it describes that *Fred* needs an hour from home *A* to work place *B*. And it's 10 minutes' walk from *A* to *C*, 40 minutes' by train from *C* to *D*, and then 10 minutes' walk from *D* to *B*.

It can be seen from instance (3') that time information is very important while declare an action instance assertion or relation assertion, even impacts the reasoning of action. Some logical or arithmetical operations can be applied to action time, for example, in (3'), T is divided into three parts, T_1, T_2, and T_3. The time of each action can be calculated with the method in definition 6. T can also be used to describe action relations, for example, *Fred* is listening to music as he is walking can be described as:

$$walk\ (A,\ C,\ am\ T_1)\ ||\ listen\_music\ (Fred,\ am\ T_1)$$

3.2 Inference Services of Action

The effects of action executed are such that they can transform one states of the world into another one. That is to say, there are states changing after action executed. In this formalism, the static concepts and roles which defined in general TBox, the instances in ABox in *Pre* and *Post* sets must satisfy the base DL inference services, such as satisfiability and subsumption of concepts and roles, instance checking and consistence of knowledge base. For action, the inference services are executability, action's possible effects, and satisfiability of intermediate processes in composite action.

(1) The inference services in *Pre* set

There are many static concepts and roles in *Pre* set of action. Basic *tableau* algorithm in DL can be applied to satisfiability and instance checking of concepts and roles [13]. So the satisfiablity and instance checking in *Pre* set must be satisfied before the action time *before T* at first. For example, the definition of "*driver*" can be described in TBox as follows:

$$driver(c) \equiv \exists x.(vehicle(x) \cap driving(c,\ x))$$

We can come to the conclusions that *driver*(a) and *driver*(b) are satisfied *before T* through the definition of *Pre* set in "*collision*", where *Pre*={*vehicle*(x), *vehicle*(y), *driving*(a, x), *driving*(b, y), *at_place*(x, $place_1$), *at_place*(y, $place_1$)}.

(2) Executability of action

Before trying to apply the action, we want to know whether it is indeed executable, i.e., whether all pre-conditions are satisfied in the states of the current world. This problem is called executability [6]. If A is an action, all conditions in *Pre* set of A are satisfied *before T*, the action A is executable.

(3) The inference services in *Post* set

Similar to *Pre* set, there are also many static concepts and roles in *Post* set of action. But *Post* set contains all the possible effects after an action executed which defined in Action-TBox. There may be some inconsistent concepts in *Post* set. So the *Post* set doesn't need to satisfied consistency testing of concepts and roles but to satisfied satisfiability *after T* which is the time of action. But in the *Post* set of an action instance which defined in Action-ABox, both satisfiability and consistency testing should be carried out *after T*. For another example, an instance of action "*collision*" is described as follows:

$$collision(car_1,\ car_2,\ at\ t) \equiv (\{vehicle(car_1),\ vehicle(car_2),\ driving(Mary,\ car_1),\ driving(Fred,\ car_2),\ at\_place(car_1,\ Nanjing\_Road),\ at\_place(car_2,\ Nanjing\_Road)\},\ \{\varnothing\},\ \{damaged(car_1),\ damaged(car_2),\ died(Mary),\ injured(Fred)\})$$
$$at\ t=(2010\text{-}5\text{-}10\ 14{:}25,\ 2010\text{-}5\text{-}10\ 14{:}25) \qquad (2')$$

Instance (2') indicates that *Mary* is driving car_1 and *Fred* is driving car_2 *before T*. They are colliding at Nanjing Road, at 14:25 on May 10th. After the collision, two cars are damaged, *Mary* is died, and *Fred* is injured *after T*. So we can come to the conclusions that the instances of *driver*(*Mary*) and *driver*(*Fred*) are satisfied *after T*.

(4) Instance checking of action

If A_1 is an instance of action A, there are three steps in the instance checking of A_1. First, the action A_1 must be executability. Second, the *Post* set of A_1 must be a subset of the *Post* set of A. Third, the *Post* set of A_1 must be satisfiability and consistency.

(5) action's possible effects in *Post* set

As described above, the *Post* set is the set of all the possible effects after an action executed. How to select proper effects from the *Post* set is our main work. Our solution is to introduce some constraint conditions to knowledge base to make sure that it is feasible to reason out the right effects, at the same time, the *Post* set must be satisfied. This problem will be discussed in detailed in section 3.3 below.

(6) Satisfibility of intermediate processes in composite action

This inference service is customized for composite action. The intermediate processes of composite action may change over time, and the composite action can be divided into atomic-actions. According to the time factor of action, we can infer some concepts and roles are satisfied among time T. For example, in the instance of "*go_to_work*", the set of {*at_place*(*Fred*, C)} is satisfied *at* ($end(T_1) \cup begin(T_2)$), the set of {*at_place*(*Fred*, D)} is satisfied *at* ($end(T_2) \cup begin(T_3)$), the set of {*at_place*(*Fred*, B), *work_place*(B)} is also satisfied *after T*.

3.3 Action's Possible Effects in Post Set

The main task for action reasoning is to reason out what results in *Post* set is true after an action executed. This problem is called projection [6]. In other word, if the action is executable, we want to know whether applying it achieves the desired effect, i.e., whether an assertion that we want to make true really holds after executing the action. Obviously, it is not enough to achieve the desired effect though the existing definitions of action. So we can instantiated an action through adding constraint conditions. Following are three guidelines for the instantiation of action.

(1)Add predicates which describe the degree of action

While named an action instance, add an adverb or adjective in it which describe the degree of action. At the same time, the *Post* set will be reduced. For example, an action "*serious_collision*" can be described as follows:

$$serious\_collision(x, y, at\ t) \equiv collision\ (x, y, at\ t) \cap \exists a.((driver(a) \cup passenger(a)) \cap died(a))$$

It indicates that there are some persons died after a "*serious_collision*" action executed. These death persons may be drivers or passengers. So, we can come to the conclusion that there is $\{died(a) \cup died(b)\}$ in the *Post* set of "*serious_collision*" according to the definition of *Post* set in "*collision*", where $Post=\{damaged(x), damaged(y), died(a), died(b), injured(a), injured(b)\}$.

In addition, there is a set $\{died\ (Mary)\}$ in *Post* set of instance in "$collision(car_1, car_2, at\ t)$". So, we can also come to the conclusions that "$collision(car_1, car_2, at\ t)$" is both an instance of "*collision*" and an instance of "*serious_collision*" since there is somebody death in this accident.

(2) Add predicates which describe the scope of action

While instantiated an action, add some predicates that describe the scope of action to reduce the scope of the *Post* set. For an action in specific situation, it will result in specific effects. Thus the *Post* set of the action will be narrowed and become more explicit. For example, the action "*sea_collision*" can be described as follows:

$$sea\_collision(x, y, at\ t) \equiv collision(x, y, at\ t) \cap in\_sea(x, y) \cap \exists a.(\ passenger(a) \cap died(a))$$

Where "*sea_collision*" indicates that vehicle x and y collide in the sea, it belongs to the maritime traffic accident. Colliding in the sea is generally a serious colliding according to common sense. And there may be some person died (or disappeared). So, we can come to the conclusions that $sea\_collision \subseteq serious\_collision$ and $\{died(a) \cup died(b)\}$ is satisfied in the *Post* set of "*sea_collision*" through the definitions of "*serious_collision*" and "*sea_collision*" since there is somebody death in this accident.

(3) Instantiate objects in action

Generally, there are always many objects involved in an action. So, we can instantiate part objects of an action to reduce the *Post* set, but it is different from the instantiation of an action that all objects should be instantiated. For example, an action "*call_police*" can be described as follows after action "*collision*" executed:

$$call\_police(x, n, at\ t) \equiv (\{human(x), at\_place(x, p), phone\_number(n)\}, \{\ hurry\_to(y, p, after\ t)\}, \{at\_place(y, p), police(y), firemen(y)\})$$

It indicates that someone *x* calls phone number *n* for help at place *p* after an action "*collision*" executed. The person who answers the call may be policemen or fireman and will send person *y* hurry to *p*. If we instantiate the object *n* of action "*call_police*", the *Post* of "*call_police*" may be narrowed. For example, someone calls "110" for help is described as follows:

call_police(*x*, "110", *at t*)≡({*human*(*x*), *at_place*(*x*, *p*)}, { *hurry_to*(*y*, *p*, *after t*)}, {*at_place*(*y*, *p*), *police*(*y*)})

It indicates that if someone *x* called "110" for help, the policemen will come to the scene. In another case, someone called "119" for help can be described as follows:

call_police(*x*, "119", *at t*)≡({*human*(*x*), *at_place*(*x*, *p*)}, {*hurry_to*(*y*, *p*, *after t*)}, {*at_place*(*y*, *p*), *fireman*(*y*)})

It indicates that if someone *x* called "119" for help, the firemen will come to the scene.

4 Related Works

To enable the computer to understand the information automatically in Semantic Web, the first is to describe the information formally. And then to conduct automated reasoning based on this formalism. The research problem on Semantic Web reasoning is mainly manifested through action reasoning. In the last few years, extensive research has been dedicated to action representation and reasoning with quite significant results, such as Situation Calculus [3], Dynamic Description Logic [4-5], integrating DLs and action formalisms which proposed by Baader et al. [6]. There are also some other methods, such as event calculus [7] which based on logic programming.

Situation calculus is a kind of formal method firstly proposed by McCarthy [3] in 1963, which aims at problem solving and logic programming in dynamic field. It can be seen as a sorted first-order logic framework that provides a methodology to axiomatics the effects of actions, and defines its semantics using second-order axioms. Thus, the translation into situation calculus does not provide us with decidability or complexity results for reasoning problems.

In order to obtain the expression ability of the action logic and the reasoning ability of description logic, SHI Zhong-zhi, etc [4] proposed a dynamic description logic, which called DDL. DDL provides syntax and semantics for representing and reasoning about action, it can be used to describe and reason about both static and dynamic knowledge. Based on DDL, Chang Liang, etc [5] proposed a kind of extended dynamic description logic, which called EDDL(X). EDDL redefined the semantics of actions in dynamic description logic (DDL). In EDDL, each action is interpreted as a set of trajectories, where each trajectory is a sequence of possible worlds of the semantic mode. Thus, the intermediate processes set of action is not defined, also the temporal information.

Baader et al. [6] make a proposal for an action formalism in which the state of the world and the pre-conditions and post-conditions can be described using DL concepts. Concerning reasoning, they focus on the basic tasks of executability and projections, which are mutually polynomially reducible. In their framework, only atomic action and sequential composite action can be represented, thus the expressivity of the formalism is limited.

Event Calculus is another logical language for representing and reasoning about actions proposed by Kowalski [7]. And it is a logical mechanism that infers what's true when given what happens when and what actions do. For example, given that "eating makes me happy and that I eat at 12:00", the event calculus concludes that "I'm happy at 12:05". The basic ontology of the Event Calculus comprises actions, fluent and time point [10]. Thus, Event Calculus can not describe the procedure of action executed.

The methods above describe and reason about action from various perspectives, but most of them neglect some factors that will impact the effects of action execution, such as the time information. In this paper, we regard action as an element of event, and define action as a 3-tuples formally with temporal information. And a principle of minimal change of action is proposed to restrain the size of *Pre* and *Post* sets. We also defined some non-taxonomic relations of events. And a transfer chain of them acts as association in brain which is a kind of deep reasoning in event ontology.

5 Conclusion

Many of the so far developed Semantic Web technologies, ontology technology in particular, provide us with tools for describing resources on the web. In this paper, a formal definition of action which is a very promising method for describing dynamic knowledge in Semantic Web is proposed based on event ontology. It overcomes current formalisms' insufficiency that can not describe temporal information of action. With this definition, both the states changing and the intermediate processes of action can be described. Especially, the principle of minimal change of action is adopted to avoid the complexity of description. As well, we analyze several action reasoning services in event ontology, and give relevant examples. Our further study work is to form a complete formal representation of dynamic knowledge in Semantic Web, which including the syntax and semantics of action, the decidability and the computation complexity of this formalism.

Acknowledgement. This paper is supported by the Natural Science Foundation of China, No. 60975033 and Shanghai Leading Academic Discipline Project, Project Number: J50103.

References

1. Berners-Lee, T., Hendler, J., Lassila, O.: The Semantic Web. Scientific American 284, 28–37 (2001)
2. Luo, X., Yu, J.: Building Web Knowledge Flow based on Interactive Computing with Semantics. New Generation Computing 28, 113–121 (2010)
3. McCarthy, J.: Situations, Actions and Causal Laws. Stanford Univ. Calif. Dept. of Computer Science, pp. 410–417 (1963)
4. Shi, Z.-z., Dong, M.-k., et al.: A Logic Foundation for the Semantic Web. Science in China, Series E 34(10), 1123–1138 (2004)

5. Chang, L., Shi, Z.-Z., et al.: Family of Extended Dynamic Description Logics. Journal of Software 21(1), 1–13 (2010)
6. Baader, F., Lutz, C., Milicic, M., et al.: Integrating Description Logics and Action Formalisms: First Results. In: Proceedings of the Twentieth National Conference on Artificial Intelligence (AAAI 2005), pp. 572–577 (2005)
7. Kowalski, R., Sergot, M.: A Logic-based Calculus of Events. New Generation Computing 4, 67–95 (1986)
8. Liu, W., Xu, W., Fu, J., Liu, Z., Zhong, Z.: An extended description logic for event ontology. In: Bellavista, P., Chang, R.-S., Chao, H.-C., Lin, S.-F., Sloot, P.M.A. (eds.) GPC 2010. LNCS, vol. 6104, pp. 471–481. Springer, Heidelberg (2010)
9. Liu, Z., Huang, M., et al.: Research on Event-oriented Ontology. Computer Science 36(11), 189–192 (2009)
10. Shanahan, M.: The event calculus explained. In: Veloso, M.M., Wooldridge, M.J. (eds.) Artificial Intelligence Today. LNCS (LNAI), vol. 1600, pp. 409–430. Springer, Heidelberg (1999)
11. Baader, F., Calvanese, D., McGuinness, D., Nardi, D., Patel-Schneider, P.: The Description Logic Handbook. Cambridge University Press, New York (2007)
12. Huang, Z.-s.: Reasoning about action. Computer Science 20(3), 7–13 (1993)
13. Baader, F., Sattler, U.: An Overview of Tableau Algorithms for Description Logics. Studia Logica 69(1), 5–40 (2001)

Building the Association Catalog for Books Based on Association Linked Network

Xiao Wei, Wei Wu, Jiyan Xu, and Zheng Xu

College of Computer Science and Information Technology,
Shanghai Institute of Technology, Shanghai, China
{xwei,weiwu,xjy,zx}@sit.edu.cn

Abstract. Current library catalogs, such as author catalog, title catalog and so on, index the books from one aspect but cannot reflect the relations among relevant book classifications. In this paper, the association relations among book classifications are mined from a large amount of borrowing logs of readers. Based on the mined relations, the Association Linked Network of book classifications is built to present the association relations among book classifications. A new type of library catalog named Association Catalog for books (ACB) is proposed based on the association linked network of book classifications. By means of ACB readers can also get the books about the related disciplines, which are closely related to this book. The experiment results show that ACB can help the readers retrieve the related books in interdisciplinary learning and researching.

Keywords: Library Catalog, Library Classification, Association Catalog for Books, Association Linked Network.

1 Introduction

Nowadays, the development trend of disciplines is increasingly interdisciplinary, which leads researchers and students to have great demand of retrieving books about different disciplines that are related to each other to some degree. Although there are several types of library catalogs in the current library, such as author catalog, title catalog, keyword catalog, dictionary catalog and so on, they only index the books from one aspect and cannot be used to retrieve the interdisciplinary and closely related books. So a new type of library catalog holding the association relations among library classifications should be designed to provide interdisciplinary retrieval for the relevant classifications.

The relations among books can be mined from the mass borrowing logs of the readers and the new library catalog, Association Catalog for Books (*ACB*), can be constructed based on the mined relations. Although there is much work about mining the relations between books, such as book recommendation of online book store [1] and the search recommendation of library [2], our work is quite different from them. The goal of the our mining is not to recommend books but to build a common library catalog for book search; that is to say, a new type of library catalog for library will be

X. Luo et al. (Eds.): ICWL 2010 Workshops, LNCS 6537, pp. 102–111, 2010.

designed based on the mined relations. And the experiment results show that ACB can improve the efficiency of book resources and help the readers retrieve the related books.

The rest of this paper is organized as follows. In Section 2, Chinese Library Classification is reduced by pruning. In Section 3, Association Linked Network of books is defined and the construction methods are discussed. In section 4, the Association Catalog for Books is defined based on the Association Linked Network of Books. Experiments and analysis are discussed in section 5. Finally, the conclusion is reached in Section 6.

2 Chinese Library Classification

2.1 Structure of Chinese Library Classification

There are many library classifications, such as CLC (Chinese Library Classification) [3], PACC (Physics Abstracts Classification and Contents), EEACC (Electrical and Electronics Abstracts Classification and Contents), PACS (Physics and Astronomy Classification Scheme) and so on [4][5][6]. Among these classifications, CLC is a common one and widely used in most of Chinese libraries. CLC and most of the library classifications are organized in classification tree (as Figure 1 shows).

CLC consists of five basic classifications and twenty-two big classifications. Each classification is represented by letters and Arabic numerals. All the classifications are organized in a classification tree. In the CLC tree there are about 50000 nodes (classifications) and the depth of the tree is eight. The lower level node has smaller scope than the higher ones. So it is best to classify the book in the leaf class in CLC tree. But in the library when it is difficult for the staffs to classify a book in an exact class, he usually groups it into a higher classification. As a result, the real classification tree looks like Figure 1, in which both the leaf nodes and branch nodes have the books belonging to them.

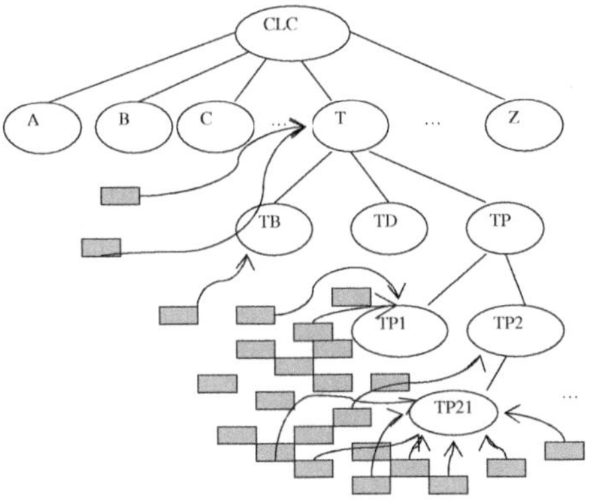

Fig. 1. CLC tree (Each ellipse represents a classification and each rectangle represents a book)

Fig. 2. BC-ALN (Each node represents a library classification)

2.2 CLC Tree Pruning

The classifications of CLC are too detailed and very great in quantity. Some problems will arise if the mining is directly done based on CLC, so it is necessary to select an appropriate layer as the research object. By analyzing the real experimental data from two libraries, the fourth level classifications are selected as the research objects for two reasons. (1) The depth of CLC tree is about eight and the fourth is just the middle layer. (2) Most of the books are exactly classified into the forth level or lower levels in CLC tree in library.

After the classification layer is selected, books distributed in the CLC tree can be merged in the fourth layer classifications. The merger rules are (1) all the books above the fourth layer are ignored; (2) all the books of lower layers are merged to the fourth level classifications by finding the parent nodes in the CLC tree.

The merger can be realized by prune the branches lower than level 4. The pruning can be realized by DSF (Depth-First Search) or BFS (Breadth-First Search) on the CLC tree. It is noticeable that the deleted node and the ancestor node of the 4 level should be recorded in order to merge the books of the deleted node to the pruned CLC tree.

After pruning, the CLC tree is a four-level tree and all the books are classified into the leaf classifications. Each leaf level classification can be represented by all the books belonging to it. Suppose there are n books in a classification, the classification can be defined as

$$C = \{b_1, b_2, \cdots, b_i, \cdots, b_n\} \tag{1}$$

In equation (1), b_i is a book of classification C and n is the number of books in C. The following steps only focus on the leaf classifications of the pruned CLC tree and mine the relations between them.

3 Association Linked Network of Book Classifications (BC-ALN)

3.1 Definition of *BC-ALN*

In the pruned *CLC* tree, the number of leaf nodes is about 5000 and each one presents a classification. In order to present the relations between classifications, Association Linked Network (ALN)[7][8][9][10] is used to organize these classifications and named as Association Linked Network of Book Classifications *(BC-ALN),* which is defined as

$$BC - ALN = (N, L) \tag{2}$$

In equation (2), N is the set of classifications, which is denoted as

$$N = \{C_1, C_2, \cdots, C_m\} \tag{3}$$

In equation (3), C_i presents a classification defined in equation (1). In equation (2), L is the set of relations among classifications, which is denoted as

$$L = \begin{pmatrix} caw_{11} & \cdots & caw_{1n} \\ \vdots & \ddots & \vdots \\ caw_{n1} & \cdots & caw_{nn} \end{pmatrix} \tag{4}$$

In (4), caw_{ij} is the association weight between classification C_i and classification C_j.

3.2 *BC-ALN* Construction

The construction of *BC-ALN* consists of four steps. The first step is to group the readers into different virtual readers. The second step is to shift borrowing logs into transactions set for mining algorithms. The third step is to mine association rules. The fourth step is to construct *BC-ALN*. Among these steps, in step 3, we use the traditional mining algorithm to mine the *ARs*, and just focus on how to generate the formatted data structure for mining algorithms. In step4, the construction of *BC-ALN* is the same as *ALN* [7], so we just give the construction result.

3.2.1 Virtual reader (v-reader)

Because the number of borrowing logs of a reader may be limited in a short period, if selecting a single reader as a mining unit, it is difficult to find useful rules. In fact, the readers of university library usually have some common characters and so they can be classified into different groups. For example, the students of the same major and class usually have the same learning processes and projects, so they have much in common in terms of the focus of books in a short period. If we merge the readers with the same characters into one virtual reader, the borrowing log of the virtual reader will increase to a large degree.

Because different readers have different knowledge background and different amount of borrowing logs, compared with the students, the teachers and researchers make more contributions to the mining results. Also we adopt different principles related to teacher and students respectively. The merge principles are:

- Each teacher or researcher is regarded as a virtual reader alone.
- The students are grouped by major, grade, class and sex. Each group is regarded as a virtual reader.

3.2.2 Generate Transaction Set Based on Time Segment of Borrowing Log

The borrowing logs of library have many differences from basket data which refers to cash register tapes of supermarket. A basket data is the list of merchandises bought by a user. Each basket can be seen as a transaction, and frequent pattern and association rules can be mined with traditional mining algorithms based on the transactions. But in most libraries each borrowing log records just one book that a reader borrows at a certain time, which cannot be used as a transaction directly. So it needs to translate borrowing logs into normal mining transaction set.

Normal logs are organized as log set *B* and each item of *B* presents a book a reader borrows at a certain time. The log item is defined as,

$$Logitem=\{LogID, ReaderID, BookID, BorrorwTime, ReturnTime\} \tag{5}$$

There are two main jobs to do to translate log set *B* to transaction set *D*.

The first job is to translate original readers to virtual readers. In (5), '*ReaderID*' is the original reader which needs to be replaced by the Virtual Reader gotten by last section. The job is easy to do but very time-consuming. It is easy because it is just a replacing operation. It is time-consuming because the time complexity is *O(m*n)*, where *m* is the number of readers and *n* is the number of log items. In fact the number of the reader is about 10^4 and the number of log items is about 10^6 per year.

The second job is to group log items into transactions based on readers and log time. The value of a transaction is that there may be some potential relations among the items of a transaction. So the direct idea is that log items in a short period can be seen as a transaction. For example, a day, a week, a month even a longer period can be seen as a transaction time unit. If the period is too short, there will be few items in a transaction. On the other hand, if the period is too long, there will be too many items in transactions which will lead too many *ARs* to be mined. So it is important to select an appropriate period to generate transactions.

In our method, the dynamic time segment is used to solve this problem. A dynamic time slot replaces the fixed time slot to group the borrowing logs. A day (24hours) is selected as the basic slot because a reader generally goes to library once a day. Then the average number of daily borrowing logs of all readers is counted. Because some readers may borrow many books a day, it should reduce the time slot for them. For those readers with few borrowing logs, it is necessary to increase the time slot. Especially, the max slot should be set because if the time slot is too long, the relation among the items will be too weak to mine. Here we select 7 days as the maximal time slot.

Algorithm 1. Transaction Set Generating Algorithm

```
- Input: Borrowing log set B, Virtual Reader Set VR
- Output: Transaction Set: D
- Description: Translate borrowing log set B to
transaction set D based on the dynamic time slot.
MinTimeSlot = 0.5 // Minimal time slot is 0.5 hour
MaxTimeSlot = 7 * 24 // Maximal time slot is 7 days
CurrentTimeSlot = 24
AverageItems = 0;
Group B according to Virtual Readers, B'={B_i | i∈VR}
Group Bi according to CurrentTimeSlot,
B_i'={B_ij | j∈SlotID}
AverageItems = average of |Bij|
For each Bij in B'
if  |Bij| > AverageItems
{CurrentTimeSlot'= CurrentTimeSlot'}
end
```

At the same time, we select 30 minutes as the minimal time slot. That is to say, the time slot varies from 30 minutes to 7 days for difference readers according to the average number of log items.

3.2.3 Generate Association Rules

After the borrowing logs set *B* has been translated into Transaction Set *D*, the normal Association Rules (*ARs*) mining algorithms can be used to mine *ARs*. For the mining technology is feasible, the detailed mining process is not discussed here. We only describe the prepared data to be mined.

The formal statement of mining association rules is represented in [11]: Let $I = \{i_1, i_2, \cdots, i_m\}$ be a set of literals, called items. Let *D* be a set of transactions, where each transaction *T* is a set of items such as $T \subseteq I$. Association with each transaction is a unique identifier, called its *TID*. We say that a transaction *T* contains *X*, a set of some items in *I*, if $X \subseteq T$. An association rule is an implication of the form $X \Rightarrow Y$, where $X \subset I$, $Y \subset I$, and $X \cap Y = \emptyset$. The rule $X \Rightarrow Y$ holds in the transaction Set *D* with confidence *c* if *c*% of transactions in *D* that contains *X* also contain *Y*. The rule $X \Rightarrow Y$ has support *s* in the transaction set *D* if *s*% of transactions in *D* contains $X \cup Y$.

In the above statement, the input data are organized as *literals*, *Items*, *Transaction T*, Transaction Set *D*, *X*, *Y*. The represents of these notations in our method are described as follows.

1) Items, *I*

In book borrowing log mining, the items consist of books. That is to say, each book is an item of *I* and *I* is the set of all books in the library. Particularly, items can be represented by

$$I=\{bookID_1,\ bookID_2,\ldots bookID_m\} \tag{6}$$

2) Transaction *T*

In book borrowing log mining, a transaction *T* is a virtual reader's borrowing logs set in a time slot.

$$T = B_{ij} \tag{7}$$

3) Transaction Set *D*

In book borrowing log mining, the transaction set *D* is the set of *T*.

$$D= B' \tag{8}$$

As a result, by Equations (6)(7)(8), the miming algorithm can get the source data for mining the relation among books. Suppose the results of mining algorithm, called *AR* set, as denoted as *ARs*.

$$ARs= \{X=>Y\} \tag{9}$$

In *ARs*, we only focus on the first order Association Rule, which means both *X* and *Y* only have one item. That is to say, it is the relation between a pair of books.

3.2.4 Construction of *BC-ALN*

Because *BC-ALN* is the set of nodes which is represented by a set of books, the relations between nodes can be gotten from the *ARs* between books. *BC-ALN* has the same structure as *ALN*, so the construction of *BC-ALN* is also the same as that of *ALN*. The construction of *ALN* is represented in [7]. According to this the construction of *BC-ALN* is as follow:

Suppose C_1 and C_2 are a pair of classifications. C_1 includes books $\{b_i, b_j, b_k, \ldots\}$ and C_2 includes books $\{b_m, b_n, \ldots\}$. According to association rules set *ARs*, check each items pair from C_1 to C_2, such as $b_i \rightarrow b_m, b_i \rightarrow b_n, \ldots, b_j \rightarrow b_m, b_j \rightarrow b_n, \ldots$, if a pair is included in *ARs*, then count 1. In the end, the number of *ARs* appearing from C_1 to C_2 can be gotten, notated as x. The total number of all *ARs* is notated as y. The association degree from C_1 to C_2 is x/y which is the rate of the appeared *AR* and the total *ARs*. Using this method, the *BC-ALN* can be gotten and shown in figure 2.

4 Association Catalog for Books

In the previous sections, the classifications set and the *BC-ALN* of the classifications are defined, from which we can search a classification and get the associated classifications with it. However the search process is not formal and complex (It needs operation the matrix of figure 2).

In the section, Association Catalog for Books (*ACB)* will be defined, which is the formal style of the classifications set and the *BC-ALN*. *ACB* should be designed for fast search and easy application.

4.1 Structure of *ACB*

ACB is a set of items C_{ACB} defined as.

$$ACB = \{C_{ACB}\} \tag{10}$$

In equation (10), each item C_{ACB} consists of a keyword K and a list of association items C.

$$C_{ACB} = \{k, C\} = \{k, \{c_1, c_2, c_3, \ldots c_m\}\} \tag{11}$$

In equation (11), k is the keyword of classification item (Here k is also the classification name), and c_i is the classifications related to k.

4.2 Generation of *ACB*

In fact, *ACB* is the serialization of figure 2 and another representation of Equation (2). It is easy to realize the translation from (2) to (10). In (2), N is the classifications set and each node C_i in (2) is an item C_{ABC} in (10). The name of C_i is used as the keyword k of the item in (11), such as *'TP311'*, *'H12.1'* and so on. The related classification set C $\{c1, c2, c3, \ldots, cm\}$ in (11) can be gotten from the matrix L. In L, the *ith* line (notated R_i here) represents the association weight from the *ith* classification with all the other classifications. C is the top m items of R_i which can be gotten by ordering R_i by the weight and selecting the top m ones.

4.3 Using of ACB

ACB as a new type of library catalog, it is mainly used to retrieve books. The typical modes of *ACB* are as follows:

(1) Query associated classifications
A reader inputs a classification name k and system gives the associated items C to the reader by searching *ACB*. After *ACB* is indexed on k, the retrieval of *ACB* is fast enough.
(2) Book retrieval recommendation
When a reader retrieves books in library system by traditional retrieval methods, *ACB* can be recommended. Suppose the book that a reader retrieves is b_i, the classification C_i of the book is easy to find in *CLC* Tree. The next step is to find the association classes of C_i. And all of the books are the candidate set for recommendation.

4.4 Analysis

Since the *ACB* is mined from the readers' borrowing log, it is unavoidable that the *ACB* is somewhat unilateral according to the readers. The mined results from different libraries and readers may be different. Furthermore, as the time goes on, the mined results may be different, too. All of these factors are considered and the *ACB* is not a static catalog but a dynamic one.

For the first question, a certain number of different data sources are needed. In a big library, the number of readers and the borrowing logs are enough. The mined results have some statistical characters and reliability. If we mine in several libraries and integrate the results, the reliability will increase to a great extent. In our experiment, the source data come from two libraries.

For the second question, in order to reflect the dynamic change of *ACB*, it needs to generate *ACB* periodically. The items of *ACB* are steady because the classifications of subjects change slowly. The relations between classifications are dynamic because the development and fusion of disciplines are comparatively fast. So periodic mining and updating are very important for *ACB*. In our method, we plan to select 6 month as a period for ACB updating. However, because the time is limited we do not get the second mining results to present in this paper.

5 Experiments

All the experimental data used in this paper come from two universities' libraries: Shanghai University Library and Library of Shanghai Institute of Technology. Shanghai University Library has over 3.6 million books and over 1 million records of book circulations per year. Library of Shanghai Institute of Technology has about 1 million books and over 100 thousand records of book circulations per year.

Based on the proposed *ACB* structure and the methods to generate *ACB*, we developed an experimental system of *ACB*. This system provides two types of search: search by classification name and by book title. If classification name is adopted to search books, the corresponding books of the classification and associated classifications will be provided together. If book title is employed, it first works as a traditional search. And then relevant books are recommended to the readers based on the *ACB*.

The subjective evaluation is used to evaluate the ACB. A score system is embedded in the *ACB* system. The scope of score varies from 0 to 5 to indicate the relevant degree between the results given by ACB and the reader wanted. Score 0 means irrelevant and score 5 means most relevant.

After retrieval is completed every time, the user is asked to score the results and all the scores given by the user are averaged. The final score is weighted average of all the scores of each user. The final score is defined as

$$S = \frac{1}{n}\sum_{i=1}^{n} w_i \times s_i \qquad (12)$$

In (12) s_i is the *ith* user's average score and w_i is the weight of the *ith* user. Here the weight is assigned according to the identity of user. Generally, the teacher has bigger weight than the student; the professor has higher weight than the lecturer.

After being evaluated by 500 users, the final score is 3.7, which means the accuracy of *ACB* is equal to 0.74. There is still much space to improve the accuracy of *ACB* and the available methods are

(1) Reader classification. In this paper, the differences of readers are not considered drastically. Indeed, the contribution of different readers for *AR* mining should be discussed in detail.

(2) The source data are still limited. In the future, we plan to unite more libraries to realize the projects together.

6 Conclusions

In this paper, a new type of library catalog named Association Catalog for Books (*ACB*) is proposed which holds the association relations between classifications. Using *ACB* readers can not only accurately find the books they want, but also the most closely related disciplines and other subjects in the bibliography.

The contributions of the paper are

(1) Proposed a new type of library catalog *ACB*. Compared with the traditional library catalogs, *ACB* holds the relations among classifications and has the ability of interdisciplinary search.

(2) Proposed the construction method of *ACB* based on *ALN*. *ALN* is the effective tool to organize the objects with association relations. Based on ALN, the construction of ACB is easy to build.

Although *ACB* is an available library catalog and can help the readers in interdisciplinary book search, there is still much work to improve the accuracy of *ACB*.

Acknowledgements. Research work reported in this paper is supported by key Foundation of Shanghai Educational Committee under grant NO.06OZ019, and key subject of Shanghai Institute of Technology (Computer science and technology).

References

1. Cui, B., Chen, X.: An Online Book Recommendation System Based on Web Service. In: FSKD 2009, Sixth International Conference on Fuzzy Systems and Knowledge Discovery, pp. 520–524 (2009)
2. Yao, C.-b.: Personalized guidance and ubiquitous learning in intelligent library with multi-agent. In: The 2nd International Conference on Computer and Automation Engineering (ICCAE), pp. 578–582 (2010)
3. Wu, H.: On the Revision of The Chinese Library Classification (4th edition). Journal of Academic Libraries (March 2004)
4. Chan, L.M.: Cataloging and Classification: An Introduction. McGraw-Hill, New York (1994)
5. Micheau, F.: The Scientific Institutions in the Medieval Near East, pp. 988–991 in (Morelon & Rashed 1996, pp. 985–1007)
6. Strout, R.F.: The development of the catalog and cataloging rules. Library Quarterly 26(4), 254–275 (1956)
7. Luo, X., Xu, Z., Yu, J., Liu, F.: Discovery of association topics for the intelligent browsing. In: Proceedings of the First IEEE International Conference on Ubi-Media Computing and Workshops, pp. 119–125 (2008)
8. Xu, Z., Luo, X.: Association Link Network: an Incremental Semantic Data Model on Organizing Web Resources. In: 15th International Conference on Parallel and Distributed Systems, pp. 793–798 (2009)
9. Zhuge, H.: Autonomous semantic link network model for the Knowledge Grid. Concurrency and Computation: Practice and Experience 7(19), 1065–1085 (2007)
10. Zhuge, H.: Communities and Emerging Semantics in Semantic Link Network: Discovery and Learning. IEEE Transactions on Knowledge and Data Engineering 21(6), 785–799 (2009)
11. Agrawal, R., Imielinski, T., Swami, A.: Mining association rules between sets of items in large databases. In: Proc. of the ACM SIGMOD Conference on Management of Data, Washington, D.C., pp. 207–216 (May 1993)

Factors Affecting Lifelong Learners' Intention to Continue Using E-Learning Website: An Empirical Study

Hsiu-Li Liao, Su-Houn Liu, Shih-Ming Pi, and You-Jie Chou

Department of Information Management, Chung Yuan Christian University, No. 200, Chung Pei Rd., Chung Li, 320, Taiwan, ROC
{Wenlly,vandy,smpi}@im.cycu.edu.tw
ycchou123@gmail.com

Abstract. In an era of rapid change, with a need for lifelong learning, this study aimed to explore the behaviors of lifelong learning by proposing an integrated theoretical framework for the lifelong learners' usage behavior on web-based e-learning. The research model draws on TAM and integrates with TPB to predict the lifelong learners' intention to continue using e-learning. Subjects were randomly selected from the members of the SME Online University in Taiwan and analyzed using partial least squares structural model (PLS). Results showed that course flexibility, course quality, system functionality and system response significantly affect learners' perceptions. Both the perceived usefulness and perceived ease-of-use have positive effects on users' intentions of continued use of the e-learning website. Additionally, our research findings indicated that for lifelong learning, learners' perceived behavioral control should be considered in the model for their planned behavior of e-learning activities.

Keywords: Lifelong learning, e-learning, small and medium enterprises (SME).

1 Introduction

Nowadays, learning can no longer be divided into a place and time to acquire knowledge (school) and a place and time to apply the knowledge acquired (the workplace) [5]. Lifelong learning is a term recognized that learning is not confined to childhood or the classroom, but takes place throughout life and in a range of situations. One of the most convenient delivery formats for lifelong learning is e-learning [9]. E-learning can be highly personal and interactive, enabling learners to attain an intimate out-of-classroom learning style. Self-paced e-learning allows learners to assimilate content at their own speed-often 20 percent to 50 percent faster than in a classroom [16].

The US market for Self-paced eLearning will projected to grow to $23.8 billion by 2014 according to a new report by Ambient Insight. The demand for online education products in America is growing by 7.4% [2]. Business spending on e-learning is expected to reach approximately $19.6 billion by 2010, according to IDC [8].

X. Luo et al. (Eds.): ICWL 2010 Workshops, LNCS 6537, pp. 112–119, 2011.

However, compare to the continuous growth of the e-learning market for the lifelong learning of adults, there are relatively few studies are available on the learning behaviors of these learners on the e-learning website.

The rapid technology development of lifelong learning has made learners' intention to continue using e-learning an increasingly critical issue. Previous research done under different task environments has suggested a variety of factors affecting user satisfaction with e-Learning. These factors that affecting students' satisfaction of using e-learning can categorized into six dimensions: student, teacher, course, technology, system design, and environment dimension [3], [17]. On a preliminary study, after interviewing 40 lifelong learners, the researchers have identified that the student, teacher, course, and technology dimensions are the major factors that influence the continued use of e-learning for these learners [11].

To explain learner's behavioral intention in using e-learning technology, the Technology Acceptance Model (TAM) has been prevailing in the area. Perceived ease-of-use and perceived usefulness have played important roles in affecting e-learning adoption decisions [12]. Since late 1980s, information technology adoption and use have remained a central concern in the field of information systems research. For this reason, some influential theories in other areas, such as theory of planned behavior (TPB) were borrowed into the studies of technology adoption. The theory of planned behavior (TPB) is an extension of the theory of reasoned action made necessary by the original model's limitations in dealing with behaviors over which people have incomplete volitional control [1]. TPB is more important in a person's behavioral intention particularly when the behavior is not wholly under volitional control. For example, when conducting lifelong learning, learners may need not only more resources (time, information, etc.), but also more self-confidence in making a proper decision.

In sum, this study intends to propose an integrated theoretical framework for the lifelong learners' usage behavior of web-based e-learning. Therefore, our research framework draws on TAM for its basic model and then integrates it with TPB so as to predict the lifelong learners' intention to continue using e-learning.

2 Research Methodology

2.1 The Research Model

Fig. 1 represents the proposed research model drawn from the constructs of student, course, and technology dimensions, perceived usefulness, perceived ease of use, perceived behavioral control, and intention of continued use as discussed above. The research model is empirically tested in this study.

2.2 Characteristics of the Sample and Study Context

To test the research model, users from the SME Online University (http://www.smelearning.org.tw) in Taiwan was chosen as a representative of e-learning users for the lifelong learning. The SME Online University has been recognized as the

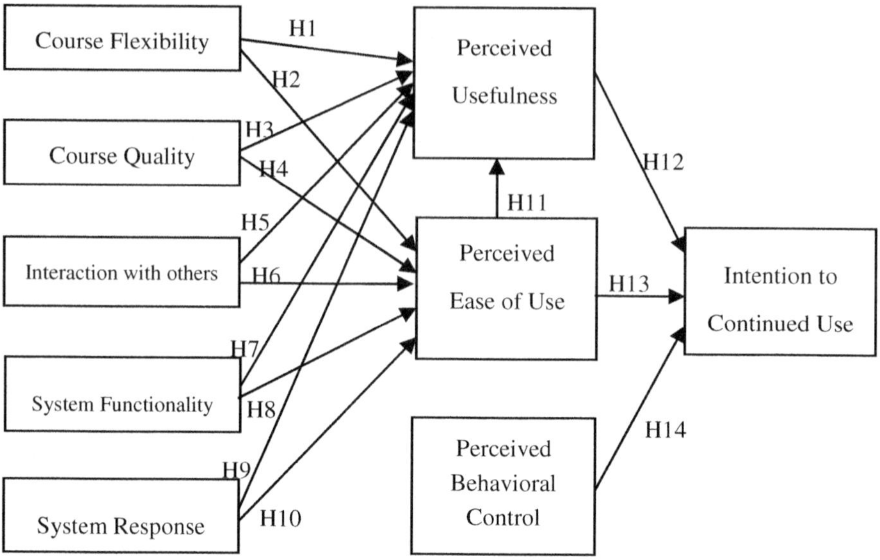

Fig. 1. Research Model

first e-learning website developed for small and medium enterprises (SME) in Asia and one of the biggest in the world. There are now more than 800 free online courses in five major categories. Today, the SME Online University has served over 300,000 SME employers and employees around the world. 500 subjects were randomly selected from the members of SME Online University. A total of 178 surveys were voluntarily completed, resulting in a response rate of 35.6%. The age range of the sample was 20–50 years old (Table 1). Of the 178 respondents, 98 were females (45%) and 80 were males (55%).

Table 1. Subject demographic (n=178)

Measure and items	Frequency	Percentage
Gender		
Male	98	55%
Female	80	45%
Age		
20-30	66	37%
31-40	69	39%
41-50	43	24%
Prior e-learning experiences		
< 1 year	109	61%
1~2 year	31	17%
2~3 year	17	10%
3~4year	12	7%
> 4 year	9	5%

2.3 Instrument Development

The survey questionnaire included a combination of items derived from earlier studies and newly developed items. Arbaugh [3] and Sun et al. [17] questionnaire items of course flexibility, course quality and interaction with others, Pituch and Lee [14] questionnaire items of system functionality and system response as well as Lee [10] questionnaire items of Perceived behavioral control was used in this study. Additionally, perceived usefulness, perceived ease of use and adult learner's intention to continued use were following the recommendations of Davis et al. [6] as the foundation for the development of the survey instrument. Respondents scored on a seven-point Likert-type scale with the end points being "strongly disagree" and "strongly agree", except for items intended to collect demographic data.

3 Analysis and Results

The research models were measured with the partial least squares (PLS) structural modeling analysis approach. PLS is appropriate for predicting highly complex models [4] and maximizing the variance explained for the constructs in a model [15].

3.1 Measurement Model

Table 2 presents the numbers of items, means, standard deviations and reliabilities of the constructs. The alpha-level of the sample indicates a reasonable level of reliability (α>0.70) [13], revealing adequate internal consistency.

Table 3 shows the each variable' the square root of AVE and intercorrelations, ranging from -0.078 to 0.795. Convergent validity of the instrument is appropriate when the constructs have an average variance extracted (AVE) of at least 0.5 [7]. The square root of AVE should exceed the intercorrelations for satisfactory discriminant validity [18]. The AVE for every construct is larger than the correlation between the construct and other constructs in the model. All items loadings of each construct are larger than cross-loadings of that construct with all other constructs in the model. Hence, the convergent validity and discriminant validity in the research model were adequate.

3.2 Structural Model

The result of the structural model testing includes the path coefficients and the R^2 values. Fig. 2 illustrates the results of the structural model for the research model. Course quality (β=0.305, $p<0.01$), system functionality (β=0.364, $p<0.01$), and system response (β=0.123, $p<0.05$) positively influence perceived usefulness. The three variables account for 71.2% of the variance in perceived usefulness. Hypotheses about Course quality (H3), system functionality (H7), and system response (H9) were

Table 2. Construct Means, Standard Deviations, and Reliabilities

Construct	Number of Items	Mean	Standard Deviation	Cronbach Alpha
1. Course Flexibility (CF)	3	5.742	1.589	0.794
2. Course Quality (CQ)	3	5.146	1.624	0.819
3. Perceived interaction with others (PIO)	2	3.905	2.284	0.879
4. System Functionality (SF)	3	5.670	1.438	0.872
5. System Response (SR)	3	4.959	1.766	0.868
6. Perceived Usefulness (PU)	4	5.650	1.409	0.948
7. Perceived Ease of Use (PE)	4	5.772	1.191	0.940
8. Perceived Behavioral Control (PBC)	3	5.749	1.367	0.929
9. Intention of Continued Use (INT)	3	5.908	1.323	0.862

Table 3. Correlations and Average Variance Extracted (AVE)

	CF	CQ	PIO	SF	SR	PU	PE	PBC	INT
CF	**0.841**								
CQ	0.580	**0.857**							
PIO	0.094	0.161	**0.944**						
SF	0.596	0.795	-0.078	**0.893**					
SR	0.560	0.562	-0.234	0.589	**0.930**				
PU	0.555	0.765	-0.183	0.783	0.627	**0.922**			
PE	0.617	0.598	-0.210	0.631	0.668	0.670	**0.895**		
PBC	0.552	0.575	-0.098	0.609	0.572	0.648	0.775	**0.929**	
INT	0.613	0.642	-0.240	0.635	0.449	0.689	0.691	0.664	**0.871**

Diagonal **bolded** elements are the square root of AVE.

supported, while course flexibility (H1), interaction with others (H5) was not supported. System functionality has the strongest impact on perceived usefulness, followed by course quality and system response.

Course flexibility (β=0.244, $p<0.05$), system functionality (β=0.213, $p<0.1$), and system response (β=0.341, $p<0.01$) positively influence perceived ease of use. The three variables account for 57.9% of the variance in perceived ease of use. Course flexibility (H2), system functionality (H8), and system response (H10) were supported but course quality (H4) and interaction with others (H6) were not supported. System response has the strongest impact on perceived ease of use, followed by course flexibility and system functionality.

Perceived usefulness (β=0.362, $p<0.01$), perceived ease of use (β=0.290, $p<0.1$), and perceived behavioral control (β=0.204, $p<0.1$) significantly influence intention of continued use. Hypotheses about Perceived usefulness (H12), perceived ease of use (H13), and perceived behavioral control (H14) are thus supported. Perceived usefulness has the strongest impact on intention of continued use, followed by perceived ease of use and perceived behavioral control. However, perceived ease-of-use did not significantly influence perceived usefulness.

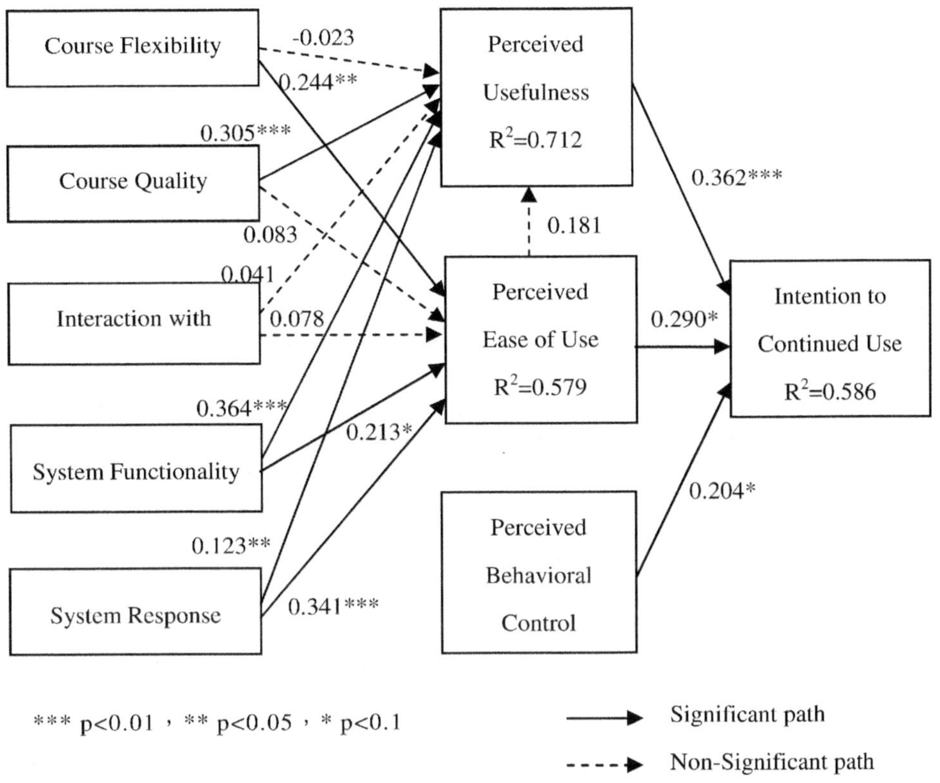

Fig. 2. The Continued Use Model of E-learning

4 Conclusion and Discussion

Our research is founded on previous researches related to the technology acceptance model as well as the theory of planned behavior. The research model considering perceptions, course and system dimensions to predict and explain the perceptions and behavior of e-learning of the lifelong learners. Course quality of an e-learning website positively influences lifelong learners' perceived usefulness of learners. Course flexibility has a significant impact on perceived ease of use of the learners. Besides, interaction with others doesn't have a direct impact on perceived usefulness and perceived ease of use of an e-learning website. The possible reason is that lots of learners came to the SME Online University with specific learning objectives (for example, to acquire knowledge that can benefit their job performance), therefore, they may not intend to spend time on interacting with other learners during their learning process.

Both System functionality and system response of an e-learning website positively affect perceived usefulness and perceived ease of use. The strong system functionality of e-learning website can offer multimedia course content and facilitate diversified ways of learning in anytime and at any place. The fast system response of an e-learning website provides learners with continuous learning process without interrupt. Therefore, these lifelong learners perceive ease of use and usefulness of an e-learning website more easily. These findings of our study were consistent with previous researches (e.g. Pituch and Lee [14]).

The results of our study demonstrate that both the perceived usefulness and perceived ease-of-use construct play important roles in predicting users' intentions of continued use of the e-learning website. Additionally, perceived behavioral control of an e-learning website has a direct influence on intention to continued use. Our research findings indicated that for lifelong learning, learners' perceived behavioral control should be considered in the model of the planned behavior of e-learning activities. The research results have shown that learner's behavior is strongly influenced by their confidence in their ability to perform e-learning activities.

The current research can lead to several further studies. First, the dependent construct here represents behavioral intention of continued use. It would be valuable that studies can be conducted to understand potential implications of other antecedents of the e-learning use model. A second concern is that the model tested here has been empirically assessed in only one conducting context. The gereralizability of the results reported here is not known beyond the current sample, e-learning context and richness antecedents. However, the proposed research model provides explanations and predictions to understand learners' behavior. Based on this understanding, system platform manager and education institution can determine how to improve the adult learners' the intention to continued use of e-learning websites.

References

1. Ajzen, I.: The Theory of Planned Behavior. Organizational Behavior and Human Decision Processes 50, 179–211 (1991)
2. Anonymous: Ambient Insight Reports Strong US eLearning Market. Business Wire (2009)
3. Arbaugh, J.B.: Managing the On-Line Classroom: A Study of Technological and Behavioral Characteristics of Web-Based MBA Courses. Journal of High Technology Management Research 13, 203–223 (2002)
4. Barclay, D.W., Higgins, C.A., Thompson, R.: The Partial Least Squares (PLS) Approach to Causal Modeling: Personal Computer Adoption and Use as an Illustration. Tech. Stud. 2(2), 285–309 (1995)
5. Minshell, C., Butterworth, C., Henderson, J.: Occupational Health 61(3), 35 (2009)
6. Davis, F.D., Bagozzi, R.P., Warshaw, P.R.: User Acceptance of Computer Technology: A Comparison of Two Theoretical Models. Management Science 35(8), 982–1003 (1989)
7. Fornell, C., Larcker, D.F.: Evaluating Structural Equation Models with Unobservable Variables and Measurement Error. Journal Marketing Research 18, 39–50 (1981)
8. Fretty, P.: Go the Distance. PM Network 20(9), 16–21 (2006)
9. Lamont, J.: E-learning: Options for Delivery. KM World 17(5), 22–23 (2008)
10. Lee, M.C.: Explaining and Predicting Users' Continuance Intention toward E-Learning: An Extension of the Expectation–Confirmation Model. Computers & Education 54(2), 506–516 (2009)

11. Liao, H. L., Chou, Y. J.: Factors Influencing Adult Learners' Continued Use of E-Learning. In: 2010 Information Management Research and Application Conference (IMRAC) proceeding (2010)
12. Liu, S.H., Liao, H.L., Pratt, J.A.: Impact of Media Richness and Flow on E-Learning Technology Acceptance. Computers & Education 52, 599–607 (2009)
13. Nunnally, J.C.: Psychometric Theory. McGraw-Hill, New York (1978)
14. Pituch, K.A., Lee, Y.K.: The influence of system characteristics on e-learning use. Computers & Education 47, 222–244 (2006)
15. Plouffe, C.R., Hulland, J.S., Vandenbosch, M.: Research Report: Richness Versus Parsimony in Modeling Technology Adoption Decisions–Understanding Merchant Adoption of a Smart Card-Based Payment System. Information Systems Research 12(2), 208–222 (2001)
16. Schooley, C.: The ROI of E-learning. KM World 18(7), 12–13 (2009)
17. Sun, P.C., Tsai, R.J., Finger, G., Chen, Y.Y., Yeh, D.: What Drives a Successful E-Learning? An Empirical Investigation of the Critical Factors Influencing Learner Satisfaction. Computers & Education 50, 1183–1202 (2008)
18. Wixom, B.H., Todd, A.P.: A Theoretical Integration of User Satisfaction and Technology Acceptance. Information Systems Research 16(1), 85–102 (2005)

Requirements of Chinese Teachers for Online Student Tracking and a Comparison to Their Western Counterparts

Xiaohong Tan[1], Carsten Ullrich[1], Oliver Scheuer[2], Erica Melis[2], and Ruimin Shen[1]

[1] E-learning Lab, Shanghai Jiao Tong University, 6th F, Haoran Building, 1954 Huashan Rd. Shanghai, China
[2] German Research Center for Artificial Intelligence (DFKI)
{Xhtan,ullrich_c,rmshen}@sjtu.edu.cn,
{Oliver.Scheuer,melis}@dfki.de

Abstract. Effective teaching requires teachers to know their students and to adapt their teaching accordingly, regardless of taking place in China or in Western countries. This raises requirements on online learning environments: they need to track online learners' actions and present these to the teachers. This paper investigates whether the requirements differ between Western and Chinese teachers. We address this question via the analysis of a questionnaire that investigates requirements collected from Chinese teacher who have been in online teaching field for several years. In this paper, we present a detailed analysis of the requirements and compare the results to the formal survey research on the requirements of student tracking system conducted by Western researchers. We found that several requirements differ significantly. The results of this work are significant as they inform the design of online learning environments in general and online learning data analysis in particular.

Keywords: Student tracking, intelligent tutoring system, online learning, requirement comparison, questionnaire, quantitative analysis.

1 Motivation

Student tracking or monitoring can be defined as "activities pursued by teachers to keep track of student learning for purposes of making instructional decisions and providing feedback to students on their progress" [1]. Research on student tracking in Web-based Learning Management Systems (LMS) started at the time these systems were first developed. Peter T. Ewell, Ronald Parker, and Dennis P. Jones discuss basic principle and techniques for constructing a student tracking system [2]. Information on student achievement, effectiveness of educational programs, student retention and persistence is addressed. Goldberg discusses tracking information in the LMS WebCT [3]. Wang predict student performances early by tracking the data on student online activity in a web-based learning management system (LMS) [4] [5]. More recently, John Campbell

X. Luo et al. (Eds.): ICWL 2010 Workshops, LNCS 6537, pp. 120–128, 2011.

proposed that the academic analytics of LMS data can identify students at risk of attrition or course failure [6]. Other research shows that teachers could conduct teaching strategies from the analysis of LMS data [7] [8] [9].

In this paper, we investigate whether Chinese and Western teachers have different requirements for student tracking. This paper contributes to learning about cross-cultural difference by investigating the different requirements of Chinese and Western teachers. The work will provide guidance for designing effective educational technology that respects cultural differences. To our knowledge, the work in this paper is the first that investigates this particular question.

The paper is structured as follows. Section 2 discusses related work on student tracking. Section 3 describes the teacher's questionnaire, summarizes the results from the Western teachers and presents the new results gained with Chinese teachers. From this raw data, Section 4 distills the requirements of Chinese online teachers. Section 5 analyzes and compares the requirements of Western and Eastern teachers. Section 6 gives the conclusions.

2 Related Work on Student Tracking

Research on student tracking in Web-based Learning Management Systems (LMS) started at the time these systems were first developed. Goldberg discusses tracking information in the LMS WebCT [3], for instance the progress of each student through the course material and how often each component is used.

Recent work focuses on providing the teacher further information. ADVisor generates advice on the level of individual students, groups and the whole class [11]. The Classroom Sentinel detects critical teaching and learning patterns, informs the teacher and takes appropriate proactive actions to alleviate detected problems [10]. An "early warning system" for educators predicts at-risk students based on LMS data and allows for more timely pedagogical interventions [12]. The course tracking variables selected from LMS includes detailed logs, number of online sessions, total time online, mail message send and read, total discussion messages posted, etc.

Survey-based research on the requirements of student tracking systems was published, such as [13], [14], [15] and [16]. Mazza and Dimitrova ([13]) found out that information of cognitive and behavioral aspects is of high interest to instructors. On the other hand, social aspects like email and chat have been rated as less relevant for teaching purposes. Zinn and Scheuer's survey ([14]) indicates a high interest in tracking data about student performance, such as success rate in exercises, mastery level for a concept, skill or method, and frequent errors. While teachers expressed less interest in social networks, navigation pattern, and historical usage data. The 15 participants in the survey of [15] were mainly from Canada and Great Britain. Their findings are in accordance with the former empirical studies. Maite Martin carried out an informal survey to detect teacher needs about student mastery and performance [16]. Their results show that student behaviors during learning activities, the characteristics of individual students, and the characteristics of groups of students are the detailed information that teachers want to understand.

However, all previous studies disregard cultural differences and focus on Western teachers. The participants in the survey of [13] were mainly from Swiss, Canada, and UK. The 49 teachers in the study of [14] represent 10 Western countries (USA: 63%, United Kingdom: 12%, Germany: 8%, and others).

3 Teacher's Questionnaire and Feedback

3.1 Description of the Teachers' Questionnaire

Our work uses the questionnaire by Zinn and Scheuer as basis. This allows us to compare the requirements collected from the two clusters and to detect significant differences. Nevertheless, in order to cope with the cultural differences in learning and teaching, parts of it needed to be adapted. Three questions had to be replaced due to differences in LMS functionalities and online behavior:

Firstly, the question "List of most frequently looked-up terms (when a dictionary is available)" is too specific for Chinese learning environment. Often, many learning management systems in China do not have a dictionary, but a question & answer center. We therefore changed this question to "List of most frequently asked questions"

Secondly, in the question "Number of sessions", session is not widely used in Chinese learning systems, we changed this to "Current learning schedule (such as how many lectures have been learned)".

Thirdly, the question "Ratio of social activities to all activities" is about communicational tools. Social activities in the Web in China differ from those in the West. In China, the main Web social communication tools are forums. In forums, students discuss the content of online course and other issues not related to learning courses. So we replaced this item by "Percentage of topics in the course forum that discuss learning material"

As a result, all the 35 items used in this questionnaire got fairly good approved rate. This also corresponds to the text feedback from the some response.

3.2 Statistical Results

The teachers could rate their answer on a 5 point scale, with the values "very interesting" (weight 5), "interesting" (4), "not very interesting" (2), and "not at all interesting" (1). The calculation method is the same as that used in [14]. The score value for a given proposal resulted from the addition of all votes with their corresponding weights, and a subsequent linear transformation that yielded a scale from 0 to 100. Table 1 shows the 10 highest ranking proposals with the highest scores. Table 2 shows the bottom ten proposals with the lowest scores.

4 Requirement Deduced from the Questionnaire Data

According to Chinese teachers' feedback to this questionnaire, we infer the following requirement for online student tracking:

1) The online learners' problems and mistakes

"The list of most frequently asked questions in Q&A center" (rank 1) and "the list of n most frequent diagnosed mistakes and misconceptions" (rank 2) are the most popular proposals according to the survey. This clearly shows that Chinese online teachers want to be informed about their learners' difficulties and mistakes in the online learning process. This information is particularly interesting for teachers while teaching students in online courses since it allows a timely recognition of and response to current learning problems.

2) Basic information about the learning state

In the free feedback sections of the survey, several teachers commented that "the learner's basic learning state, coverage of learning material, types of learning activities are particularly important" (translated from Chinese). Accordingly, the survey data shows a high interest in basic and overview information. For instance, the items "Percentage of available exercises tackled" and "Amount of time spent in the learning system per week" ranked 4 and 6.

3) Basic learning activities

Similar to the information about the basic learning state, Chinese teachers consider information about basic learning activities as an important feature of student tracking. The corresponding items "Activity type distributions" (rank 5) and "Number of learner actions with the system (per week)" (rank 3) were highly ranked. Overall, the top

Table 1. Top ten highest ranking proposals

Question No.	Proposal	Score
q7_3*	List of most frequently asked questions	91.5
q5_7	List of n most frequent diagnosed mistakes and misconceptions	91.5
q1_2	Number of learner actions with the system (per week)	87.5
q2_2	Percentage of available exercises tackled	86.9
q4_2	Activity type distributions	83.3
q1_1	Amount of time the learner spends in this course with the system (per week)	82.9
q10_1	Percentage of students communicating on forum (student's percentage)	82.8
q9_2	Allow automatic group clustering by systems	82.7
q8_1	Learner classification (to know different types of students)	82.4
q7_4	List of most frequently trained concepts/skills/methods/competencies	81.5

Table 2. Bottom ten proposals with the lowest scores

Question No.	Proposal	Score
q1_3*	Current learning schedule(e.g. how many lectures have been learned)	70.7
q4_1	Amount of time per activity type	70.2
q3_3	History of past learning contents (e.g. the time spent on different contents last week)	68.6
q3_2	Number of learner activities per section	65.9
q10_2*	Percentage of topics underlying on learning content on forum	64.4
q5_4	Ratio of correct to incorrect steps	63
q5_6	Replay of exercises (in discrete steps)	61.3
q3_1	Amount of time spent per section	56.2
q5_3	Number of steps done	56.2
q9_1	Allow manual definition of group by teacher	54.6

ten proposals reflect that Chinese teachers pay detailed attention to basic learning activities, such as "exercise tackled," "asking questions in Q&A center," and "communications on course forum".

4) Group learning

Two of three items about group learning asked in the questionnaire rank among the top ten. The item "Allow manual definition of groups by teachers" got the lowest score of all items. We assume that this is due to the fact of the large number of students (remember: a large majority of participants teaches classes with more than 100 students). All in all, group learning is not widely adopted in online learning in China: the survey result shows that only 20% of the participants have used group work in their online teaching. Despite that, the two high-ranking items show that Chinese teacher have an interest in group learning.

5) Fine-grained tracking information is regarded as unimportant

Compared to the high interest in basic learning state, fine-grained tracking information is regarded as being unimportant. The items "Amount of time spent per activity type," "Number of learner activities per section," "replay of exercises (in discrete steps)," "Number of steps done (exercises)," and "Amount of time spent per section" are all ranked in the bottom ten proposals. This is a clear indication that currently it is not highly relevant to record and analyze learners' learning activities in too much detail. Again, the large number of students that Chinese teachers have to support makes a detailed activity analysis impracticable and calls for a more focused or condensed presentation of tracking data.

5 Comparison and Discussion

In order to find out whether there are any differences between the needs of Chinese and Western teachers, we compared our results to previous research. Since the findings of several recent empirical studies ([14] [15] [16]), are, by and large, in accordance with one other [14], we focus on a quantitative comparison between our Chinese sample and the Zinn and Scheuer ([14]) sample.

5.1 Comparison the Profiles of Two Different Groups

Similarities: Some of the profiles of participants from China and Western are similar. Such as, most of the respondents are teachers/instructors/tutors/facilitators, some of them are course coordinators. More than 50% of respondents are involved in 2 to 5 online courses. The facilities that have been used in online courses are all included content material, discussion forum, e-mail, chat, and dictionary. They all have experience in different learning systems including WebCT, Blackboard, Moodle and others developed by different institutions.

Differences:

1) There are more higher education students participating in online courses in Western countries. While in China, Half of teachers worked with junior college students. And only 5% of all the participants have the work experience with postgraduate students.

2) The online class in China is larger a lot than Western's. 85% of the Chinese teachers taught classes with more than 100 students. While the largest classes of 50% of the Western teachers had 20 to 50 students.

3) More pure distance learning via web-based environment conducts in Western. 65% Western teachers involve in pure distance teaching. As for teaching model, traditional face to face teaching, online teaching, video lecture provided in website, broadcast via satellite and, lectures in CD, and online tutoring are all adopted by NECs. Blending learning is a popular teaching model in China.

5.2 Comparison the Requirements of Two Different Groups

Similarities: There were no significant differences regarding student's achievement tracking information. Teacher want to have information about their students' problems and mistakes, their mastery of individual concepts/skills/methods/ competencies, and their performance in learning system. The findings are in accordance with other western studies, like [15] [16].

Differences: Figure 1 provides the proposals that got different approval rates from Chinese and Western teachers. The main three differences are the following.

Some fine-grained information is of high interest to the Western teachers but not to Chinese teachers, such as "number of learner activities per concept/skill/ method/competency," "amount of time spent per concept/skill/ method/ competency," and "number of learner activities per section". This is mainly because the different classes scale in Western and China. The online class in China is larger a lot than Western's. Even some of the Chinese online classes have several hundred students.

Chinese teachers want to teach online student in group. They like to classify students according to different types, such as interest, knowledge status, or preferences. Large scale online classes make it necessary for teachers to apply a variety of teaching strategies to adapt to the different needs and backgrounds of learners [17]. Group teaching is essential for effective online tutoring, but it is hard for them to group such a large number of students without system help. So automatic group clustering by some intelligent technologies is a welcomed method.

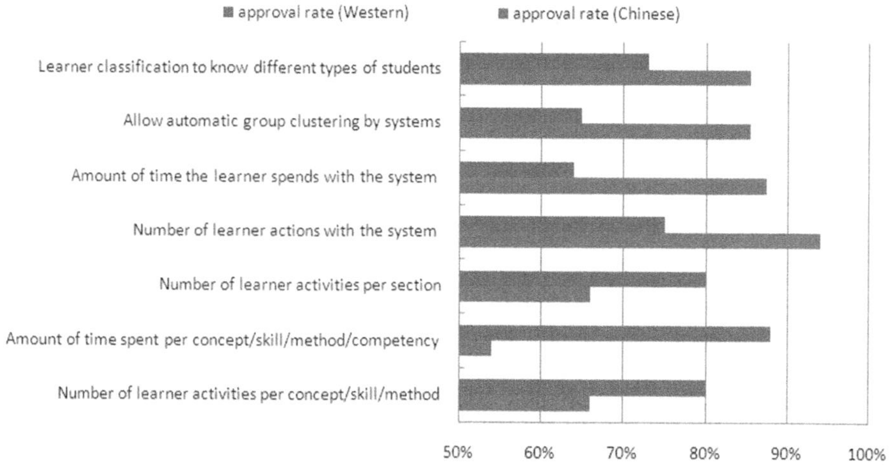

Fig. 1. Proposals with different approval rate from Chinese and Western teachers

6 Conclusion

This paper investigates differences on online student tracking. Being able to track student's misconceptions and mistakes is of high interest to all teachers, in both, China and Western countries. For Chinese teachers, the basic learning activities and learning state are highly valued information about students. Information on the coverage of learning material, percentage of available exercises tackled, is helpful to teachers to know whether students study or not and how much effort they put into learning. The information of the types of activities, the amount of time spent in the learning system per week, can teachers inform about the interest of the students in their course. Because Chinese classes often have a very high amount of students, teachers prefer to teach in groups and thus automatic group clustering preferred over a manual definition of groups. Compared to the Western teachers, Chinese teacher value less of fine-grained tracking information.

The information in this paper contributes to the design of cross-cultural technology-enhanced learning systems and meaningful online learning data analysis.

Acknowledgement

This work was supported by the German Ministry of Education and Research, research grant CHN 08/013.

References

1. Cotton, K.: Monitoring student learning in the classroom, school improvement research series (SIRS). Northwest Regional Educational Laboratory, US Department of Education (1988), http://www.nwrel.org/scpd/sirs/2/cu4.html (retrieved 7.3.2009)
2. Ewell, P.T., Parker, R., Jones, D.P.: Establishing a Logitudinal student tracking system: an implementation handbook. NCHEMS publications, P.O. Drawer P, Boulder, CO 80302-9752 (1988)
3. Goldberg, M.W.: Student Participation and Progress Tracking for Web-Based Courses using WebCT. In: Proceedings of the Second International N.A. WEB Conference, Fredericton, NB, Canada, October 5-8 (1996), http://www.uvm.edu/~hag/naweb96/zgoldberg.html (retrieved 7.3.2009)
4. Wang, A.Y., Newlin, M.H.: Characteristics of students who enroll and succeed in web-based psychology classes. Journal of Educational Psychology 92(1), 137–143 (2000)
5. Wang, A.Y., Newlin, M.H.: Predictors of performance in the virtual classroom: Identifying and helping at-risk cyber-students. The Journal of Higher Education. Academic Matters 29(10), 21–25 (2002)
6. Campbell, J.: Utilizing student data within the course management system to determine undergraduate student academic success: An exploratory study. Doctoral thesis, Purdue University, Indiana, USA (2007)
7. Campbell, J., Oblinger, D.: Academic analytics. EDUCAUSE Center for Applied Research (2007), http://connect.educause.edu/library/abstract/AcademicAnalytics/45275
8. Goldstein, P.J., Katz, R.N.: Academic analytics: The uses of management information and technology in higher education. EDUCAUSE Center for Applied Research, Washington (2005)
9. Mazza, R., Dimitrova, V.: Visualizing Student Tracking Data to Support Instructors in Web-Based Distance Education. In: The 13th International World Wide Web Conference, New York, USA (2004)
10. Singley, M.K., Lam, R.B.: The Classroom Sentinel: Supproting Data-Driven Decision-Making in the Classroom. In: Proceedings of the 14th International Conference on World Wide Web (2005)
11. Kosba, E., Dimitrova, V., Boyle, R.: Using Student and Group Models to Support Teachers in Web-Based Distance Education. LNCS, pp. 124–133. Springer, Berlin (2005)
12. Macfadyen, L.P., Dawson, S.: Mining LMS data to develop an early warning system for educators: A proof of concept. Computers & Education 54(2010), 588–599 (2010)
13. Mazza, R., Dimitrova, V.: Informing The Design of a Course Data Visualisator: an Empirical Study. In: 5th International Conference on New Education Environments (ICNEE 2003), pp. 215–220 (2003)

14. Zinn, C., Scheuer, O.: Getting to know your student in distance learning contexts. In: Nejdl, W., Tochtermann, K. (eds.) EC-TEL 2006. LNCS, vol. 4227, pp. 437–451. Springer, Heidelberg (2006)
15. Jovanovic, J., Dragan Gasevic, D., Christopher Brooks, C., Vladan Devedzic, V., Marek Hatala, M.: LOCO-analyst: A tool for raising teachers' awareness in online learning environments. In: Duval, E., Klamma, R., Wolpers, M. (eds.) EC-TEL 2007. LNCS, vol. 4753, pp. 112–126. Springer, Heidelberg (2007)
16. Maite, M., Alvarez, A., Fernandez-Castro, I., Urretavizcaya, M.: Generating Teacher Adapted Suggestions for Improving Distance Education Systems with SIgMa. In: IEEE International Conference on Advanced Learning Technologies, pp. 449–453. Santander, Cantabria (2008)
17. Zhang, J.: A cultural look at information and communication technologies in Eastern education. Education Tech. Research Dev. 55, 301–314 (2007)

Model-Based Cognitive Diagnosis of Students' Test Performance in an E-Learning Environment

Rong Chen*, Junjie Xu, Yingjie Song,
Wu Deng, and Yanheng Li

College of Information Science and Technology,
Dalian Maritime University, Dalian 116026, China
{rchen.cs,tsmc.dmu}@gmail.com

Abstract. Cognitive diagnosis is the process of inferring a cognitive state from observations of performance. This paper considers the problem of cognitive diagnosis as an instance of model-based diagnosis, as studied in artificial intelligence for many years. The model-based cognitive diagnosis we present runs on a model of students' courses in terms of knowledge items that they may learn, tests them and helps them to understand their faults in cognition, and thus improve their learning performance in an E-learning environment. To do so, courses are formally defined as set of knowledge items with requirement constraints, knowledge items are associated with a set of exam questions. Moreover, diagnostic algorithms are used to help a student understand what knowledge item within a course the student does not master, the root reason of his/her test errors, and the recommendations like what should be done next. Experimental results show that the group of students with such understanding can improve their testing performance greatly in an E-learning environment.

Keywords: model-based cognitive diagnosis, computer adaptive assessments, course model, knowledge items, E-Learning.

1 Introduction

Educational researchers have investigated Intelligent Tutoring Systems (ITS) as a means of providing cost effective yet personalized tuition for many years. ITS implementations have demonstrated student learning improvements comparable to the assistance of a human tutor with intermediate expertise [1]. In an ITS cognitive diagnosis is often used synonymously with 'student modeling' that builds a representation of the student's knowledge from the evidence provided by student inputs to solve problems [2]. A widely accepted definition of *cognitive diagnosis* has been given by Ohlsson [6]: "*cognitive diagnosis* is the process of inferring a person's cognitive state from his or her performance." It is widely accepted that cognitive

* This work is supported by National Natural Science Foundation of China (60775028), the Major Projects of Technology Bureau of Dalian No.2007A14GXD42, and and IT Industry Development of Jilin Province.

X. Luo et al. (Eds.): ICWL 2010 Workshops, LNCS 6537, pp. 129–138, 2011.

diagnosis can help in personalized tuition an ITS must know, in particular what the student knows, what misconceptions he/she has, and thus help him/her improve learning outcomes.

Cognitive diagnostic modeling has become an exciting new field of psychometric research. Cognitive diagnostic models aim to diagnose students' status of a group of discretely defined skills, thereby providing them with detailed information regarding their specific strengths and weaknesses [10]. To date, at least fourteen distinct cognitive diagnostic models have appeared in the literature [5]. The NIDA model and the Fusion model are good examples of these models [9]; they can be thought of as a Q matrix, each row of which is a list of the cognitive attributes that an examinee needs to have mastered in order to give a correct response to the item. Rule-based models are also used to depict both desired students' knowledge and common mistakes [5], thereby student performance is monitored by comparing actual student problem solving sequences against the known production rules.

Although a number of methods for cognitive diagnosis have been developed, these methods have not been placed on a more rigorous rooting until John Self placed this problem in a general theoretical framework in 1993. He considered the problem of cognitive diagnosis as an instance of Model-Based Diagnosis (MBD)[2]. To illustrate the problem of diagnosing students' attempts to solve problems, a three-column subtraction is modeled a subtraction problem-solving 'circuit' and a form of heuristic search is used in [6] to find plausible sequences of actions that lead to a known solution. However, as an infinite number of ineffective behavior sequences are possible, such a cognitive diagnostic model is time consuming and rarely complete.

As the precise cognitive modeling of a student is likely to be intractable, adaptive remediation methods have been used successfully by applying instructional techniques appropriate to the current student context rather than requiring complex cognitive student and domain modeling. This paper considers the problem of computerized cognitive diagnosis by combining model-based reasoning with a traditional testing system in order to provide the Computerized Adaptive Testing (CAT). Like Self, we put this problem in a MBD framework to better define the nature of the cognitive diagnosis problem in CAT; we recast an adaptive course testing as a diagnosis system in MBD; a course description is mapped onto the system description, knowledge items onto components, and observations are students' inputs that indicate their test performance. As distinguished from Self's work, we seek to use model-based cognitive diagnosis with hierarchical course modeling and employ adaptive remediation based upon the student's current state and learning difficulties encountered revealed by his/her test behavior.

To do so, courses are formally defined as set of knowledge items with requirement constraints, knowledge items are associated with set of *exam questions*, and thus diagnostic algorithms are used help the student improve learning outcomes. Also we develop a diagnostic system that runs on a course model and a computer testing system of exam questions. The diagnostic system can help the student understand what knowledge item he/she does not master within a course teaching, what difficulties he/she has, what he/she should do next. Such a system may act like a human tutor who can let students be aware of their knowledge state and the root reason of their test errors. Such awareness is proved to benefit students because they are guided by the diagnosis to concentrate on the problem they are encountering, and thus improve their learning outcome afterwards. As the experimental results show, the group of students using our diagnostic system can improve their testing performance greatly in terms of time and effort.

The rest of the paper is organized as follows: Section 2 provides more discussion on related work. Section 3 presents our method on model-based cognitive diagnosis of students' test errors. In Section 4 we think about experiments and evaluation of our cognitive diagnostic system, and finally we conclude with some future work.

2 Model-Based Cognitive Diagnosis from Performance Evidence

To describe our approach, we recast an adaptive course testing as such a diagnosis problem, address a hierarchical course model with the right grain size that is efficient to analyze, and a small sample case study is devised to show the application of our approach to the Computer Network course.

2.1 Course Modeling

In our framework, knowledge is represented by atomic elements, called *Knowledge Items* (*KI*), and a course composed by a set of *Learning Components* (*LC*), each of which specifies the knowledge that it requires, the knowledge that it will eventually provide and the related learning resources [3].

Definition 1. (Knowledge Item [3]) A *knowledge item* is an expression meaning the (sufficient) knowledge about a certain topic.

Definition 2. (Component) A *component* specifies a problem-solving module which has input, output, attributes, behavior and identity. A component uses input and output for passing data values, it also provides a number of operations which define its behavior.

Definition 3. (Learning Component) A *learning component* is a component that is associated with an identifier (*ID*) denoting its identity, with the *Required Knowledge* (*RK*) denoting its input, with the *Acquired Knowledge* (*AK*) denoting its output, and optionally with a set of low-level subcomponents. The behavior of a learning component is to count the number of passed exam questions and to output the count and *AKs*.

Definition 4. (Course) A *course* is modeled as a directed acyclic graph (DAG for short) such that every vertex is a learning component and every arc depicts the dependence between two learning components.

2.2 Hierarchical Models of Computer Network Course

An obvious difficulty in course modeling lies in deciding the 'grain size' of the system description. To do so, we build a hierarchical course model heuristically, i.e., and select the *KIs* that are prone to cause students' faults at the cognitive level. Such *KIs* are modeled as atomic learning components and can have low-level modeling, whereas other knowledge may have a coarse description.

Table 1. Learning components in a course model

LCs	Component name	RK	AK
C1	MAC_addr	nil	C1
C2	ip_addr	nil	C2
C3	login	nil	C3
C4	subnetting	C2	C4
C5	route_selection	C4,C6	C5
C6	gateway	C4	C6
C7	protocol/port	C1,C2	C7
C8	proxy_http/socks	nil	C8
C9	proxy_connection	C3,C4,C7,C8	C9
C10	connection	C2,C3,C5,C11	C10
C11	HTTP	nil	C11

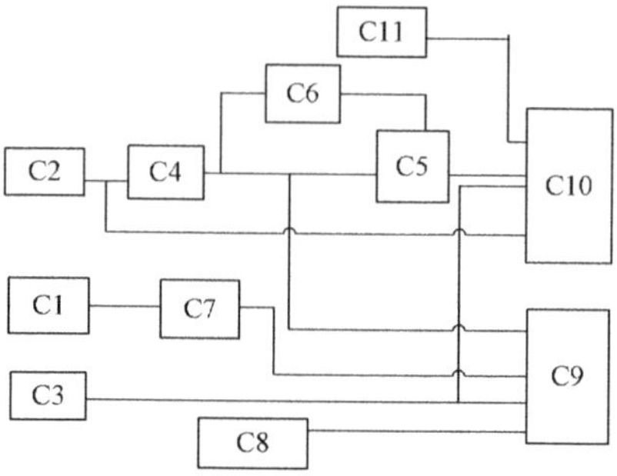

Fig. 1. A course model

We consider a course P{MAC_addr, ip_addr, login, subnetting, route_selection, gatewagy, protocol/port, proxy_http/socks, proxy_connection, connection, HTTP}, each *KI* in P is treated as a *LC* in our system, the course model can be pictured as a graph in Figure 1, where each vertex is a *LC* and every arc depicts the dependence between two *LCs*. All *LCs* are put together in Table 1. For example, the arc from C2 (denoting the 'ip_addr' *LC*) to C10 (denoting the 'connection' *LC*) means that one of the required knowledge for 'connection' is 'ip_addr' (i.e. IP address).

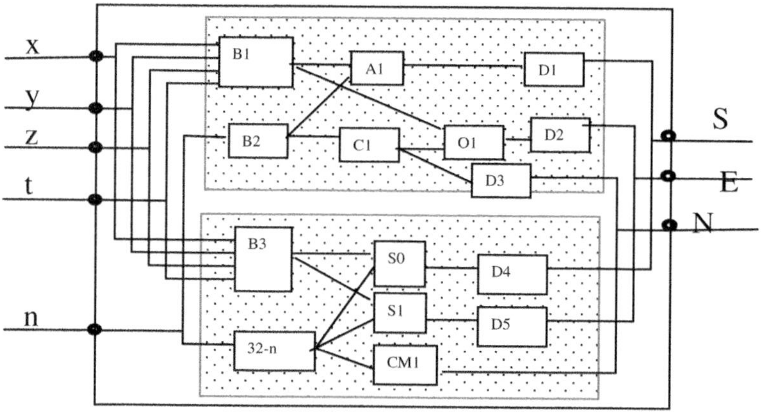

Fig. 2. An abstract CIDR calculator

As mentioned before, some of these learning components can have a fine description (i.e. a low-level model). In Figure 2 is the learning component 'ip_addr', which takes either IP address in dot-decimal form of x.y.z.t/n and computes the start address (denoted as S), the end address (Denoted as E), and the number of hosts on such a network (denoted as N). Since there are two ways to compute such S, E and N, we model this as two separate composite components (pictured as two shadowed rectangles in Figure 2). Clearly the upper component consists of several subcomponents, among which are B1 (to convert four decimals into a binary number), B2 (to convert a decimal into a binary), A1 (denoting and), C1 (denoting complement), O1 (denoting or), D1, D2 and D3 (to convert a binary into a decimal).

2.3 Cognitive Diagnosis

Like Self, we consider the problem of cognitive diagnosis as an instance of consistency-based diagnosis. The development and improvement of such diagnosis techniques are built upon the strict logical foundation provided by Reiter (in [4]). Formally, a diagnosis system is described as a triple (*SD*, *COMPS*, *OBS*), where the device under consideration is modeled as a set *COMPS* of components, *OBS* denotes the observed inputs and outputs, and the working of the device and its components is specified by a set of logical clauses with default assumptions, referred to as a system description (*SD*)[4].

For cognitive diagnosis in our framework, *SD* represents a hierarchical course modeling, *COMPS* are learning components that make the course, and *OBS* depicts the evidence of students' test performance.Given *SD* of a course, we assume by default that all components works normally. For example, the knowledge acquired upon a learning component can be predicated by dependency rules.

Definition 5. (System Description) A *system description* is set of logical rules produced in a course.

Definition 6. (Observation) An *observation* is set of predicates that hold for some components.

A diagnosis problem arises when the student's test performance violates what expected, i.e., there is a discrepancy between what are inferred from logical rules and the evidence in *OBS*. So we can figure out one or more sets of *ok*(*c*)–like assumptions that support such the discrepancy. When it comes to learning components, such assumptions reveal students' cognitive state, and they are logically inconsistent.

Definition 7. (Cognitive State) A student's *cognitive state* is a set of *ok*(*c*)–like assumptions that the student correctly masters the *AK* associated with some learning component *c*.

Definition 8. (Diagnosis [4]) A *diagnosis* for (*SD*, *COMPS*, *OBS*) is a minimal set $\Delta \subseteq COMPS$ such that $SD \cup OBS \cup \{\neg ok(c) \mid c \in \Delta\} \cup \{ok(c) \mid c \in COMPS\text{-}\Delta\}$ is consistent.

Formally the set of such components are called hitting set, which makes a diagnosis as proved in the following theorem[9,10]. Briefly a hitting set contains suspicious component such that they covers all conflict sets (see [4] for the formal definition and the HS-tree algorithm for computing hitting set).

Theorem 1. [4] A set $\Delta \subseteq COMPS$ is a diagnosis for (*SD*, *COMPS*, *OBS*) iff Δ is a minimal hitting set for the collection of conflict set.

With the hierarchical models above, we might start diagnosis from a high-level model in terms of learning components, progressively expand 'suspicious' *LCs*, and continue diagnosing with a low-level model of 'suspicious' *LCs* in order to explain students' cognitive faults. To illustrate this method, we consider an example.

Example 1. There is an evidence that a student fails to answer exam questions about KIs like {route_selection, proxy_connection}, i.e., OBS={¬K(route_selection), ¬K(proxy_conneciton)}. We have the following dependency rules in SD that are related to the evidence about "route_selection":

1. K(subnetting) $\wedge$ K(gateway) $\wedge$ ok(C5) $\Rightarrow$ K(route_selection)
2. K(subnetting) $\wedge$ ok(C6) $\Rightarrow$ K(gateway)
3. K(ip_addr) $\wedge$ ok(C4) $\Rightarrow$K(subnetting)
4. ok(C2) $\Rightarrow$K(ip_addr)

If we now assume that ok(C2), o*k*(C4), *ok*(C5) and *ok*(C6) hold, *K*(route_selection) holds, i.e., the student masters the knowledge of route selection. Obviously this violates the evidence. So we think of {C2,C4,C5,C6} as a conflict. Similarly we have another conflict {C1,C2,C3,C4,C7,C8} when it comes to the evidence about "proxy_conneciton". One hitting set of such conflicts is {C2}, so C2 is suspicious according to theorem 1. Therefore, our system suspects that the student has some difficulties dealing IP address and asks the testing system to generate a set of exam questions.

3 Experimental Results

In this section we present our experiments that show the performance of the MBCD in our system, also we evaluate whether it can help in improving students' learning performance. We have implemented our system MBCD in Smalltalk using VisualWorks 7.3 non-commercial, and it acts as a model-based diagnosis engine [9,10] that uses either a theorem prover or a constraint propagator to find conflict sets and thus to make diagnosis by using algorithms for computing hitting sets [4,5]. In our experiments, the MBCD runs on a PC (Pentium(R) Dual-Core E5200, 2.50GHz CPU speed, 2G memory, running on Windows XP), and works together with a testing system running on a server (450MHz CPU speed, 2G memory, running on Linux), which provides exam questions in Web pages and checks students' answers.

3.1 Diagnosing Students' Test Performance

In our next experiment, we have 20 students who are new to Computer Network which has been manually modeled like Figure 2. To evaluate the MBCD's value, we put them into two groups, each with 10 students. The group who uses the MBCD is called group A, while the other is called group B who are not assisted with the MBCD and are expected to be capable of self-learning. Without ambiguous, all students are sequentially named Ti, where T is either A or B denoting which group the student belongs to, and i is the student's number in his/her group.

Before the testing, all students take 8 hours to study the knowledge items in the Computer Network course. Then they are asked to test themselves with questionnaire containing exam questions generated by the testing system according to what they have learned. Each test paper contains 100 exam questions, either single choice questions or multiple choice questions, each concerning about the *KIs* that students are expected to have acquired so far. Since our experience with our exam questions shows that it is hard for a student to obtain a score higher than 94, we think that the student is excellent and can be exempted from testing if he/she achieves such a score.

3.1.1 First Testing

The first experiment we do is to examine all students' test performance on the same test paper after their 8-hour study. Table 2 shows the test performance of students in group A, throughout this section, the "Score" is the student's points obtained in testing, the "Failed *KIs* (*ID*)" are knowledge items on which the student fails and *ID* is the identifier of a learning component possessing such *KIs*, the "Conflicts" and the "Diagnosis" respectively refer to the conflict set and the hitting set, both computed by the MBCD. In contrast, Table 3 shows the test performance of students in group B.

Table 2. First test performance of group A

Who	Score	Failed *KIs* (*ID*)	Conflicts	Diagnosis
A1	98	Nil	Nil	Nil
A2	89	MAC_addr (C1)	$\{ok(C1)\}$	$\{\neg ok(C1)\}$
A3	90	subnetting (C4)	$\{ok(C2) \vee ok(C4)\}$	$\{\neg ok(C2)\}$, $\{\neg ok(C4)\}$
A4	80	protocol/port (C7), gateway (C6)	$\{ok(C1) \vee ok(C2) \vee ok(C7)\}$, $\{ok(C4) \vee ok(C2) \vee ok(C6)\}$	$\{\neg ok(C2)\}$, $\{\neg ok(C1) \wedge \neg ok(C4\}$, $\{\neg ok(C1) \wedge \neg ok(C6)\}$, $\{\neg ok(C7) \wedge \neg ok(C4)\}$, $\{\neg ok(C7) \wedge \neg ok(C6)\}$
A5	72	ip_addr(C2), subnetting (C4)	$\{ok(C2) \vee ok(C4)\}$, $\{\mathrm{ok}(C2)\}$	$\{\neg ok(C2)\}$
A6	70	subnetting(C4), protocol/port(C7) gateway (C6)	$\{ok(C2) \vee ok(C4)\}$, $\{ok(C1) \vee ok(C2) \vee ok(C7)\}$, $\{ok(C4) \vee ok(C2) \vee ok(C6)\}$	$\{\neg ok(C2)\}$, $\{\neg ok(C4) \wedge \neg ok(C1)\}$, $\{\neg ok(C4) \wedge \neg ok(C7)\}$
A7	85	ip_addr(C2), MAC_addr (C1)	$\{ok(C1)\}$, $\{ok(C2)\}$	$\{\neg ok(C1) \wedge \neg ok(C2)\}$
A8	90	route_selection (C5)	$\{ok(C4) \vee ok(C2) \vee ok(C6) \vee ok(C5)\}$	$\{\neg ok(C2)\}$, $\neg ok(C4)\}$, $\{\neg ok(C6)\}$, $\neg ok(C5)\}$
A9	70	connection(C10), login(C3), HTTP (C11)	$\{ok(C3) \vee ok(C2) \vee ok(C5) \vee ok(C11) \vee \mathrm{ok}(C10)\}$, $\{ok(C3)\}$, $\{ok(C11)\}$	$\{\neg ok(C3) \wedge \neg ok(C11)\}$
A10	79	proxy_connection (C9), proxy_http/socks (C8)	$\{ok(C7) \vee ok(C4) \vee ok(C3) \vee ok(C8) \vee ok(C9)\}$, $\{ok(C8)\}$	$\{\neg ok(C8)\}$

In Table 2, the group's average score is 82.3, in particular, student A1's 98 points suggests that A1 has almost mastered all *KIs*, so A1 is excluded from the second examination whereas others are enforced.

In contrast, Table 3 shows the test performance of students in group B, the average score is 84.8, which implies students in group B generally behaves better than those in group A. In particular, student B1's 99 points suggests that B1 has almost acquired all *KIs*, so B1 is excluded from the second examination.

Table 3. First test performance of group B

Who	Score	Failed *KIs*
B1	99	Nil
B2	90	MAC_addr
B3	89	subnetting
B4	83	protocol/port, gateway
B5	80	route_selection, ip_addr
B6	75	Subnetting, protocol/port, gateway
B7	82	ip_addr, MAC_addr
B8	84	route_selection,
B9	86	connection, login, HTTP
B10	80	Proxy_connection, proxy_http/socks

3.1.2 Second Testing

Before starting the second testing, all students are allowed to spend another 4 hours on learning from their faults in the first experiment. Provided with the diagnosis which explains their faults, group A are assisted by the MBCD to further analyze their cognitive faults in some *KIs*, whereas group B resort to their textbooks and the answer to the first test paper in order to understand the faults they have made.

After four-hour learning, both groups take the second examination of the *KIs* that students are expected to have acquired so far. Like Table 2, Table 4 shows the test performance of students in group A, where more of them are proved to have acquired the *KIs*; their average score of these *KIs* is increased from 82.3 to 91.7, and students A2, A4, A9, A10 have 10 points increase in comparison with their scores in the first testing. This is consistent with our understanding that they improve themselves greatly due to the awareness of their faults committed in the first testing, no matter such faults are made either by carelessness or by misconception.

In contrast, Table 5 shows the group B's test performance in the second testing. Their average score is 90.2 (vs. 84.8 in the first testing). Whereas student B2 achieves 96 points, student B6's 85 suggest that he still has some difficulties in understanding subnetting, protocol and port as well as gateway along the way.

By comparing students test performance, we find that students in group A do a great job since the average increase is 9.3 points, compared with 5.4 points in increase for group B. Group A benefit from the course of understanding faults and learning from them, whereas some students in group B were expecting a certain amount of tutoring in their exercises. Indeed, students A2, A4, A9, A10 believe that the MBCD is useful in terms of time to find the root reason of their misunderstanding.

Table 4. Second test performance of group A

Who	Score	Failed *KIs*	Conflicts	Diagnosis
A2	99	Nil	Nil	Nil
A3	95	ip_addr(C2)	$\{ok(C2)\}$	$\{\neg ok(C2)\}$
A4	90	protocol/port (C7)	$\{ok(C1) \vee ok(C2) \vee ok(C7)\}$	$\{\neg ok(C1)\}$, $\{\neg ok(C2)\}$, $\{\neg ok(C7)\}$
A5	91	Nil	Nil	Nil
A6	80	subnetting(C4) gateway(C6)	$\{ok(C4) \vee okC2)\}$, $\{ok(C2) \vee ok(C4) \vee ok(C6)\}$	$\{\neg ok(C2) \wedge \neg ok(C4)\}$
A7	94	Nil	Nil	Nil
A8	94	route_selection (C5)	$\{ok(C2) \vee ok(C4) \vee ok(C5) \vee ok(C6)\}$	$\{\neg ok(C2)\}$,$\{\neg ok(C4)\}$ $\{\neg ok(C5)\}$, $\{\neg ok(C6)\}$
A9	90	HTTP(C11)	$\{ok(C11)\}$	$\{\neg ok(C11)\}$
A10	92	Nil	Nil	Nil

Table 5. Second test performance of group B

Who	Score	Failed *KIs*
B2	96	Nil
B3	93	ip_addr
B4	90	protocol/port, gateway
B5	89	Nil
B6	85	subnetting, protocol/port, gateway
B7	88	Proxy_connection
B8	90	route_selection
B9	91	login, HTTP
B10	90	Proxy_connection

4 Conclusion

This paper considers the problem of cognitive diagnosis of students' test performance in the setting of E-learning. As an application of model-based diagnosis, we present an approach on model-based cognitive diagnosis by running a logical representation of a course against the student's test performance in order to pinpoint their faults in cognition and thus to improve their learning performance. Experimental results show that the group of students with such understanding can improve their testing performance greatly in an E-learning environment. This is consistent with our understanding that one-on-one exercise tutoring can be much more effective than traditional classroom instruction. Although the demo system has been integrated with a specific computerized adaptive testing system, the general technique could be applied to a broad class of ITS.

We are working on interactive cognitive diagnosis from multiple observations, and how to extend our course modeling with fault mode describing that the learning components tend to fail in specified ways. Motivated by course configuration in [3], we also consider how to enhance our MBCD system through test planning. Recent developments in cognitive psychology suggest models for knowledge and learning that often fall outside the realm of standard test theory, so there is always space for improvement when it comes to cognitive diagnostic modeling [8], probabilistic cognitive diagnosis, systematic faults and slips [2].

References

1. Graesser, A., Wiemer-Hastings, P., Wiemer-Hastings, K., Harter, D., Person, N.: Using Latent Semantic Analysis to evaluate the contributions of students in AutoTutor. Interactive Learning Environments 8(2), 129–147 (2000)
2. Self, J.: Model-based cognitive diagnosis. User Modeling and User-Adapted Interaction, John 1993 (1993)
3. Sterbini, A., Temperini, M.: A logical framework for course configuration in e-learning. In: Proc. International Conference on Information Technology Based Higher Education and Training (ITHET 2003) (2003)
4. Reiter, R.: A theory of diagnosis from first principles. Artificial Intelligence 32(1), 57–95 (1987)
5. McLaren, B.M., Koedinger, K.R., Schneider, M.: Toward cognitive tutoring in a collaborative webbased environment. In: The Workshop on Adaptive Hypermedia and Collaborative Web-Based Systems (AHCW 2004), Munich, Germany (July 2004)
6. Ohlsson, S.: Some principles of intelligent tutoring. Instructional Science 14(3), 293–326 (1986)
7. Xu, X., Chang, H., Douglas, J.: A simulation study to compare CAT strategies for cognitive diagnosis. In: the Annual Meeting of the National Council of Measurement in Education, Chicago (April 2003)
8. Huebner, A.: An Overview of Recent Developments in Cognitive Diagnostic Computer Adaptive Assessments. Practical Assessment, Research & Evaluation 15(3), 1–7 (2010)
9. Fleischanderl, G., Havelka, T., Schreiner, H., Stumptner, M., Wotawa, F.: DiKe - A Model-Based Diagnosis Kernel and Its Application. In: Baader, F., Brewka, G., Eiter, T. (eds.) KI 2001. LNCS (LNAI), vol. 2174, pp. 440–454. Springer, Heidelberg (2001)
10. Chen, R., Wotawa, F.: Diagnosing program errors with light-weighted specifications. In: Ali, M., Dapoigny, R. (eds.) IEA/AIE 2006. LNCS (LNAI), vol. 4031, pp. 639–649. Springer, Heidelberg (2006)

Issues of Interaction in Pure-Online English Learning Environment through Perspectives of Cognitive Constructivism and Social Constructivism: A Case Study for Non-formal Learning

Yanhui Han

Faculty of Foreign Languages, The Open University of China,
160, Fuxingmennei Street, Beijing 100031, China
hanyh@crtvu.edu.cn

Abstract. Most previous studies on the use of Internet technology and computers for second language learning have been conducted in blended learning environments. Although much research has been undertaken into interactions in online learning, little work has focused on online English learning, let alone the pure-online (ie non-blended) English learning environment with no face-to-face element. This paper investigates the English-language learning interactions in one of our projects that has been running for ten years continuously in cooperation with the BBC and British Council. Our pure-online English-language learning environment for non-formal learning is at in2english.com.cn. This study further aims to explore how the interactions work in such an environment, and investigates the related issues and peculiar characteristics of the interactions in practice.

Keywords: interaction, CALL, feedback, cognitive constructivism, social constructivism, non-formal learning, SLA.

1 Introduction

Over the last decade, "the Internet and the World Wide Web have fundamentally altered the practice of distance teaching and learning" [2] and great efforts of researchers have been put into studies on the use of Internet technology and computers in second language learning. Previous studies have recognized the value of online English education that can provide distant and interactive English learning activities and promote knowledge construction of English language and meaningful English learning [3,16,36]. It is noted that most past studies on the use of computers and Internet technology have been carried out in Computer Assisted Language Learning (CALL) within a blended learning setting with clear-cut pedagogic purposes. Interaction, a critical issue in online learning, has received a growing number of studies [2,11,29]. However, there has been little research to date conducted to investigate the issues of Interaction in online second language learning without face-to-face tutorials. The paper is just such an attempt to address the issues and peculiar characteristics of

X. Luo et al. (Eds.): ICWL 2010 Workshops, LNCS 6537, pp. 139–150, 2011.

Interaction in a pure-online English learning environment of in2english.com.cn[1]. It should be noted that all the multimedia and interactive resources offered on the website are not curriculum-based. In this sense, the pedagogic relations on the website are not as eminent as in traditional institutions.

2 Literature Review

A review of the literature indicates that the theoretical framework of online second language learning or web-based second language learning is still situated at the exploratory stage with varieties of theories and approaches [35].

2.1 The Prevalent Theory of Second Language Acquisition (SLA) from the Perspectives of Cognitive and Social Constructivism

The mainstream theories and approaches of Second Language Acquisition (SLA) are generally developed from cognitive theories and constructive approaches [15,17,26,30].

Most of the literature has contributed to the research into SLA from the perspectives of constructivism. According to constructivism, "the learner builds an internal representation and interpretation of knowledge by internalizing and transforming new information" [8] and "[t]he significance of the learner's interaction with his/her social and physical environment is here of great importance" [30]. Consequently, "language learning theory has seen a paradigm shift in which the learner becomes the centre of learning and is no longer a passive recipient of knowledge" [30]. The shift in the paradigm of education and language learning can find its root from "the constructivist philosophy" that "encourage[s] the use of computers in second language acquisition"[30].

The social constructivist approaches revolve overwhelmingly around Vygotsky's theory of 'zone of proximal development' which indicates the important role of social interaction in students' cognition development through collaboration with more experienced peers.

Amongst the various constructivism paradigms are the two leading schools of cognitive constructivism and social constructivism and "the most significant, yet still fairly simplistic difference" between the two schools of thought is that the cognitive constructivism approaches centre on group individualities "believing that cognition occurs in the head of the individual and that learners make intellectual sense of the materials on their own" while the social constructivism lays great emphasis on the social interaction of cognition [10]. The approaches of "Learning based on constructivist principles" are winning increasing recognition and deemed in the realm of education "as a suitable framework for the learning environment of the future" and "the constructivist paradigm is seen as an important methodological basis for a real innovation in foreign language learning" [9].

The proposition of combining social and cognitive constructivism approaches in e-learning is based on an analysis of the characteristics of education and educational institutions [10]. This proposition is still at a tentative stage, and Felix has not formulated how exactly the social and cognitive approaches can be applied to e-learning.

---

[1] `in2english.com.cn` is a Sino-British online English learning project which provides free supplementary English learning resources to Chinese English learners featuring multimedia and interactive technology.

2.2 Issues in Computer Assisted Language Learning (TESOL) in the Framework of the Prevalent SLA Theory

CALL research and studies have greatly developed over the last decades [18,22,25,30]. However, there are few studies on the emerging issues and solutions concerning the impact of networked computers on TESOL in the Chinese context, and most of the CALL literature has been on blended learning, with very little research on resource-based pure-online second language learning environment such as in2english.com.cn.

In traditional second language acquisition, amongst the critical elements are learner autonomy and motivation [19]. How do the elements work and what are the similarities and dissimilarities in CALL?

Some research has looked at learner autonomy in a successful distance learning environment [9,23]. However, learner autonomy and its related issues in practice have not yet received sufficient investigation in the context of a pure-online second language learning environment.

The significance of learner autonomy and motivation is acknowledged in JoblineLMU [25]. However, the main learning practice in the process occurred via email and face-to-face tutorials. Further research is needed into how learners can maintain autonomy at a high level in a single online mode without any face-to-face tutorials. Even though "Research has indicated that learners are highly motivated by the use of technology" [24], it has to be noted that the research "is tied very closely to specific uses" (ibid). Therefore it definitely lacks the adequate ground for the generalizations of the relationships between learner motivation and technology in the context of second language learning.

It has been noticed that the great majority of studies and research upon how Asian students learn English as a second language are based on stand-alone software development for CALL rather than the online learning through networked computers [14]. Two studies are located relevant to online second language learning in Asian context but still limited to blended learning environments. Loucky's study [20] fails to explore how the feedback works without face-to-face tutorials. Lim and Shen's studies [18] are confined to reading classes, and it offers the scope of question upon the effects of the use of technology in other aspects of TESOL and upon what kinds of interaction would happen if the reading classes were located online.

2.3 Interaction and Feedback in Online Language Learning

"Interaction has always been valued in distance education, even in its most traditional, independent study format" [2]. The main challenges the online instructors have to face nowadays are how to create "a consistent level of interaction that fosters genuine learning and cultivates a community atmosphere" [23]. The literature also indicates that asynchronous and synchronous communications can facilitate SLA both in writing and speaking and implies the importance of interaction in online language learning [13,24,27,28,34). But further research needs to be conducted especially in a pure-online English language learning environment.

Also, the crucial element of 'feedback' has to be taken in particular account. "[S]tudents quite like receiving instant feedback in self-access activities" and "the

Web has the potential to engage students more fully in the construction of knowledge, especially at an intermediate and advanced level" [9]. "[T]he interactive nature of CALL" can enhance learners' memorizing, recalling and producing of "newly learnt words" [1]. It has to be pointed out that the studies are limited to initial vocabulary learning, "[T]he interactive nature of CALL" was not explored in other aspects of second language learning and the relations between feedback and motivation need further studies.

Then how does the Interaction work in a pure-online second language learning environment like in2english.com.cn? This is the main research question of the paper. The two sub-questions are: a. What are the related issues of the Interaction? and b. What are the peculiar characteristics of the Interaction?

3 Research Methodology

Due to the nature of the data required, online recorded synchronous interviews and online text-based asynchronous discussions with in2english users were used in this study. Both the methods would minimize costs, as both the interviews and discussions were carried out online. Also the methods would suit the users geographically since they are located in different regions of China.

The reason why the two approaches of interviews and discussions were employed is to minimize "the inevitable shortcomings of any particular approach" [6] and to cross check information collected [9] in respect of reliability and validity. This involves the "methodological triangulation", according to Brown and Dowling [5].

"Many interviewers recruit on-line participants using the Internet itself" [21]. The author recruited the target users through a new section 'Research' in the in2english Community. The participants were divided into two groups, one for the online recorded synchronous interviews and the other for the online asynchronous discussions. Opportunity sampling was used. It has been noted by the author that opportunity sampling may produce some biased samples; however, "Opportunity samples ... are generally acceptable as long as the make-up of the sample is clearly stated and limitations of the data are realized" [4].

The registration and use of the in2english Community is free of charge. The free chat software called Tencent QQ[2] was used for the synchronous recorded interviews.

4 Findings

First of all, the recording of the interview and threads of the discussion were transcribed. Then the author reviewed all the ideas and opinions expressed by the participants during the interviews and discussions. The important sentences and key words/phrases related to the research questions were highlighted. Through the process of "open coding" [31], the highlighted sentences were compared, and the similarities and differences between the participants' interview replies and discussion posts were

---

[2] Tencent QQ, often referred to as QQ, is the most popular free instant messaging tool in China. It supports comprehensive basic online communication functions, including text messaging, video and voice chat as well as online (offline) file transmission.

summarised. The coding was mainly carried out upon the key words/phrases into discrete concepts that revolve around the research questions. The words/phrases that are supposed to pertain to the same concept were then categorized together into the identical label. All the concepts were regarded as the prospective or temporary categories of description that classified the perception towards the research questions. A further attempt was made to trace back to the concepts through the original data collected from the interviews and discussions in order to attain the verification of the concepts [12].

4.1 Tensions between Community Motives and Language Learning

Of the 8 participants, 6 of them regard the Community as the place of social interaction. They tend to agree that in the Community they can not only improve their English level but also communicate with others just like "a big and friendly family".

Shirley happened to know in2english through "searching translation exercises on the Internet and found such exercises in in2english Community". She said, "In the Community each day I post some messages to communicate with other users. Gradually I fell in love with in2english". On being asked why she fell in love with the Community, she explained, "Because I can post my ideas there and other users will reply to your posts just like the chat on the QQ or blog." She added that she loves the kind of communication because her English level can be improved. In particular, she stressed that "at least each day I feel very happy to communicate with other learners and look forward to other learners' replies". The communications through posting are done between the user and tutors and amongst the users themselves.

Henry, Tony, Stephen, Shirley, Eric and Mark clearly stated that their main purpose of coming to in2english is to visit the Community. The interviews and discussions indicate it is evident that all of them have formed a habit of keeping writing English articles there just because other users read them and the articles obtain comments from both the users and tutors/editors. Shirley spoke out the learners' expectations, "I do think most of the learners expect editors' comments to their posts". Her idea is confirmed by Tony, when he explained why he prefers the Community, "Generally I visit the Community where I write articles, nearly one article a week, because my articles got replies, so I kept writing".

Mark placed emphasis on the interaction between the user and tutor, "Interaction is one of the most important things to keep me writing here." In addition, he mentioned that he can make friends in "this lovely community". Henry expressed the same idea proudly, "I've made many friends there in the Community" and further added, "The Community is just like a big and friendly family where people help each other. I really love the atmosphere". The friends include not only the users but also the tutors/editors.

4.2 Feedback and Motivation

All of them recognized the great importance of feedbacks either in flash exercises or in the Community. The consensus reached by all of them is that they are motivated by the feedbacks.

Rob loves the detailed feedbacks as in *David's London* (http://www.in2english.com.cn/living/living.php?pageid=1358) and considered that in2english editors must have done a lot of work on them, "Feedbacks are very important to online English learners. ... If all the flash exercises are provided with such detailed feedbacks, it will do take a lot of time either in maintenance or design". On being asked why the feedbacks are important, he answered, "Because firstly it can fortify what I've learned, secondly it can check how I've learned and finally it can stimulate my motivation." When pressed further on what kind of online English learning resources he expects best, he accentuated the feedbacks again, "The exercises must be various and offer timely feedback".

Shirley admitted that her interest in English learning can be motivated. On the one hand, she expects "other learners' replies" and on the other hand, she makes efforts to "post more messages to their replies". The feedbacks, in her opinion, are interactive.

When pressed more on what she thinks of the flash exercises, she iterated the significance of the feedbacks of the flash exercises, "The advantage of the site's exercise is that it provides feedbacks telling you whether your choice is right or wrong and explaining why you get a wrong answer, the usage of the word or expressions".

Quite obviously, the elaborated feedbacks of the flash exercise motivated her interest in English learning online. She particularly recognized the use of interactive flash technology which enables the elaborated and timely feedbacks.

Tony's interview also echoes the relations between feedback and motivation; he said he kept writing in the Community just because his articles got replies. Further, he added that the ordinary replies are not very helpful and strongly suggested that the articles be revised by tutors/editors of the site.

Interestingly, Mark doubted whether the author would reply to his first post in the Community, he said, "Actually, I don't think you will respond to my post, which I finished late last night quickly. What you have done will let me come here everyday and ASAP". Later on, he clarified his main purpose of visiting the Community, "I find I can get more than I expect. I also find the interaction here is one important drive for me to stay and keep writing here often".

4.3 Feedback in Flash Exercise and Virtual Tutor

One of the most striking findings to come out of these interviews and discussions is that almost half of the participants put forward such an idea that detailed and timely feedbacks in flash exercises can act as a virtual tutor.

On being asked the usefulness of the feedbacks in flash exercises, Stephen elicited the concept of 'virtual tutor', "I think the feedbacks are very helpful for me to reflect on the question and it's just like studying with a virtual tutor".

The idea was agreed on in some way with Shirley and Alice. Shirley claimed that the elaborated and timely feedback is the advantage of the website.

Asked upon whether she expects detailed feedback when giving a wrong answer in a flash exercise, Alice gave an affirmative answer, "Of course, if I cannot find the right answer, I wish somebody could help me. It's a good idea to refer to the hints or feedbacks for the choices to get a detailed explanation."

For those users who encounter a problem in the course of doing the flash exercise, the detailed and timely feedbacks can offer them instant assistance. Even though at that time the user cannot directly obtain a tutor's assistance, the feedback acts as a tutor even though it is virtual.

4.4 Reluctance of Seeking Assistance from the Website

Amongst the findings, what surprises the author a lot is the reluctance of nearly all the participants in seeking assistant from the website when coming across a question in studying the resources on in2english or encountering a technical problem. Interestingly, most of them chose dictionary as the consultant. The other alternative is to seek assistance from friends or colleagues around them.

4.5 Synchronous Communications and Oral English

One finding is that most of the participants reached the consensus on the urgency of improving oral English and the greatest challenge of improving oral English in pure-online learning environment.

On being asked the greatest challenge for learners in a pure-online English learning environment, Shirley answered without any hesitation, "I think it's the challenge of how to improve oral English abilities". When explaining why he kept writing in in2english Community, Mark emphasized the urgency of practicing oral English, "To study English well mean I have to use it. It goes without saying that writing here is better way while I can't find a place to speak English".

Tony's interview echoes their ideas, he suggested setting up a chat room for practicing oral English. Stephen also recognized the great importance of Chat Room and the feasibility of setting up a chat room on in2english.

4.6 Interface Design and Motivation

One point in Shirley's interview is her frequent stress on the importance of interface design. When explaining why she lost favour in the Community after it was revised, Shirley said, "I don't like the changed layout and I think it was not convenient to use any more". On being asked her opinions on the widely-used flash exercise, she highly praised the use of flash, "it makes me feel relaxed. I think if the flash can be designed more beautiful, more interests will be motivated from the users".

When asked about comparing in2english with other English learning websites, she confirmed again the advantage of the interface design on in2english, "the interface design of other websites looks in disorder while in2english looks comfortable; its colour blocks are well matched, so it produces good environments for English learning". The idea of Shirley is also echoed by Stephen.

4.7 Learner Autonomy and Technology

Amongst the participants, it was Eric who mentioned learner autonomy in online English learning. When asked his understanding of the Interaction in online learning, he said, "Regarding 'interaction', I think that being interesting is most important fact of success. A little bit compulsion is necessary for me to learn English, and then more interaction can be achieved".

The 'compulsion' here can be understood as learner autonomy or self-regulation, the vital element in online learning. In his opinion well-designed resources must meet the standards of 'interests' and 'compulsion'. He also implied the importance of design in the interface and content.

4.8 Interaction as Apprenticeship

Another finding is the interaction as apprenticeship. Shirley and Tony both emphasized the great importance of negotiation of meaning and feedback from tutors in the social interaction in the Community.

On being asked if she expects the editors' or foreign experts' feedback to her posts in order to help her improve your English writing, she commented, "Sure. It'll be very helpful to my writing skills. But it seems the site doesn't provide such services a lot. I do think most of the learners expect editors' comments to their posts".

In her opinion, the comments from the editors or foreign experts on the website will help her improve writing skills. Learners expect more feedback from more experienced or more capable experts so that their errors could be identified and then resolved. In the process, their input could be modified for more comprehensible output.

She then went on to iterate her expectations, "I prefer the feedback from online tutors, because sometimes I would like to write some articles in English, as you know English is different from Chinese in the way of writing, so I would like the expert's comments so that I could improve my English writing ability instead of writing some sentences similar to oral conversation".

Tony complained about the lack of tutor's feedback and revisions in the Community.

It implies that tutor's feedback can help them to modify their input and then generate comprehensible output through the social interaction among non-native speakers and native speakers or more experienced tutors.

5 Discussion of Findings

On in2english, the overwhelming interactions are the ones between users and content and amongst users themselves. Most of the participants visited the Community before studying the online English learning resources on the website. This seems to agree to greater extent upon ideas of participants' "feelings of belonging" in online communities [37]. On the other hand, much less Interaction between users and the tutors/editors happens in the Community since the participants complained about the lack of feedback and revisions from tutors/editors. The participants recognized the great importance of negotiation of meaning and input modification in second language learning through the social interaction with more experienced or more capable tutors/editors. This agrees with Vygotsky upon the important role of social interaction in the development of student's cognition through the scaffolding of more capable tutors [33]. Admittedly, in the Community it is predominant that the users themselves who interact with each other in posting messages or articles and conducting discussions.

The interactions amongst the users in the Community can be considered from the perspective of the social constructivism. The users interact with each other through posting feedbacks to others' articles and reading each other's articles. In the process of writing articles and feedback and reading others' articles and feedback, it seems to agree, to some extent, with Vetter [32] and Chun [7] that in synchronous communications participants' oral English benefits from text-based communication in language learning. Although the communications and interactions between the users in the Community are not synchronous, the findings indicate the benefits of the users' oral

English from posting articles as a sort of writing practice. One of the most surprising findings that come out of the interviews and discussions is the participants' preference for the Community and greatest desire for the setting up of a Chat Room. The users intend to minimize the absence of face-to-face tutorials through the use of a Chat Room. However, the need for a Chat Room reflects the lack of the opportunities for practicing oral English and the general low level of Chinese learners' oral English. The asynchronous Community has gained the support of most of the participants as it is the only place for them to communicate and interact with each other socially. In addition, it establishes a firm link between online learning and the need of social interaction [22]. In a pure-online learning environment, obviously the users hope they can obtain online support and assistance from other users, tutors/editors especially more professional people.

The interaction between the users and the content can be regarded as the exercise of cognitive constructivism. The users construct meaning in their own mind through the interaction with the resources. It has to be noted the users can hardly acquire any assistant from tutors/editor of the website. Nearly all of them could carry on learning the content by themselves with the facilitation of feedback, online support or content design. Feedback was important to strengthen the interaction between the users and the content [1]. The recognition of the significance of the elaborated and timely feedback by most of the participants indicates the online learners' dependence on the interactions enhanced by technology particularly interactive flash technologies. Since the online users cannot obtain tutors' instant feedback, it is the course design through the employment of the interactive flash technology that helps to maintain learners' autonomy and stimulate their motivation. This agrees with most research on the significance of the feedback in online learning, but it has to be pointed out that in pure-online second language learning, the detailed and timely feedback plays a much more important role than in general online learning. Admittedly, the proper use of the widely-employed interactive flash technology either in flash exercises or flash courses determines, to some extent, the success of the online resources. This could be regarded as a new finding especially for pure-online second language learning. In addition, the findings can help remove the inconsistency on the relationships between learner motivation and technology by different researchers. Apart from the studies of feedback in exercises which have been carried out by a few researchers, this study concluded the importance of feedback through other communication ways such as the BBS. The course design with the appropriate use of the interactive technology facilitated the users' motivation. The course design with the use of interactive technology produces a virtual tutor scaffolding English learning in such a pure-online English learning environment. In this sense, the interaction between the users and content is intertwined with the virtual interaction between the user and tutor.

Issues were discovered in the pure-online second language learning environment. Most of the participants tended not to consult the tutors/editor directly when encountering a question or problem. Probably they are rather worried about the delays in feedback. It appears to echo participants' call for the need of synchronous communication and interaction. The limit in human resources is also reflected in the participants' complaints upon the lack of tutors/editors' feedback and revisions in the Community.

6 Conclusion

This study set out to explore how the interaction works in a pure-online English-language-learning environment, and to investigate the related issues and peculiar characteristics of these interactions. Online interviews and online discussions with eight Chinese users of in2english, aged from 19 to 35, were investigated from the in2english community. Naturally the two predominant interactions were between the users and content and amongst the users themselves. The interactions in such an environment can seek its theoretical support from the cognitive and social constructivism approaches. The interaction between the users and content reveals the process of individual cognition through the facilitation of course design and especially elaborated and timely feedbacks backed by the interactive flash technology. During the course of personal construction of English language knowledge, both the learner autonomy and motivation can be ensured. The elaborately designed feedback functioned as a virtual tutor scaffold for these English learners. The interaction between users enabled the process of co-construction of knowledge in social interaction through the use of the community as asynchronous communication. The users expressed a need for more synchronous communication, due to the absence of face-to-face tutorials compared with blended learning or conventional face-to-face teaching and learning. In this pure-online English learning website, the eminent issue is the lack of tutor support and tutor interaction. Findings supported adding a new Chat Room for more academic issues to be discussed. Such findings indicate a shift in the users' concept of online learning for improving English abilities. The opportunity sampling in the study brought some limitations. The participants were confined to the active users of the community of in2english, their ideas and opinions in the interviews and discussions may have been unrepresentative of the average users. Further studies are warranted to involve a wider range of users including those who are not active users of the community.

References

1. Allum, P.: Evaluation of CALL: initial vocabulary learning. ReCALL 16(2), 488–501 (2004)
2. Anderson, T., Elloumi, F. (eds.): Theory and Practice of Online Learning. Athabasca University Press, Athabasca (2004)
3. Bax, S.: CALL - past, present and future. System 31(1), 13–28 (2003)
4. Bell, J.: Doing your research project: a guide for first-time researchers in education, health and social science, 4th edn. Open UP, Maidenhead (2005)
5. Brown, A., Dowling, P.: Doing Research/Reading Research: a mode of interrogation for education. Falmer Press, London (1998)
6. Blin, F.: CALL and the development of learner autonomy: towards an activity- theoretical perspective. ReCALL 16(2), 377–395 (2004)
7. Chun, D.M.: Using computer networking to facilitate the acquisition of interactive competence. System (22), 17–31 (1994)
8. Chun, D., Plass, J.: Networked Multimedia Environments for Second Language Acquisition. In: Warschauer, R.K.M. (ed.) Network-Based Language Teaching: Concepts and Practice. Cambridge University Press, New York (2000)

9. Felix, U.: The Web as a Vehicle for Constructivist Approaches in Language Teaching. ReCALL 14(1), 2–15 (2002)
10. Felix, U.: E-learning pedagogy in the third millennium: the need for combining social and cognitive constructivist approaches. ReCALL 17(1), 85–100 (2005)
11. Garrison, D.R., Anderson, T.: E-learning in the 21st century: a framework for research and practice. RoutledgeFalmer, London (2003)
12. Glaser, B.G.: Theoretical Sensitivity. Sociology Press, Mill Valley (1978)
13. Hampel, R.: Rethinking task design for the digital age: A framework for language teaching and learning in a synchronous online environment. ReCALL 18(1), 105–121 (2006)
14. Hansson, T.: English as a second language on a virtual platform: Tradition and innovation in a new medium. Computer Assisted Language Learning 18(1), 69–79 (2005)
15. Hemard, D.: Evaluating hypermedia structures as a means of improving language learning strategies and motivation. ReCALL 18(1), 24–44 (2006)
16. Jung, U.O.H.: CALL: past, present and future - a bibliometric approach. ReCALL 17(1), 4–17 (2005)
17. Kaufman, D.: Constructivist Issues in Language Learning and Teaching. Annual Review of Applied Linguistics 24(1), 303–319 (2004)
18. Lim, K.-M., Shen, H.Z.: Integration of computers into an EFL reading classroom. ReCALL 18(2), 212–229 (2006)
19. Little, D.: Learner autonomy and second/foreign language learning. In: Bickerton, D., Brown, K., Flood, C. (eds.) The Guide to Good Practice for learning and teaching in Languages, Linguistics and Area Studies. LTSN Subject Centre for Languages, Linguistics and Area Studies, Southampton (2002)
20. Loucky, J.P.: Combining the benefits of electronic and online dictionaries with CALL web sites to produce effective and enjoyable vocabulary and language learning lessons. Computer Assisted Language Learning 18(5), 389–416 (2005)
21. Mann, C., Stewart, F.: Internet Interviewing. In: Gubrium, J., Holstein, J. (eds.) Postmodern Interviewing, pp. 81–105. Sage, Thousand Oaks (2003)
22. McInnerney, J.M., Roberts, T.S.: Online Learning: Social Interaction and the Creation of a Sense of Community. Educational Technology & Society 7(3), 73–81 (2004)
23. Muirhead, B.: Encouraging Interaction in Online Classes. International Journal of Instructional Technology and Distance Learning 1(6) (2004)
24. Murray, D.E.: Technologies for Second Language Literacy. Annual Review of Applied Linguistics 25, 188–201 (2005)
25. Neumeier, P.: A closer look at blended learning — parameters for designing a blended learning environment for language teaching and learning. ReCALL 17(2), 163–178 (2005)
26. Pujola, J.T.: Did CALL feedback feed back? Researching learners use of feedback. ReCALL 13(1), 79–98 (2001)
27. Roed, J.: Language learner behaviour in a virtual environment. Computer Assisted Language Learning 16(2-3), 155–172 (2003)
28. Scheffel-Dunand, D.: Bimodal communication over webcasts: from CSCL to CALL. Computer Assisted Language Learning 19(4-5), 341–355 (2006)
29. Shank, P., Sitze, A.: Making sense of online learning: a guide for the beginners and the truly skeptical. Pfeiffer, San Francisco (2004)
30. Simina, V., Hamel, M.-J.: CASLA through a social constructivist perspective: WebQuest in project-driven language learning. ReCALL 17(2), 217–228 (2005)
31. Strauss, A., Corbin, J.: Basics of Qualitative Research: Grounded Theory, Procedures and Techniques. Sage, London (1990)

32. Vetter, A., Chanier, T.: Supporting oral production for professional purposes in synchronous communication with heterogenous learners. ReCALL 18(1), 5–23 (2006)
33. Vygotsky, L.S.: Mind in society: The development of higher psychological processes. Harvard University Press, Cambridge (1978)
34. Wang, Y.: Negotiation of Meaning in Desktop Videoconferencing-Supported Distance Language Learning. ReCALL 18(1), 122–146 (2006)
35. Warschauer, M.: Online Learning in Sociocultural Context. JSTOR 29, 68–88 (1998)
36. White, C.: Distance learning of foreign languages. Language Teaching 39(04), 247–264 (2006)
37. Wilson, B.G.: Sense of Community as a Valued Outcome for Electronic Courses, Cohorts, and Programs (2001), `http://carbon.cudenver.edu/~bwilson/SenseOfCommunity.html`

The Virtual Learning Commons Architecture Based on Semantic Technologies

Shuhuai Ren[1] and Jialin Cao[2]

[1] Shanghai University Library, Shanghai, 200444 China
[2] Shanghai University, Shanghai, 200444 China
{rensh,caojl}@shu.edu.cn

Abstract. Virtual Learning Commons (VLC) is a new web-based virtual learning environment to support learning, teaching, research and knowledge sharing by integrated digital library, e-learning system, social network, academic support tools, and so on. In this paper, a new semantic based VLC architecture is proposed, which reveals the logical relationship among the virtual environments, the functional levels, the virtual service organization, and other components. The five-layer structural model is described in detail. Finally, a prototype system of the semantics-based VLC is implemented. The case study shows that the proposed semantics-based architecture and structural model have great theoretical and practical value in guiding the construction of VLC.

Keywords: Virtual Learning Commons, E-Learning, Resource Organization, Semantic technology.

1 Introduction

Virtual Learning Commons (VLC) is a new web-based virtual learning environment that can meet modern learners' needs for learning, interaction, collaboration and research by integrating digital library, e-learning system, social network, academic support tools and so on. With the rapid development of the Internet and information technology, the learning modes and pedagogical models have made great changes in universities. Especially the wide use of Constructivism Learning Theory in education, the collaborative learning outside the classroom becomes more popular [1]. The library plays an increasingly important role in supporting students' study, as it works as the literature center, information center, learning center and cultural center in the campus. Thus, many university libraries redefine their missions, expand their services, and collaborate with departments for information technology, teaching, academic support and student affairs to build a new learning spaces named Learning Commons (LC). It consists of the physical layer, virtual layer, support layer and others. VLC mainly refers to the virtual layer of LC[2].

There are many factors to be considered when building a VLC. The system architecture, structural model and implementation techniques are more important aspects. After a wide range of literature search, it is found that, except the literature [3] and [4], there is little literature concerning the VLC's architecture. Because there is

X. Luo et al. (Eds.): ICWL 2010 Workshops, LNCS 6537, pp. 151–160, 2011.

no good system architecture and structural model to guide the construction of VLC, and the traditional technologies for existing VLC systems are weak at interoperability and semantics and lack of context-sensitive semantic-driven mechanism as well. It is urgent to build a comprehensive system architecture and structural model for VLC, and to research into a new approach for the realization of VLC, which should be based on new technologies, especially the semantic technologies.

Semantic technologies can enhance the semantic and intelligence ability of the VLC. Many researches about semantic technologies will be helpful in improving VLC performance. The internet interactive computing laboratory of Shanghai University has done a lot of work on "human-web interaction", which will do great work for the intelligent VLC, such as Element Fuzzy Cognitive Maps [5], Web knowledge flow [6], Automatic Discovery of Semantic Relations [7], Textual knowledge flow [8][9], Collaborated Semantic Link Network [10], Semantic Cloud based on SLN and ALN [11], and so on, which are good technical support for building semantics-driven VLC.

The rest of this paper is organized as follows. In Section 2, a semantics-based architecture of the VLC for e-learning is proposed. In Section 3, the VLC structural model based on semantic technology is proposed and discussed in detail. In Section 4, a case study is given. Finally, the paper is concluded in Section 5.

2 A Semantic-Based Architecture of VLC for E-Learning

An architecture is defined by the recommended practice as the fundamental organization of a system, embodied in its components, their relationships to each other and the environment, and the principles governing its design and evolution [12]. System architecture plays an important role in guiding the successful construction of VLC. The goal of VLC is to provide a seamless access to the virtual learning environment of learning, communication, collaboration and sharing for learners, teachers and service team beyond time and space required by integrated digital libraries, e-Learning systems, social networks, virtual communities, academic resources and tools. According to the existing research results [13], this paper proposes a new semantic based VLC architecture for e-learning shown in Figure 1. For narrative convenience, we define the VLC system architecture as following.

Definition: Virtual Learning Commons VLC: ={U, {Pt, Vc, Sm, Ot, Vr}, {Dl, El, Sn, It}, Up, Vo}, in which U:={St, Te, Li}, U is user, the generalized concept which includes all the participants in learning activities. St: Students or Learner; Te: teachers, counselors, peer counselors; Li: librarians, IT support staff, and other staff. In the VLC, students are the learning subjects, while teachers, counselors, librarians, IT support staff and other support staff are supporters of the learning activities, and also learning partners of students for improving learning effect through exchange and interaction.

{Pt, Vc, Ot, Sm, Vr} are the five functional layers. Pt: portal, Vc: virtual community, Ot: online collaboration and learning tools, Sm: Semantic construction, Vr: virtual resources.

{Dl, El, Sn, It} are the four virtual sections to support learning. Dl is Digital Library (service environment to provide digital resources and reference work). El is E-Learning system (theory and regulatory environment to support learning, teaching and academia). Sn is social networks (social and cultural environment to support learning). It is a modern information technology (technology environment to achieve systems integration and hosted learning, especially the semantic technology). Here El: = {IS, PM, LT}. IS is instructional Strategies (e.g., collaboration, articulation, reflection, role-playing, exploration, problem solving). PM is pedagogical model or construct (e.g., open/flexible learning, distributed learning, knowledge building communities). LT is learning technologies (e.g., asynchronous & synchronous communication tools, hypermedia & multimedia tools, Web authoring tools, course management systems) [14].

Vo is virtual service organization which is the human-machine integration service organization supported by information technology and composed of human resources through a virtual way.

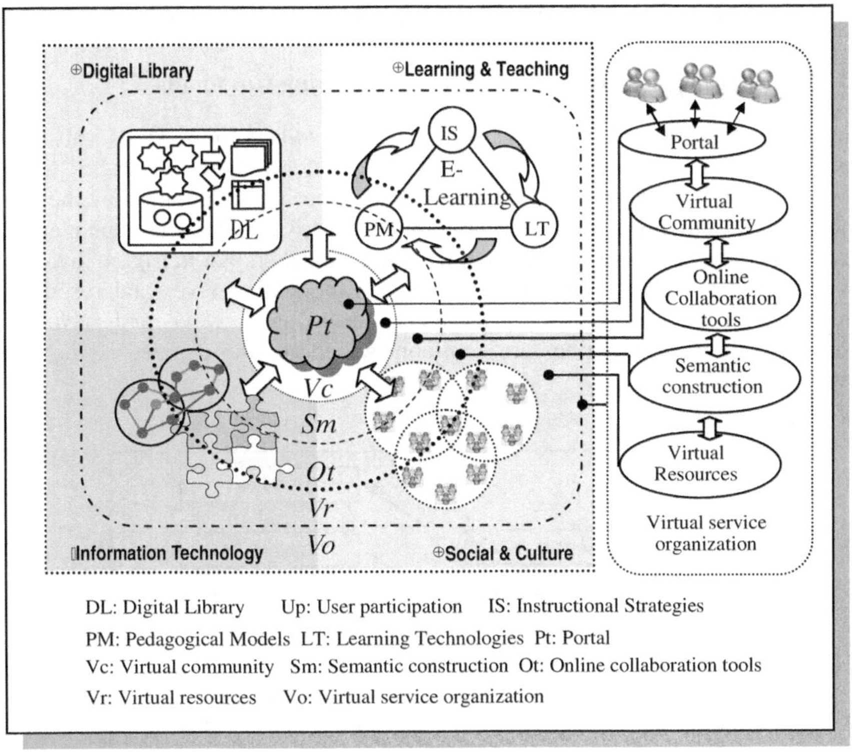

Fig. 1. A semantic-based architecture of VLC for e-learning

In the VLC architecture, the elements are not mutually independent, but can be an organic whole by interaction. Virtual communities include virtual learning communities, communities of interest, communities of practice, knowledge communities and social networks, etc. To enable learners who have common interests, common hobbies, common vision or common goals to get together across time and space, the learning, coordination and communication of teachers, librarians, technicians and other staff in virtual organization will achieve collaborative learning and research goals through exchanging experiences, sharing resources, sharing ideas, etc. Online communication and learning tools include online learning software, communication tools, software of information sharing and accessing, multimedia tools, search engines, knowledge navigation, and other network software, which are the necessary means to achieve collaborative learning. Digital resources and online learning courses include digital library resources, online resources, learning knowledge repository, online learning and training courses, which are sources for learners to construct knowledge framework and learning environment, and essential conditions of self-learning and collaborative exploration. The structure integrates the digital library with e-Learning seamlessly, so it may become an appropriate learning environment to support a variety of study modes.

3 VLC Structural Model Based on Semantic Technologies

3.1 Shortcomings of the Current Virtual Learning Commons

An architecture describes logical relationship between the various subsystems or components and external environment. The structural model describes the system hierarchy of components, order, processes, and the implementation of the roadmap. Therefore, the structural model has an important role in guiding implementation of the VLC. The current VLC's hierarchical structure model shown in Figure 2(a) is mainly divided into the user layer, interaction layer, application layer and resource layer. Although different VLCs are constructed in different ways and have different functions, some shortcomings are common, which are summarized in the following several aspects.

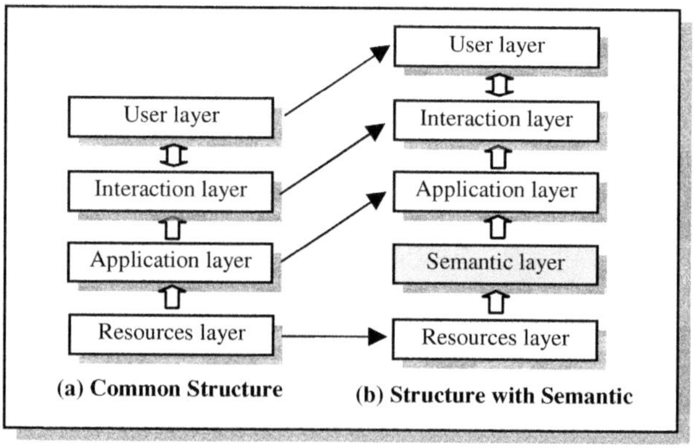

Fig. 2. The hierarchical structure of VLC

1) Poor interoperation. VLC needs to integrate various data sources or application systems which are often distributed and heterogeneous. The data organization standards of different systems are quite different and it is not easy to make a seamless integration among these systems, which leads to poor interoperability of VLC. For example, as described in the literature [3], although the digital library portal and WebCT are integrated on the same page, but the user still has to log in the digital library system to make another retrieve when a user needs digital library resources from WebCT. It cannot make a convenient back and forth visit between the two different systems.

2) Lack of semantics. The methods of information organization and retrieval of VLC are still based on the keywords, mainly relying on string matching identity, lacking of semantic comprehension of the keywords, which can't realize concept retrieval and semantic retrieval. Therefore, it is difficult to improve the recall ratio and the precision ratio, which restricts user accessing relevant information accurately and quickly.

3) Lack of Context-driven mechanism. Learning and knowledge acquisition is a complicated process of interaction, communication, collaboration and meaning construction between learners and learners or between learners and learning object in a certain context. If the system could perceive the context of learners and provide personalized recommendation of knowledge, learning objects and information resources, it will be of great practical significance for improving learning efficiency and quality. However, the current VLC still lacks of such a mechanism.

In addition, the current VLC also has other shortcomings, suca as functional decentralization, poor reuse of knowledge resources, poor interaction, and weak personalization features.

In order to eliminate these defectives, the proposed solution of this paper is to add a semantic construction layer between resource layer and application layer, to extend the functions of application layer and interaction layer, and to enhance virtual service organization's support for users at the user layer. This new layer structure is shown in figure 2(b). The purpose of adding a semantic layer is to build a semantic space based upon the resource layer, to add semantic indexing, to support the concept of semantics-based browsing, semantic search, semantic navigation, semantic reasoning and semantic perception. To expand the application layer would enhance scenario-driven and semantic reasoning mechanism to enable the system automatically to perceive the context of learner's interaction, conversation and collaboration process, to realize the individualized and intelligentized knowledge delivery to learners.

3.2 The Structural Model of Semantic VLC

Based on the above analysis, a structural application model of semantic VLC is proposed, which is shown in Figure 3. The model is composed of 5 logical levels, which are the Virtual Resource Layer, Semantic Construction Layer, Application Link Layer, Interactive Display Layer and User Layer. The lower layer is the foundation of the upper layer. On the contrary, the upper layer is the extension of the lower layer.

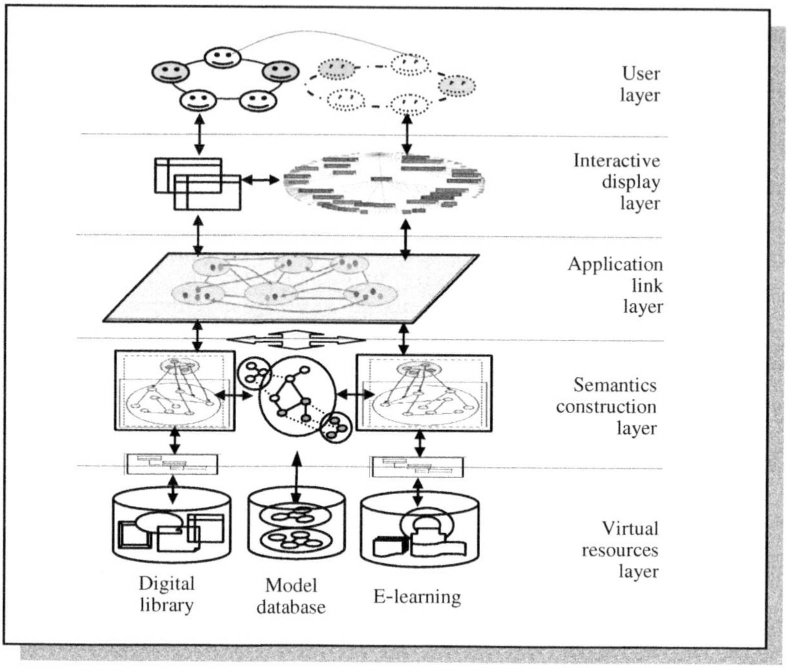

Fig. 3. A VLC structural model based on semantic technologies

1) Virtual resource layer. Virtual resource layer taking advantage of virtualization technology could map heterogeneous and distributed resources of multiple systems into a unified virtual resources space, form a consistent logical structure with standardized interface and facilitate management and operation of virtual resource layer. The metadata mapping mechanism and the interoperability protocol based on Web Service are the foundations of the information resource virtualization. On one hand, these technologies can cover the heterogeneity among the various data, solve the integration problems of heterogeneous and distributed information resource; on the other hand, the information resources can be cut into smaller resource units in order to be better managed and used, which could be used for the upper semantic space. Information resources include digital library resources, e-learning repository, institutional repository and network information resources. Digital library resources include electronic journals, Internet databases, CD-ROM databases, electronic books, streaming media, subject navigation, knowledge navigation, knowledge base, institutional repository, etc.; e-learning resources include learning documents, learning objects, courseware, school assignment and question bank, lesson plans, educational software, program, online training and counseling resources and the social and cultural resources as well. These resources are stored in different places in a distributed way or stored in the pattern of cloud storage.

2) Semantics construction layer. Semantics construction layer is the core layer to achieve the semantic system, and it is also the functional layer that uses semantic technology to build semantic space and increase semantic index in the virtual resource layer. In other words, it takes advantage of semantic technology for analyzing the data elements to establish semantic association between the concepts of metadata, and then builds ontology and semantic knowledge base. Ontology is the abstraction and description of the domain knowledge and it is also the method to express, share and reuse knowledge, which provides a tool for extraction, understanding and dealing with the domain knowledge. The function of semantic structure layer includes knowledge discovery, knowledge mining, ontology construction, and semantic-based user-model construction, etc. In order to make its function come true, a variety of methods and techniques can be used synthetically, such as Semantic association rules [7], Knowledge Flow[8], Semantic Cloud Based on SLN and ALN [11], and other semantic technologies.

3) Application link layer. Application link layer is composed of functional mapping, inference, intelligent agents, social networks, virtual communities, online tools, semantic search and knowledge of navigation and other components. The knowledge of resource layer can be connected to the appropriate user and appropriate context through functional mapping and knowledge inference. Virtual communities are all kinds of virtual places for users to share and collaborate, such as interest community, learning community, knowledge community, subject community, student community, etc. The system can configure online tools dynamically according to the user's tasks and individual needs. Online tool is the application software or tool for users to achieve communication, cooperation, learning, transaction processing, resource acquisition and other operations, including communication tools, learning tools and information sharing tools, such as synchronous or asynchronous communication tools, e-learning, software of information sharing and accessing, search engines, knowledge navigation tools, multimedia tools and other network software, which are the essential means of collaborative learning.

4) Interactive display layer. Interactive display layer is composed of login and validation, human-computer interface, interactive and collaborative course processing and visual display, etc. Interactivity and interoperability are the key features of interactive display layer which should be designed to break the constraints of time and space of traditional classroom teaching. So learners can carry out multi-level and multi-role interactions and form a distributed cognitive environment to support learner-centered teaching ideas. Collaboration will offer learners more opportunities to participate in the social learning activities and encourage them to frequently elaborate, discuss, and rethink on learning strategies and change themselves to promote their knowledge construction. The use of knowledge building theory and visualization techniques can reduce the cognitive burden of learners, so that they can concentrate their attentions on the much more complex learning task.

5) User layer. User layer is the core element, which is extendedly defined as all the people involved in the learning process including learners, teachers, counselors, librarians, experts of special field and so on. See the definition of user above in Section 2.

4 Case Study

Based on the above architecture and structural model, a prototype system of semantic VLC is developed. A frequently used database of digital library of Chinese colleges and universities, Chinese Scientific Journals Database (CSJD), is taken as a metadata source. This database contains 24.5 million articles from 13.6 thousands of journals from the year of 1989 to now. Metadata mapping follows DC (Dublin Core) rules and 15 elements such as Title, Creator, Date, Subject, Publisher, Type, Description, Contributor, Format, Source, Rights, Identifier, Language, Relation, and Coverage when the element set are selected. RDF (Resource Description Framework) is taken to describe, store, change, compute and inquire the metadata. In the semantic layer structure, the method proposed by document [11], which is based on Association Link Network (ALN) and Similarity Link Network (SLN), is used to construct a semantic layer for connecting resources from different domains. This method utilizes E-FCM (element fuzzy cognitive map) to represent resources such as digital documents, learning objects, webpages, etc. E-FCM is the building block of SLN and ALN. And it is a kind of fuzzy cognitive map and a representation approach of resources. The relations between E-FCMs can be efficiently computed. The SLN and ALN, which are based on the similarity and association relations respectively, form SLN-cloud and ALN-cloud which make the semantic cloud layer with rich abilities. Accurate and continuous results can be provided to users depending on the global view of resources. As Figure 4 shows, there exist two levels of resource flows- oriented clouds. The lower level is SLN-cloud and the higher is ALN-cloud. The fine-grained one consists of resources from SLN-clouds, while the coarse-grained one just consists of SLN-clouds.

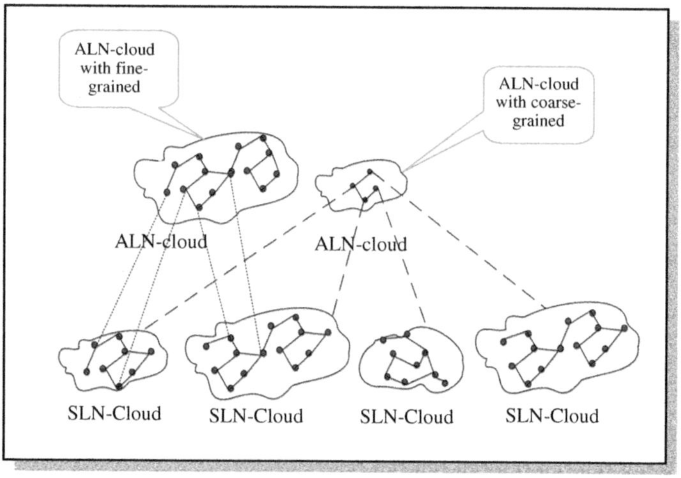

Fig. 4. The relations of ALN-cloud and ALN-cloud

The application layer is to integrate social network with academic support tools through the technologies of web 2.0, semantic based algorithms construction and reasoning exploration of repository. The result is context driven and shown in visualization navigation framework on the interactive layer, an interface for semantic search as the figure 5 shows.

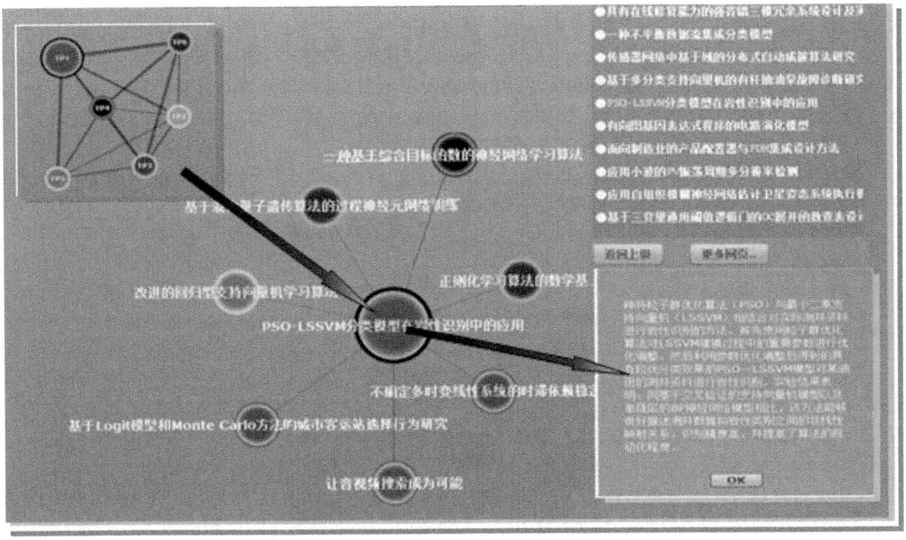

Fig. 5. An interface for semantic search

5 Conclusion

Virtual Learning Commons is a new virtual learning environment designed to support learning, teaching, research and knowledge sharing. This paper presents a new semantics-based VLC architecture which reveals the logical relationship among the four virtual environments (Digital Library, e-Learning, Social & Culture, and Information Technology), the five functional levels (Portal, Virtual Community, Online Collaboration tools, Semantic Making, and Virtual Resources), a virtual service organization, and other components. In order to overcome the weakness of poor interoperation, lack of semantic relations, and lack of Context-driven mechanism, we present a five-layer structural model of VLC based on semantic technologies. Finally, a prototype of the semantics-based VLC is implemented. The case study shows that the proposed semantics-based architecture and structural model has great theoretical and practical value in guiding the construction of VLC. Semantic technologies can be used to enhance the semantic and intelligence level of the VLC. However, VLC is still a new field to explore, especially when it comes to integrate the semantics- based e-learning system, digital library and virtual services and so on, and there is still a great deal of work to do in solving technical problems.

References

1. Koohang, A., Riley, L., Smith, T., Schreurs, J.: E-learning and constructivism: from theory to ap-plication. Interdisciplinary Journal of E-Learning and Learning Objects 5, 91–109 (2009)
2. Ren, S., Sheng, X.: Learning Commons Building Collaborative and Interactive Learning Environments. Journal of Academic Libraries 26(4), 20–26 (2008)
3. Braaksma, B., et al.: Building a Virtual Learning Commons: What Do You Want to Do? In: The World Library and Information Congress: 73rd IFLA General Conference and Council, Durban, South Africa, August 19-23 (2007)
4. Session, D., Douglas, R.: Xavier University's Web 2.0 Strategy: The Virtual Learning Commons, EDUCAUSE Annual Conferences, `http://connect.educause.edu/library/abstract/XavierUniversitysWeb/45371`
5. Luo, X., Zhang, J., Liu, F., Du, Y., Yu, Z., Xu, W.: Merging Textual Knowledge Represented by Element Fuzzy Cognitive Maps. JSW 5(2), 225–234 (2010)
6. Luo, X., Xu, Z., Li, Q., Hu, Q., Yu, J., Tang, X.: Generation of similarity knowledge flow for intelligent browsing based on semantic link networks. Concurrency and Computation: Practice and Experience 21(16), 2018–2032 (2009)
7. Luo, X., Yan, K., Chen, X.: Automatic Discovery of Semantic Relations Based on Association Rule. Journal of Software 3(8), 11–18 (2008)
8. Luo, X., Hu, Q., Xu, W., Yu, Z.: Discovery of textual knowledge flow based on the management of knowledge maps. Concurrency and Computation: Practice and Experience 20(15), 1791–1806 (2008)
9. Luo, X., Yu, J.: Building Web Knowledge Flow based on Interactive Computing with Semantics. New Generation Computing 28, 113–121 (2010)
10. Liu, F., Luo, X., Xu, Z., Liu, X.: Discovery of Web Services Based on Collaborated Semantic Link Network, wscs. In: IEEE International Workshop on Semantic Computing and Systems, pp. 89–94 (2008)
11. Liu, F., Luo, X., Yu, J., Liang, G.: Semantic Cloud Based on SLN and ALN, skg. In: Fifth International Conference on Semantics, Knowledge and Grid, pp. 314–317 (2009)
12. ANSI/IEEE Std 1471-2000: IEEE Recommended Practice for Architectural Description of Software-Intensive Systems. The Institute of Electrical and Electronic Engineers, Inc., New York, NY (2000)
13. Ren, S., Sheng, X.: Information Commons: Theoretical Modeling and Dynamic Mechanisms. Journal of Library Science In China 34(4), 34–40 (2008)
14. Dabbagh, H.: Pedagogical Models for E-learning: A Theory-based Design Framework. International Journal of Technology in Teaching and Learning 1(1), 25–44 (2005)

OCL-Based Testing for E-Learning Web Service

Jin Liu[1,3,4], Xiaoming Lu[1], Xiguang Feng[2], and Jianxun Liu[2]

[1] State Key Lab of Software Engineering, Computer School, Wuhan University, China
[2] Key Lab of Knowledge Processing and Networked Manufacturing,
Hunan University of Science and Technology, 411201, China
[3] State Key Lab. for Novel Software Technology, Nanjing University, 210093, China
[4] Lab. of Complex Systems and Intelligence Science, Institute of Automation,
CAS, 100190, China
mailjinliu@yahoo.com

Abstract. As testing has been playing an important role in guaranteeing quality of Web service in respect of E-learning, the traditional testing of Web services presents its inability such as time-consuming and flawed testing procedures as opposed to desired measures in quickly and thoroughly scanning Web services for detects. To reduce testing cost and enhance testing efficiency, our testing measure for E-learning Web services is to describe services with an annotation mixed with the Object Constrain Language (OCL) and Semantic Annotations for WSDL and XML Schema (SAWSDL), parse OCL pre-conditions and OCL post-conditions, and generate test cases with class division and boundary values. An experimental case indicates the feasibility of the proposed approach.

Keywords: E-learning, Web service, OCL-based testing.

1 Introduction

Serving as specific media to implement the learning process, E-learning has been playing an important role in effecting the construction of knowledge with reference to individual experience, practice and knowledge of the learner [1]. In addtional to interoperability across various computing platforms through networks due to their conformity to open standards such as HTTP and XML-based protocols as SOAP and WSDL, Web service also owns positive characteristics such as versatile design, convenient application and data integration, code reuse, and cost reduction [2, 3]. Adopting Web service as a form of electronically supported learning and teaching, E-learning Web service has attracted a lot of public attention as well as concerns from modern educators. E-learning as Web service can employ Service-oriented architecture (SOA) to quickly and flexibly implement E-learning solutions with loose coupling communication [4].

As an important measure to guarantee the quality of service, testing has been playing a vital role in developing E-learning Web service. Unlike traditional manual methods in laboursome and flawed testing procedures, a desired testing measure can reduce testing cost and enhance testing efficiency due to its ability of quickly and thoroughly scanning E-learning Web services for detects.

X. Luo et al. (Eds.): ICWL 2010 Workshops, LNCS 6537, pp. 161–168, 2011.

As a de facto language for describing Web services, Web Services Description Language (WSDL) is not able to provide detailed information of service interfaces for service testing, so that the correctness of testing results is usually spoiled and testing cost is dramastically raised. Academic efforts of WSDL dominant testing have been made but taken no significant effect. An extended WSDL measure introduced testing on input-output dependency, functional hierarchy and the sequence of operation invocation [5]. A mutation based testing employes mutation operators on WSDL documents to generate mutated interfaces for testing WSDL described service interfaces [6]. Another attempt is to generate test cases automatically by parsing and transforming WSDL interface documents into structured DOM trees [7]. Contract variations together with WSDL documents are used to produce testing data only in simple data type such as int, float and double [8]. A static analysis parses WSDL schema recursively and extracts basic XML elements and their correspongding value [9].

Thus other related research activities that take different approaches may be regarded as benefit remedies for the inability of the above mentioned WSDL-syntax based analysis to generate valid test cases. Web service operations are expressed as input, output, pre-conditions and post-conditions with Semantic Web Rule Language (SWRL) and Web Service Semantics Language (WSDL-S), so that a limited decision table is used consequently to generate test cases [10, 11]. A contract-based measurement that describes service interfaces with OWL-S checks the consistency between Web service instances with their corresponding service profile [12]. Taking an ontology-based testing approach, an OWL-S specification of a Web service is divided into two sub-specifications [13]. One is for input-output information; the other is for operational behavior described as a formal state-machine. The analsis of paths in the state-machine together with the inputs and outputs of atomic processes would generate testing cases.

Even though these efforts, a formal notation set with more powerful description ability is still required to competent for generating valid testing cases. For this reason, this paper introduced Object Constraint Language (OCL) in the Unified Modeling Language community for testing E-learning Web services [14], because OCL provides more expressive ability than those ever in this field. Further, an OCL-based testing measure for E-learning Web services is proposed, which describs Web services by an annotation mixed with OCL and SAWSDL, parses OCL pre-conditions and OCL post-conditions, and generate test cases with class division and boundary values.

2 Technical Background

Though the WSDL standard, as a XML based language, clearly describes the syntax specification such as the structure, tags and attributes of valid WSDL documents, it also defines descriptive constraints on the XML elements in natual language. Some of them are too ambiguous to accurately express service interfaces. Moreover, some constraints are so complex to understand the literal meanings that it is easy to generate formally valid but logically conflicting documents. Therefore, OCL and SAWSDL are introduced to solve the problem.

2.1 Object Constraint Language

OCL language as a constriction language is originally designed for representing the well-formedness rules of models in Unified Modeling Language (UML) community. A well-formedness rule as an OCL expression is an invariant for the involved class, which is a triple of preconditions, postconditions and invariants. The validation of an object model can be validated by checking these constrictions imposed on this model. The formal OCL avoid ambiguity in stating constrictions and can automatically be processed by computer. The set theory and the predicate logic are the basis of OCL, which makes it easier to be understood and handled than other formal restrictive language. Additonally, OCL is a declarative language so that it is free from side effect on target models. We use OCL to enhance the accuracy and legibility of interface description.

2.2 Semantic Annotations for WSDL and XML Schema

The Semantic Annotations for WSDL and XML Schema (SAWSDL) W3C Recommendation provides mechanisms of referencing concepts from semantic models within WSDL components by annotating these concepts to WSDL components [11]. These semantics when expressed in formal languages can disambiguate the description of Web services during service testing for the Web services. With extended attributes such as "modelReference", "liftingSchemaMapping" and "loweringSchemaMapping" in SAWSDL, the complementary semantics regarding input and output messages, interfaces and operations can be associated with WSDL documents for service testing.

```
<wsdl:types>
    <xsd:element name="Discount">
       <xsd:complexType>
          <xsd:element minOccurs="1" name="pAge" type="xsd:int" />
          <xsd:element minOccurs="1" name="pAmount"type="xsd:int"/>
       </xsd:complexType>
   </xsd:element>
   <xsd:element name="DiscountResponse">
       <xsd:element name="out" type="xsd:int"/>
   </xsd:element>
</wsdl:types>
<wsdl:message name="DiscountResponse">
   <wsdl:part name="parameters" element="tns:DiscountResponse" />
</wsdl:message>
<wsdl:message name="DiscountRequest">
     <wsdl:part name="parameters" element="tns:Discount" />
</wsdl:message>
<wsdl:operation name="Discount"
   sawsdl:modelreference=
   "http://125.221.235.156:8080/DiscountService/DiscountService.ocl">
<wsdl:input name="DiscountRequest" message="tns:DiscountRequest"/>
<wsdl:output name="DiscountResponse" message="tns:DiscountResponse"/>
</wsdl:operation>
<wsdl:service name="DiscountPasswod">
```

Fig. 1. WSDL Description of Web service

3 OCL Description of Web Service

Since WSDL owns only primitive discriptive ability of web service, such as name, summary description, calling address and input-output parameter for the service, qualified testing data can not be generated by analizing primitive WSDL documents of Web services. A typical example is datatype mismatch that can be seen in the case of a web service for converting postcode into address information. The datatype of input parameter is “string” in the WSDL file of this service as apposed to type “integer” in targeted testing data set. While the string “086430072” with 9-character length will perform a valid transformation, the string “hereweare” can fail in this tranformation. Similar problems stemmed largely from the lack of rigid restriction mechanism and ambiguous expression for Web services, which makes for inefficiency and high cost of service testing. Figure 1 gives a WSDL segment describing a Web service that discounts prices according to serveral conditions, such as 60% discount for people between 50 to 100 years old and purchasing commodities more than 500 Yuan RMB. In this case, only the types of input parameters and output parameters can be obtained, but the lack of the range for input parameters is ambiguous to support the discounting rule.

When we use OCL to express restrictions on Web services, the pre-conditions containing restrictions is attached to operations that can be invoked only if the pre-conditions are valid. The post-conditions describe the expected effects or behaviors of operation output. The absence of restrictions in Figure 1 can be remedied by using OCL to describe the Web services in Figure 2, where the keyword “context” defines the service name as “DiscountService”, the operation name as “Discount” and two input parameters “pAge” and “pAmount”. The keyword "pre" defines the pre-conditions of the operation as well as constraints of input parameters. The keyword "post" grammar defines the post-condition and the expected output of the operation.

```
context DiscountService:Discount(pAge:int,Amount:int):int
pre: 50<=pAge <=100 and Amount >=500
post:if(50<=pAge <=100 and Amount >=500)
        then result= “0.6* Amount”
    else if(pAge<=0 or pAge>100 or Amount<0)
        then result=”0.0”
    else   then discount=”1* Amount”
```

Fig. 2. OCL Description of Web service

To associate primitive WSDL segment with the extra “semantic model” DiscountService in OCL, the "ModelReference" property of SAWSDL extends the primitive WSDL segment as underlined in Figure 1.

4 OCL-Based Testing for E-Learning Web Service

We propose an OCL-based testing framework in Figure 3, which is mainly consisted of three components: testing case generation, testing execution and testing analysis.

Testing case firstly generation parses a WSDL document and gets the type of input parameters. We developed a WSDL parser with WSDL4J API, which takes advantage of characters of WSDL documents. That is six main elements of a WSDL document:

"definitions", "types", "message", "porttype", "binding" and "service". Service interface name, parameter name and the type of these names can be obtained from "types", because "types" defines all data types in clients and servers. Information of operations can be found in "porttype" since "porttype" reprents the abstract set of operations. "service" as a collection to access related services provides service call address as well as service type name and Web service calling URL.

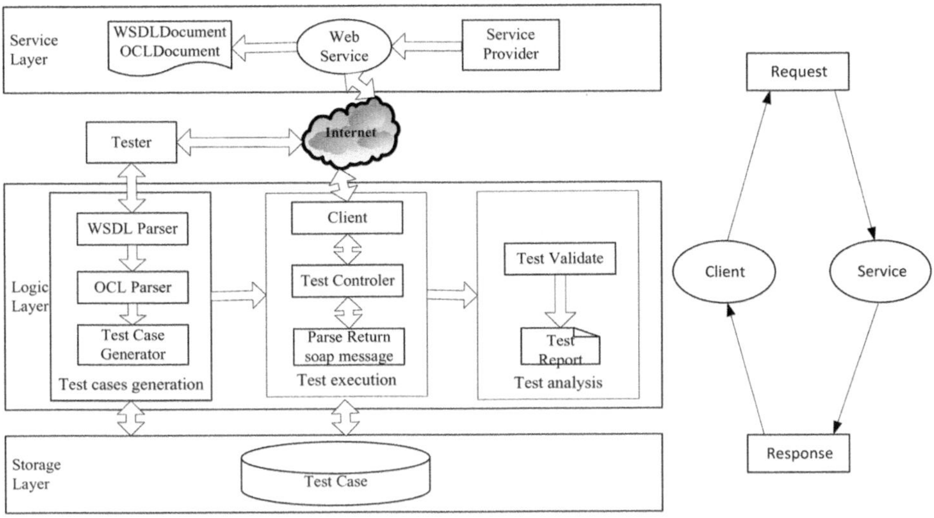

Fig. 3. OCL-based Testing Frame for E-learing Web service

The procedure of testing case generation further parses the OCL components and gets the constraint rules of operations. The restrictive specifications of pre-conditions and post-conditions are obtained by parsing OCL documents according to the following procedure:

(1) Lexical analysis analyzes the OCL text and verifies its legality. OCL expressions are extracted to establish an OCL lexical analysis tree.
(2) Syntax analysis checks the legality of class name, method name, and the property name, and further extracts invariant class, pre-conditions and post-conditions to form a syntax tree.
(3) OCL constraint expressions are extracted by traversing the syntax analysis tree.

Following that, a black-box testing approach generates the testing cases according to the equivalence class partitioning and boundary value analysis method. The equivalence class partition divides all possible input data into several subsets from which representative data as testing case are selected. The equivalent class is valid when input data set is logically reasonable for service interface specification. So the valid equivalence class can be used to verify the consistency of service interfaces with their specification. Boundary value analysis uses the boundaries value as input data for testing. The algorithm of testing data generation is described in Process 1.

Process 1. TestingDataGeneration(WSDL doucement, OCL doucement)

```
TestData= Ø;                        // initialization Test Data
Type=GetType(WSDL);                 // get the data type name from WSDL
Restrition=GetRestriction(OCL); //get OCL constraint
switch(Type)
case: String // generate test data with equivalence class and boundary value method
TestData=GenTestDataForString(Type, Restrition);
case:  int
   TestData=GenTestDataForInt(Type, Restrition);
case: boolean
   TestData=GenTestDataForBoolean(Type, Restrition);
Return TestData;
```

Table 1. Testing data for Web service "Discount"

ID	test data		ID	test data	
	pAge	Amount		pAge	Amount
1	49	600	12	60	501
2	50	499	13	60	600
3	50	500	14	100	499
4	50	501	15	100	500
5	50	600	16	100	501
6	51	499	17	100	600
7	51	500	18	99	499
8	51	501	19	99	500
9	51	600	20	99	501
10	60	499	21	99	600
11	60	500	22	101	600

For the case of Web service for making discount in Figure 1, Table 1 gives its testing data set. The testing data set can further be divided into an effective equivalent class "50<=pAge<=100" and "Amount>=500" and two invalid equivalent classes for "pAge<50", "pAge>100" and "Amount <500".

Moreover, testing execution establishes the client to send SOAP message containing testing cases and performs the testing procedure. Testing analysis compares the execution result and the expected output to complete testing reports.

5 Experiment

A simple OCL-based testing tool for E-learing Web services has been developed by Dresden OCL2 plug-ins for Eclipse programming platform. A Web service "ValidPassword" that checks the identity of two passwords is tested. Firstly, the SAWSDL document is parsed to get service name, operation name, input parameters, other information and pre-conditions by SAWSDL4J API and this Dresden OCL tool. The parsing result is indicated in Figure 4.

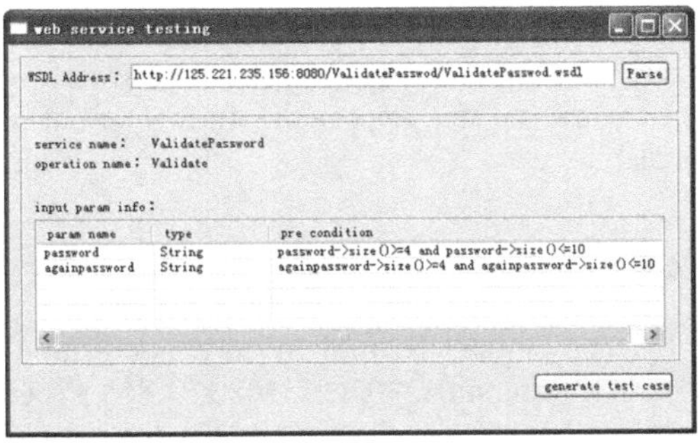

Fig. 4. Parsing result of the SAWSDL document by the OCL-based testing tool

Following the thought of the OCL-based testing for E-learning Web Service in section 5, the testing case is generated with equivalence class partitioning and boundary value approach. The Web service "ValidPassword" was invoked by sending SOAP message with SAAJ API. Figure 5 indicates the testing report in comparing results between testing output and desired output. This primitive experiment supports that our OCL-based testing can generate valid testing data for testing E-Learning Web service.

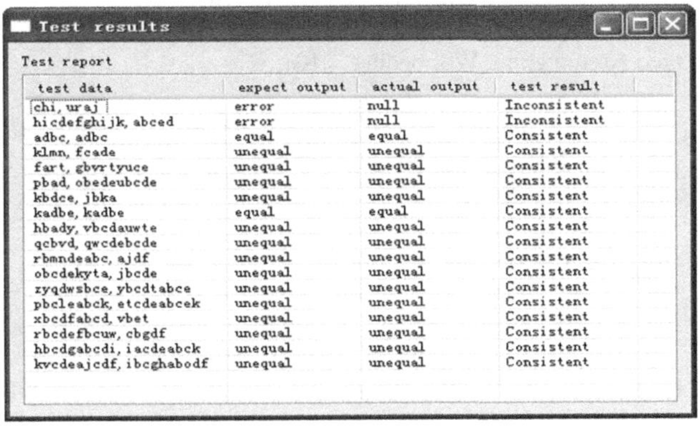

Fig. 5. Testing report comparing results between testing output and desired output

5 Conclusions

Although current semantic Web language mechanism such as WSDL provides limited ability of simple semantic description, it is inadequate to testing E-learning Web services where the ability of representing more complex and formal semantics is required. Our research extends the ability of semantic representation by introducing restrictive formal language and associates WSDL with OCL semantic model by SAWSDL mechanism. Consequently, the testing framework and the procedure of generating testing data and implementing are also explained. A primitive testing case indicates the feasibility of our method to some extent. The competence of OCL in complex testing for E-learning Web services depends very much on OCL's ability of semantic representation and computational characters.

Further research and experiments, such as the loose organization of Web applications, data security and mixture with different network programming language, are to be carried out to work out this approach's full potential in complex testing for E-learning Web services.

Acknowledgement

This work is funded by the National Natural Science Foundation of China (60703018; 61070013; 90818004), 973 Program (2007CB310800), 863 Program (2008AA01Z208; 2009AA01Z405), Open Fund Project of State Key Lab. for Novel Software Technology, Nanjing University, the Science and Technology Commission of Wuhan Municipality "Chenguang Jihua" (201050231058), and Doctoral Fund of Ministry of Education of China (20090181110053).

References

1. E-learning. Wikipedia (2010), http://en.wikipedia.org/wiki/E-learning
2. Web service. Wikipedia (2010), http://en.wikipedia.org/wiki/Web_service
3. Web Services Description Working Group. W3C (2010), http://www.w3.org/2002/ws/desc/
4. Service-oriented Architecture. Wikipedia (2010), http://en.wikipedia.org/wiki/Service-oriented_architecture
5. Tsai, W.T., Paul, R., Wang, Y., Fan, C.: Extending WSDL to Facilitate Web Services Testing. In: 7th IEEE International Symposium on High Assurance Systems Engineering, pp. 171–172 (2002)
6. Siblini, R., Mansour, N.: Testing Web Services. In: Proc. of IEEE International Conference on Computer Systems and Applications, pp. 135–143 (2005)
7. Bai, X.Y., Dong, W., Tsai, W.T., Chen, Y.N.: WSDL-Based Automatic Test Case Generation for Web Services Testing. In: Proc. of IEEE International Workshop on Service-Oriented System Engineering (SOSE 2005), pp. 215–220 (2005)
8. Jiang, Y., Xin, G.: A Web Service Method of Automatic Generation of Test Data. Journal of Computers 28(4), 568–577 (2005)
9. Sneed, H., Huang, S.: WSDLTest-A Tool for Testing Web Services. In: Proc. of the Eighth IEEE International Symposium on Web Site Evolution, pp. 14–21 (2006)
10. Noikajana, S., Suwannasart, T.: Web Service Test Case Generation Based on Decision Table. In: Proc.of the 8th International Conference on Quality Software, pp. 321–326 (2008)
11. Semantic Annotations for WSDL and XML Schema (SAWSDL). W3C (2010), http://www.w3.org/2001/sw/wiki/SAWSDL
12. Dai, G., Bai, X., Wang, Y., Dai, F.: Contract-Based Testing for Web Services. In: Proc. of IEEE International Computer Software and Applications Conference, pp. 517–526 (2007)
13. Wang, Y., Bai, X., Li, J., Huang, R.: Ontology-based Test Case Generation for Testing Web Services. In: Proc of the Eighth International Symposium on Autonomous Decentralized Systems, pp. 43–50 (2007)
14. Gogolla, M., Kuhlmann, M., Büttner, F.: A Benchmark for OCL Engine Accuracy, Determinateness, and Efficiency. In: MODELS 2008. LNCS, vol. 5301, pp. 446–459. Springer, Heidelberg (2010)

The Application of Moodle in Computer English Teaching

Yihai Chen[1,2] and Huaikou Miao[1,2]

[1] School of Computer Engineering and Science, Shanghai University, Shanghai 200072, China
[2] Shanghai Key Laboratory of Computer Software Evaluating and Testing, Shanghai 201112,China
{yhchen,hkmiao}@staff.shu.edu.cn

Abstract. With the rapid development of China's software outsourcing industry, it is essential for IT industry to recruit IT professionals with adequate English proficiency, which undoubtedly brings English for computer a booming era. But the current computer English teaching method is teacher-centered and is criticized as deaf and dump English. In view of the problems of traditional English teaching and the advantages of E-learning, the new published College English Curriculum Requirements proposes suggestions on using the Web as a medium to improve English teaching and learning in higher education. Moodle is one of the fastest growing free, open-source virtual learning environments. This paper mainly focuses on how Moodle can be effectively used in a college computer English teaching classroom. First of all, the current computer English teaching situation will be introduced. Next the reasons for choosing Moodle at our school are presented. Then the design and implementation of Moodle based computer English teaching environment will be introduced. Finally, the author concludes the paper and proposes future work.

Keywords: Moodle, CMS, blended-learning, computer English.

1 Introduction

During the past ten years, China software outsourcing industry is developing rapidly. According to the latest statistics provided by China's Ministry of Commerce, the contract value of China's software exports in 2009 reached 10.15 billion U.S. dollars, and the contract value of service outsourcing agreement reached 20.01 billion U.S. dollars [1]. It is estimated that till 2013, there will emerge 15000 new IT enterprises. However Chinese IT companies are now at the lowest ring of the world software outsourcing chain. One of the main reasons for this situation is that current university English education fails to provide large quantities of qualified software professionals with good English proficiency for the software outsourcing industry [2].

Specialized English for computer is widely taught in almost every Chinese computer school, some schools are also providing bilingual courses for students. However the great achievements in English teaching in recent years have been overshadowed by the gap between students' knowledge of English and their ability of

X. Luo et al. (Eds.): ICWL 2010 Workshops, LNCS 6537, pp. 169–176, 2011.

using English in real situations. The current English teaching at colleges and universities is test-oriented. Even the students can pass the CET-4 and has high score, students lack the English language abilities for IT industry. Their incompetence in English may reflect some weaknesses in specialized English for computer teaching.

With the rapid development of Internet and communication technology, computer assisted language teaching is getting more and more attention from educationists in China. The new issued College English Curriculum Requirements stipulates that, "The new model should be built on modern information technology, particularly network technology, so that English language teaching will be, to a certain extent, free from the constraints of time or place and geared towards students' individualized and autonomous learning."

The following paper is organized as follows: section 2 discusses the background information about the specialized English for computer course and introduces the theory of blended learning. Section three introduces our practice of using Moodle to build a computer English online teaching platform. The final section concludes the paper and proposes further work.

2 Course Objectives and Blended Learning

2.1 Course Background

The English education of a computer major student received at our school include two stages: In the first phase, is a general English learning through two years of study, students are required to pass the country English Test(CET) Band 4, some excellent students can pass CET 6. The second stage is to learn special English for computer, the learning objectives are: This course mainly aims at improving students' ability of studying computer and technology in English and using English to the course study, scientific research, academic exchange and cooperation, and business activities.

The course involves fundamental knowledge and development of the computer science and technology, and discusses some questions of computer science and technology related to society, economy, moral, ethic, law, and so on. Especial emphasis is placed in scientific research, academic exchange and cooperation, interview and presentation, software development and project management, etc, on English environment.

Over the years, the school of computer engineering and science has always focused on the importance of computer English teaching. As an elective course, because the course playing important role in student's academic learning, the course is welcomed by students. In addition our school also offers a course on Japanese for computer and three English-Chinese bilingual professional courses.

2.2 Difficulties Encountered

The first difficult we counter during the teaching process is lack suitable textbook for computer English teaching. Also there are many textbooks available on the market. Most of them focus on the English grammar and translation, so the requirements of other basic skills, such as listening, speaking and writing are not tackled. Moreover, the text materials are often out of date. Although we have attempted to provide some extracurricular materials on the school's Lefu online forum, the effect is not good as expected. The over stress of only reading and translation abilities make the class dull and boring. Thus the students lost interest in leaning computer English, they just think learning computer English is just memorize the key terms and vocabulary and doing English to Chinese translation. After complete the course, some students still can't master the basic frequently used computer terms and vocabulary, not even to mention how to apply computer English in real situations and using English as a tool to acquire new knowledge. Another difficulty is the teacher lack effective tools to monitor the students to finish their assignments. In addition, the teaching hour for computer English is only 30 hours, how to reach to the teaching objective of the course is a great challenge for the teacher.

2.3 Brief Introduction of Blended Learning

In recent years, blended learning is attracting more attentions in second language teaching as it incorporates the benefits of traditional teacher-centered classroom teaching and web-based learning. The approach of combining face to face instruction with computer mediated instruction is called blended learning. As an alternative to traditional face to face instruction, blended learning has been adopted by more and more educators and learners in recent years, and the trend towards blended learning systems will increase [3]. Some of the advantages blended learning includes: (1) Students can learn synchronically and asynchronically. (2)Blended Learning can satisfy learners' individualized needs and interest. (3) Students can acquire knowledge systematically and have opportunities to apply them. (4) Blended Learning can help develop learner autonomy. (5) Blended Learning provides more language input and output opportunities. (6) Blended Learning helps create a favorable and harmonious learning environment [4]. Considering the benefits of blended learning, so we are exploring blended learning approach in our computer English course.

3 Why Moodle

Moodle[5,6,7](abbreviation for Modular Object-Oriented Dynamic Learning Environment) is a free and open-source e-learning software platform, also known as a Course Management System, Learning Management System, or Virtual Learning Environment (VLE). As of September 2010 it had a user base of about 50 thousand registered and verified sites, serving 36.9 million users in 3.7 million courses. The localization of Moodle begin in December 2005. Li Ling coming from Beijing Institute of Technology initiated the Chinese Moodle project(cn-moodle)	since then Moodle is gaining its popularity among Chinese educators.

Moodle is a dynamic and powerful Learning Management System built on social constructionist pedagogy that supports the building of learning communities. Moodle encourages teachers to go beyond using the LMS as a file repository and instead to create opportunities for interactive collaboration that supports the development of learning resources. In the teaching process, teachers and students are equal entity, they can collaborate and work together to construct knowledge and solve the problems according to their experience.

Moodle has several features typical of an e-learning platform. Its rich course functions cover all the functions needed to support teaching and learning online. For example Forum, Choice, Resource, Lesson, Assignment, Glossary, Blog, Wiki, WebQuest etc. The teacher can upload learning materials in forms of Word document, Power Point presentation, Flash, Video and Audio in Resource module. The assessment function provided by Moodle allow teacher to provide detailed feedback to his students on specific areas of language performance. Moreover Moodle provides rich collection of plug-ins particular to facilitate English teaching. For example the FLAX[8](Flexible Language Acquisition) helps automate the production and delivery of practice exercises for learning English. Teacher can create exercises from the textual content of digital libraries. Gong[9] is a free system for voice communication on the Web. It allows groups of people such as students and teachers to participate in discussion groups using their computers, using both synchronous (real-time) and asynchronous chat. All these features make Moodle an ideal platform for language teaching.

4 The Design and Implementation of Moodle Based Computer English Teaching Environment

The realization of the learning environment design relies on the activity-modules supported in Moodle. In our current work, the GLOSSARY, FORUM, RESOURCE and QUIZ modules are selected. The design and implementation of Moodle based computer English teaching environment is discussed below.

4.1 Course Design

The book used in our current course is Computing Essentials [10]. The book mainly introduces the key concepts and terminologies related to computer and information technology. The main content include information technology, Internet, Web and electronic commerce, computer software and hardware, communication and networks, information system, system analysis and design, database, programming and languages etc. The course content is closed related to computer major; besides this book provide a Resource CD and a accompany web site to assistant student learning.

Moodle support three course formats, according to our teaching need, we select the Topics format. Each chapter in Computing Essential book is related to the corresponding topic in Moodle. The topic content is organized as follows: The first part is online learning section; the other is self assessment section. The online learning section is to supplement to teacher's class teaching, it contains the learning objectives of each chapter, chapter overview and online resources etc. The self assessment section contains the Listening Exercise, Choice & Matching Quiz, Crossword Puzzle, reading and writing exercise etc.

4.1.1 Vocabulary Learning

According to "The College English Curriculum Requirements", the vocabulary for higher demand should reached 6500 words and 1700 phrases. But there still a lot of special computer terminologies and abbreviations in computer English. Mastering the vocabulary and in particular the active vocabulary is basis to improve computer English language proficiency. There are several ways to use Moodle to assistant vocabulary learning. One is the Hot Potatoes[11], which is a free and easy to use quiz program, it enabling you to create interactive multiple-choice, short-answer, jumbled-sentence, crossword, matching/ordering and gap-fill exercises for the World Wide Web. Currently, we use it to design the crossword exercise for the students. The other Moodle activity used to support vocabulary learning is the Glossary. The Glossary in Moodle is used to provide the related words and phrases to the students.

In addition, the students can also make comments to the keywords and provide feedback by using the glossary rating facility. We have made the Chinese translation to all the keywords in the textbook. The interface of Moodle system, for glossary, is depicted in Figure 1.

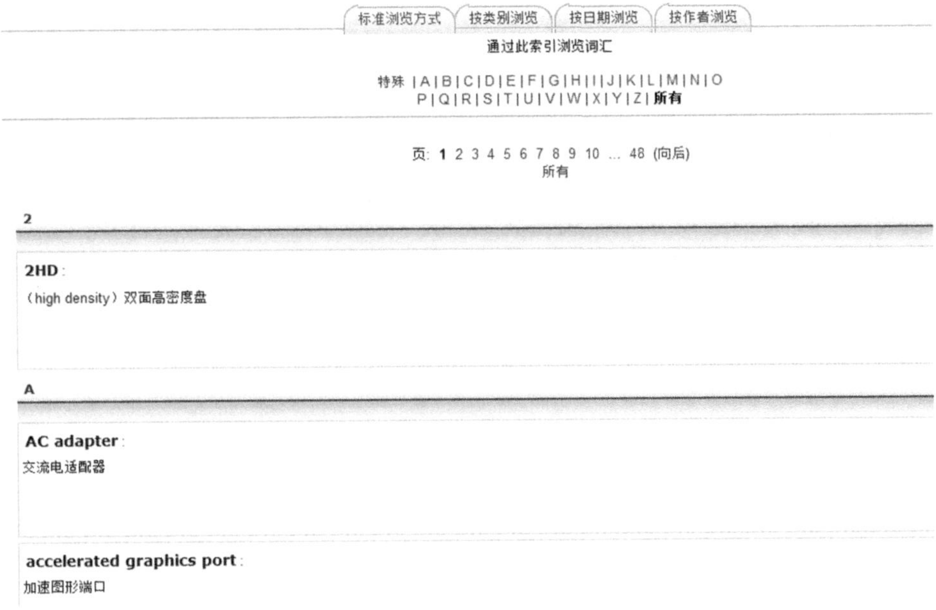

Fig. 1. The Moodle Glossary

4.1.2 Listening Compression Exercise

During the traditional computer English teaching process, subject to the limitations of the classroom and time constraints, listening compression exercise can hardly be tackled in classroom teaching. Using Moodle, students can listen to the recording and making online test to judge how well they understand the recording. Inserting audio recording in Moodle is rather simple. You can insert audio recording in the HTML instruction box using Moodle Flash player. In addition, the Quiz module can be used to help students test how well they understand the recording, after which they are likely to understand the whole recording better. Following figure show the gap-fill exercise for the Listening compression.

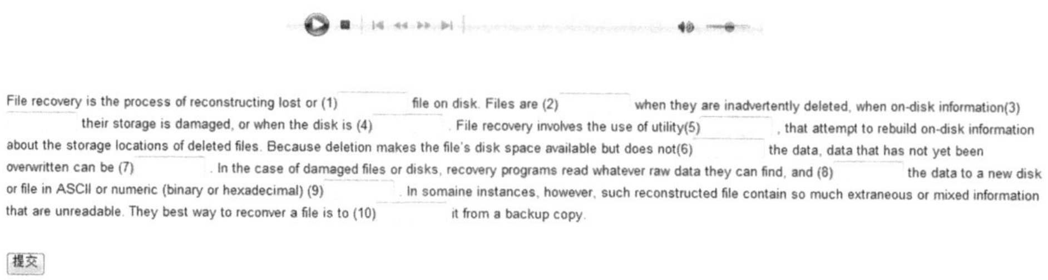

Fig. 2. The Gap-Fill Exercise

Besides the Gap-fill exercise, the Moodle also support reviewing recordings using Choice and Questionnaire.

4.1.3 Self Assessment Exercise

According to the teaching requirement of the Computing Essential textbook, each chapter provides some after class exercises. These exercises can be integrated into a small test. We use the Quiz module to provide the students text-related exercises to consolidate what they have learned from class. In the process of doing the quiz, the students can get immediate feedback of and hints on their work. After they complete the quiz, the scores of the whole quiz is presented on the screen, and the tutorial instruction of each item is also present, so that the students can go over what they have done and think over their learning reflectively. The interface of Moodle system, for self assessment, is depicted in Figure 3.

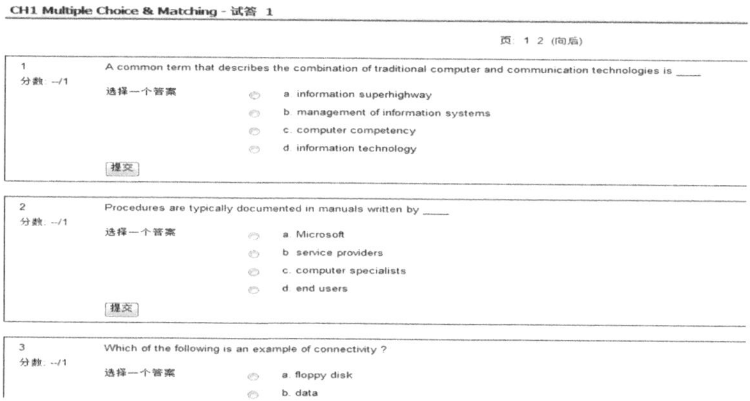

Fig. 3. The self assessment module

4.1.4 Writing and Translation

Writing and translation ability are another skills students should acquire. We use the Assignment activity to support writing and translation exercise. Moodle supports four types of assignments: upload a single file, advanced uploading files, online text and offline activity. For the English to Chinese translation, we use the 'Online text' assignment. Using this type assignment, we can edit the student's online text pages.

When the students clicks the on the assignment, he or she will the see the grade and compare the edited versions of their page with their original one. Every chapter in Computing Essential book has Web-related end-of-chapter exercises directing students to prepare and to write a one- or two-page paper on critical technology-related issues. Some questions require students to summarize and analyze select emerging technologies addressed in the chapter. We select the 'Upload a single file' assignment for the writing exercise. The due time is set for each assignment. As the students submitted their assignment, we can grade the student's submission.

5 Conclusions

Both theoretically and practically, teachers and researchers from home and abroad have made great efforts to study Moodle based English teaching and have achieved a lot. For example, John Brine et al.[12] reported using Moodle and other software tools in EFL courses in a Japanese IT university, Moodle was used to enhance EFL reading, writing and pronunciation courses. In university of Waikato, New Zealand, researchers are exploring using Moodle to provide academic literacy development for students [13]. Some Chinese researchers are also exploring using Moodle to assistant college English teaching[4, 14]. Above research work are close related to ours. But English for computer has its own characteristic and features. Currently the college English teaching is not gear to the needs of the IT outsourcing industry. More work need be done to formulate the knowledge points, vocabulary, textbook and syllabus for computer English course. We have constructed a web-based English Learning Environment to support teaching computer English. The system which builds on Moodle platform provides a self-contained computational environment in which students may carry out autonomous learning related to computer English course. This web-based learning environment has features to support computer English vocabulary learning, computer knowledge self assessment and self learning etc. The environment is also extensible and evolving. With the help of Moodle, new teaching materials and exercises can be added into the system easily. Currently, the system is used on trail basis; we are trying to incorporating more computer English learning materials into the system and put into use on more large scales. We envision seeking international cooperation and incorporating the Open Educational Resources [15] in our computer English course. Currently, we have only utilized small portion of Moodle functions, further works includes exploring how to utilize Moodle to assistant student to learn academic English writing.

Acknowledgment

This work is supported by National Natural Science Foundation of China(NSFC) under grant No.60970007, the Natural Science Foundation of Shanghai Municipality of China under Grant No.09ZR1412100, Project of Science and Technology Commission of Shanghai Municipality under Grant No. 10510704900 and Shanghai Leading Academic Discipline Project(Project Number: J50103) and Shanghai education committee fourth undergraduate education high land project.

References

1. Sina News, http://tech.sina.com.cn/it/2010-06-22/10144335550.shtml (June 22, 2010, in Chinese) (retrieved July 1, 2010)
2. Zhang, H.: The analysis of China's software outsourcing industry's demands for foreign language skills. Computer Education 9 (2009) (in Chinese)
3. Bonk, C.J., Graham, C.R. (eds.): Handbook of blended learning: Global perspectives, local designs. Pfeiffer Publishing, San Francisco (2005)
4. Yin, L.: An Empirical Study of Blended Learning in College English Education, Master thesis of Nanjing University of Aeronautics and Astronautics (March 2008)
5. Moodle definition, http://en.wikipedia.org/wiki/Moodle
6. Moodle Foundation. Moodle Version 1.9, http://moodle.org
7. Stanford, J.: Moodle 1.9 for second language teaching. Packt publishing (October 2009)
8. The Flax project homepage, http://flax.nzdl.org/greenstone3/flax
9. The Gong Project homepage, http://gong.ust.hk/index.html
10. O'Leary, T.J., O'Leary, L.I.: Computing Essentials 2008. McGraw-Hill, New York (2007)
11. Hot Potatoes Home Page, http://hotpot.uvic.ca/
12. Brine, J., Wilson, I., Roy, D.: Using Moodle and Other Software Tools in EFL Courses in a Japanese IT University. In: Proceedings of the 7th IEEE International Conference on Computer and Information Technology (2007)
13. Gilliver-Brown, K., Jonhson, E.M.: Academic literacy development:A multiple perspectives approach to blended learning. In: Proceedings of ascilite Aucklang (2009), http://www.ascilite.org.au/conferences/auckland09/.../gilliver-brown.pdf (retrieved from WWW)
14. Bai, X.: Moodle based environments for College English Learning, master thesis of University of Electronic Science and Technology of China (2008)
15. Open Educational Resources, http://www.oercommons.org/

A Web Services Matchmaking Engine for AFlow

Zhongwei Yang[1], Zhaoteng Song[1], Xin Li[1], Xinhuai Tang[1],
Xiaozhou Yuan[2], and Delai Chen[3]

[1] School of Software Engineering Shanghai Jiao Tong University Shanghai, China
yang_zhongwei@hotmail.com, songdragon@sjtu.edu.cn,
Shine.li@live.cn, tang-xh@cs.sjtu.edu.cn

[2] School of Mechanical and Dynamics Engineering Shanghai Jiao Tong University
Shanghai, China
Colin_yuan@hotmail.com

[3] Shanghai Key Lab of Advanced Manufacturing Environment
China Telecom Shanghai Branch
Shanghai, China
dlchen.2005@hotmail.com

Abstract. The web service composition plays more and more important role in SOA environment nowadays. Composing Web services on user's demand will prove to be essential. AFlow is such an automated web service composition system. In this paper, we first represent our separation model for web service modeling and give an overview to the AFlow. After giving web service definitions and matchmaking rules, we give the description of our web services matchmaking engine. Finally we give the analysis and give the experimental comparison, which shows our method has a better performance and scalability.

Keywords: matchmaking engine, web service composition, AFlow, workflow.

1 Introduction

Web services are self-contained, self-describing, modular applications that can be published, located, and invoked across the Web [1]. With a rapid development of internet technology, a large number of web services have been developed and deployed over the internet. However, it becomes more and more difficult to find a single web service to satisfy users' specific requests. Furthermore, the demand of quickly delivering new services becomes a business imperative today gradually. In order to solve these problems, the most common approach is to adopt Web Service Composition.

Service matchmaking is an important step to the process of Web Service Composition, and it needs formally representation of web service functionalities and non-functionalities. Currently, there are mainly two ways to describe a web service: Web Description Language [2] and Ontology Web Language for Service (OWL-S) [3]. However, matchmaking is often outside the representation capabilities of registries such as UDDI and WSDL. They are important but insufficient because matchmaking process based on these methods is taken place on the basis of keywords

X. Luo et al. (Eds.): ICWL 2010 Workshops, LNCS 6537, pp. 177–184, 2011.

but not semantic. So many of researchers have focused on semantic web since an advanced matchmaking facility requires the description of a web service to be only machine readable, but also machine understandable [4].

On the other hand, OWL-S is a markup language defined for facilitating the creation of web service ontology. It is designed to model a single web service. The main drawback of this approach is that OWL-S does not capture the notion of service type and instance, which will affect the performance and scalability of facilities in a Web Service Composition System.

The rest of this paper is organized as follows. In next section, we review our previous work: an extended OWL-S model for separating service type and instance and AFlow — and Web Service Composition System. In section 3, we describe the matchmaking process of the Service Matchmaking Engine in detail including the matchmaking rules. In section 4, we analyze this Matchmaking Engine and give the experimental report. Finally, Section 5 concludes our work.

2 Background

In this section, we first review the model which was extended the OWL-S for separating service type and instance; then we briefly review the automated web service composition system, AFlow.

2.1 Service Modeling

Many web services offer same functionalities, such as multiple flower shop services are all flower shops though they maybe offer different flower packages. This fact could be very useful for efficient representation of these services. Unfortunately, OWL-S does not capture the notion of types and instances.

So we introduced the separation model based on multi-type. This model separates the representation of web service type definitions from instance definitions according to the instance different functions. But the instance has a service type sequence instead of belonging to only one service type.

Thus we add Service Type class hierarchy to the Service hierarchy, as shown in Figure 1. According to this model, we can split the service registry into two parts: the type ontology and instance ontology.

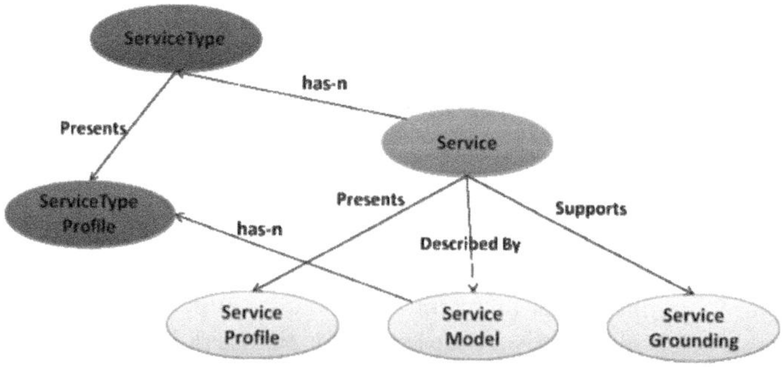

Fig. 1. Speration Model Based on Multi-Type

There are several benefits in our approach which was also described in our previous work. First, it is proven to be useful for organizing the expected thousands of web services. Second, by extracting services as a sequence of service types, it can not only reduce the planning domain scope to enhance the performance and efficiency of the planner, but also distinguish the service and a sequence of services which provide the same functions. Third, a new service, whose functions are the union of the existing service types' functions, needs to be added into the instance ontology, while the type ontology will not be affected.

2.2 Overview of AFlow

Aflow is an automated web service composition system which combines the AI Planning and workflow together based on the separation model above. It divided the web service composition into two phases. Thus, it consists of two parts: AI Planning Subsystem and Service Matchmaking Subsystem, as shown in Figure 2.

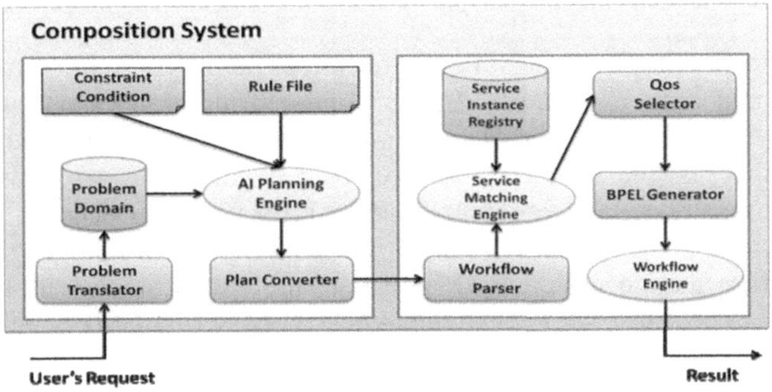

Fig. 2. The Overview Of Aflow

The AI Planning Subsystem takes the user's request as input, using an AI Planner to construct an Abstract Workflow which consists of a sequence of service types, and the Service Matchmaking Subsystem selects the most suitable web services according to this sequence of service types and execute via workflow engine.

The Service Matchmaking Engine is the core of Service Matchmaking Subsystem since it provides the functionality to bind proper service instances for workflow engine to execute, such as JBoss [5].

3 The Service Matchmaking Engine

Service matchmaking is often considered as the precondition of web service composition [4]. But service matchmaking takes place in the Service Matchmaking Subsystem of Aflow. At this stage, we will select the most suitable service instance to match the abstract workflow, generate an executable workflow described by BPEL and finally take it to execute, as shown in Figure 3.

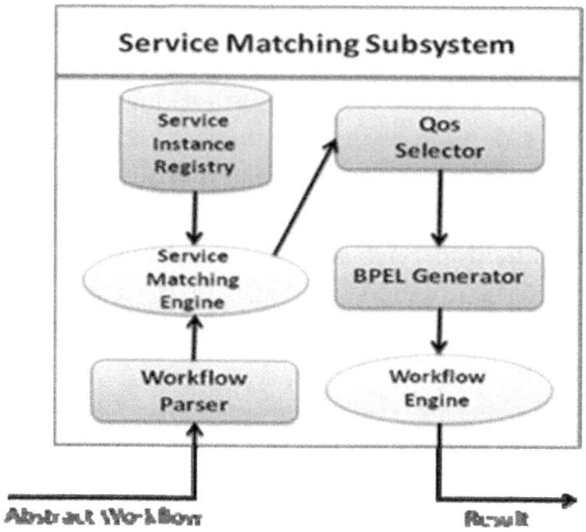

Fig. 3. Servive Matchingmaking Subsystem

For a matchmaking process, there are three parts: service consumer, service provider and matchmaking facility. In our approach, the service consumer is the AI Planner Subsystem. It sends the abstract workflow to the matchmaking engine. The service provider is the service instance ontology, which provides the enough information for matchmaking engine to bind the proper web services.

Thus, the process of bind the proper services is the matchmaking engine receive the abstract workflow and generate the BPEL according to the instance ontology.

Before discussing the whole matchmaking process of our service matchmaking engine, we first give related assumptions, definitions and rules.

3.1 Web Service Definition

Definition 1: Web Service Type (WST) = <I,O,P,E,T>, Where I, O, P, E, describing input, output, precondition and effect of service, are functional property of service. T is service type, which owns a unique identifier. A particular service instance can own multiple service types, and vice versa. Web service type, describing the function of service, can reduce the quantity of service in composition phase and accelerate the progress.

In the process of service instance registration, service suppliers choose service types existed or create a new service type.

Definition 2: Abstract Workflow (AW) = < Composite-service-name, Description, WS-nodes, IN, OUT >, Where WS-nodes is a partial ordering set. An abstract workflow node corresponds with a service type.

Definition 3: C (T) is the set of case of service type T.

Definition 4: Equivalence. In a service type sequence $STS=\{ST_1,ST_2,ST_3...ST_m\}$, which is a POset, $A=\{ST_1,ST_2,ST_3...ST_n\}(n<m)$, $B=\{ST_{n+1},ST_{n+2},ST_{n+3}...ST_m\}$,

$C=\{ST_1, ST_2, ST_3...ST_j\}(j < m \cap j \neq n)$ and $D = \{ST_{j+1}, ST_{j+2}, ST_{j+3}...ST_m\}$ all are subsets of STS. Sequence <A,B> and sequence <C,D> are equivalence iff when A, B, C and D each stands for a service instance.

Definition 5: P(T) is the subset of POset T and the first element in P(T) is the same as in T.

3.2 Matchmaking Assumption

A registered web service with multiple service types is considered as atom service maintained by a provider. And the service's availability is better than atom services having the same function after composited. Hence, the former is a better choice, and we give it a higher priority.

3.3 Matchmaking Rules

Steps of matchmaking rules using in our engine are as follows:

Step 1: Eviscerate all service types in WS-nodes, get partial ordering set WST, and the number of service type is n.

Step 2: Init the variables ($k = n$, $m = n$, $RWST = \varphi$, $T_0 = \varphi$).

Step 3: If $k>1$, $WS=C(T_m)$, $m = m - 1$, execute step 4); otherwise, execute step 6.

Step 4: If $WS \cap C(T_m)$ is not φ, $WS = WS \cap C(T_m)$, $m = m - 1$, execute step 4; if $WS \cap C(T_m)$ equals φ, execute step 5.

Step 5: If $WST = WST - \cup Ti$ ($i=k, k+1 ... m+1$), $k = m$, $RWST = RWST \cup <WS>$, execute step 3).

Step 6: If every element of RWST is a single-element set, the matching progress ends. Cases matched are recorded and part executable workflow is generated; otherwise, execute QoS matching.

Assumption. ST_xstands for a service type, while S_x is a service instance. Planning result is {ST1, ST2, ST3...STn}, the optimal result is OR = { S1, S2, S3, ... Sk}, and the result obtained from the above algorithm is $R = \{ S_1', S_2', S_3'... S_m'\}$.

Proof. Apply transformation to R as follow:

From S1' or Sm', if P(S1') is a service instance and (S1'- P(S1')) $\cup$P(S2') is another service instance, then split the S_1' as $P(S_1')$ and $S_1'- P(S_1')$.

Repeat the transformation, the partial order set (POset) R can convert to its equivalent POSets $ER= \{ S_1'', S_2'', S_3''... S_l'' \}$.

When there are three or more service instances in R, set AR contains all equivalent sets to R after the above transformation. Each element in AR satisfies any condition as follow:

a) l=m, the R is an optimal result;
b) l<m, the R is also an optimal result;
c) l>m, for three adjacent service instance, the transformation result is at least two service instance, so $m \geq (2n/3)$. Hence, the matching algorithm has two competitive ratio.

3.4 QoS Matching

QoS, referring to a Web Service's ability to meet customers, is the key for Web Services to success in business [6]. This paper mainly uses guild line made by International Standards Organizations for QoS (cost, time, availability, reliability). QoS for Service Matching is calculated as follows;

$$Q=(Q_{ai}*W_{ai} + Q_{ri}*W_{ri})/(Q_{ci}*W_{ci} * Q_{ti}*W_{ti}) \quad (1)$$

Q is availability and reliability in unit time and unit cost. Choose the Web Service instance corresponding to max value of Q as matching result. In formula (1), I is the ith Web service in the set of web service instance. Meanwhile, Q_a is availability index, and Q_r is reliability index, and Q_c is cost of service, Q_t is execution time of service. W_a, W_r, W_c, W_t are weights of Q_a, Q_r, Q_c, Q_t.

3.5 Matchmaking Process

Figure 4 depicts the whole matchmaking process as follows:

a) Matchmaking of Service Instance

This Web Services Matchmaking Engine accesses the Service Instance Registry and selects the most suitable service instance to bind.

If there is only one result, this matchmaking engine will transfer this result to BPEL Generator directly; otherwise, the matchmaking engine will transfer the results into the QoS Selector to select the service instances which have the highest performances and give the match result to BPEL Generator.

b) Generating of Executable Workflow and Executing it

The BPEL generator will receive the match result to produce an executable workflow described by BPEL, which is deployed onto a workflow engine (such as JBoss [5]) later to execute it.

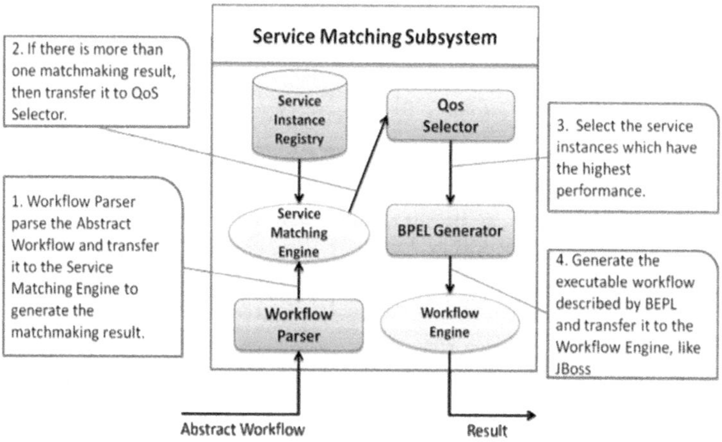

Fig. 4. Matchingmaking Process

4 Analysis and Experimental Evaluations

4.1 Analysis

We choose three aspects to analyze the performance of this matchmaking engine. They are precision, recall and executing time.

In precision, this engine's final results are the best performance of the matched services and the system matched the services based on the complete IOPE. As a result, these result services must be consistent with the users' request. So the system's precision is 100%. While, this causes that some similar result will be dropped, because we defines one service type has its own IOPE. Thus the recall is lower.

The matching's time is also less than the similar matching model. That's because we defines the atomic service as one type, which decreases the number of types and this system needn't to match all the service instances. So this executing time is much shorter and it grows slowly. Here we choose the OWL-S Matcher to make a compare. This is the compare below.

4.2 Experimental Evaluations

In our simulated experimental, we choose the OWL-S Matcher to make a compare.

All the tests have been performed on Intel Core2 Duo 1.66GHz, with 2 GB of RAM under the Windows XP operating system.

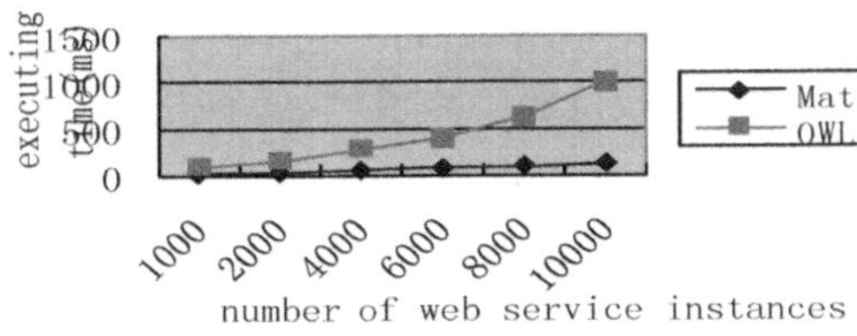

Fig. 5. The evaluation of Matchmaking Engine to OWL-S Matcher

In Figure 5, the X axis denotes the number of web service instances, and the Y axis shows the executing time. With the growing of the number of service instances, the OWL-S Matcher's time increases remarkably. However, this system's time grows with the number of service types. Since the number of type grows slowly, the executing time of this system increase slowly too.

5 Conclusion

In this paper we have proposed a web services matchmaking engine for AFlow, which is an automated web service composition system. We first represent our separation model for web service modeling and give an overview to the AFlow. Then we give the description of our web services matchmaking engine, including the web service definitions, matchmaking assumptions and matchmaking rules. Finally, we analyze this matchmaking engine and give the experimental results of our work by comparing to other matchmaking engine. The result shows that our web services matchmaking engine has better performances and scalability to large number of web services.

However, there are still some limitations in our web service matchmaking engine. First, there is more work to maintain the relationship between the service type and service instance. Second, to improve performance, AFLOW stops matchmaking once it finds a right service instance to bind. However the rest candidate service instances may contain a better choice, and there may be more than one appropriate result of matchmaking. We would like to refine AFLOW further, and consider these two problems as our future work.

References

1. Sirin, E.: Automated Composition of Web Services using AI Planning Techniques [EB/OL] (2004), http://www.cs.umd.edu/Grad/scholarlypapers/papers/aiplanning.Pdf
2. Chinnici, R., Moreau, J., Ryman, A., et al.: Web Services Description Language (WSDL) 2.0 (2007), http://www.w3.org/TR/wsdl20/
3. OWL-S: Semantic Markup for Web Services (November 2003), http://www.daml.org/services/owl-s/1.0/owl-s.html
4. Sun, S., Tang, X.: A Symmetric Matchmaking Engine for Web Service Composition. In: 15th International Conference on Parallel and Distributed Systems (2009)
5. JBoss JBPM WS-BPEL Runtime User Guide. Introduction to jBPM BPEL (2008), http://docs.jboss.com/jbpm/bpel/v1.1/userguide/introduction.html
6. Yq, J.G., Yin, S.: Web Service Composition Method Based on OWL. IEEE, Los Alamitos (2008)
7. Business Process Execution Language for Web Services (2007), http://www.ibm.com/developrworks/library/specification/ws-bpel/
8. Li, L., Horrocks, I.: A Software Framework For Matchmaking Based on Semantic Web Technology. In: Proceedings of WWW 2003, Budapest, Hungary (May 2003)
9. Paolucci, M., Kawamura, T., Payne, T.R., Sycara, K.: Semantic Matching of Web Services Capabilities. Springer, Heidelberg (2002)
10. Facciorusso, C., Field, S., Hauser, R., et al.: A Web Services Matchmaking Engine for Web Services. Springer, Heidelberg (2003)

A Mobile Course Coordinator System

Youngseok Lee[1], Jungwon Cho[2,*], Seungdo Jeong[3],
Sungjae Han[1], and Byung-Uk Choi[1]

[1] Department of Electronics Computer Engineering, Hanyang University,
17 Haengdang-dong, Sungdong-gu, Seoul, 133-791 Korea
{yslee38,sjhans,buchoi}@hanyang.ac.kr
[2] Department of Computer Education, Jeju National University,
66 Jejudaehakno, Jeju-si, Jeju-do, 690-756 Korea
jwcho@jejunu.ac.kr
[3] Department of Information & Communication Engineering, Hanyang Cyber University,
17 Haengdang-dong, Sungdong-gu, Seoul, 133-791 Korea
sdjeong@hycu.ac.kr

Abstract. The rapid progress of IT technologies has enabled users to access 'any service, anytime, anywhere', and wireless Internet services have enabled users to access Internet services even while traveling. Cellular phones have evolved to smart phones, and act as computers. Users can now access service categories that offer new possibilities and which are accessed and used in ways different from traditional services anytime, anywhere. Previous academic administration management systems had migrated from wired to wireless technology but were restricted to specific equipment, as such systems were not based on industry standards. The course coordinator plays a significant role in managing the curriculum and counseling students on academic matters, with a view to fostering their academic progress. However, the coordinator does not have the time to advise individual students on the details of which fields and courses they should pursue. This paper proposes a mobile course coordinator system (MCCS) to help students to choose and access the courses necessary for their major fields of study. When students apply, the MCCS recommends the most suitable subjects, using an inference engine that considers not only course sequences but also the student's information. The performance of the MCCS in tests was very good, coinciding 89.5% of the time with an expert's recommendations. In particular, our method was more effective than the Intelligent Online Academic Management System (IOAMS) in related research. Students can use their personal cellular phones to track their courses and receive course recommendations from the MCCS.

1 Introduction

The requirement for mobile data access is increasing as the amount of information available on the Internet grows. Today's web applications are designed for a wide range of target devices ranging from mobile phones to web browsers in PC environments.

* Corresponding author.

X. Luo et al. (Eds.): ICWL 2010 Workshops, LNCS 6537, pp. 185–194, 2011.

The availability of mobile services presents new opportunities and challenges for service users and service providers. Users can access services that offer new possibilities and methods that differ from traditional services. Service providers creating value-added mobile services face challenges during the development stage because they must adapt services to new devices and media.

Universities offer a wide selection of courses to students studying in various fields; however this has generated several unintended problems. Students may choose a course based on the reputation of the professor, the course time, the course difficulty, or other factors that are not directly related to a specific field of study. Although they may achieve the required number of credits to graduate, the breadth of knowledge that they acquire may not equip them well for the professional world that they face after graduation [1, 2]. To address this problem, guidance professors should check students' study majors and recommend suitable courses or subjects. However, delivering this assistance to students is not an easy task.

In this paper we propose a Mobile Course Coordinator System (MCCS) that focuses on the relation between course categories and students' preferences when it comes to subject recommendation. The MCCS has been developed to recommend suitable subjects to individual students, taking into consideration courses already taken, with the aim of maximizing students' professional foundation. We analyzed senior student participants to evaluate the performance of the proposed system, and examined the number of participants who took the subjects recommended. Thus, we were able to analyze the proportion of lectures accessed that were appropriate to individual subject fields.

2 Review of Pertinent Literature

2.1 Course Coordinators

Course coordinators create and manage course curricula. They are appointed from the group of senior lecturers, associate professors, and professors belonging to the faculty. Coordination of a registered degree course is the responsibility of one particular course coordinator who is responsible to the head of the academic unit offering the course [3]. The appointment of course coordinators enhances inter- and intra-faculty course coordination. A course coordinator's role includes the following [3]:

- developing and monitoring efforts for continuous course improvement, and reporting on course improvement projects to the faculty advisory committee through the department head;
- determining appropriate course plans (in consultation with department heads, study center directors, and other coordinators) for students transferring to the course from another course or institution, once exemptions and credits have been determined;
- counseling students on academic matters and encouraging their progress in the course;
- providing appropriate information on the course, and promoting the quality and range of students enrolled in the course;

- ensuring that student enrollments conform with the course structure and prerequisites, and that students have met all course requirements before being certified eligible for graduation;
- negotiating teaching allocations for the course with relevant department heads and center directors;
- providing leadership in the course development and approval process.

2.2 Related Works

The Intelligent Online Academic Management System (IOAMS) is an intelligent web-based system, which offers an effective tool for the higher education sector. It is designed to provide academic advice and to monitor progress [4]. It provides functions such as automated enrollment, tracking of enrollment variations, providing academic advice based on students' personal profiles and interests, creating study plans for students according to current stage of progress, calculating credits, and final sign off from the institution. The system contains a powerful inference engine based on Resolution with Partial Intersection and Truncation (PT resolution) [5]. It periodically updates its database from the university's student administration system. There is a course finder that recommends suitable courses, based on the prospective student's field of interest, military merit, and career history [6].

A course recommendation system is used to provide students with suggestions when they have trouble choosing courses. One such system has been designed [1]. That particular study presented a system based on the Prediction Methodology proposed [7]. To adapt teaching to individual abilities in the distance learning environment, it used a method to construct personalized courseware by building a personalized web tutor tree, and mining both the context and structure of the notion of similarity. It included the Naïve Algorithm for tutor topic trees, and level_generate Algorithms to generate web tutor topic of K+1 levels, as well as experimental results [7].

The course coordinator should check students' study majors and recommend suitable courses or subjects. However, delivering this assistance to students is not an easy task. So, the MCCS has been developed to recommend suitable subjects to individual students, taking into consideration courses already taken, with the aim of maximizing students' professional foundation.

3 System Design and Implementation

3.1 Recommendation Algorithms for MCCS

Step 1: The importance of certain subjects in all fields

The recommendation algorithm displays the importance of a subject when considered in the context of all fields in the department. The relevant term is the one that applies to the courses taken.

$$wField_j = \sum_{i=1}^{n} C(i, j) \quad (1 \le j \le m) \tag{1}$$

i: Field index j: Index of optional subjects available in relevant term
n: The number of relevant fields in the faculty
m: The number of optional subjects
C(i, j): The importance of each subject in each field
Compulsory and core subjects: 4 points
Subjects that are to be encouraged: 2 points General subject: 1 point

If a subject's value is high, MCCS will determine that it is an important subject in its field. This classification is useful for making recommendations when information about which fields are the most suitable for a particular student is lacking. Table 1 shows the lectures that students in the third grade have taken and Table 2 shows an example of the first step of the recommendation algorithm for the second semester in the third grade.

Table 1. Subjects that students in third grade have taken

Term	Subjects
Second grade: first semester	Circuit Theory, Electromagnetism, Electrical and Electronic Instrumentation
Second grade: second semester	Signals and Systems, Internet Programming
Third grade: first semester	Computer Architecture, Electronic Circuits

Table 2. Example of the first step of the recommendation algorithm

Subject	Fields						$wField_j$	Rank
	Signal processing	Com-munication	Energy & Controls	Com puter	High-frequency	Semi-conductor		
Computer Networks	2	4	2	4	1	1	14	3
Antenna Engineering	2	1	1	1	4	1	10	2
Control Engineering	2	1	4	1	1	1	10	2
Algorithms	1	1	1	4	1	1	9	1
Quantum Optoelectronics	1	1	1	1	4	1	9	1
Energy Conversion Devices	1	1	4	1	1	1	9	1
Electric System Controls	1	1	4	1	1	1	9	1

Step 2: The importance of the connectivity of each subject

The recommendation algorithm displays the importance of prerequisite subjects, considering the relevant fields in the department. Relevant fields are those that apply to the courses taken.

$$w\Pr erequisite_j = \frac{\sum_{i=1}^{n} CCP_i}{\sum_{i=1}^{n} PCP_i} \quad (1 \leq j \leq m) \tag{2}$$

i: Field index j: Index of optional subjects available in relevant term
n: The number of relevant departments m: The number of optional subjects
CCP_i: Completed subject points PCP_i: Prerequisite subject points
Essential prerequisite subject: 1 point
Optional relevant prerequisite subject: 0.5 point

If a subject has a particularly high value, MCCS determines whether the student has accumulated a certain amount of knowledge about that subject. MCCS then estimates whether a given subject is suitable for the student.

Step 3: The importance of the recommended fields
The recommendation algorithm displays the importance of recommended fields in the department. In other words, the algorithm indicates which fields in the user's faculty are the most appropriate.

$$wSuitability_j = \frac{\sum_{i=1}^{n} \sum_{k=1}^{Ci} CP(i,k)}{\sum_{i=1}^{n} \sum_{k=1}^{Fi} FP(i,k)} \quad (1 \leq j \leq m) \tag{3}$$

i: Field index j: Index of optional courses in the relevant term
n: The number of relevant departments m: The number of optional subjects
k: Subject index of specific fields
F_i: The number of subject fields until previous semester or grade
C_i: The number of subject fields completed by the previous semester or grade
FP: Fields point CP: Complete point
The core subject: 1 point Subjects to be encouraged: 0.5 points

This value indicates the fields in the department that are the most suitable for the student. Each course is organized by considering a subject tree; the tree of recommended subjects and which subjects have or have not been completed. Because each user has a user profile, the algorithm's recommendations are customized to individual users.

Step 4: Recommends suitable subjects
Finally, the recommendation algorithm recommends suitable subjects.

$$w_{sum\ j} = Rank(wField_j) + Rank(w\Pr erequisite_j) + Rank(wSuitabukuty_j) \tag{4}$$

MCCS assigns the rank in each part of the algorithm based on a weighting, such as a first-order subject is k rank points, a second-order subject is k-1 rank points, a third-order subject is k-2 rank points, and the remainder are converted to 0 points. The final values are summed and the choices are presented to the user in descending order.

3.2 Implementation Results

Figure 1 shows the results of the interface implemented on a cellular phone. The system provides menus once the user login has been completed. This system works through the response to menus. If a student selects the "Information" menu, he or she can view and update basic user information. The "Apply Lectures" menu displays courses in which the student is already enrolled; he or she can cancel them if so wished. If the user wishes to take a course, he or she selects from a specific field and then a course tree. The "Score" menu shows credits and grades for every term. The "Timetable" menu shows lecture times and classrooms.

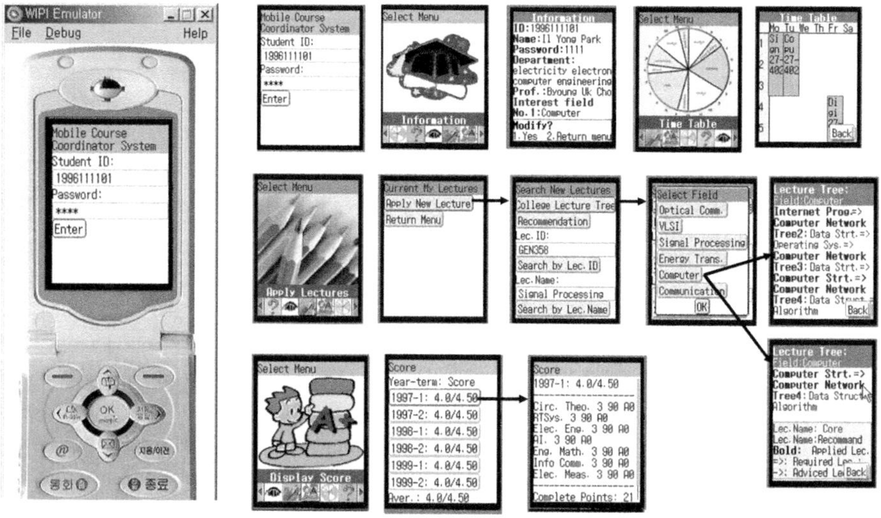

Fig. 1. Cellular phone interface

4 System Evaluation and Relevance Analysis

4.1 System Analysis

Table 3 shows a comparison of MCCS with EzHub[8], IOAMS[4], and CourseFinder[6]. MCCS allows convenient user mobility, so that students can access the faculty information system through the wireless internet services. Existent course coordinators' functions are considered profession and interest field that player subject and individual do by target. If existent course coordinator system select interest field, it is lack to estimate suitable subject.

However, MCCS identifies a field using a course tree and individual course enrollment information and then presents appropriate curriculum information to individual learners by composing a reasoning engine on the basis of the course tree, the student's record of courses taken, the relative importance of individual subjects and relation of major/minor subjects. Thus, MCCS presents appropriate course and subject selections to facilitate individualized learning.

Table 3. Comparison with other faculty systems

Functions \ Kinds of System	MCCS	ezHub	IOAMS	Course-Finder
User Mobility	O	△	△	X
Guidance major subject of User	O	X	△	△
Display Course Tree	O	O	X	O
Consideration of user preference	O	X	O	O

4.2 System Evaluation

To evaluate the effectiveness of the system presented in this paper, we conducted a survey of 214 senior students and 18 graduate students in the Electrical Engineering Department of Hanyang University. Two professors with experience as course coordinators were selected as curriculum experts. MCCS recommended options for majors on the basis of the tree of courses already taken. In the case of students in the first semester of the fourth grade, they were able to select the subjects that they wanted to take in the following term.

First, among the weak point of faculty, because it is difficult to do systematic subject selection about a major field, table 4 shows the result of correspondence analysis between the recommendation result of the system and course taken.

Table 4. The number of course taken within a system recommendation subject order

Term \ The order of priority	1st	2nd	3rd	4th	5th	6th
Second grade: first semester	199	93	32	201	-	-
Second grade: second semester	179	172	-	-	-	-
Third grade: first semester	153	49	68	108	-	-
Third grade: second semester	90	95	41	41	-	-
Fourth grade: first semester	47	58	117	34	36	20
Fourth grade: second semester	100	79	28	27	19	-

According to the result of an attending lecture requisition of a second term of three year, students could select 4 subjects. About subject that system presents, 90 students who take a course 1st order recommendation subject, 2nd orders 95 students, 3rd orders 41 students, it was not more in 4th orders 41 people. If there was course coordinator system that recommend course and inform student's major field, then they will be able to learn about a major field.

For the 18 graduate students, Table 5 shows the relationship between the subjects recommended by the curriculum experts and those recommended by the system.

Table 5. The relationship between subjects recommended by the curriculum expert and those recommended by the proposed system

Term	Student No.1	···	Student No.18	Average
Second grade: second semester	100.0%	···	100.0%	94.4%
Third grade: first semester	66.7%	···	66.7%	78.2%
Third grade: second semester	100.0%	···	66.7%	87.0%
Fourth grade: first semester	100.0%	···	100.0%	94.4%
Fourth grade: second semester	100.0%	···	50.0%	97.4%
Total	92.3%	···	76.9%	89.5%

The degree of conformity between subjects recommended by curriculum experts and those recommended by MCCS averaged 89.5%. Therefore, MCCS functions well as a course coordinator; it not only helps with course-selection choices but also improves the proportion of courses taken that are relevant to each student's major field, thus helping students to accumulate knowledge in their major field.

To analyze the performance of the proposed system, it was compared with the Intelligent Online Academic Management System (IOAMS) [4]. Students deciding their courses for the second semester of the fourth grade completed a survey, and a course

Table 6. Comparison of accuracies of the proposed system (MCCS) and IOAMS (%)

System Student	The Proposed System (MCCS)	IOAMS
No. 1	88.1	88.1
No. 2	83.3	45.8
No. 3	95.2	80.9
No. 4	78.6	59.5
No. 5	95.2	80.9
No. 6	83.3	91.7
No. 7	94.4	63.9
No. 8	100.0	42.9
No. 9	93.3	86.6
No. 10	94.4	36.1
No. 11	94.4	66.7
No. 12	88.1	78.6
No. 13	95.2	80.9
No. 14	100.0	80.9
No. 15	86.1	58.3
No. 16	95.2	42.8
No. 17	100.0	94.4
No. 18	72.2	44.4
Average	91.4	67.1

coordinator recommended subjects. After the proposed system and IOAMS had also recommended subjects, the accuracy of selection relative to that of the course coordinator was examined. A comparison of the performance of the proposed system and that of IOAMS is shown in Table 6.

The average accuracy of the proposed system was 91.4%, whereas that of IOAMS was 67.1%. In most cases, the proposed system matched students with subjects better that IOAMS. However, in the case of student No. 6, the performance of IOAMS was better than that of the proposed system. Student No. 6 was simultaneously attending lectures in subjects that were and were not in the subject tree. The proposed system recommended subjects adaptively, but IOAMS recommended subjects based on the first configured field. The proposed system can diagnose and recommend appropriate subjects for students, which is usually the role of a course coordinator.

5 Conclusion and Discussion

Faculty systems provide opportunities for students to make informed selections of academic courses from a broad range of fields. This has meant that students, generally, did not acquire expert knowledge in any particular field of the kind that is expected of a graduate student. The course coordinator plays a significant role in building and managing curricula, and counseling students about these items. However, the course coordinator does not have the time to advise individual students on which fields of study are suitable and which courses they should take. A number of academic administration management systems set up previously have offered the function of tailoring personal curricula for individual students. These systems have a very large knowledge base and infer courses using students' subjective data.

This paper has proposed a mobile course coordinator system to help students select course majors. The system has an inference engine that considers not only course trees, which hold information about courses in every field, but also personal courses that students have already taken. The system has an inference engine that considers not only course trees that hold information about available courses in all fields but also personal histories of the courses those students have already taken. The system acts as a substitute for a course coordinator in the role of counseling students. Students are able to keep track of their courses by using their cell phones, anytime and anywhere, and to improve their overall knowledge by taking the courses that the system's inference engine has recommended.

References

1. Chu, K., et al.: Designing a Course Recommendation System on Web based on the Students Course Selection Records. In: Kommers, Richards, G. (eds.) Proceedings of World Conference on Educational Multimedia, Hypermedia and Telecommunications, pp. 14–21 (2003)
2. Dabner, N., Davis, N.E.: Developing best practices in online teaching and learning to impact students and their organisations. In: Proceedings ascilite Auckland (2009), http://www.ascilite.org.au/conferences/auckland09/procs/dabner-poster.pdf (retrieved January 2010)
3. Queensland University of Technology, Manual of Policies and Procedures, Chapter B - Human resources, http://www.mopp.qut.edu.au/B/B_03_05.html

4. Ivanto, I.J., et al.: Intelligent Online Academic Management System. In: Zhou, W., Nicholson, P., Corbitt, B., Fong, J. (eds.) ICWL 2003. LNCS, vol. 2783, pp. 320–326. Springer, Heidelberg (2003)
5. Liu, F., Moore, D.H.: GOPT-Resolution and Its Applications. In: Proceedings of the Eighth International Conference on Artificial Intelligence Applications, pp. 9–14 (1996)
6. La Trobe University, Course Finder, `http://www.latrobe.edu.au/courseDB/courseFinder/courseFilter.jsp`
7. Changjie, T., et al.: Personalized courseware construction based on Web data mining. In: Proceedings of the First International Conference on Web Information Systems Engineering, pp. 204–211 (2000)
8. Hanyang University, EzHub, `http://ezhub.hanyang.ac.kr`

A Research of the Internet Based on Web Information Extraction and Data Fusion

Yajun Jiang, Zaoliang Wu, Zengrong Zhan, and Lingyu Xu

School of Information Engineering, Guangzhou Panyu Polytechnic College,
No.1342, Shiliang Road, Panyu District, 511483 Guangzhou, P.R. China
{jiangyj,zhanzr}@gzpyp.edu.cn,
{wzl,xly}@shu.edu.cn

Abstract. This paper proposes a strategy to personalized the Internet searching, which would help to filter, extract and integrate the massive information from the web based on the specific user requirements in the hopes that it can relieve them from the tedious process of manually selecting and retrieving the relevant information as well as the confusion caused by the inconsistencies of the information. The strategy proposed in this paper has been applied to the searching of the laptop product information and the result shows a much less human effort involved and a much more accurate price range.

Keywords: Internet, Search, Information Extraction, Intelligent Search, Information Fusion.

1 Introduction

The emergence of the search engine makes it possible to quickly extract the information that the user needs from the massive ocean of information on the Internet. The search engine employs certain strategies to understand, organize and process the information it discovers and extracts from the web so that it can provide the users with the search service they need to navigate through the Internet. According to the statistics, 90% of the Internet users nowadays use search engine to find the information they want. Search engine is the key technology in the world of Information extraction and it has become the key for opening the gate of the Internet. It plays a positive role in the acceleration of the information exchange and the appreciation of the value of information [1].

Though search engine has solved the problem of retrieving hard-to-find information from the massive Internet, and offers an efficient way to help the user to find the information they need. It is not satisfactory in terms of the resource coverage, search accuracy, results visualization, specialization, and maintainability [2][3]. Generally speaking, the shortcomings of the search engine available today are: large scale and distributed sources of information; quality of the information; lack of coverage of the dynamic web pages; heterogeneous sources of information; problem of faithful expression; duplication of the search results.

The limitation of the search engine makes the results unsatisfactory to fulfil user's requirement. As most of us have experienced, when we search the price for a certain

X. Luo et al. (Eds.): ICWL 2010 Workshops, LNCS 6537, pp. 195–206, 2011.

model of laptop in the search engine, we would probably get tens of thousands of links, with many of them irrelevant and duplicated. Even for the useful ones, the amount of information might make it impractical for us to manually check and compare them one by one in order to get a panoramic view. If the users are forced to make the random selection of the available information, it might lead to the wrong perception towards the laptop prices.

Therefore, the service that the users urgently need is how to accelerate the extraction of the product information so that they can be accumulated and compared in real time.

The authors of this paper want to take advantage of the existing information extraction and fusion technology to process the search results, hoping that the computer will be enabled to automatically extract and fuse the product information and provide the end users with a relatively trustworthy and complete view of all the available information. This will save tremendous amount of human effort and increase the extent of the automatic information extraction.

To retrieve product information, especially the price information from the search engine, and then select and fuse the relevant information before getting back a trustworthy answer to the end user is one of the latest and challenging research areas. The authors of this paper believed that the research based on the extraction and fusion of the product information got the directly from the web is the newer fusion technology. It has two aspects: one is the research of the extraction of product information; another is the research of the fusion of product information. In the following passages, the technology and current research status of these two aspects will be briefly discussed.

The extraction of the product information is carried out by the IE (Information Extraction) system. IE technology was developed in the late 1980s with the intention of finding relevant information in the navy database, thanks to the emergence of the Internet and MUC (Message Understanding Conference) which is sponsored by DARPA (the Defence Advanced Research Projects Agency, DARPA) [4].

The main functionality of the web IE system is to extract the specific factual information. For instance, to extract the details of the terrorist incidents from the news portals, like the location, time, terrorists, victims, attacking target, weapons used, etc.

The relatively mature Web IE systems available outside China right now include WHISK [5], STALKER [6-9], BYU [10], RoadRunner [11], etc. WHISK system is suitable not only for the structural, semi-structural text but also for the free text. Structural and semi-structural text is primarily used to locate the interested information based on the analysis of the context. STALKER takes the sample page tagged by the user and the structural meta information provided by the user in the form of embedded catalogue tree, applies the sequential covering algorithm to recursively generate the delimiter-based accurate extraction rules so that the multi-layer information extraction can be made possible. The approach that BYU system takes is based on the ontology methodology. RoadRunner system compares the structure of 2 or more sample pages to generate a common structural pattern that is expressed using the regular expression. The structure pattern is thereafter used to describe the structure of the similar web pages to facilitate the information extraction. Reference [12] discusses the IE for the sales information of the products, which has a strong requirement of the type of information. Reference [13] gives the Ontology for centain special area information where the range is rather special.

The research of the Web IE technology started late in China. Reference [14] studies a way to solve IE problems by using XML, proposes a system for Web IE based XML. Reference [15] conducted some preliminary research on the Web IE based on DOM technology.

The intention of this paper is to provide the user with the highly trustworthy and reliable information based on a system that analyses, extracts, de-duplicates, and fuses the information contained in the search results returned by the search engine given a particular user requirement.

2 Web Information Integration Fusion Strategy

Web IE is the foundation of this model. The pages searched from the web will go through the IE process so that a data set and a text set will be generated. At the same time, the relevant information can be defined in the corresponding data set.

Data integration or fusion is the core to the implementation of this model. The quality of the data integration or fusion has a direct impact over the quality of the view that the end-user would get. The data in the data set will be compared and fused and finally the fused data will be returned back to the end-user.

2.1 General Definition

[Def 1] Denote the data set as $S=\{S_1,S_2,S_3,...,S_i,...S_n\}(1\le i\le n)$, S_i represents one of the prices got extracted. The data set S might contain duplicated data. Denote the text set as $F=\{f_1,f_2,...,f_i,...,f_n\}(1\le i\le n)$, f_i represents the extracted information of the product configuration (other than the price). Denote the text set $F'=\{f_1',f_2',...,f_i',...,f_m'\}(1\le i\le m)$ as the detailed features of the product after fusion (other than price and configuration information), f_i' represents one feature of the product.

[Def 2] Based on the analysis of the data set s, we get: $S'=\{S_1',S_2',S_3',...S_i',...S_m'\}(i\le m\le n)$. S_i' is one of the prices after the statistics gathering. The difference between S_i' and S is there's no duplicated data in S_i'. Calculate the number of the duplications for each of the elements in the data set s, the resulting set is denoted as $R=\{r_1,r_2,r_3,...,r_i,...,r_m\}$ ($i\le m\le n$, $r_m\ge 1$), the value of r_i is the number of duplications of the corresponding element S_i'.

[Def 3] If the data set R exists and the condition is satisfied, denote the credibility of the data as:

$$C_i=\frac{r_i^2}{\sum_{i=1}^{m} r_i^2} \quad (1\le i\le m) \tag{1}$$

r_i is the number of duplications for element S_i' in the data set S'. The credibility is calculated based on the number of duplication of S_i'. The more the number of S_i' elements, the more credible it is. Denote the smallest data in data set S' as:

$$Ds=Min(S')=S_i'(1\le i\le m) \tag{2}$$

Min() is the function to return the minimal value of a set by comparing every two elements in the set. Denote the biggest data in the data set R as:

$$Rm = Max(R) = r_i \quad (1 \le i \le m) \tag{3}$$

Max() is the function to return the maximal value of a set by comparing every two elements in the set. Denote the element with the most number of duplication in data set S' as:

$$Dm = Relation(S', r_i) \quad (1 \le i \le m) \tag{4}$$

Relation() function finds the corresponding element for r_i in the data set S', which is Dm.

2.2 The Strategy for IE

Based on the structure and the HTML code of the web page for the product information, get the intermediate search results in URL by leveraging the Google SOAP Search API. Analyse and de-duplicate the set of URLs in the following steps:

1. Pass the first URL in the URL set to the HtmlParser, HtmlParser will start to analyse the Html document online, then go to step 3.
2. If there are still elements in the URL set, get the ith URL in the set and pass it to the HrmlParser, HtmlParser will start to analyse the Html document online, then go to step 3. If there's no URL left in the URL set, finish.
3. Get the keywords from the knowledge base, i.e. price, market price, reference price, etc, in addition to the name of the product, to generate the characteristics phrase. HtmlParser will parse all the table tags and check if there are any table tags that match with the characteristics phrase. If there's any, go to step 4, otherwise go to step 5.
4. For the table tag that matches with the characteristics phrase, if there's no embedded table block, parse the td tags using the HtmlParser, filter out the Html tags like <font> and then extract the detailed information of the product using the keywords in the knowledge base. Use regular expression to extract the price information and store them into the data set S after the validation and modification. Other product information will be extracted to the data set F. If the table is relatively complicated with embedded table blocks, find the table tag embedded the deepest that matches with the characteristics phrase, parse the td tags and use the keywords in the knowledge base to extract the relevant information, use regular expression to extract the price and store them into the data set S after validation and modification. Go to step 2.
5. HtmlParser checks if there is any div block that matches with the characteristics phrase. If there's any go to step 6, otherwise go to step 2.
6. Analyse the div blocks that meet the condition. Generally, div block is complicated because it usually has embedded table blocks or div blocks. The same method described in step 4 will be applied to div block here as well. The extracted price information will be stored in the data set S after the validation and modification. Other product information will be stored in F. Then go to step 2.

7. After the algorithm described above, the price data set s and the detailed product information set F will be generated.

2.3 Weighted Average Estimated Price Based on the Credibility

Calculate the weighted average of the price based on the web credibility to address the differences of the prices extracted from the web for the same product. Weighted average means the average of all the elements after applying a weight to each of them. Assuming that there's a data set like this:

$$M=\{m_1, m_2, \cdots m_i, \cdots, m_n\} \quad (0<i\leq n)$$

Weighted average model:

$$\bar{m}=\sum_{i=1}^{n} m_i \times \frac{w_i}{\sum_{i=1}^{n} w_i} \quad (0<i\leq n) \tag{5}$$

In the formula, w_i is the weight for m_i and $\sum_{i=1}^{n} w_i = 1\ (0<i\leq n)$.

2.4 Method of Credibility

Credibility indicates the reliability of the data. The data with certain extent of credibility can be used as the reference for weights. For the convenience of the calculation, the weight can be adjusted.

In this paper, the weight to be used is decided by the credibility of the data in s'. The more credible the data is the bigger weight it will be associated with, vice versa.

From formula (4), we can get the following formula:

$$Dr=\sum_{i=1}^{n} S_i \times \frac{C_i}{\sum_{i=1}^{n} C_i} \quad (0<i\leq n) \tag{6}$$

C_i is the credibility of the data.

Apply the formula (1) to formula (6), we get:

$$Dr=\sum_{i=1}^{n} S_i \times \frac{\frac{r_i^2}{\sum_{i=1}^{n} r_i^2}}{\sum_{i=1}^{n}\left(\frac{r_i^2}{\sum_{i=1}^{n} r_i^2}\right)} \quad (0<i\leq n, n\geq 1) \tag{7}$$

r_i is the number of duplication of s_i' in the data set s'. Since $\sum_{i=1}^{n}\left(\frac{r_i^2}{\sum_{i=1}^{n} r_i^2}\right)=1$ formula (7) can be simplified as:

$$Dr=\sum_{i=1}^{n} S_i \times \frac{r_i^2}{\sum_{i=1}^{n} r_i^2} \quad (0<i\leq n, n\geq 1) \tag{8}$$

2.5 Algorithm for Integration Fusion

Algorithm for fusion of the text set is as follows:

1. Get the keywords related to the properties of this product from the knowledge base, and compare the first keyword with the elements in the text set F. Go to step 3 if it matches, otherwise go to step 2.
2. Get the ith keyword ($1<i<=n$) relevant to this product and compare it with the elements in the data set F. Go to step 3 if it matches, otherwise if $i<=n$ go to step 2, if $i>n$, finish.
3. Pull out the elements in the text set F that match with the relevant keyword in the knowledge base and put them into the text set F'. Then go to step 2.

The text set F' generated from the algorithm described above should contain the detailed information of the product we are interested in.

Algorithm for fusion of the data set (price) is as follows:

1. Data set S' and R are empty in the beginning. Get the first element s_1 from the data set S and insert it into the data set S', the new element in S' is denoted as s_1'. Now in the data set R, there will be the first element r_1 with the value set to 1. Go to step 2.
2. Get the ith ($1<i\leq m$) element from S, compare it with all the elements in S' and check if they are the same. If they are not the same, insert the element s_j' ($1<j\leq i$) into data set S' and set the corresponding element in the data set R to be 1, then go to step 2. If they are the same, go to step 3. If all the elements in data set S are consumed, go to step 4.
3. If elements are the same, s_i doesn't need to be inserted into data set S', increment the corresponding element r_j in the data set R by 1, then go to step 2.
4. Process the elements in the data set S' using the formula (1) to get the credibility data set C, then go to step 5.
5. Use the minimal element in the data set S' by applying the formula (2) as the reference; apply the formula (4) to get the data s_i', which has the maximum number of duplication. Apply formula (8) to fuse the data from data set S' and R to get the fused result.
6. Return the fused result, the lowest price and the price with the maximum appearances together with the detailed information of the product back to the end-user as the trustworthy reference. End-user gets a panoramic view of the interested product information.
7. At the same time, save the fused results in the search history so that within a specific period of time user will be directed to the search history if the same keywords are queried again. This eliminates the re-integration of the data when it has already been done quite recently.

3 Demonstration System

This experiment takes the price of the laptop as an example to demonstrate the work flow of the system by extracting and fusing the relevant information.

Keyword: *Price of IBM ThinkPad T60 2007BT1*
Feature Phrases: *IBM ThinkPad T60 2007BT1 + (Price or Bidding)*
Knowledge Base: *Configuration of the laptop {Central Processing Unit/CPU, Memory, Standard Frequency/Highest Frequency, Hard Disk, Monitor, Weight}*

3.1 The Process and Analysis of the Experiment

Input the keyword "IBM ThinkPad T60 2007BT1 price", shown in Fig. 1.

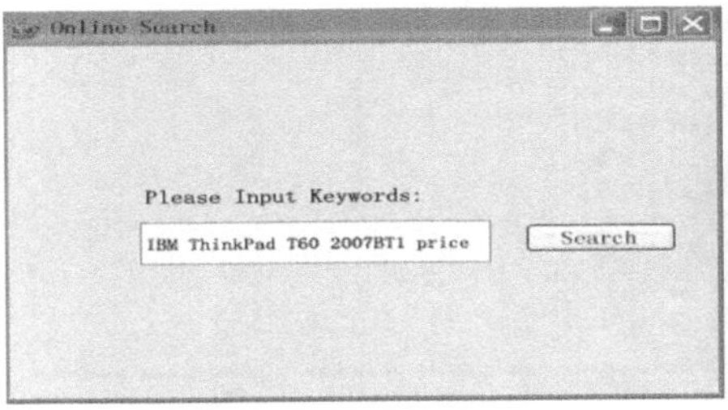

Fig. 1. Interface for keywords input

Fig. 2. URL addresses

Search the result using Google Search Soap API. After selecting and de-duplicating the results (no duplication for the URL used in here), there are 10 URLs left shown in Fig. 2.

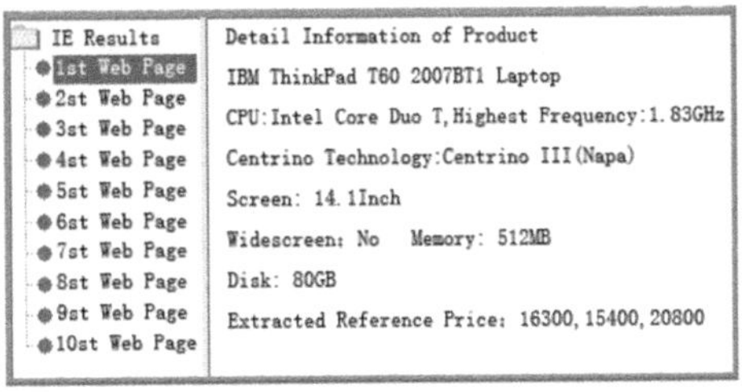

Fig. 3. IE result 1

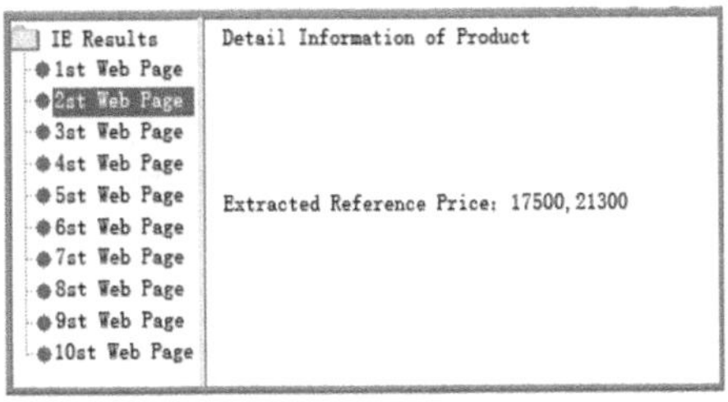

Fig. 4. IE result 2

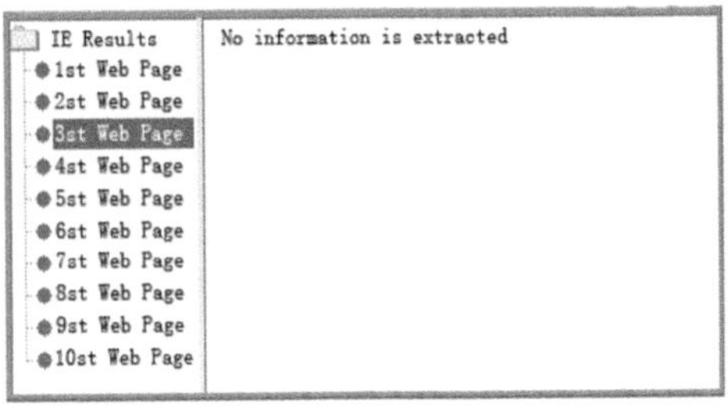

Fig. 5. IE result 3

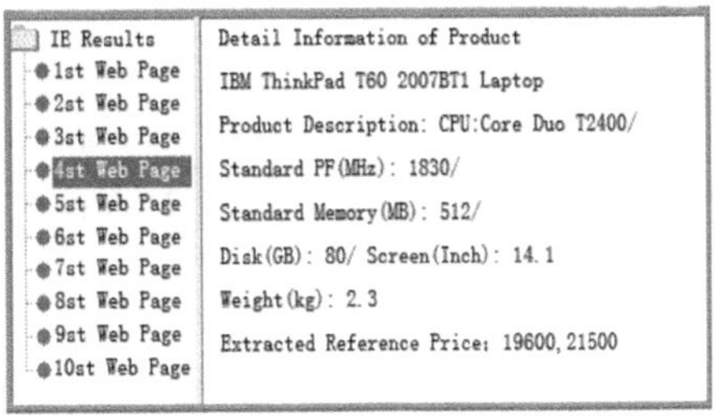

Fig. 6. IE result 4

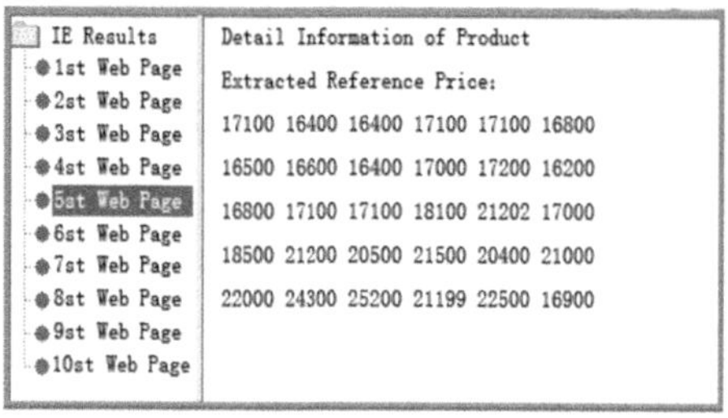

Fig. 7. IE result 5

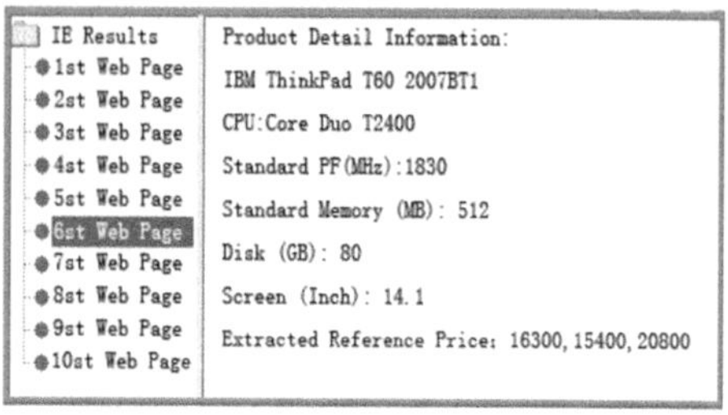

Fig. 8. IE result 6

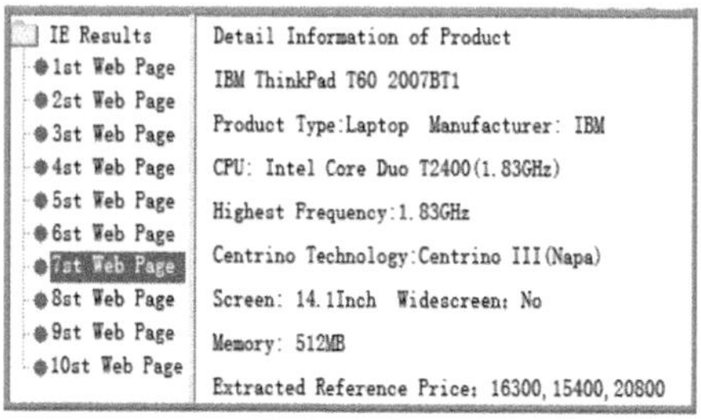

Fig. 9. IE result 7

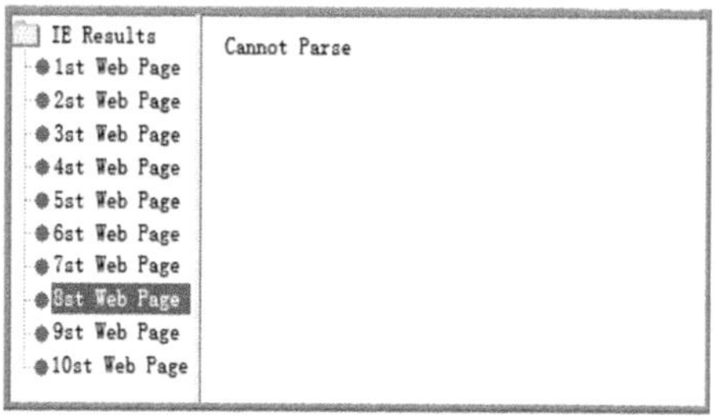

Fig. 10. IE result 8

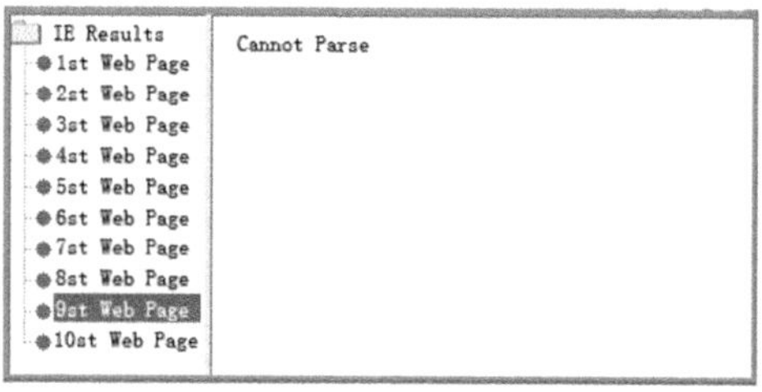

Fig. 11. IE result 9

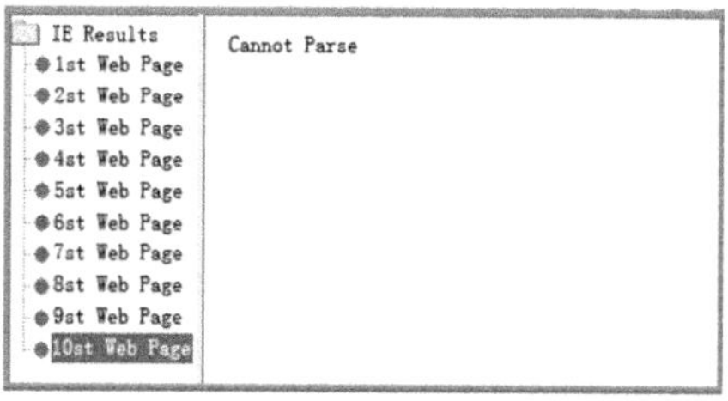

Fig. 12. IE result 10

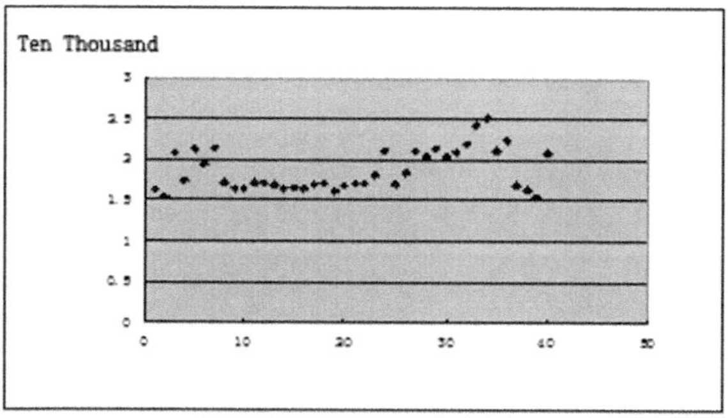

Fig. 13. Price Distributions

The intermediate results calculated from the Web IE algorithm based on the characteristics phrases used in this experiment are shown above.

From the Fig. 3 to Fig. 12, we can see that Fig. 5 indicates no data was successfully extracted; Fig. 10, 11, 12 indicates the failure of parsing. The pages that successfully went through the process of parsing might have multiple prices. Fig. 13 summarizes and visualizes all the prices.

From the figure shown above, the price of the laptop can be clearly understood. There are 40 prices ranging from 15,000 to 30,000 RMB, with the highest concentration between 15,000 to 22,000 RMB.

The system will fuse the prices based on the algorithm described in section 2-E. After the comparison and statistics compilation, the result is shown in the Table 1.

Table 1. Prices

16300	15400	20800	17500	21300	19500	21500
17100	16400	16800	16500	16600	17000	17200
16200	18100	21202	18500	21200	20500	20400
21000	22000	24300	25200	21199	22500	16900

The corresponding number of duplication for each of the prices is compiled in Table 2.

Table 2. Statistics of the number of duplicated prices

2	2	2	1	1	1	2
5	3	2	1	1	2	1
1	1	1	1	1	1	1
1	1	1	1	1	1	1

Apply the weighed average algorithm introduced in section 2-D to the data in Table 1, the results are shown in Table 3.

Table 3. Weighed coefficient

4/78	4/78	4/78	1/78	1/78	1/78	4/78
25/78	9/78	4/78	1/78	1/78	4/78	1/78
1/78	1/78	1/78	1/78	1/78	1/78	1/78
1/78	1/78	1/78	1/78	1/78	1/78	1/78

According to the formula (6), the fused price is 18,001 RMB, according to the formula (3) and formula (4), the price with the most number of duplication and the lowest price are 17,100 and 15,400 respectively.

The detailed configuration information of "IBM ThinkPad T60 2007BT1"can be compiled using the text fusion method described in section 2-B:

CPU: Intel Core Duo T2400(1.83G) Standard PF(MHz): 1830
Memory (MB): 512 Disk (GB): 80
Screen (Inch): 14.1 Weight (kg): 2.3

At last, the system integrates the detail information and prices of "IBM ThinkPad T60 2007B" and returns a complete information view (shown in Fig. 14) to user. Meanwhile, the experimental results are recorded in the history library.

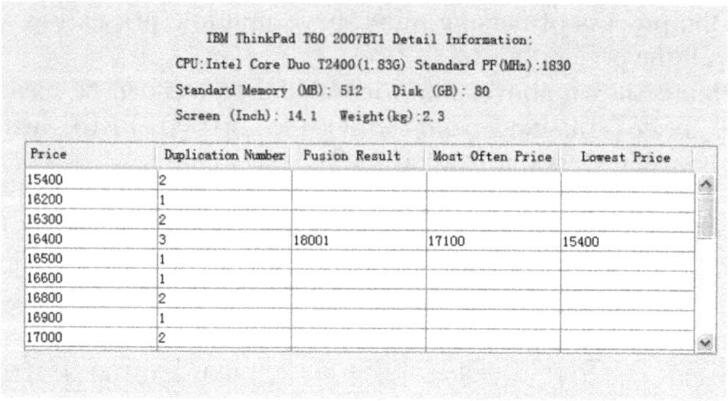
IBM ThinkPad T60 2007BT1 Detail Information:
CPU:Intel Core Duo T2400(1.83G) Standard PF(MHz):1830
Standard Memory (MB): 512 Disk (GB): 80
Screen (Inch): 14.1 Weight(kg):2.3

Price	Duplication Number	Fusion Result	Most Often Price	Lowest Price
15400	2			
16200	1			
16300	2			
16400	3	18001	17100	15400
16500	1			
16600	1			
16800	2			
16900	1			
17000	2			

Fig. 14. The complete information view

3.2 Comparative Experiment and Summary

We will use few models of laptops to conduct a comparative experiment and the models are shown below in the Table 4:

Table 4. Model of the Laptops

IBM ThinkPad T60 2007BT1	Dell Inspiron 9400(N510614)
HP Pavilion dv2113TX	BenQ Joybook R41E-107
Toshiba Statellite M100 PSMAOQ-10GOOE(Grey)	Samsung X11-CV0B

Method 1: Search manually, get the search results from the search engine, get the top 10 results with the highest ranking and make the comparison.

Method 2: Use the text system, input the model of the laptop and check the results.

The comparison result is shown in Fig. 15.

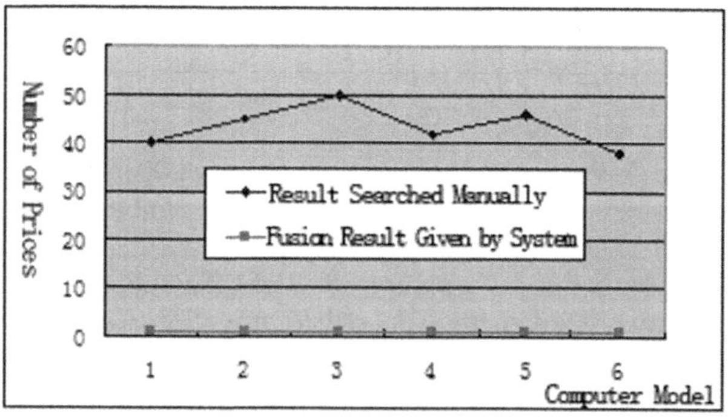

Fig. 15. Comparisons of Manual and System

In the Fig. 15, on the x-coordinate 1 represents IBM ThinkPad T60 2007BT1, 2 represents Dell Inspiron 9400(N510614), 3 represents HP Pavilion dv2113TX, 4 represents BenQ Joybook R41E-107, 5 represents Toshiba Statellite M100 PSMAOQ-10GOOE (Grey), 6 represents Samsung X11-CV0B.

From the Fig. 15, we can easily see that there will be fairly big amount of human efforts involved in the method 1 to compare big number of prices. This effort will be drastically reduced in method 2 where only the model of the laptop needs to be input to the system and the system will return a fused result as a reference for the decision-making.

If there were tens of thousands of pages, the amount of workload involved in selecting and comparing the prices would be beyond imagination. Using the system described in this paper to help automatically process, extract and fuse the search result will be very helpful if the speed of the network and processor is reasonably fast.

Although the system described in this paper cannot help to display the prices one by one for the users to browse, but it can help to extract the prices of the product that complies with the text extraction rules, the fused price also falls within the range of the concentrated distribution region, therefore is of high reference value. The system described in this paper can relieve the user from the tedious work of manually searching and increase the extent to which the automation is used in this process.

4 Conclusion

With the search engine technology prospering in today's world, the "information overload" caused by the tremendous amount of results that might be returned by the search engine often makes the users confused. This paper developed a system by using the Web information extraction and data fusion technology on top of the search engine. This system provides the user with the trustworthy, panoramic view of the information, increases the automation of the information extraction. It has got a very high opinion among all the users since its release.

Acknowledgments. This work is supported by the National Natural Science Foundation of China (No.40976108).

References

1. Fard, A.M., Ghaemi, R., Mohammad, R., Akbarzadeh, T., Kavosh, A.H.: An intelligent neuro-fuzzy search engine. Intelligent Systems Design and Application (4), 597–602 (2007)
2. Hou, J.: Research on Design of an Auotomatic Evaluation System of search engine. Future Computer and Communication, 16–18 (2009)
3. Wang, X.-Y., Hu, Q.-S., Li, B., Zhuang, Z.-Q.: A system of personalized intelligent information retrieval for Internet. Journal of Computer Research and Development 36(9), 1039–1046 (1999)
4. Wu, X.-J.: Research of named entity recognition and automatic pattern acquisition in information extraction. Northeastern University, Shenyang (2004)
5. Soderland, S.: Learning information extraction rules for semi-structured and Free Text. Machine Learning 34(1-3), 233–272 (1999)

6. Muslea, I., Minton, S., Knolock, C.: Hierarchical wrapper induction for semi-structured information sources. Autonomous Agents and Multi-Agent System 4(1/2), 93–114 (2001)
7. Knoblock, C.A., Kristina, L., et al.: Accurately and reliably extraction data from: A machine learning approach. Data Engineering Bulletin 23(4), 33–41 (2000)
8. Muslea, I., Minton, S., Craig, A., et al.: Active learning for hierarchical wrapper induction. In: Proceedings of the Sixteenth National Conference on Artificial Intelligence and Eleventh Conference on Innovative Applications of Artificial Intelligence, Orlando, Florida, USA (1999)
9. Muslea, I., Minton, S., Craig, A., et al.: A hierarchical approach to wrapper induction. In: Proceedings of the Third International Conference on Autonomous Agents, Washington, USA (1999)
10. Embley, D., Campbell, D., Jiang, S., et al.: Conceptual-model-based data extraction from multiple record web pages. Data and Knowledge Engineering 31(3), 227–251 (1999)
11. Crescenzi, V., Mecca, G.: RoadRunner: towards automatic data extraction from large Web sites. In: Proceedings of the 27th International Conference on Very Large Database, Roma, Italy (2001)
12. Doorenbos, R., Etzinoni, O., Weld, D.: A scalable comparison-shopping agent for the world-wide web. In: Proceeding of the AAAI 15th National Conference on Artificial Intelligence (1998)
13. Embley, R., Xu, L.: Locating and reconfiguring records in unstructured multiple-record web documents. In: Suciu, D., Vossen, G. (eds.) WebDB 2000. LNCS, vol. 1997, p. 256. Springer, Heidelberg (2001)
14. Lu, R.: The Research of XML-Based Web information extraction. Dalian Maritime University, Dalian
15. Chunying, K.: DOM-based web page to Detemine the structure of the similatity Algorithm. Intelligent Information Technology Application, 245–248 (2009)
16. Intelligence Fusion Pushed. Auiation Week and Space Technology, 205-211 (1979)

Internet GIS and System Dynamic Modeling in Urban Public Safety and Security Studies: A Conceptual Framework

Danlin Yu[1,*] and Jingyuan Yin[2]

[1] Center for Urban Public Safety Information Services, School of Computer Sciences; and Earth and Environmental Studies, Montclair State University, Montclair, 1 Normal Ave., USA
yud@mail.montclair.edu

[2] Center for Urban Public Safety Information Services, School of Computer Sciences, Shanghai University, Shanghai, China
jyyin@staff.shu.edu.cn

Abstract. Urban space has been a focus of various studies for centuries. In the awake of recent events, it becomes important to understand and model urban safety and security, and disseminate urban safety and security information to the decision-makers, the general public, and other interested parties in an efficient and dynamic way. This study embarks on such a task of proposing a system dynamic methodology based modeling technique, and an Internet GIS based information dissemination framework to address such an issue. In particular, we propose to establish a set of "urban safety and security information indicator system". Based on the actual scenario of Shanghai, such indicator system includes information from the urban socioeconomic development, urban crime and violence, urban tenure insecurity, and natural and manmade disasters. We will discuss its general framework and then give a thorough review of Internet GIS and its applicability to the urban safety and security domain. We conclude our research with proposed future works including data collection, modeling and simulation, and dissemination network creation.

Keywords: urban safety and security, indicator systems, system dynamics, Internet GIS.

1 Introduction

Urban space is a highly dynamic, extremely diversified, and enormously complex human habitat in the contemporary mankind history. This high concentration of human beings in relatively small pieces of land area makes great challenges for cities worldwide regarding its social, economic, and environmental safety and security. Some of such challenges come in the forms of catastrophic events such as earthquakes, tsunami, volcanic eruptions, environmental pollution, terrorist's attacks

* The study is supported by Shanghai University's Key Discipline Project Grant (#J50103), and the collaborative research grant from Montclair State University's Global Education Center.

X. Luo et al. (Eds.): ICWL 2010 Workshops, LNCS 6537, pp. 207–216, 2011.

and financial meltdown; others manifest them as urban crime, poverty and inequality, and rapid and chaotic urbanization process. Models and methods of recording, evaluating, and even forecasting such events will be of significant importance for sustainable urban planning and urban governance.

Studies of such models and methods have yielded fruitful results in recent years [1][2][3][4][5][6][7]. Many of the studies are conducted in Europe and North America concerning primarily on quality of life, health of urban population, urban crime, sustainable urban development and counter-terrorism [2][8][9][10][11][12][13] or focus on building structure [14] and natural disasters [15][16].

Chinese megacities such as Beijing and Shanghai, although under China's urban development guideline of restricting the development of megacities, maintaining the size of large and medium-sized cities and encouraging small-sized cities [17], still experience rapid development after the launch of the economic reform in 1978. This is especially so for Shanghai.

During the pre-reform period, Shanghai was largely underdeveloped despite its past glories of urbanization. The reform almost instantaneously released the enormous potential of Shanghai's development vigor. Within about 30 years, the city proper expanded from the original 660 km^2 in the late 1970s to the current megacity with a proper area of 6340 km^2. Economic status almost jumped from being a mediocre performed region to number one in China and marked as the "Dragon's Head". Such huge expansion and explosive development create not only enormous amount of opportunities for this "new Shanghai", but also bring greater challenges to the city's decision-makers regarding urban public safety, security and sustainability.

One of the imminent challenges Shanghai is facing today is the lack of a systematic, organized and central urban public safety and security information system. Such information system would potentially provide a centralized node and platform for various agents of urban Shanghai, including the general public, the government and its corresponding departments, the business owners and foreign investors to coordinate efficiently. With development of efficient visualization, prediction and analysis toolsets through the applications of Geographic Information Systems (GIS) and System Dynamic modeling, the benefits that such information system can provide are enormous for a safe, sustainable, and prosperous Shanghai.

This current study is the first step of a response to such an urgent need in Shanghai. In particular, in this stage of the study, we propose a conceptual framework for urban safety and security evaluation that is based on system dynamic simulation [18] and information dissemination with Internet GIS techniques [19]. Following this introduction, we'll discuss the significance of building an indicator system to evaluate urban safety and security, and its tentative structure. This is followed by a proposal of a conceptual framework of urban safety and security simulation model. The fourth section attempts to introduce the idea of Internet GIS and its application in urban safety and security studies. We conclude our study with future steps.

2 Urban Safety and Security with Indicator System

After the 9.11 terrorist attack of New York City, Washington DC, US in 2001, and the 2004 Southeast Asia tsunami that swept through numerous cities in the coastal regions and brought over 230,000 lives to an end, the July 5th, 2009 terrorist riots in Urumqi, Xinjiang, China, and numerous other man-made or nature-caused disasters that happened around the world in recent years, urban safety and security have become a great concern for the general public, governments worldwide and the scholarly communities as well. Being one of the largest cities in China, Shanghai is also increasingly aware of the potential natural or man-made threats that would endanger the development, lives and urban infrastructure. Developing and implementing a scientifically guided urban public safety and security evaluating, monitoring and forecasting system are hence of particular importance.

There are two basic ways from which we attempt to interpret complex systems such as cities. First is the top-down approach in which we break down the complex system into a series of subsystems that are composed of specific measurable variables or indicators. In so doing, we'll be able to see the system as a whole, and will be able to understand the inherent relationships between different indicators and subsystems during the running-down process.

The second approach is the reversed direction of the above in which we understand the system from a bottom-up perspective. In essence, with such an approach, we collect relevant indicators first, and then group them into various subsystems. With sufficient subsystems built, we'll be able to approach the understanding of the entire system. Unlike the top-down approach, however, the relationships among indicators and subsystems will be sought empirically based on data.

From a system dynamic perspective, it would be ideal to have a top-down approach to get a full understanding of the complex system. While running down to the individual indicators, we would get the inherent relationships among subsystems and indicators and build them into mathematically representative equations for simulation purposes. In reality, however, it is seldom the case that a complex system such as a city can be fully comprehended and all subsystems identified. In this regard, a bottom-up approach might be more tenable. As a matter of fact, when attempting to understand many complex systems, such as the regional socioeconomic development system [20], regional and urban sustainability system [21][22][23], regional planning system [24], scholars tend to build a so-called indicator systems from bottom-up arguing that such indicators are what the complex system manifests in specific aspects. By collecting such indicators and group them into different categories, researchers are able to create at least a partial image of the system.

Following similar arguments, we contend in this research that an indicator system for urban safety and security, specifically for Shanghai, is our best chance to evaluating and monitoring Shanghai's safety and security. It is noticed [20], however, when it comes down to individual indicators, we tend to found a huge volume of relevant information existed in various agencies. Selecting all would be unlikely a task and might lead to information repetition. Since our current purpose is to evaluate and monitor the safety and security issues of Shanghai, the selected indicators shall closely reflect that.

According to UN-Habitat's 2007 report [25], the theme of "urban safety and security" encompasses a wide range of concerns and issues. These range from basic needs such as food, shelter and health, through impacts of natural disasters, such as those triggered by earthquakes, tsunami and hurricanes, to collective security needs, such as protection from urban terrorism or war or financial meltdowns. However, as aforementioned, it will be impractical to consider all potential issues when building an indicator system. Our study attempts such an effort from a human settlement perspective through appropriate urban policy, planning, design and governance. In this regard, three major threats to the safety and security of cities are identified: urban crime and violence; insecurity of tenure and forced eviction; and natural and human-made disasters. Based on this recognition, we propose a framework of indicator system that reflects the three threats, and a general category capturing the urbanization process.

1). The general urbanization category: This first group contains a series of indicators which describe basic demographic, socio-demographic characteristics, economic development, the financial capability of local governments and services provided, urban land use information and critical environmental indicators (such as the produce of solid waste, discharge of waste water, green space, etc.) of the city. This category of indicators would provide a foundation for the general picture of the city. These indicators shall mostly serve as inputs and basic stocks.

2). Urban crime and violence category: This category of indicators attempts to capture not just the occurrence of various crimes (types and rates of urban crimes), but also focus on the potential origins that might lead to urban crimes from social, cultural and economic perspectives. In addition, the forces and resources the city can employ to fight urban crimes are also of particular importance in this category. This type of information would be critically beneficial to build a safe Shanghai when published via interactive Internet GIS services.

3). Tenure insecurity and forced eviction category: Needless to say, security of tenure is the basic attribute of human security in general. And central to the security of tenure is the availability, quality, and sustainability of housing. Being able to accommodate adequately and comfortably its citizens shall be deemed a high priority for any city aiming at improving its own safety and security. In this category, our indicators will primarily reflect the availability of housing, the cost of adequate housing, the quality of housing, the governmental programs and investment for adequate housing, and factors that have strong impact on citizens' capability of acquiring adequate housing, such as unemployment and poverty.

4). Natural and man-made disasters: The high concentration of assets, wealth and people; the rapid urbanization in the coastal regions; the modification of the urban built and natural environment through human actions; the expansion of settlements within cities into hazard-prone locations; and the failure of urban authorities to regulate building standards and land-use planning strategies are all very much the factors that put modern cities at increased risk of natural or man-made disasters. This is especially true to coastal cities like Shanghai. This group of indicators attempts to capture the occurrence possibility of potential tectonic, climatic and environmental disasters and terrorist attacks, their potential damages. More importantly, we attempt to collect and develop appropriate indicators that will be able to reflect Shanghai's preparedness towards various possible disasters, such as the efficiency of urban emergency response system and personnel, financial support to disaster preparation, and the like.

3 A System Dynamic Simulation Framework

System dynamic simulation is arguably one of the best approaches to simulate and understand complex systems [18]. System dynamic simulation is based on *system thinking* that requires the scientist to move away from looking at isolated events and their causes (usually assumed to be some other events), and start to look at the entire problem as a *system* made up of *interacting* parts [18]. The primary tasks for building a system dynamic simulation model are hence to attempt to identify influential "parts" (the events, represented by various indicators), and more importantly, the *interactions* among those events. When creating a system dynamic simulation, all the events are grouped to be either "causes" or "effects". Yet unlike in an isolated view, an event can be both a cause and an effect – a cause to some other effects, and an effect of some other causes. Such systematic view of events creates the so-called *feedback loop* interaction [18]. While building the events (indicators) and their relevant *feedback* interactions into a computer model, we are able to simulate what the real system might function and operate.

The actual simulation of the model is based upon the passage of time, while the interactions among various events work through this passage of time. The essential idea is that the model takes a number of simulation steps along the time axis. At the end of each step, some system events, which essentially represent the states of the system and usually are what we need for effective policy-making, are brought up to date for representing consequences ensued from their previous status and the various interactions among them. Except for those state indicators, there also exist other system indicators, which represent flow of information and initiation of action, arise as results of system activities and produce the related consequences (the interactions and events that govern such interactions).

One of the arguably most flexible characteristics of such system dynamic simulation is that it can incorporate both empirical relationships that are established with data or theoretical studies, and experts' subject opinions that are hard to formulate. Running the model, however, will provide validation for its performance by using historical data. The appealing point is that both the modelers and the users (the decision-makers) are able to alter some critical events to see what results might be produced, hence provide a foundation for effective policies. Based on these discussions, we propose a conceptual framework in Fig. 1.

Apparently, detailed feedback loops have to be determined once the actual indicators that represent the various aspects listed in the conceptual framework are identified and data are collected. The central idea of the conceptual framework, however, is to demonstrate what we believe in a systemic understanding of urban safety and security system. The three critical components of urban safety and security, i.e., urban crime and violence, tenure insecurity and forced eviction and natural and man-made disasters, are all linked via the urban infrastructure category. The double heads of all the arrows in the conceptual framework indicate that events can be both causes and effects. While the solid block arrows indicate a direct interaction among the components, the dashed linear arrows represent indirect interactions that might be formulated. Components within a specific category will interact with one another as well, though not explicitly expressed in the illustration. The big picture depicted in the conceptual framework is that all the components (events) are intrinsically related with one another, either directly or indirectly. For instance, when a tectonic disaster (earthquake, tsunami, etc.) hit home, it inevitably impacted upon the demographic characteristics, socioeconomic development, and the environment (apparently in a negative way). Yet in the mean time, the government's supports and services would be positively related with the disaster preparedness which in turn might be able to mitigate the negative impact the natural disaster brought upon.

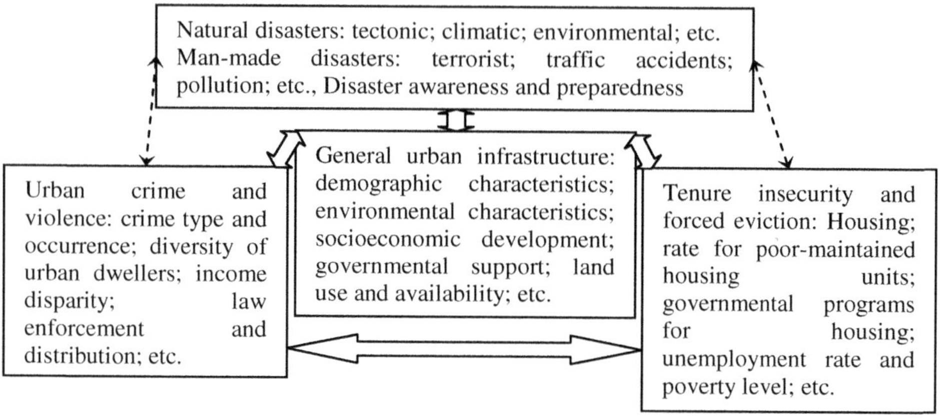

Fig. 1. Conceptual framework of the urban safety and security and simple illustrative dynamic system feedback interactions

Through carefully building appropriate indicators into the conceptual framework, we hope to present a clear and understandable picture of the real urban safety and security issues in Shanghai. It is worth noting here that the choice of indicators and building of the simulation models is never going to be a one-time business. Instead, the model will need to be run numerous times with both the modelers and the model users to determine the appropriate indicators and the realistic interactions. In addition, as the name itself might suggest, the simulation shall be dynamic, that is, the model structure shall be able to accommodate updates and changes, and the entire model might need to be adjusted or even re-built regularly to reflect the real world better. In this regard, the simulation, though theoretically can extend to as long as the modelers see fit, is not recommended to go beyond more than 10 years for complex problems as urban safety and security.

4 Disseminating the Information via Internet GIS

While not explicitly build in our indicator system, one of the most important aspects of urban safety and security is the awareness, understanding, hence better preparedness of the city's citizens. To achieve this, an efficient and fast information dissemination infrastructure needs to be constructed. There are multiple ways of information dissemination. The traditional ones include newspapers, radio, TV broadcasting, information posted at various traffic junctions, and the like. With the rapid development and diffusion of the Internet, web-publishing sees great increase for information dissemination during the past decades in China, especially in large cities like Shanghai.

The issue of urban safety and security is essentially a geographic issue. Though we don't explicitly exploit this particular characteristic of our indicators, the indicators we are eventually going to collect and build in our previously discussed system dynamic model will be collected for different zones (neighborhoods, communities, street districts, etc.) instead of the entire city. Some indicators, such as the occurrence of crimes, traffic accidents, potential locations of natural and man-made disasters, will even have their own specific coordinates. Needless to say, we would find out that the most direct representation of those types of information is a map that will be able to show the various indicators in different zones and locations in the city with different colors and symbols. Although it might not be a difficult task to disseminate static, pre-made maps via the Internet, such maps would be inadequate to reflect the dynamic characteristics of urban safety and security. Dissemination of dynamic, interactive maps, however, requires the application of Internet Geographic Information System (GIS) technique [19].

Traditional GIS has existed for decades, and made great contributions for the understanding of geographic patterns, distributions, mechanisms etc. via the powerful analytical operations such as overlay, address matching, geographic query and the like. Traditional GIS, however, run short in delivering on-line, distributed geographic information services and providing flexible, friendly GIS solutions for non-GIS-trained users such as the general public and/or the policy-makers, which is of particular importance for urban safety and security studies.

Apart from the needs of monitoring and evaluating urban safety and security dynamically, information distribution in real-time is of high demand in the face of a growing population of Internet users. Availability of real-time safety and security related information will help not only the citizens, but the various governmental and non-profit/for-profit agencies and organizations to coordinate better during critical times hence reduce potential damage and loses. In addition, with a complex and dynamic system as urban safety and security, we will expect the data volume to be huge, and analytical work based on traditional GIS techniques might take long time to produce relevant results for real-time decisions. An Internet GIS, on the other hand, utilizes distributive architecture that can take advantage of storing data at relevant data centers (such as crime data in the police department, traffic data in the transportation department, socioeconomic data in the statistic bureau, etc.) instead of at a centralized locations, while analyze them collectively when needed. This indicates the implementation of an Internet GIS information dissemination strategy must be a multi-agent, multi-department structure. Within such structure, the academic unit (universities) or relevant governmental department will provide a central node for the GIS services, while other relevant governmental departments and agencies maintain their data and link to the GIS server for real-time data processing and analyzing. The results from such operation will be published via the Internet through the GIS server in real-time.

In any implementation of an Internet GIS technique, there will be four primary components [19]: the clients (users with access to the Internet), the Web and application server, the map server, and the data server. The last two are unique to a website that provides Internet GIS services. Figure 2 illustrates a distributive architecture of an Internet GIS service that will be effectively used for disseminating urban safety and security information. Note in the figure that various data are stored in their relevant data servers while in the mean time they are connected to the map server for processing. In so doing, the quality of the data which is of critical importance in assessing urban safety and security will be guaranteed due to regular maintenance by the responsible agents instead of the data collectors. The map server, which can usually be housed in an academic unit (universities) or a governmental department, will have the GIS analysis and real-time map-rendering capability. The products from the map server are then output to the web and application server for publishing at the clients. Note the double head of the arrows from the map server to the web and application server, and from the web and application server to the clients. This indicates the information flows in both directions, i.e., the users at the client sides are able to plug in their inputs to the server for better understanding. While using the Internet GIS services, the users are able to perform basic GIS analytical operations such as geographic query, choroplethic mapping and printing.

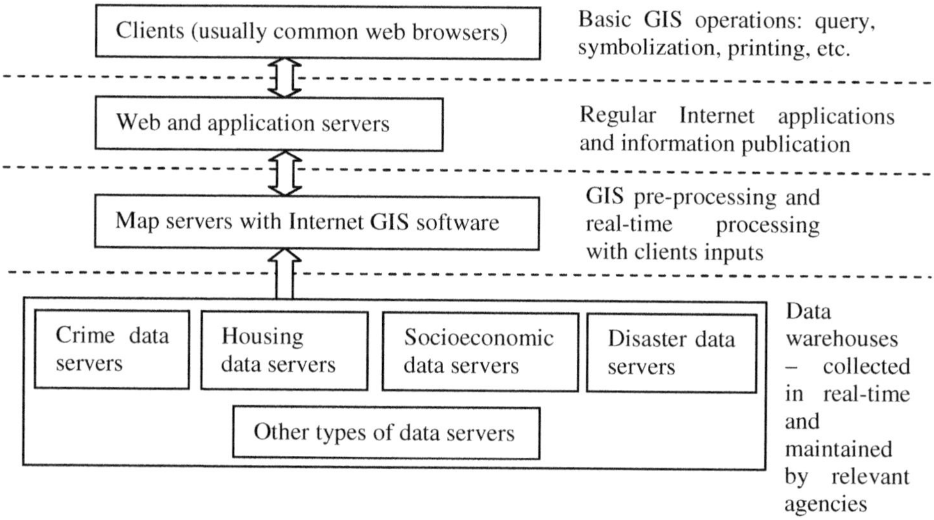

Fig. 2. Illustration of the distributive architecture of an Internet GIS service

Except for publishing the real-time urban safety and security information via the web, coupled with the system dynamic modeling technique we discussed in the previous section, the map server will be able to integrate the simulation results from the system dynamic model and create the so-called optional scenarios. In such scenarios, the user will be able to input an imaginary event and see what such event will bring upon the city's safety and security. For instance, an input indicating a large scale tsunami will trigger the map server to produce a map simulate what Shanghai would like if hit by such a disaster. Apparently, implementation details still need further discussion, yet with map servers that are capable of coupling with the system dynamic simulation, the city is at a much better position of informing, educating, and preparing its citizens for various types of urban safety and security events.

5 Conclusion

In this paper, we have discussed the importance of urban safety and security in the process of urban development and urbanization. We specifically look into the three primary aspects of urban safety and security, i.e., urban crime and violence, tenure insecurity and forced eviction, and natural and man-made disasters, from a human settlement perspective. We contend that it is crucial to build a set of indicators for better understanding urban safety and security. These indicators shall timely reflect the three aspects of urban safety and security and the general urban development and urbanization. We then proposed a framework of potential categories of indicators for such endeavor.

Based on the proposed categories of indicators, we further constructed a conceptual system dynamic model in an attempt to capture the interactions among the various indicators and simulate how the urban safety and security system might work in real world. This practice intends to build a virtual environment in which various "trial-and-error" experiments can be simulated, hence providing the general public and the decision-makers a better understanding of what the city will look like if certain events (such as tectonic disasters, environmental degradation, terrorist attacks, increased crime rates, etc.) occur. Such understanding is fundamental for creating better policies that will lead to a safe and secure urban living environment.

This paper also intends to integrate what the system dynamic simulation produces with the Internet GIS technique for the best possible information dissemination. A distributive structured Internet GIS framework is proposed in an attempt to coordinate various academic, governmental, non-profit and for-profit organizations in participating into monitoring, evaluating, simulating and understanding urban safety and security issues in megacities like Shanghai. We omit the technique details since they are beyond the scope of the current study. We do believe, however, construction of such an information dissemination venue would be of utmost importance to not just urban safety and security, but urban sustainability in the long run as well.

This study initiates an exploration to urban safety and security issues in Chinese cities from a system dynamic simulation and Internet GIS dissemination perspective. This is the first attempt in this direction. The current study intends to provide a conceptual framework which we hope will be the foundation of future works. We do not, however, delve into details about how the urban safety and security indicator-system is constructed; how the system dynamic simulation model is built; and how the Internet GIS distributive structure is established. These tasks are apparently our immediate next goals in the line of studying urban safety and security.

References

1. Sharma, V., Al-Hussein, M., Safouhi, H., Boufergubene, A.: Municipal infrastructure asset levels of service assessment for investment decisions using analytic hierarchy process. J. Infrastruct. Syst. 14(3), 193–200 (2008)
2. Maas, J., Spreeuwenberg, P., Van Winsum-Westra, M., Verheij, R.A., de Vries, S., Groenewegen, P.P.: Is green space in the living environment associated with people's feelings of social safety? Environ. Plann. A 41(7), 1763–1777 (2009)
3. Dumbaugh, E., Rae, R.: Safe urban form: revisiting the relationship between community design and traffic safety. J. Am. Plann. Assoc. 75(3), 309–329 (2009)

4. Hubbard, P., Matthews, R., Scoular, J.: Legal geographies-controlling sexually oriented businesses: law, licensing, and the geographies of a controversial land use. Urban Geogr. 30(2), 185–205 (2009)
5. Korving, H., Van Noortwijk, J.M., Van Gelder, P.H.A.J.M., Clemens, F.H.L.R.: Risk-based design of sewer system rehabilitation. Struct. Infrastruct. E. 5(3), 215–227 (2009)
6. Suddle, S.: The weighted risk analysis. Safety Sci. 47(5), 668–679 (2009)
7. Thiessen, K.M., Arkhipov, A., Batandjieva, B., Charnock, T.W., Gaschak, S., Golikov, V., Hwang, W.T., Tomas, J., Zlobenko, B.: Modeling of a large-scale urban contamination situation and remediation alternatives. J. Environ. Radioactiv. 100(5), 413–421 (2009)
8. Van den Berg, L., Pol, M.J., Mingardo, G., Speller, C.J.M.: The Safe City Safety and Urban Development in European Cities. Ashgate, London (2006)
9. Bramley, G., Dempsey, N., Power, S., Brown, C., Watkins, D.: Social sustainability and urban form: evidence from five British cities. Environ. Plann. A 41(9), 2125–2142 (2009)
10. Duncan, D.T., Johnson, R.M., Molnar, B.E., Azrael, D.: Association between neighborhood safety and overweight status among urban adolescents. BMC Public Health, 9: Art. No. 289 (2009)
11. Kullberg, A., Karlsson, N., Timpka, T., Lindqvist, K.: Correlates of local safety-related concerns in a Swedish Community: a cross-sectional study. BMC Public Health, 9: Art. No. 221 (2009)
12. Senlier, N., Yildiz, R., Aktas, E.D.: A perception survey for the evaluation of urban quality of life in Kocaeli and a comparison of the life satisfaction with the European cities. Soc. Indic. Res. 94(2), 213–226 (2009)
13. Coaffee, J., O'Hare, P., Hawkesworth, M.: The visibility of (in)security: the aesthetics of planning urban defenses against terrorism. Secur. Dialogue 40(4-5), 489–511 (2009)
14. Wu, Z.S., Fahmy, M.F.M., Wu, G.: Safety enhancement of urban structures with structural recoverability and controllability. J. Earthq. Tsunami. 3(3), 143–174 (2009)
15. Keeley, J.E., Safford, H., Fotheringham, C.J., Franklin, J., Moritz, M.: The 2007 Southern California wildfires: lessons in complexity. J. Forest. 107(6), 287–296 (2009)
16. Koetse, M.J., Rietveld, P.: The impact of climate change and weather on transport: An overview of empirical findings. Transport. Res. D-Tr. E. 14(3), 205–221 (2009)
17. Wei, Y.H.D., Yu, D.L.: State policy and the globalization of Beijing: emerging themes. Habitat. Int., 377–395 (2006)
18. Hannon, B., Ruth, M.: Dynamic Modeling, 2nd edn. Springer, New York (2001)
19. Peng, Z.R., Tsou, M.H.: Internet GIS: Distributed Geographic Information Services for the Internet and Wireless Network. Wiley, New York (2003)
20. Mao, H.Y.: Indicator systems for sustainable development in Shandong Province. Geographic Research 16(4), 19–22 (1996)
21. Roseland, M.: Toward sustainable cities. Ecodecision 3, 48–52 (1991)
22. Huang, S.L., Wong, J.H., Chen, T.C.: A framework of indicator system for measuring Taipei's urban sustainability. Landscape Urban Plan. 42, 15–27 (1998)
23. Maclaren, C.W.: Urban sustainability reporting. J. Amer. Plan. Assoc. 62, 184–202 (1996)
24. Fang, C.L.: Theories of Regional Planning. Science Press, Beijing (2000)
25. United Nations Human Settlements Programme: Enhancing Urban Safety and Security Global Report on Human Settlements 2007. Sterling, London (2007)

The Detection of Scene Features in Flickr

Chunjie Zhou[1], Pengfei Dai[2], and Jianxun Liu[3]

[1] School of Information, Renmin University of China, Beijing, China
[2] School of Software, Beijing University of Posts and Telecommunications, Beijing, China
[3] Hunan Knowledge Grid Lab, Hunan University of Science and Technology, China
{lucyzcj,dzcouple,ljx529}@gmail.com

Abstract. Detecting events from web resources has attracted increasing research interests in recent years. Flickr is one of Web resources, which is used to share photos. Complex event detection on Flickr includes the detection of tourist features, user's interest, and so on. With the increasing user requirements of efficient and personalized services, the detection of scene features in Flickr is urgently needed. In this paper we propose a novel method to detect tourist features of every scene, and its difference in different seasons as a probabilistic combination of tags. The use of topic models enables the automatic detection of such patterns, which can translate unstructured tag information into structured event form. The experimental evaluation using real datasets in Flickr show the feasibility and efficiency of the proposed method.

Keywords: complex event detection, Flickr, topic model, tag, scene feature.

1 Introduction

Due to the rapid advancement of digital technology in the last two decades, Internet can provide billions of photos and videos contributed by Web users. As a popular online photo sharing platform, Flickr allows users to store, search, sort and share their photos. It collects not only photos, but also textual information such as keywords and comments. In this work, we focus on temporal and spatial tags of photos. A spatial tags represents a location where the corresponding photo was taken. An accurate spatial tag can be obtained with a GPS device or a location-aware camera-photo. The temporal tag allows to track the difference of scene features over time. In our work, we capture the content of Flickr photos by exploiting user-supplied tags.

Detecting events from web resources has attracted increasing research interests in recent years. Our focus in this paper is to detect scene features from photos and tags on Flickr. The problem is challenging considering: 1) Flickr data is noisy, because there are photos unrelated to scenes; 2) It is not easy to capture the content of photos; 3) It is hard to extract structured knowledge from the unstructured set of tags. This paper presents our effort in detecting scene features from Flickr photos by exploiting the tags supplied by users to annotate photos. In particular, the temporal and spatial distributions of tag usage are analyzed.

We propose a topic model-based method to detect tourist features of each scene in each city, and store them in a database. Furthermore, we analyze the difference of scene

X. Luo et al. (Eds.): ICWL 2010 Workshops, LNCS 6537, pp. 217–226, 2011.

features in different seasons. For this we propose to leverage the power of probabilistic topic models 1) to automatically extract scene features from photos and tags; 2) to express scene features as a composition of tags; 3) to illustrate the difference of scene features in different seasons. Efficient scene feature evaluation could become a new important feature of advanced services in Flickr. The quality of these services can be greatly improved by supporting more advanced query types.

Contributions: This paper proposes a novel method to detect scene features in Flickr and studies its difference in different seasons. In particular:

- We provide a data expression model of picture-tag-scene in Flickr, give a formal definition, and provide the matrix to express their relationships.
- We propose a novel method to detect tourist features of every scene as a probabilistic combination of tags.
- We analyze the difference of scene features in different seasons, which can be achieved without users' annotation.
- We perform an extensive experimental evaluation of the proposed algorithms on real datasets in Flickr.

Paper Organization: The rest of the paper is organized as follows: Section 2 gives the problem definition and introduces the related works. The topic model-based detection method of mining scene features and its difference in different seasons is presented in Section 3. An experimental evaluation of the proposed approach using real datasets is presented in Section 4. Finally, we give the conclusion and future works.

2 Preliminaries

This section formally defines the data expression model and the problem definition. Furthermore, the basic notation that will be used in the rest of the paper are introduced. A concise overview of related works is also presented.

2.1 Problem Definition

Table 1 lists the main symbols we use throughout this paper. Following standard notation, we use capital letters for sets (e.g., P is a set of all photos), and lowercase letters for vectors (e.g., o_i).

The datasets are collected at different scenes, where each scene consists of many photos. Each photo p_i is associated with a location $l(p_i)$ and a timestamp $t(p_i)$. $l(p_i)$ refers to the location where the photo was taken, and $t(p_i)$ stands for the time when the photo was taken. Each photo $p_i \in P$ is correlated with a subset of tags $Z(p_i) = \{z_1, z_2, ..., z_x\} \subseteq Z$. One tag $z_j \in Z(p_i)$ of the photo p_i is also correlated with the location and time. The tag $z_j \in Z$ can be used to label several photos in P. We use $P(z_j)$ to denote the set of all photos which are labeled by the tag z_j, then $P(z_j) = \{p_1, p_2, ..., p_y\} \subseteq P$. So the tag z_j has relationships with a set of location and time, that is $L(z_j) = \{l(p_1), l(p_2), ..., l(p_y)\}$, and $T(z_j) = \{t(p_1), t(p_2), ..., t(p_y)\}$.

Table 1. Symbols

Symbol	Definition and Description
R	a set of all scenes $\{ R_1, ..., R_m \}$
P	a set of all photos $\{ p_1, ..., p_n \}$
Z	a set of all tags $\{ z_1, ..., z_t \}$
$W^{x,y}$	the adjacency matrix of object x and y
o_i	the ith chosen scene
m	the number of all scenes
n	the number of all photos
t	the number of all tags

In Figure 1, we observe 8 photos $(p_1, ..., p_8)$. These photos are spreaded among 5 scenes $(o_1, ..., o_5)$, and each photo involves 2 tags. To simplify the description, we regard 'scene', 'photo' and 'tag' as different types of objects. Furthermore, the relationships among different types of objects are modeled by the adjacency matrices $(W^{x,y})$. For example, we can use $W^{o,p}$ to model the relationship between the 'scene' object and the 'photo' object, where $W^{o,p}(i,j) = 1$ iff the jth photo was taken at the ith scene; $W^{o,p}(i,j) = 0$ otherwise. Similarly, we can use $W^{p,z+x}$ to model the relationship between the 'photo' object and the xth 'tag' object, where $W^{p,z+x}(i,j) = 1$ iff the ith photo involves the jth instance of the xth type of tags; $W^{p,z+x}(i,j) = 0$ otherwise.

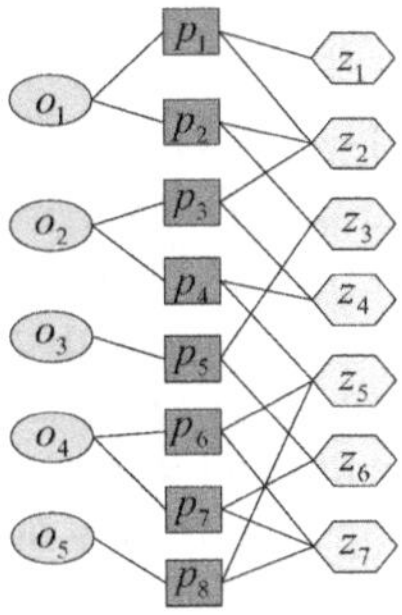

$$W^{o,p} = \begin{bmatrix} 11000000 \\ 00110000 \\ 00001000 \\ 00000110 \\ 00000001 \end{bmatrix} \quad \text{(rows: scene, columns: photo)}$$

$$W^{p,z} = \begin{bmatrix} 1100000 \\ 0110000 \\ 0101000 \\ 0001100 \\ 0010010 \\ 0000101 \\ 0000011 \\ 0000101 \end{bmatrix} \quad \text{(rows: photo, columns: tag)}$$

Fig. 1. The Data Expression Model

Here we use a model like data cube which is a three-dimensional array of values. The three dimensions are tag, time and scene separately. As in Figure 2, a snapshot of the model taken at time t_i contains the distribution of all scenes and all tags at that time. Based on the distribution of photo-tag and scene-photo, we can analyze the probabilistic distribution of scene-tag. For simplicity, we call each such snapshot a world W and it can be expressed as $W = \{1 \leq i \leq n | < Z_i, R_i >\}$. Different tags of the same scene at different time is called a stream. That is, a stream shows different probabilistic distribution of tags of the same scene in different seasons. A flow of tags is a set of scenes which are expressed by the tag at distinct timestamps. The weight of the same tag in different scenes is different. The weight of the same tag in the same scene at different seasons is also different.

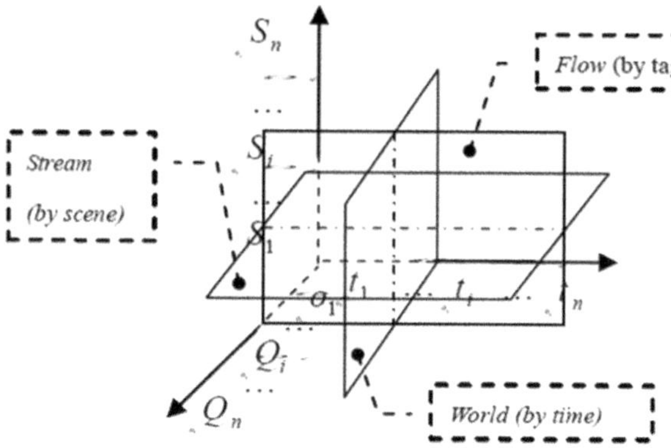

Fig. 2. The event model

2.2 Related Work

The objective of event detection is to discover new or previously unidentified events, where each event refers to a specific thing that happens at a specific time and place[1]. In particular, event detection can be divided into two categories: retrospective detection and on-line detection[2]. The former refers to the detection of previously unidentified events from accumulated historical collection, while the latter entails the discovery of the onset of new events from live feeds in real-time. We here concentrate on both retrospective detection and on-line detection approaches.

Existing algorithms of retrospective event detection can be generally classified into two categories: document-pivot approaches and feature-pivot approaches. The former detects events by clustering documents (e.g., news stories) based on semantics and timestamps[2], while the latter studies the temporal and document distributions of words and discovers events of words[3]. Considering that not every Flickr photo is related to some real scenes, adopting a document-pivot approach and directly clustering photos based on content and timestamps may lead to non-optimal results involving photos irrelevant with scenes. Therefore, we follow the fashion of feature-pivot approaches by detecting event-related tags before detecting scene features.

As one of the very first several efforts of event detection, in [2] a simple agglomerative clustering algorithm, called augmented Group Average Clustering, is used to discover events from the corpus. A probabilistic approach which models both content and time information of documents explicitly is given in [4]. Recently, there has been another research direction which detects events from text streams using feature-pivot approaches, This line of research is inspired by Kleinberg's seminal work that describes extracting bursty features using an infinite automaton model [5]. The work presented by He et al. [3] also detects events by examining features first. They analyzed every feature using Discrete Fourier Transformation and classified features to different categories.

Lately, many known social networking websites like Flickr and Last.fm offer users the opportunity to tag Web resources by supplying textual labels. This service has attracted not only individual users to contribute tags but also researchers to investigate the structure, dynamics, and applications of collaborative tagging data. Halpin et al. used the results of tag data at the bookmarking site Del.icci.us. They confirmed these results in [6], which showed additionally that tags follow a power law distribution. The wide usage of this emerging metadata has been explored by various applications such as navigation [7], enterprise search [8] and Web search [9]. One recent work [10] attempted to extract semantics from Flickr tags. There are also some researches on Flickr data which focus on finding images of scenes and landmark [11]. Such works usually rely on not only the user-supplied tags, but also the content of images. The challenge of tagging systems is to extract structured knowledge from the unstructured set of tags. We are interested in the problem of mining travel sequence from tags in Flickr. So we focus on both spatial and temporal tags. Based on the temporal and spatial distribution of tags, we attempt to detect scene features and its difference in different seasons.

In the context of Flickr, the scene feature detection has not been addressed before. Rattenbury et al. [12] was an early attempt to discover both event and place names from Flickr geolocated textual metadata, resulting in an application [13] for geographic image retrieval, with representative and popular tags overlaid on a scalable map. Quack et al. [14] downloaded 200,000 georeferenced Flickr images from nine urban areas and clustered them using local image descriptors to discover place names and events, linking some places to their Wikipedia articles. In contrast to [14] and [15], we do not limit ourselves to geographic information of photographs since temporal information are also important for detecting scene features.

3 Scene Feature Detection

Our detection approach involves three steps: Firstly, we analyze tags and express photos as a probabilistic combination of tags. As described above, each tag is associated with a set of locations and timestamps. We aim to discover photo-related tags based on their temporal and locational distributions. Secondly, using a probabilistic topic model, we analyze logical relationships between tags and scenes, in order to find a combination of tags to represent scene features. Given a set of tags, we should classify these tags before achieving scene features. However, these scene features cannot be achieved simply from the corresponding tags, because: 1) the same tag may belong to different scenes; 2) the same scene involves many tags; 3) the features of the same scene may be different in different seasons. Finally, from the aspect of time, we can find the difference of scene features in different seasons according to photos taken in different times.

We first discuss the basic statistical topic models, which stem from the text processing community [25]. The basic idea of these models is to model documents with a finite mixture model of k topics and estimate the model parameters by fitting the data with the model. They regard a document as a collection of words, discarding all positional information. This is called a "bag-of-words" representation.

Based on the topic model, scene features and its difference in different seasons can be detected automatically without any user annotation or intervention. To illustrate how this can be achieved, we describe the process of making a tourist plan. Assuming that different photos have different impact factors on the same scene. We model the photos as a probability distribution $p(p_i|R)$ over scenes R, where $i \in [1,n]$. Similarly, the

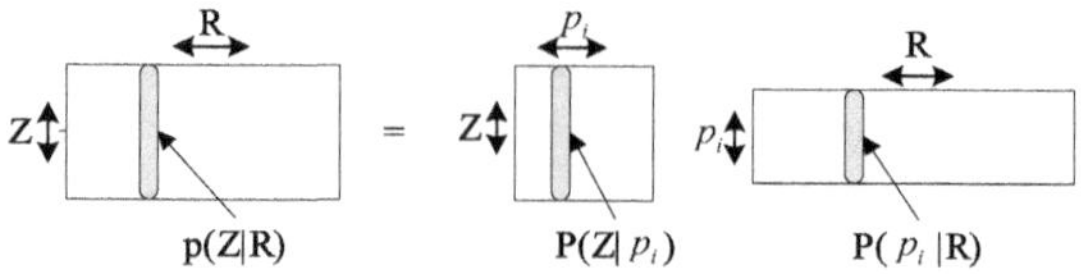

Fig. 3. Intuition of Scene Feature Decomposition

importance of each tag for each photo p_i is also modeled as a probability distribution $p(Z|p_i)$ over the photo p_i. Given these two distributions, we can compute the probability of tags Z occurring in scenes R:

$$p(Z|R) = \sum_{i=1}^{n} p(Z|p_i)p(p_i|R) \tag{3}$$

n is the number of photos in scenes R. This probability distribution $p(Z|R)$ does not include any notion of photos any more. Having many scenes, we observe a data matrix of observed $p(Z|R)$ as depicted on the left hand side of the equation in Figure 3. According to the equation of the topic model, the data matrix can be reconstructed by a matrix product of the tag relevances for each photo and a mixture of photos $p(p_i|R)$ for each scene. Estimating the topic model means doing the reverse. The data matrix on the left-hand side is decomposed into the two matrices on the right-hand side. Then recover the characteristic tags for each photo and the mixture of photos for each scene.

In the following experiments we use a particular instantiation of topic models - called Latent Dirichlet Allocation (LDA) [25]. LDA works under the assumption that documents in a corpus are a low-dimensional mixture of hidden topics of interest. LDA learns, in an unsupervised way, a word-topic and a topic-document distribution from a document corpus. The latter can be used to represent a document based on its topic distribution. β is the control parameter of probability distribution between scenes and photos, while γ is the control parameter of photos and tags. Fitting the model is equivalent to find the parameter β for the dirichlet distribution and the parameter γ for the photo-tag distributions $p(Z|p_i, \gamma)$ that maximize the likelihood in Eq.(4), where n is the number of photos, t is the number of tags, and m is the number of scenes.

$$p(Z|\beta,\gamma) = \prod_{r=1}^{m} \int p(\theta_r|\beta)(\prod_{j=1}^{t} \sum_{i=1}^{n} p(z_j|p_i,\beta)p(p_i|\theta_r))d\theta_r \tag{4}$$

4 Experimental Evaluation

This section presents a comprehensive performance evaluation of the proposed methods for STS using Flickr datasets.

Experimental Setup. We crawled photos from the Flickr site using the available Flickr API. Specifically, we collected photos from the two-year-period starting from Jan 01,

2008, until Dec 30, 2009. We obtained the real dataset in the city of Beijing with 286 scenes and 658 edges. A total 7,000,000 photos were collected, where 3,200,000 photos belong to the year 2008 and 3,980,000 photos were taken in 2009. These photos cover a temporal range of 730 days. The average number of photos per day is 9600,with a minimum of 2360 and a maximum of 16300. These photos are annotated with 40,100,000 tags. On average, each photo is annotated with 5.96 tags, with a minimum of 1 and a maximum of 226. each tag is used to annotate 48.65 photos on average and at most 507.51 photos. The dirichlet parameter β is set as 0.01.

Performance Results

In this part we study the performance of the scene feature detection method.

Table 2 shows the distribution of photos and tags (Here we only list some tags with probability $p(z_i|p_j)\geq 0.1$, where $i \in [1,t], j \in [1,n]$). From the table we can see the same photo involves many tags, which have different probabilities. So only tags with larger probabilities are chosen to make probabilistic combination. Meanwhile, different photos may share the same tag, for example, z_1.

The proportion relationships of different photos which are taken in the scene o_i are shown in Figure 4. From the figure, we can see different photos have different impact factors on scene features.

Table 2. Distribution of Photos and Tags

ID	Photo	Tag	Probability
1	p_1	z_1	0.4402
2	p_1	z_2	0.2396
3	p_1	z_3	0.1088
4	p_1	z_4	0.0727
5	p_1	z_5	0.0482
6	p_1	z_6	0.0224
7	p_1	z_7	0.0105
8	p_2	z_1	0.3427
9	p_2	z_3	0.2456
10	p_2	z_7	0.1176
11	p_2	z_8	0.0858
12	p_2	z_9	0.0476
13	p_2	z_{10}	0.0354
14	p_2	z_{11}	0.0206

Correspond to the intuition of scene feature decomposition in Figure 3, we have already achieved the decomposition matrixs $p(Z|p_i)$ and $p(p_i|R)$ on the right hand of the equation. The next objective is to analyze the matrix $p(Z|R)$ on the left hand of the equation. Figure 5 gives the distribution of scenes and tags. Different scenes have different probabilistic combination of tags. The probability of the same tag in different scenes also exist great difference. For example, tag z_1 can better reflect the tourist feature of scene o_1, while z_5 is suitable to reflect scene o_3.

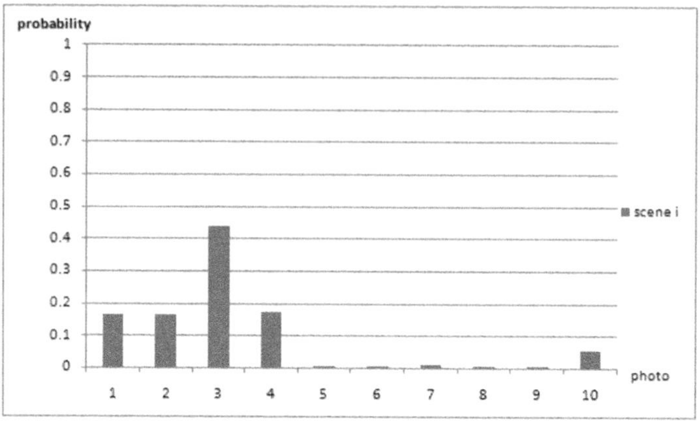

Fig. 4. Distribution of scenes and photos

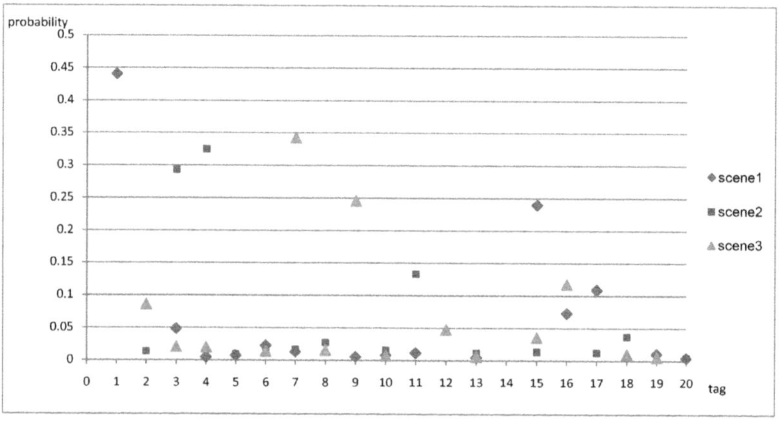

Fig. 5. Distribution of Scenes and Tags

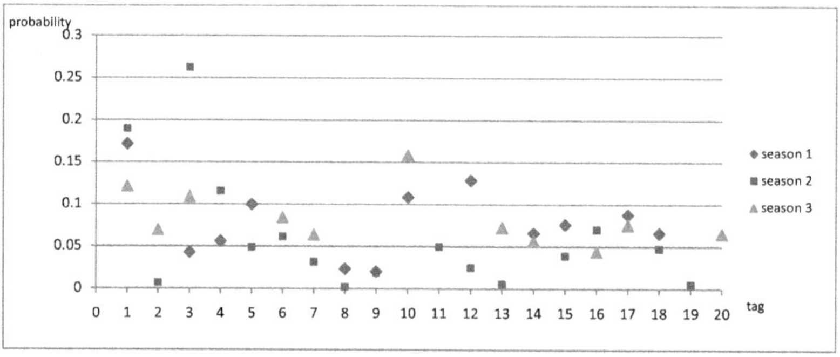

Fig. 6. Distribution of Scenes in different seasons

Figure 6 gives the different distribution of scene o_i in different seasons. Tag z_3 is the best one to reflect its tourist feature in season 2. In season 1 and 3, the probability of z_3 decreases, while the probability of z_1, z_4, z_7 and z_{10} increases.

5 Conclusions and Future Work

The goal of this paper is to detect scene features and its difference in different seasons. We formally defined the problem, and gave the data expression model of photo-tag-scene. The topic model-based method for detecting scene features was provided, which mainly includes three steps. The experimental study using real datasets in Flickr demonstrated the effectiveness of our proposed approach.

In the future work, we will combine scene features and users' profile to provide users with the optimal spatio-temporal sequence that passes through as many chosen scenes as possible with the maximum weight and the minimum distance within a limited travel time. For further research, the offline together with online methods will also be studied, which can greatly improve the performance of mining STS.

Acknowledgement

This paper was supported by NSFC, under grant number 90818004, Program for New Century Excellent Talents in University, under grant number: NCET-10-0140, and Scientific Research Fund of Hunan Provincial Education Department, under grant number: 09K085.

References

1. Allan, J., Carbonell, J.G., Doddington, G., Yamron, J., Yang, Y.: Topic Detection and Tracking Pilot Study: Final Report. In: DARPA Broadcast News Transcription and Understanding Workshop (1998)
2. Yang, Y., Pierce, T., Carbonell, J.G.: A Study of Retrospective and On-line Event Detection. In: The 21th Annual International ACM SIGIR Conference (SIGIR), pp. 28–36 (1998)
3. He, Q., Chang, K., Lim, E.P.: Analyzing Feature Trajectories for Event Detection. In: The 30th Annual International ACM SIGIR Conference (SIGIR), pp. 207–214 (2007)
4. Li, Z., Wang, B., Li, M., Ma, W.Y.: A Probabilistic Model for Retrospective News Event Detection. In: The 28th Annual International ACM SIGIR Conference, SIGIR (2005)
5. Kleinberg, J.M.: Bursty and Hierarchical Structure in Streams. In: The 9th ACM SIGKDD International Conference on Knowledge Discovery and Data Mining (KDD), vol. 7(4), pp. 373–397 (2003)
6. Halpin, H., Robu, V., Shepherd, H.: The Complex Dynamics fo Collaborative Tagging. In: The 16th International Conference on World Wide Web (WWW), pp. 211–220 (2007)
7. Dubinko, M., Kumar, J., Magnani, J., et al.: Visualizing Tags over Time. In: The 15th International Conference on World Wide Web (WWW), pp. 193–202 (2006)
8. Dmitriev, P.A., Eiron, N., Fontoura, M., Shekita, E.: Using Annotations in Enterprise Search. In: The 15th International Conference on World Wide Web (WWW), pp. 811–817 (2006)
9. Bao, S., Xue, G.R., Wu, X., Yu, Y., Su, Z.: Optimizing Web Search Using Social Annotations. In: The 16th International Conference on World Wide Web (WWW), pp. 501–510 (2007)

10. Rattenbury, T., Good, N., Naaman, M.: Towards Automatic Extraction of Event and Place Semantics from Flickr Tags. In: The 30th Annual International ACM SIGIR Conference (SIGIR), pp. 103–110 (2007)
11. Popescu, A., Grefenstette, G., Moellic, P.A.: Mining Tourist Information from User-Supplied Collections. In: The 18th ACM Conference on Information and Knowledge Management (CIKM), pp. 1713–1716 (2009)
12. Rattenbury, T., Good, N., Naaman, M.: Towards Automatic Extraction of Event and Place Semantics from Flickr Tags. In: Proceedings of the 30th Annual International ACM SIGIR Conference (2007)
13. Ahern, S., Naaman, M., Nair, R., Yang, J.: World Explorer: Visualizing Aggregate Data from Unstructured Text in Georeferenced Collections. In: Proceedings of the ACM IEEE Joint Conference on Digital Libraries, JCDL (2007)
14. Quack, T., Leibe, B., van Gool, L.: World-Scale Mining of Objects and Events from Community Photo Collections. In: Proceedings of the 7th ACM International Conference on Image and Video Retrieval, CIVR (2008)
15. Crandall, D., Backstrom, L., Hutternlocher, D., Kleinberg, J.: Mapping the World's photos. In: Proceedings of the 18th International World Wide Web Conference, WWW (2009)
16. Zheng, I., Zhang, L., Xie, X., Ma, W.Y.: Mining Interesting Locations and Travel Sequences from GPS Trajectories. In: Proceedings of the 18th International World Wide Web Conference, WWW (2009)
17. Gonotti, F., et al.: Trajectory Pattern Mining. In: Proceedings of the 13th ACM SIGKDD International Conference on Knowledge Discovery and Data Mining (KDD), pp. 330–339 (2007)
18. Girardin, F., Dal, F., Blat, J., et al.: Understanding of Tourist Dynamics from Explicitly Disclosed Location Information. In: Proceedings of the 4th International Symposium on LBS and Telecartography (2007)
19. Chen, Z., Shen, H.T., Zhou, X., Zheng, Y., Xie, X.: Searching Trajectories by Locations-An Efficiency Study. In: Proceedings of the 36th SIGMOD International Conference on Management of Data, SIGMOD (2010)
20. Home and Abroad, `http://homeandabroad.com`
21. Popescu, A., Grefenstette, G.: Deducing Trip Related Information from Flickr. In: Proceedings of the 18th International World Wide Web Conference, WWW (2009)
22. Popescu, A., Grefenstette, G., Alain, P.: Mining Tourist Information from User-Supplied Collections. In: Proceedings of The 18th ACM Conference on Information and Knowledge Management, CIKM (2009); SIGMOD (2004)
23. Shekhar, S., Liu, D.: CCAM: A Connectivity Clustered Acccess Method for Networks and Network Computations. IEEE Transactions on Knowledge and Data Engineering (TKDE), 102–119 (1997)
24. Li, F., Cheng, D.: On trip planning queries in spatial databases. In: Anshelevich, E., Egenhofer, M.J., Hwang, J. (eds.) SSTD 2005. LNCS, vol. 3633, pp. 273–290. Springer, Heidelberg (2005)
25. Blei, D., Ng, A., Jordan, M.: Latent Dirichlet Allocation. The Journal of Machine Learning Research, 993–1022 (2003)

QoS-Based Probabilistic Fault-Diagnosis Method for Exception Handling

Zhen Zhu and Wanchun Dou*

State Key Laboratory for Novel Software Technology,
Nanjing University Nanjing, China 210093
douwc@nju.edu.cn

Abstract. Fault-diagnosis is an essential prerequisite for exception handling. There are several attempts to apply it in the decentralized systems like Web Service. However, few of them discuss the fault-diagnosis technics along with QoS. In this paper, we base our work on an existing framework, and employ the Bayesian Network which takes QoS under consideration to operate a probabilistic analysis. We aim to evaluate the precedence of each diagnosis returned after the diagnostic procedure with a posterior probability and thus provide more support for exception handling.

Keywords: Fault-Diagnosis, QoS, Bayesian Network, Probabilistic Analysis.

1 Introduction

Fault-diagnosis is one key phase in exception-handling [6], it concerns the technics to detect the originating fault or faults for an already happened exception in order to recover from it. Fault-diagnosis is a particularly challenging task for web services due to intrinsic properties of Service Oriented Architecture (SOA). The traditional model-based fault-diagnosis methods require a global sight to detect fault across services which is unrealistic under SOA while each component service must protect its inherent logics from disclosing for privacy or business reasons.

A framework is proposed in literatures [1], [3] for adding diagnostic capabilities to web services without unveiling the private information. In their framework, all global consistency-based diagnoses are supposed to be returned after a diagnostic process which is triggered by exception. In each diagnosis, one or several services are suspected to have malfunctioned so as to result in the exception.

Nevertheless, they didn't discriminate each of those diagnoses from another. The services with suspected malfunctions in different diagnoses may have enormous differences in their stabilities. According to definitions in QoS area, stability which is one of the most important QoS dimensions of services measures how often one service may cause a fault during its execution. So it is natural that one diagnosis caused by services with lower stabilities has a higher probability to occur and should take precedence over other diagnoses.

---

* Corresponding author.

X. Luo et al. (Eds.): ICWL 2010 Workshops, LNCS 6537, pp. 227–236, 2011.

In this paper, we aim to base our work on the existing investigations [1], [3] and operate a probabilistic analysis on the all possible diagnoses so as to provide a more tractable fault-diagnosis result for exception handling strategies [8]. In our method, the Bayesian Network which takes QoS values under consideration is applied as a probabilistic model to evaluate the importance of each possible diagnosis.

The paper is organized as follows: in the next section, we describe the proposed diagnostic framework [1], put emphasis on our extensions. In section 3, a Bayesian Network based probabilistic method is introduced, we describe it in details. And then the feasibility of our approach is demonstrated by a case study in section 4. At last, we conclude our discussion in section 5.

2 The Diagnostic Framework

The original diagnostic framework in literature [1] mainly comprise an architecture of two roles and an algorithm referred as the Supervisor Algorithm that regulates how the two roles coordinate with each other in order to get the global diagnoses. In this section, this framework [1] along with our own extensions is generally described as the prerequisite of the later discussion.

2.1 Diagnostic Architecture

The proposed architecture [1] which we intend to keep unchanged is constituted by two roles: the Local Diagnoser (LD) and the Supervisor. The LDs are assumed to be associated with the corresponding component services and independent to each other, capable to operate the local fault-diagnosis. In consideration of clarity, the input to invoke one LD is referred as the **hypothesis**, while the output is referred as **explanation** throughout this paper. The LD is supposed to behave as follows: given one hypothesis, LD returns the complete set of possible explanations that are consistent to its private structure and behavioral model along with its local observations.

The Supervisor is located above the LDs, and possesses information of the data dependencies between component services. The Supervisor doesn't engage in the specific diagnostic actions, it operates the Supervisor Algorithm to coordinate the LDs and produce the global diagnoses [1].

2.2 Supervisor Algorithm

The original Supervisor Algorithm [1] is actually a hypothesis propagation process, it operates as follows:

(i) Both hypothesis and explanation are partial assignments to the relative variables. Hypothesis for LD_i is a partial assignment to the outputs (denoted in the form of $O_{i,j}$) of WS_i. Each explanation returned from LD_i is a partial assignment to the inputs (in the form of $I_{i,j}$) and the functionality (F_i) of WS_i.

(ii) All the evaluations of variables throughout the diagnostic process are simplified to be binary. As a matter of notation, $X_V=x_V$ or simply x_V denotes that the variable X_V has an expected value, and similarly $X_V=\overline{x}_V$ or simply $\overline{x}_V$ stands for the contrary situation. Otherwise, $X_V=*$ or simply $*$ is used to indicate that the correctness of variable X_V can not be determined.

(iii) The whole diagnostic procedure is triggered by an exception which will be referred as *DSource* for the rest of this paper. When service WS_i detects the *DSource* during its execution, its corresponding Local Diagnoser LD_i is awakened to give the initial explanations.

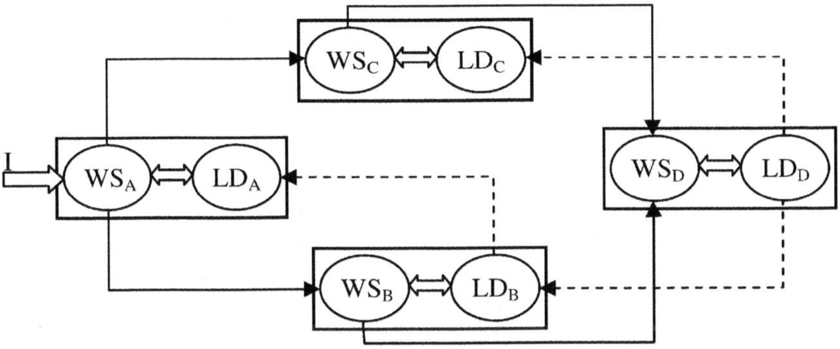

Fig. 1. A simple web service WS (represented by solid lines) and its diagnostic process (the dash lines) derived from LD_D. The symbol *I* denotes the initial inputs.

(iv) LD sends all its explanations to the Supervisor. Then Supervisor transforms the inputs variables of one service into other services' outputs variables in all explanations according to data dependency knowledge between services. Since this transformation is trivial, we neglect it and assume that all explanations are transformed automatically.

(v) After the variable transformation in part (iv) has been finished, the Supervisor generates a new set of hypotheses from the explanations, and then those hypotheses are used to invoke the corresponding LDs to get another set of explanations (we formalize this hypothesis generation process in later discussion). The Supervisor Algorithm repeats this process until no more hypotheses can be obtained.

It's worth nothing that the original literature [1] uses qualitative models to give further evaluation to the variables in part (ii), but for the purpose of simplicity, we assume they are all binary in our discussion. And the concept of functionality in part (i) is applied to build connections with QoS knowledge.

In order to conduct a probabilistic analysis to the diagnostic result in the next section, we make our own assumptions on the Supervisor Algorithm [1] as follows: $E_{i,j}$ denotes the complete set of the explanations that returned from LD_i when it is invoked with one hypothesis $H_{i,j}$ and let $e \in E_{i,j}$, if $F_i(e) \neq *$, a conditional probability $P(H_{i,j}|e)$ is supposed to be returned along with this explanation, where $F_i(a)$ is a function that returns the evaluation of variable F_i in the partial assignment a. We will give our interpretation of this assumption in section 3.

2.3 A Fault-Diagnosis Example

In this section, the fault-diagnosis procedure depicted in Fig. 1 is described in details according to our extended Supervisor Algorithm [1] as follows:

At the beginning, WS_D detects the *DSource* and then arouses LD_D to analyze this abnormality and give the initial explanations as:

Table 1. Complete set of explanations returned from LD_D

explanation	hypothesis	F_D	$I_{D,1}$ ($O_{B,1}$)	$I_{D,2}$ ($O_{C,1}$)	cp
$e_{D,1}$	*DSource*	$\overline{f}_D$	$\overline{i}_{D,1}$ ($\overline{o}_{B,1}$)	*	v_1
$e_{D,2}$	*DSource*	*	$\overline{i}_{D,1}$ ($\overline{o}_{B,1}$)	$\overline{i}_{D,2}$ ($\overline{o}_{C,1}$)	*

Each row in Table 1 represents one explanation. The hypothesis element in one row denotes which hypothesis this explanation is used to explain for, it also implies which explanation set this explanation belongs to. *DSource* acts as an input of LD_D, thus it's regarded as a hypothesis in Table 1. As mentioned before, the explanation returned by LD_i is a partial assignment to the inputs and the functionality of WS_i which are $I_{D,1}$, $I_{D,2}$, and F_D respectively in Table 1. The symbols $O_{B,1}$ and $O_{C,1}$ represent the corresponding outputs of $I_{D,1}$ and $I_{D,2}$ according to the data dependencies between services. And since $F_D(e_{D,1})\neq*$, a conditional probability v_1 is also returned from LD_D with $e_{D,1}$.

The Supervisor gives rise to a set of new hypotheses ($H_{B,1}$, $H_{C,1}$) on the basis of received explanations $e_{D,1}$ and $e_{D,2}$. Then LD_B and LD_C are invoked with the new hypotheses.

Table 2. Complete set of explanations returned from LD_B

explanation	hypothesis	F_B	$I_{B,1}$ ($O_{A,1}$)	$I_{B,2}$ ($O_{A,2}$)	cp
$e_{B,1}$	$H_{B,1}:(\overline{o}_{B,1})$	*	$\overline{i}_{B,1}$ ($\overline{o}_{A,1}$)	*	*
$e_{B,2}$	$H_{B,1}:(\overline{o}_{B,1})$	*	*	$\overline{i}_{B,2}$ ($\overline{o}_{A,2}$)	*

Table 3. Complete set of explanations returned from LD_C

explanation	hypothesis	F_C	cp
$e_{C,1}$	$H_{C,1}:(\overline{o}_{C,1})$	$\overline{f}_C$	v_2

Similarly, the Supervisor constructs the new hypotheses ($H_{A,1}$, $H_{A,2}$) from explanations $e_{B,1}$ and $e_{B,2}$, and then LD_A is invoked. However, the explanation $e_{C,1}$ for $H_{C,1}$ only blames the functionality of WS_C, as a result, no more hypothesis can be produced from this explanation.

Table 4. Complete set of explanations returned from LD_A

explanation	hypothesis	F_A	cp
$e_{A,1}$	$H_{A,1}:(\overline{o}_{A,1})$	$\overline{f}_A$	v_3
$e_{A,2}$	$H_{A,2}:(\overline{o}_{A,2})$	$\overline{f}_A$	v_4

At the end, none of explanations returned from LD_A can be used to generate new hypothesis, the fault-diagnosis procedure terminates.

3 The Probabilistic Fault-Diagnosis Method

In this section, at first, some fundamental theories of Bayesian Network are summarized. And then we illustrate how to build a Bayesian Network for fault-diagnosis which is referred as BN-D in this paper. At last, the method to operate a probabilistic analysis on the BN-D is introduced in details.

3.1 Preliminaries

The Bayesian Network (BN) is a directed acyclic graph which is often used to manifest the conditional dependencies between a set of random variables, given x_p, random variables x_m and x_n are said to be conditional independent to each other, if

$$P(x_m,x_n|x_p)=P(x_m|x_p)P(x_n|x_p)\ . \tag{1}$$

Each node in BN represents a random variable (this paper doesn't make difference between node and random variable concepts in BN), while a directed edge represents a conditional dependency between two nodes. The Bayesian Network expresses one way to decompose the joint probability and thus facilitates the probabilistic inference [7] as

$$P(X)=\prod_{x\in X}P(x\,|\,\pi(x))\ , \tag{2}$$

where $\pi(x)$ represents all the parent nodes of x in the network.

3.2 Bayesian Network for Fault-Diagnosis

The Supervisor needs to split an explanation into several disjoint parts in order to generate new hypotheses. We formalize this hypothesis generation process as: Given an explanation $e\in E_{i,j}$, if conf$_k(e)$ is not empty and there is at least one variable v in conf$_k(e)$ that is not assigned as$*$, then conf$_k(e)$ is regarded as a new hypothesis, where conf$_k(a)$ stands for a function that returns a sub-assignment of a that only contains output variables of WS_k.

We depict the BN-D construction procedure as follows:

(i) Each hypothesis $H_{i,j}$ is represented as a node $NH_{i,j}$ in BN-D. $NH_{i,j}$ is also binary; $NH_{i,j}=h_{i,j}$ or simply $h_{i,j}$ stands for the same partial assignment as hypothesis $H_{i,j}$, whereas $NH_{i,j}=\overline{h}_{i,j}$ or simply $\overline{h}_{i,j}$ denotes all the other partial assignments.

(ii) As mentioned before, *DSource* is regarded as a specific hypothesis, and according to the properties of fault-diagnosis, this *DSource* variable in BN-D has only one evaluation representing the occurrence of the exception.

(iii) Given a hypothesis $H_{i,j}$, if it is generated from explanation $e\in E_{m,n}$ which means $H_{i,j}$=conf$_i(e)$, a directed edge is added that leads from $NH_{i,j}$ to $NH_{m,n}$.

(iv) If there exists at least one explanation e that $e \in E_{i,j}$ and $F_i(e) \neq *$, add one directed edge leads from the functionality node F_i (construct it if there is not one in the network) to $NH_{i,j}$.

(v) Given an explanation $e \in E_{i,j}$, if the evaluation is not $*$ in e for a initial input $I_p \in I$, add one directed edge leads from the initial input node I_p (construct it if there is not one in the network) to $NH_{i,j}$.

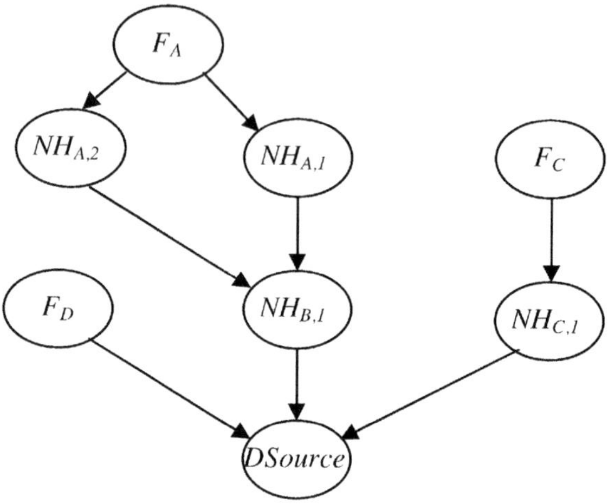

Fig. 2. The BN-D built in accordance with the diagnostic procedure depicted in Fig. 1 and Tables 1-4

Several details are worth to take notice about one BN-D, and the consideration of the initial inputs to start with:

i) The initial input nodes may not appear in the BN-D. For instance, in the diagnostic procedure depicted in Fig. 1, the hypothesis propagations terminate at LD_A and LD_C respectively.

ii) Taking each initial input under elaborate consideration is too complicated to explore. In order to reduce the complexity and without losing generality, we assume that all initial inputs are independent to each other and share a same probability P_I to be abnormal.

Nodes in BN-D are divided into four categories according to the construction method, i.e., the *DSource* set named in accordance with its only member, the *HYP* set contains all hypothesis nodes, the *I* set contains all initial input nodes and the *FUN* contains all functionality nodes respectively.

Only the initial input nodes and the functionality nodes can be leaf in the BN-D. For instance, if LD_i returns no explanation for hypothesis $H_{i,j}$ (equals to that $NH_{i,j}$ is a leaf node) indicates that this hypothesis could not happen in any conditions, and this $NH_{i,j}$ node should be removed. Thus the BN-D needs to be pruned after the construction, until all the unnecessary leaf nodes are removed.

3.3 Probabilistic Analysis

As a review of our aforementioned extensions on the Supervisor Algorithm [1], a value v is associated with explanation $e \in E_{i,j}$ when $\mathrm{F}_i(e) \neq *$ to represent the probability of hypothesis $H_{i,j}$ given the occurrence of e. And we lay down the underlying assumptions here to give an interpretation:

i) Only the random variables of functionality (F_i for instance) can contribute uncertainty to the conditional probabilities in the BN-D. For example, let $e \in E_{i,j}$, if $\mathrm{F}_i(e)=*$, which means that LD_i only blames inputs in this explanation e for hypothesis $H_{i,j}$, then $P(H_{i,j}|e)=1$. There is a similar assumption appears in literature [2].

ii) One functionality variable contributes the same uncertainty in different explanations for the same hypothesis which means that for two explanations e, e', if $e \in E_{i,j} \wedge e' \in E_{i,j}$ and $\mathrm{F}_i(e)=\mathrm{F}_i(e') \neq *$, then $v=v'=v_{i,j}$, where v and v' are the conditional probabilities associated with e and e' respectively, $v_{i,j}$ is a general representation for those equivalent values.

The definition of ***conflict***: let a be a union of a set of assignments, if there exists a variable v that possesses different evaluations in these assignments (all the $*$ evaluations are ignored), this a is said to contain a conflict. If a contains a conflict, $P(a)=0$.

Thus, $(HYP,I,FUN,DSource)$ might contain a conflict, in this case $P(HYP,I,FUN,DSource)=0$. Otherwise, it is calculated as follows:

Inputs: $(HYP,I,FUN,DSource)$, the hypothesis $H_{i,j}$ along with its explanation set $E_{i,j}$ and perhaps the conditional probability $v_{i,j}$.
Outputs: $P(NH_{i,j} \mid \pi(NH_{i,j}))$ under $(HYP,I,FUN,DSource)$.

If $\exists e(e \in E_{i,j} \wedge ((HYP,I,FUN,DSource)$ satisfies $e) \wedge \mathrm{F}_i(e)=*)$
  If $NH_{i,j}=h_{i,j}$, $P(h_{i,j} \mid \pi(NH_{i,j}))=1$.
  else if $NH_{i,j}=\bar{h}_{i,j}$, $P(\bar{h}_{i,j} \mid \pi(NH_{i,j}))=0$.
  endif.
else if $\forall e((e \in E_{i,j} \wedge ((HYP,I,FUN,DSource)$ satisfies $e)) \rightarrow \mathrm{F}_i(e) \neq *)$
  If $NH_{i,j}=h_{i,j}$, $P(h_{i,j} \mid \pi(NH_{i,j}))=v_{i,j}$.
  else if $NH_{i,j}=\bar{h}_{i,j}$, $P(\bar{h}_{i,j} \mid \pi(NH_{i,j}))=1-v_{i,j}$.
  endif.
else
  if $NH_{i,j}=h_{i,j}$, $P(h_{i,j} \mid \pi(NH_{i,j}))=0$.
  else if $NH_{i,j}=\bar{h}_{i,j}$, $P(\bar{h}_{i,j} \mid \pi(NH_{i,j}))=1$.
  endif.
endif.

Fig. 3. An algorithm to compute $P(NH_{i,j} \mid \pi(NH_{i,j}))$ under $(HYP,I,FUN,DSource)$

The definition of ***satisfy*** (appears in lines 1, 6): as it is mentioned before, the explanation $e \in E_{i,j}$ can be split into several disjoint parts, and each part is an evaluation to the according node in BN-D. If *(HYP,I,FUN,DSource)* contains all these evaluations, it is said to satisfy *e*.

Line 1 demonstrates the situation where there exists one explanation for hypothesis $H_{i,j}$ satisfied by *(HYP,I,FUN,DSource)* doesn't blame the functionality F_i, the conditional probability is computed according to our aforementioned assumption (i). When the explanations satisfied by *(HYP,I,FUN,DSource)* all blame F_i for hypothesis $H_{i,j}$ (line 5), the conditional probability can be calculated according to our assumption (ii). If there is not explanation satisfied at all by *(HYP,I,FUN,DSource)* (line 9), the hypothesis $H_{i,j}$ $(NH_{i,j}=h_{i,j})$ can not happen in this situation which indicates $P(h_{i,j} \mid \pi(NH_{i,j}))=0$ and $P(\overline{h}_{i,j} \mid \pi(NH_{i,j}))=1$.

The stability of one service WS_i is also written as the success rate denoted as $q_{\text{rat}}(WS_i)$ in some literatures [4]. Now we introduce stability here to calculate the probability $P(F_i)$ for all $F_i \in FUN$:

$$P(F_i = f_i) = q_{\text{rat}}(WS_i) \qquad P(F_i = \overline{f}_i) = 1 - q_{\text{rat}}(WS_i)\,. \tag{3}$$

The final diagnosis concerns the assumptions over *FUN*. We adopt the same definition of **diagnosis** Δ that appears in literature [2] as:

$$\Delta = \{f_i \mid F_i \in Fun\} \cup \{\overline{f}_i \mid F_i \in FUN \setminus Fun\},$$

where *Fun* represents a subset of *FUN*. Since a diagnosis is a complete assignment over *FUN*, thus *(HYP,I,FUN,DSource)* is substituted by *(HYP,I,Δ,DSource)* for the rest of this paper. Now the joint probability P*(HYP,I,Δ,DSource)* is computed according to Equations (2), (3) as

$$P(HYP,I,\Delta,DSource) = P_I^{\,m}(1-P_I)^n \prod_{NH_{i,j}\in HYP} P(NH_{i,j} \mid \pi(NH_{i,j})) \prod_{F_i\in Fun} q_{\text{rat}}(WS_i) \prod_{F_i\in FUN\setminus Fun} (1-q_{\text{rat}}(WS_i)) \tag{4}$$

where symbols *n* and *m* represent total numbers of the initial inputs to be assigned as regular and irregular respectively in *(HYP,I,Δ,DSource)*. In the end, the final posterior probability *P(Δ|DSource)* to evaluate the importance of each diagnosis Δ can be obtained

$$P(\Delta, DSource) = \sum_{HYP,I} P(HYP,I,\Delta,DSource), \tag{5}$$

$$P(\Delta \mid DSource) = \frac{P(\Delta, DSource)}{P(DSource)} = \frac{P(\Delta, DSource)}{\sum_{\Delta} P(\Delta, DSource)}\,. \tag{6}$$

4 A Case Study

In this section, we exhibit a probabilistic analysis on the BN-D depicted in Fig. 2 to demonstrate the feasibility of our proposed method.

Apply the symbols defined in section 3 as: $HYP=\{NH_{A,1},NH_{A,2},NH_{B,1},NH_{C,1}\}$, $I=\varnothing$, $FUN=\{F_A,F_C,F_D\}$.

Each possible diagnosis Δ and its corresponding joint probability in the form of $P(\Delta, DSource)$ according to Equations (4), (5) are listed in Table 5 as follows:

Table 5. All possible diagnoses and their joint probabilities P(Δ,*DSource*). $M=(1-v_3)v_4+(1-v_4)v_3+v_3v_4$

daignosis	$P(\Delta, DSource)$
(f_A, f_C, f_D)	0
$(f_A, f_C, \overline{f}_D)$	0
$(f_A, \overline{f}_C, f_D)$	0
$(f_A, \overline{f}_C, \overline{f}_D)$	0
$(\overline{f}_A, f_C, f_D)$	0
$(\overline{f}_A, f_C, \overline{f}_D)$	$(1-q_{\text{rat}}(WS_A))q_{\text{rat}}(WS_C)(1-q_{\text{rat}}(WS_D))v_1M$
$(\overline{f}_A, \overline{f}_C, f_D)$	$(1-q_{\text{rat}}(WS_A))(1-q_{\text{rat}}(WS_C))q_{\text{rat}}(WS_D)v_2M$
$(\overline{f}_A, \overline{f}_C, \overline{f}_D)$	$(1-q_{\text{rat}}(WS_A))(1-q_{\text{rat}}(WS_C))(1-q_{\text{rat}}(WS_D))[v_1(1-v_2)+v_2]M$

We set the success rate values of services and conditional probability values returned from LDs separately in Table 6 and Table 7 as follows:

Table 6. The success rate of services

service	WS_A	WS_C	WS_D
success rate	0.87	0.90	0.99

Table 7. The conditional probabilities appear in Tables 1-4

variable	v_1	v_2	v_3	v_4
conditional probability	0.60	0.75	0.82	0.90

Apply values in Table 6 and Table 7 to joint probabilities in Table 5, and according to Equation (6), the final posterior probabilities of all diagnoses can be obtained.

diagnosis	$P(\Delta \mid DSource)$	diagnosis	$P(\Delta \mid DSource)$
(f_A, f_C, f_D)	0	$(\overline{f}_A, f_C, f_D)$	0
$(f_A, f_C, \overline{f}_D)$	0	$(\overline{f}_A, f_C, \overline{f}_D)$	0.067039
$(f_A, \overline{f}_C, f_D)$	0	$(\overline{f}_A, \overline{f}_C, f_D)$	0.921788
$(f_A, \overline{f}_C, \overline{f}_D)$	0	$(\overline{f}_A, \overline{f}_C, \overline{f}_D)$	0.011173

5 Conclusion

In this paper, a method is introduced to evaluate the returned diagnoses from fault-diagnosis procedure. We extended the existing diagnosis framework [1] and then build a Bayesian Network according to the returned information form Local Diagnosers [1] in order to operate a probabilistic analysis. Our method evaluates the precedence of each possible diagnosis with a posterior probability, and thus provides more tractable diagnostic results for exception handling.

References

1. Console, L., Picardi, C., Dupre, D.T.: A Framework for Decentralized Qualitative Model-Based Diagnosis. In: Proceedings of the 20th International Joint Conference on Artificial Intelligence, pp. 286–291 (2007)
2. Flesch, I., Lucas, P., van der Weide, T.: Conflict-based Diagnosis: Adding Uncertainty to Model-based Diagnosis. In: Proceedings of the 20th International Joint Conference on Artificial Intelligence, pp. 380–385 (2007)
3. Ardissono, L., Console, L., Goy, A., Petrone, G., Picardi, C., Segnan, M., Dupre, D.T.: Enhancing Web Services with Diagnostic Capabilities. In: Proceedings of the Third European Conference on Web Services, pp. 182–192 (2005)
4. Zeng, L., Benatallah, B., Ngu, A.H.H., Dumas, M., Kalagnanam, J., Chang, H.: QoS-Aware Middleware for Web Services Composition. IEEE Transactions on Software Engineering 30(5), 311–327 (2004)
5. Hagen, C., Alonso, G.: Exception Handling in Workflow Management Systems. IEEE Transactions on Software Engineering 26(10), 943–958 (2000)
6. Friedrich, G., Fugini, M.G., Mussi, E., Pernici, B., Tagni, G.: Exception Handling for Repair in Service-Based Processes. IEEE Transactions on Software Engineering 36(2), 198–215 (2010)
7. Zhang, L., Guo, H.: Introduction to Bayesian Networks. China Science Press, Beijing (2006)
8. Liu, A., Li, Q., Huang, L., Xiao, M.: FACTS: A Framework for Fault-Tolerant Composition of Transactional Web Services. IEEE Transactions on Services Computing 3(1), 46–59 (2010)

A Knowledge-Driven Approach to Web-Based Learning for Formal Algorithm Development*

Yujun Zheng, Haihe Shi, and Jinyun Xue

Provincial Key Lab of High Performance Computing Technology, Jiangxi Normal University, Nanchang 330027, China
yujun.zheng@computer.org, haiheshi@163.com, jinyun@jxnu.edu.cn

Abstract. The paper reports an effort to construct a Web-based environment for teaching/learning algorithm design. The semantic web version of PAR platform, a practical platform for formal algorithm development, consists of structural knowledge models for effectively organizing and managing learning concepts in the domains of problem specification, algorithm calculation, algorithm reuse, and program transformation, and provides effective learning paths for synthesize and transmit these concepts meeting the requirements of Web users. The e-learning PAR platform has been successfully applied in undergraduate and graduate courses, and demonstrated its effectiveness in improving algorithm learning.

Keywords: Web-based learning, algorithm design, formal methods, PAR method.

1 Introduction

Web-based learning provides a whole new approach to eliminate the time and distance barriers of learning and to improve the subjective activity and responsibility of the learners. During the last years, the expanding population of students in higher education also significantly increases the demand for effective, flexible, and user-friendly Web-based learning. Among the majors in higher education, computer science is one of the most successful areas for the application of digital learning techniques [10, 12, 13], perhaps mainly because computer science educators have an enviable position in building learning tools and environments to meet their pedagogical goals. A number of successful and impressive cases have been reported on different major courses such as programming language (e.g., [2, 5, 7, 11]) and database (e.g., [3, 9]). However, few researches have been reported on the Web-based environments for learning algorithm design and analysis, which is considered as the "spirit" of computing [6].

Obviously, the complexity of combinatorial problems and the delicate subtlety of problem-solving algorithms hinder the existing e-learning systems to

* Supported by grants from Natural Science Foundation (No. 60773054) and International Science & Technology Cooperation Program (No. 2008DFA11940) of China.

X. Luo et al. (Eds.): ICWL 2010 Workshops, LNCS 6537, pp. 237–245, 2011.

process, organize and transmit knowledge fast and effectively. According to the High/Scope Educational Research Foundation [8], it is suggested that active learning is a methodology that:

1. Exercises and challenges the capacities of the learner that are emerging at a given developmental level;
2. Encourages and helps the learner to develop a unique pattern of interests, talents, and goals;
3. Presents learning experiences when learners are best able to master, generalise, and retain what they learn and can relate it to previous experiences and future expectations.

PAR method [15–17, 21] is a formal algorithm design method developed under continuous support from the National Science Foundation (Grant No. 69783006, 69983003, 60273092, 60573080, 60773054) of China. It covers main algorithm design techniques including divide-and-conquer, dynamic programming, greedy, backtracking, etc., and supports the whole development process from formal problem specifications to executable algorithmic programs. Besides a series of impressive industrial applications (see [19] for examples), PAR has also been successfully practised in teaching and learning of the "algorithm and data structure" course in computer science major.

Since 2008, with support from the Ministry of Science and Technology of China, a semantic web version of PAR platform has been constructed in support of both undergraduate and graduate students as well as other researches in the area of formal algorithm development[1]. In this paper we report the architectural design of the Web-based system, putting emphasis on the modeling and use of algorithm-design knowledge for visual illustration, participatory training, and interactive learning.

2 E-Learning PAR Platform

The e-learning version of PAR platform is constructed and used as the vehicle for the learning of the formal algorithm development method through the internet. Fig. 1 presents an architectural overview of the e-learning system.

The system is based on algorithm design knowledge including formal specification knowledge, algorithm calculation knowledge, algorithm reuse knowledge, and program transformation knowledge, which is modeled as an integrated concept map. From the perspective of learners, the concepts in the knowledge map can be elicited and synthesized into their learning paths. As shown in Fig. 2, there are two general learning paths that both start from a set of learning objects of in the context of formal problem specifications: the first passes through learning objects of algorithm calculation and program transformation, and the second passes through learning objects of existing algorithm design techniques

[1] A preview version of the Web-based system can be visited at: `http://www.jxcsst.com/ParandPlatform/parplatform.html`

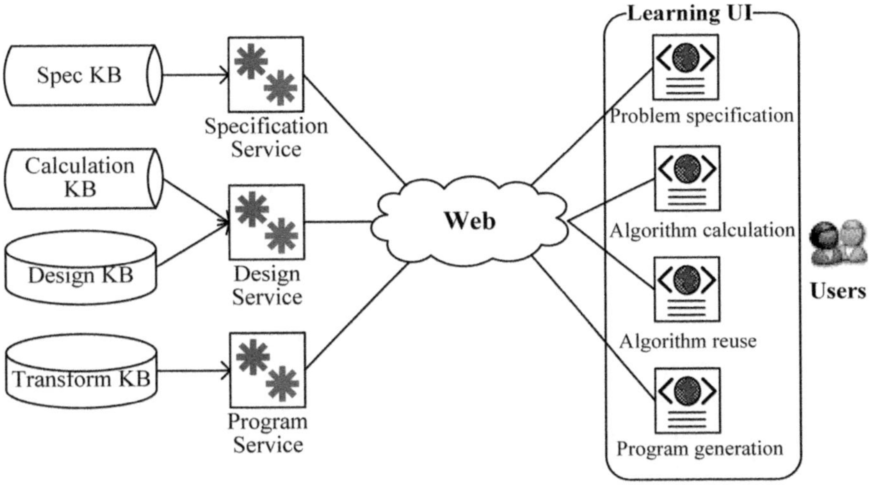

Fig. 1. The architectural overview of the e-learning PAR platform

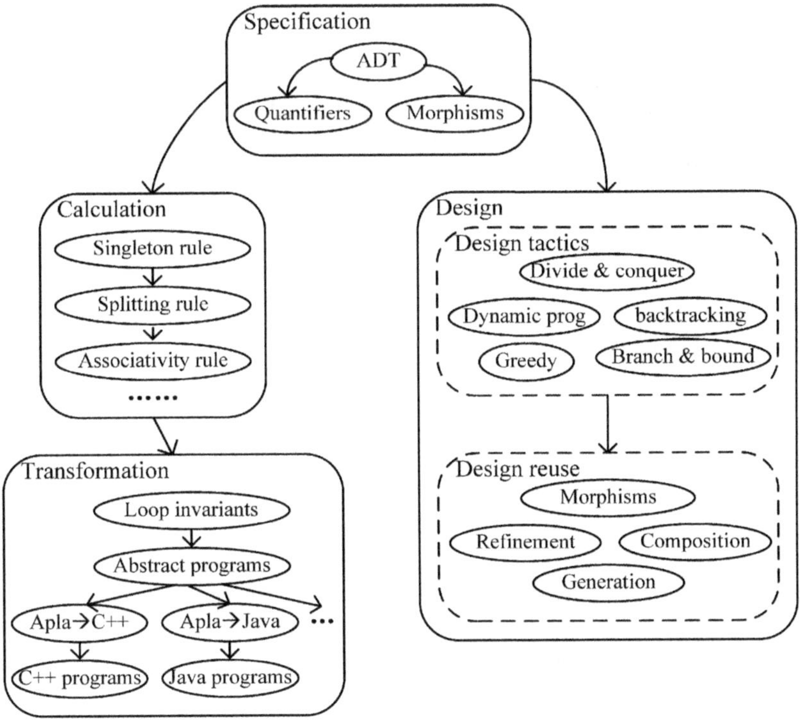

Fig. 2. The general learning paths of the e-learning PAR platform

and algorithm reuses. The three kinds of web services, i.e., specification service, design service, and program service, trace the progress of the learners and use corresponding learning objects based on appropriate concepts selected from the knowledge bases.

2.1 Specification Knowledge

The specification knowledge base (Spec KB) consists of concepts of formal specifications, which can be divided into the following three parts.

- Abstract data types (ADT): The learners start from the concepts of algebraic specifications of data types, which consist of sorts, functions (operators), and axioms. They first learn basic ADT such as *Boolean* and *Integer* and then generic ADT such as *List*, *Stack*, and *Queue*. The specification service selects typical types from the ADT library in Spec KB and transforms them into XML format; The user interface interprets them into visual presentations to illustrate their structures; Afterwards, the learners can try to define new ADT, which are verified by the specification service.
- Quantifier expressions: In PAR method the problem specifications are expressed using the Eindhoven quantifier notation [1], the components of which including generalized quantifiers, free and bounded variables, range expressions, and goal expressions, are visually illustrated step by step. Similarly, the specification service can verify user-defined expressions.
- Morphisms: A specification morphism maps the sorts and operators from one specification to another such that the axioms hold in translation. The concepts include refinement morphisms that extend existing specifications, instantiation morphisms that bind actual values to formal parameters in generic specifications, and reduction morphisms that describe recurrence relationships between the combinatorial problems.

Fig. 3 presents an example of concept map for constructing specification of the knapsack problem, which is composed by learning objects of maximum quantifier, ADT *Set*, operators and functions on *Set*, etc.

2.2 Calculation Knowledge

The calculation knowledge base (Calculation KB) consists of a set of algorithm calculation rules for reducing the problem into subproblems and constructing problem recurrences. At the beginning stage of learning algorithm calculation, the design service provides a number of exercises for learners to use individual calculation rules; After a period of ordinary training, the design service creates purposeful exercises on how to apply a set of calculation rules on a specific problem specification. For example, the following presents a calculation process on the knapsack problem, which employs the rules of *function decomposition, range splitting, single range, separate condition, and fold.*

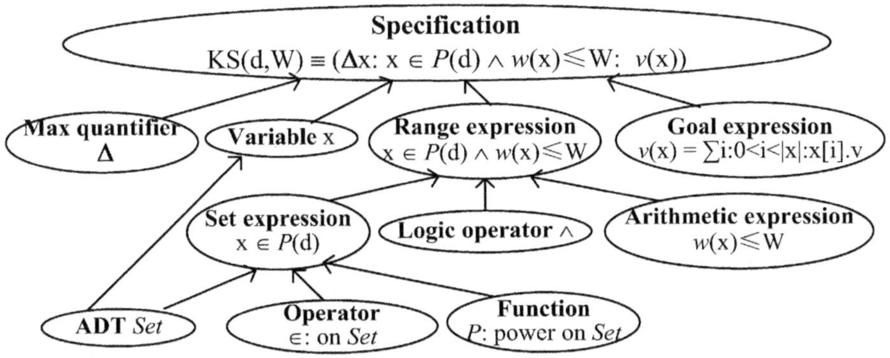

Fig. 3. The concept map for constructing the knapsack problem specification

$$
\begin{aligned}
& KS(S_n, W) \\
\equiv\ & [\text{function decomposition } \mathcal{P}(S_n){=}\mathcal{P}(S_{n-1}){\cup}\{z|z{=}z' \cup \{s_n\} \wedge z' \in \mathcal{P}(S_{n-1})\}] \\
& (\triangle z : w(z) \le W \wedge (z \in \mathcal{P}(S_{n-1}) \cup \{z|z = z' \cup \{s_n\} \wedge z' \in \mathcal{P}(S_{n-1})\}) : v(z)) \\
\equiv\ & [\text{range splitting}] \\
& max((\triangle z : w(z) \le W \wedge z \in \mathcal{P}(S_{n-1}) : v(z)), \\
& \qquad (\triangle z' : w(z' \cup \{s_n\}) \le W \wedge z' \in \mathcal{P}(S_{n-1}) : v(z' \cup \{s_n\}))) \\
\equiv\ & [\text{fold}] \\
& max(KS(S_{n-1}, W), \\
& \qquad (\triangle z' : w_n \le W \wedge w(z') \le W - w_n \wedge z' \in \mathcal{P}(S_{n-1}) : v(z') + v_n)) \\
\equiv\ & [\text{single range}] \\
& max(KS(S_{n-1}, W), \\
& \qquad (\triangle z' : w_n \le W \wedge w(z') \le W - w_n \wedge z' \in \mathcal{P}(S_{n-1}) : v(z')) + v_n) \\
\equiv\ & [\text{separate condition on } w_n \le W] \\
& \begin{cases} max(KS(S_{n-1}, W), \\ \qquad (\triangle z' : w(z') \le W - w_n \wedge z' \in \mathcal{P}(S_{n-1}) : v(z')) + v_n) & \text{if } w_n \le W \\ KS(S_{n-1}, W) & \text{else} \end{cases} \\
\equiv\ & [\text{fold}] \\
& \begin{cases} max(KS(S_{n-1}, W), KS(S_{n-1}, W - w_n) + v_n) & \text{if } w_n \le W \\ KS(S_{n-1}, W) & \text{else} \end{cases}
\end{aligned}
$$

2.3 Transformation Knowledge

An appropriate calculation result contains the recurrence relationship(s) between the original problem and its subproblems (including direct subproblems and/ or derivative subproblems [21]), which implicitly represents a recurrence-based (and in most cases recursive) algorithm. The next step is to develop the algorithm's loop invariant, based on which the algorithm can be transformed into an iterative program.

Similarly, the program service provides tutorials on loop invariant development techniques [4, 14] and purposeful exercises based on library and user-defined algorithms.

In order to support multi-language programming and reuse key components of transformation tools, PAR introduces an intermediate abstract programming language named Apla, and provides a semi-automatic software tool for transforming recurrence-based algorithms to Apla programs and several automatic tools for transforming Apla programs to other executable programs including C++, C#, Visual Basic and Java. The e-learning PAR platform integrates these tools as well as their online tutorials and help documents as web services to support both the learning and practice activities. Fig. 4 shows the web user interface of the transformation tool from Apla to C++.

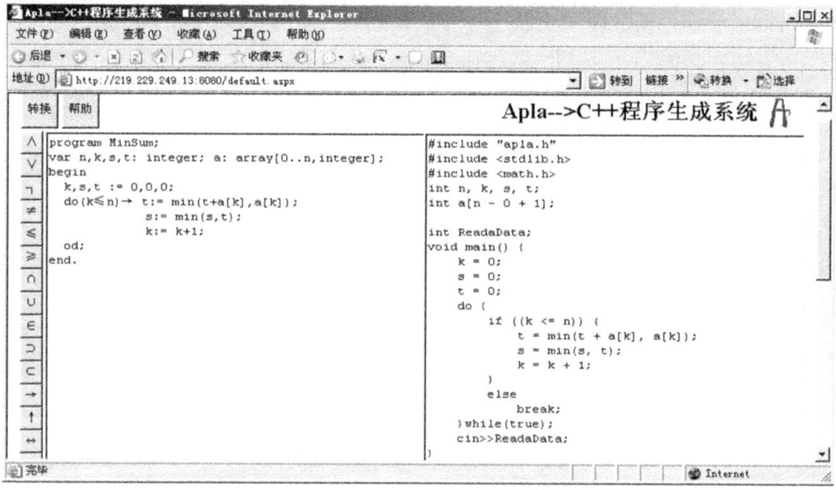

Fig. 4. The web UI of Apla→C++ program transformation tool

2.4 Design Knowledge

The design knowledge base (Design KB) consists of the following two parts:

- Design tactics knowledge: Design KB constructs structural models of knowledge from traditional algorithm design tactics (e.g., divide-and-conquer, dynamic programming, greedy, branch-and-bound and backtracking), which are saved as an integrated refinement route from generic algorithms to abstract programs and constrains on generic instantiations mapping into concrete problems (see [18, 20] for examples).

- Design reuse knowledge: For a concrete problem that fall into the category of a specific design tactic, the learners should (1) select a specific refinement morphism from the generic algorithm to generic program; (2) construct the instantiation morphism from generic types and operations to concrete ones which characterizes the application of the tactic on the problem; (3) compose the refinement and instantiation to computes abstract program for the problem; (4) transforms the abstract program to an executable program.

Take the knapsack problem for example, the learners can select the refinement from the generic dynamic programming algorithm [18] to the generic Apla program that utilizes a backward dynamic programming procedure and searches for maximum objective function values, construct a morphism that maps the generic algorithm to the recursive knapsack algorithm by instantiating generic *SolutionNode* data type and its operations, and thus work out the iterative knapsack program, the process of which is illustrated in Fig. 5.

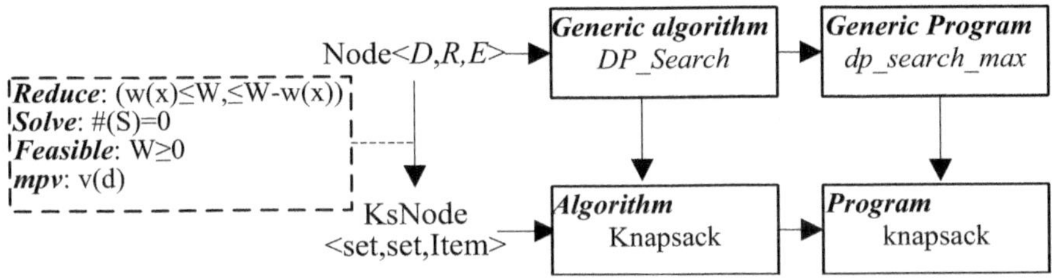

Fig. 5. Reuse of a generic dynamic programming algorithm to solve the knapsack problem

3 User Experiences and Learning Effects

Since 2009, the e-learning PAR platform was opened for use in Jiangxi Normal University, in particular for assisting the students in the undergraduate course *Programming Methodology*. We collected data on learning effects of a class of 56 students, among which 23 chose "heavily rely on the e-learning platform in study", 25 chose "sometimes use the e-learning platform to improve study", and 8 chose "never use e-learning platform". The final exam contained ten non-trivial problems, and the results of different groups of the students were given in Table 1, from which we can see that e-learning acted as a very positive force for improving scores. In more details, the results also revealed that the e-learning platform was more helpful to problems to be solved by tactics such as dynamic programming and branch-and-bound than problems that can be solved by simple tactics including divide-and-conquer and greedy, which demonstrated that the formal algorithm development method is more powerful and cost-effective on complicated problems.

Table 1. The number of students solved the problems and the average student scores in different groups

Problems \ Platform usage	Heavily use (23)	Sometimes use (25)	Never use (8)
Quick sort	18	21	6
Shortest path	19	19	6
Traveling salesman	20	18	5
Minimum spanning tree	19	17	6
Minimum vertex cover	18	15	3
Set cover	21	20	2
Maximum clique	22	17	4
Integer knapsack	16	15	2
Bin packing	18	14	1
Average Score	83.0	70.4	51.25

4 Conclusion

Nowadays, the semantic web technologies are considered the most promising solutions to effectively organize and manage available e-learning resources, meeting the peculiar requirements of both teachers and students. The paper reports the e-learning PAR platform, a semantic web based system for teaching and learning formal algorithm development. The system models knowledge of different domains of algorithm design including problem specification, algorithm calculation, algorithm reuse, and program transformation, and provides effective learning paths for synthesize and transmit key concepts to Web users step by step. The system has been successfully applied in undergraduate and graduate courses, and demonstrated its effectiveness in improving algorithm learning.

Currently, the e-learning PAR platform mainly focuses on the development of exact algorithms, i.e., working out the exact (optimal) solutions for the problems. Currently we are extending our algebraic approach to meta-heuristic methods including tabu search [22], simulated annealing, genetic algorithms, and ant colony optimization, in order to effectively tackle hard problems that are polynomial-time intractable. Our platform will also construct knowledge models and learning maps to support teaching and learning these meta-heuristics, and thus provides a more comprehensive set of algorithm design paradigms in an integrated environment.

References

1. Dijkstra, E.W., Scholten, C.S.: Predicate Calculus and Program Semantics. Texts and Monographs in Computer Science. Springer, New York (1990)
2. Ellis, A., Hagan, D., Sheard, J., Lowder, J., Doube, W., Carbone, A., Robinson, J., Tucker, S.: A collaborative strategy for developing shared Java teaching resources to support first year programming. In: 4th Annual SIGCSE/SIGCUE ITiCSE Conf. Innovation and Technology in Computer Science Education, pp. 84–87 (1999)

3. Georgiev, N.: A Web-Based Environment for Learning Normalization of Relational Database Schemata. Master Thesis, Department of Computer Science, Umea University, Sweden (2008)
4. Gries, D.: The Science of Computer Programming. Springer, New York (1981)
5. Haataja, A., Suhonen, J., Sutinen, E.: How to learn introductory programming over the Web. Informatica 25, 165–171 (2001)
6. Harel, D., Feldman, Y.: Algorithmics: The Spirit of Computing. Addison-Wesley, Reading (2004)
7. Lavonen, J., Meisalo, V., Lattu, M., Sutinen, E.: Concretizing the programming task: a case study in a secondary school. Computers & Education 40, 115–135 (2003)
8. Lee, J.A.N.: Interactive learning with a Web-based digital library system. In: 9th DELOS Workshop. Digital Libraries for Distance Learning, pp. 61–70. Bno, Czech Republic (1999)
9. Kung, H.J., Tung, H.L.: A Web-based tool to enhance teaching/learning database normalization. In: Proc. 2006 Southern Association for Information System Conference, pp. 251–258 (2006)
10. Mahmoud, M.E.: Web-based graduate diploma in computer sciences. E-Learning and Digital Media 4, 464–470 (2007)
11. Sitthiworachart, J., Joy, M.: Web-based peer assessment in learning computer programming. In: 3rd IEEE Int'l Conf. Advanced Learning Technologies, pp. 180–184 (2003)
12. Suhonen, J., Sutinen, E.: Learning computer science over the Web: The ViSCoS Odessey. In: Sharma, R.C., Mishra, S. (eds.) Cases on Global E-Learning Practices: Successes and Pitfalls, pp. 176–188 (2007)
13. Sutinen, E., Torvinen, S.: The candle scheme for creating an on-line computer science program - experiences and vision. Informatics in Education 2, 93–102 (2003)
14. Xue, J.Y.: Two new strategies for developing loop invariants and their application. J. Comput. Sci. & Technol. 8, 95–102 (1993)
15. Xue, J.Y.: A unified approach for developing efficient algorithmic programs. J. Comput. Sci. & Technol. 12, 103–118 (1997)
16. Xue, J.Y.: A practicable approach for formal development of algorithmic programs. In: 1st Int'l Symposium. Future Software Technology, Nanjing, China, pp. 158–160 (1999)
17. Xue, J.Y.: PAR method and its supporting platform. In: 1st Int'l Workshop of Asian Working Conference on Verified Software, pp. 11–20 (2006)
18. Zheng, Y.J., Shi, H.H., Xue, J.Y.: Toward a unified implementation for dynamic programming. High Technol. Lett. 12, 31–34 (2006)
19. Zheng, Y.J.: Formal Calculation of Highly-Dependable Materiel Support Algorithms Based on PAR. PhD Thesis, Institute of Software, Chinese Academy of Sciences (2009)
20. Zheng, Y.J., Xue, J.Y., Zuo, Z.K.: Toward an automatic approach to greedy algorithms. In: Deng, X., Hopcroft, J.E., Xue, J. (eds.) FAW 2009. LNCS, vol. 5598, pp. 302–313. Springer, Heidelberg (2009)
21. Zheng, Y.J., Xue, J.Y.: A problem reduction based approach to discrete optimization algorithm design. Computing 88, 31–54 (2010)
22. Zheng, Y.J., Shi, H.H., Xue, J.Y.: An algebraic approach to mechanical tabu search algorithm generation. In: 2010 IEEE Int'l Conf. Progress in Informatics and Computing, pp. 1172–1176 (2010)

The Research and Implementation of Web Subject Fusion Based on Information Fusion

Feiyue Ye[1] and Jiayong Du[2]

[1] School of Computer Engineering and Science, Shanghai University, Shanghai, China
[2] School of Computer Engineering and Science, Shanghai University, Shanghai, China
{Yefy,dujiayong}@shu.edu.cn

Abstract. This paper proposes web information fusion concept, and uses it by means of evidence reasoning and dynamic clustering algorithm to fusion web subjects, access to the effective expression of the relevant web pages, so that when Internet users use search engine, the search engine will reduce large numbers of redundant and bad pages, and feedback more useful information to users.

Keywords: web information fusion, search engine, dynamic clustering, evidential reasoning, web subject.

1 Introduction

The main channel that people use the Internet to obtain information is search engine. However, as web information itself incompleteness, inaccuracies, inconsistencies and other flaws, so much of the information doesn't need for users. Thus the search engine needs to take some web information integration rules to obtain more valuable and meaningful information, then feedbacks it to the network users.[1]

This paper uses web information fusion concept, by means of evidence reasoning and dynamic clustering algorithm to fusion web topics, access to the effective expression of the relevant web pages. When users enter a keyword to find information, search engine first searches such theme based on the keyword, and then retrieves the websites of the theme, lastly feedbacks these websites to the user, so it will reduce large numbers of redundant and bad feedback to the users, enable users to obtain more accurate information they need faster.

2 Web Information Fusion

2.1 Information Fusion

Information fusion is just to combine or integrate multi-source data and information, in order to obtain more accurate, more reliable estimates or reasoning decision-making

[1] This research work obtained the Shanghai science and technology commission's subsidization, the project number is 09JC1406200.

X. Luo et al. (Eds.): ICWL 2010 Workshops, LNCS 6537, pp. 246–253, 2011.

than single source of information [3] [9], to get high quality useful information. Information fusion is the basic function in biological or other logic system. The basic principle of information fusion [11] is like the human brain as an integrated information process, taking full advantage of multiple resources, and then using these resources and their observation information, to combine the redundant of multiple resources in space or time, or complementary information by some criteria, in order to get the consistency interpretation or description about the object.

[1][4][5] Show many information fusion functions. Common information fusion model [7]: JDL model, Boyd model and waterfall model, and so on. Common Information fusion algorithms[4][5][6]: dynamic clustering, the weighted average, neural network, least squares, probability theory, evidence reasoning, and so on.

2.2 Web Information Fusion

Based on the definition and concept of information fusion, we define the web information fusion is, to combine or integrate multi-source internet data and information, in order to obtain more accurate, more reliable estimates or reasoning decision-making than the sole network information source, to get high quality and useful network information.

The basic principle of web information fusion is similar to information fusion, the differences and similarities between web information fusion and information fusion as follows:

(1) Web information fusion is a new concept based on information fusion, its thinking and algorithms are based on the information fusion, it is a subset of information fusion, a part of information fusion.

(2) Web information fusion is not limited to information fusion; it is mainly used in the Internet, and is the integration of network information. It removes many redundancy and error messages from the exist network information, which makes Internet information more useful and effective.

Based on the JDL, Boyd model and [2] [5] [8] [10], we propose a web information fusion model (as Figure 1), the modal is: 1) Information collection. 2) Information clustering. Cluster analysis multiple web information sources with their relevance, then to get some classes of data associated. 3) Fusion. To confirm the information analysis, add an integrated, coordinated changes and estimated different information sources, to generate comprehensive information. 4) Establish information database. To store the generated integration information in a database or network file.

2.3 The Application of Web Information Fusion

The web information fusion is aims at fusioning Internet information to obtain more meaningful expression about the information. The Internet is a huge database, inside of which much information can fusion, so the application of Web information fusion is very widespread. Among them, the search engine has the best application prospect.

The search engine is the most main channel we obtains the information from the network, it provides many conveniences for our life. However, when we develop the

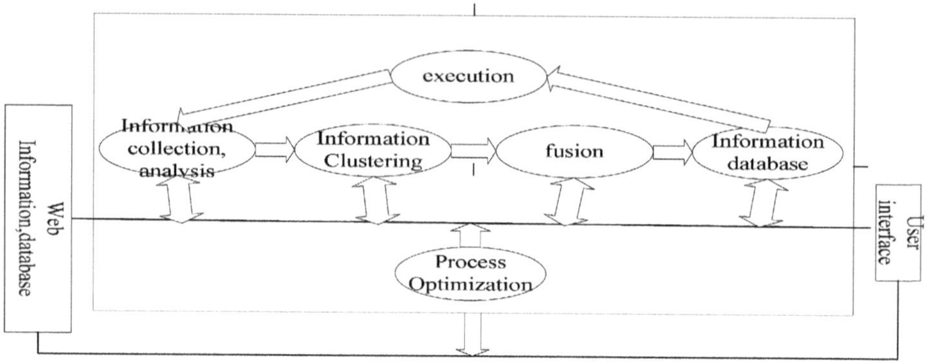

Fig. 1. Web information fusion mode

petroleum search engine project, we saw that the feedback information for users existences much redundant and inaccurate one, which enormous reduces users' search experience, also causes our database pressure to be very big. If using the web information fusion to fusion the information that web spider carried from the network according to certain rule, which will remove much redundant or bad information. So when user using search engine to search information, it will present to the user less, but more useful information, which enormous enhancement users' search experience, also enabled the search engine to have greater value. In the third part of this article has studied the web subject fusion by the web information fusion in the petroleum search engine.

3 Web Subject Fusion Algorithm

3.1 The Introduction of Evidence Reasoning

Evidence reasoning has introduced the trust function; it establishes on a non-null set Θ, Θ is called the identification frame. Regarding question territories in random proposition A, which should belong to the power collection 2^{Θ}. Define the trust distribution function basically on 2^{Θ} may be m: $2^{\Theta} \rightarrow [0,\ 1]$, m satisfies ① m(Θ)=0; ② $\sum_{A \subset \Theta} m(A) = 1$, m(A) expresses the degree of support for proposition A, but does not support any real subset of A. If A is subset of Θ, and m (A)>0, which is called focal element of the evidence. Belief function Bel (A) [12] is all degree of support for proposition A, plausibility function Pl (A) is the degree of unopposed to proposition A. [Bel (A), Pl (A)] constitutes uncertainty interval of evidence, and expresses the evidence degree of uncertainty.

In [11] shows the basic strategy of evidence reasoning.

3.2 The Introduction of Dynamic Clustering

Dynamic clustering logic diagram shown in Figure 2 [12] :

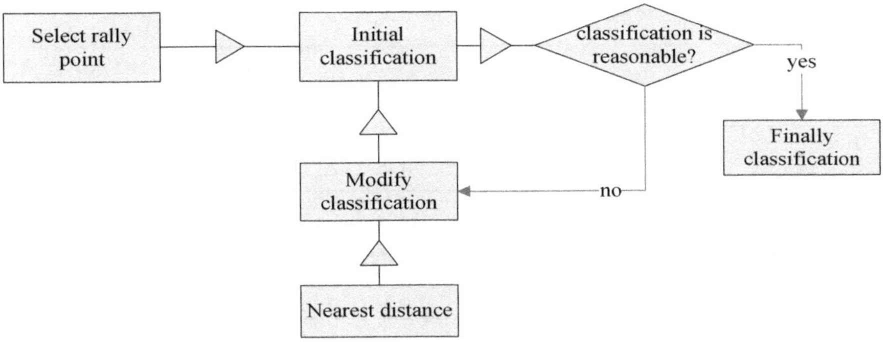

Fig. 2. Dynamic cluster logical diagrams

The so-called rally point is the first to be formed as the representative center point of the class. Usually the method of choosing a rally point as follows: (1) According to the experience of pre-determined number of categories and initial classification. (2) By the experience of all samples. (3) pre-K samples as the rally point.

In [12] shows some ways of initial classification.

3.3 The Principle of Web Subject Fusion

Thanks to the thought of evidence reasoning and the dynamic clustering, we propose the web subject fusion algorithm. Its mainly principle is: to cluster the homepage title, then to fusion each class, finally to obtain the subject of this kind of homepage. The algorithm uses alternately the thought of evidence reasoning and the dynamic clustering, thus realizes to get the subject of relevance web pages.
There are some definitions in the algorithm as follows.

Definition 1. The participle is to segment the sentence into one by one word with the je-analysis-1.4.1 participle package, for example "we are Chinese" is divided into "we", "are", and "Chinese".

Definition 2. The term frequency is times of a word which appears in sentences; in a sentence it is only count one time for each word.

Definition 3. The match is the inclusion relation between sentence and words.

3.4 The Realization of Web Subject Fusion Algorithm

To realize this algorithm, we designed two data tables, the title table for storing each webpage title and the class table for storing the depositing classification.

Table 1. Title table

filed	type	length	Initial value	explanation
url_id	Int	20		webpage ID
title	varchar	100		webpage title
count	int	4	0	Term frequency
classId	int	4	0	Class ID

Table 2. Class table

filed	type	length	Initial value	explanation
classId	Int	20		Class ID
url_id	int	20		webpage ID
title	varchar	100		Matched title
subject	varchar	100	Null	Class subject
sum	int	4	0	Total number

The flow chart of the algorithm as shown in Figure 3:

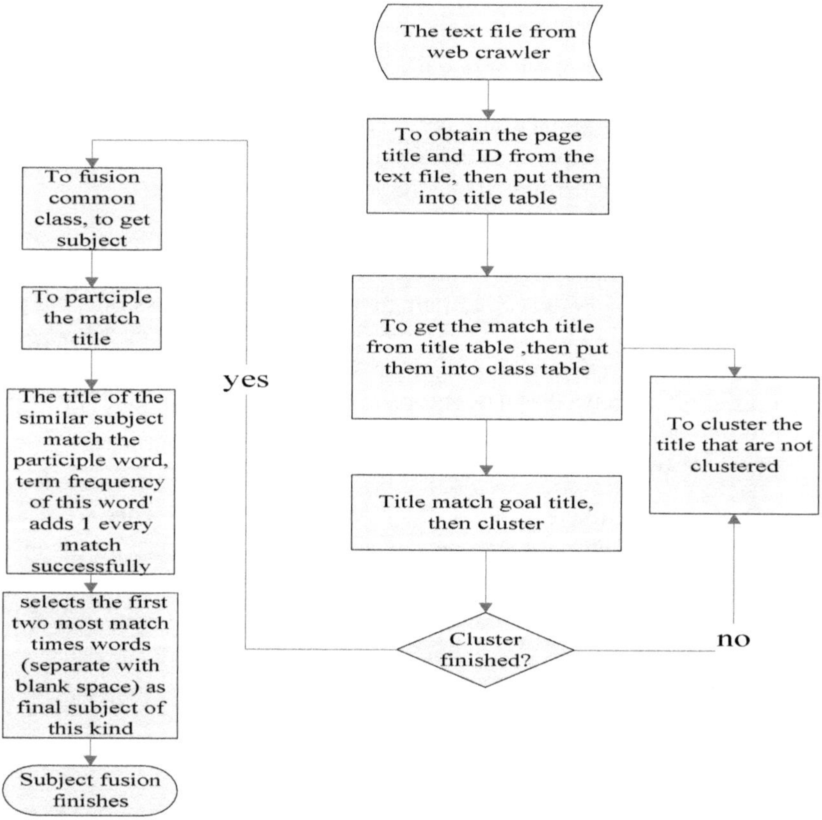

Fig. 3. Web subject fusion algorithm flow char

4 Experimental Result and Analysis

In order to examine the feasibility and the practical application value of the web subject fusion algorithm, and can use this algorithm in ours petroleum search engine, we have done many experiments. The experimental data is mainly from news homepages and other homepages about oil, we selected 10000 texts which through spiders crawling and then the processor extract the title, content and other information.

Experiment environment is: Operating system is Windows XP, development platform is eclipse, development language is JAVA, and database is MySql5.0.

Through to the massive news homepage subject fusion, the experiment effect is very good. The following figure 4 and figure 5 is a part of our experimental results, Figure 5 is the result of subject fusion, Figure 4 is the fusion homepage heading message.

id	url_id	title	count	classId
2017	10	中国石油大学举行校庆	3	223
2018	11	伊拉克成为石油大国	1	223
2019	12	大庆油田使中国生机勃勃	1	223
2020	13	第一届石油峰会成功举行	2	223
2021	14	中国如何才能成为石油大国	2	223
2022	15	大庆油田成立大会	2	226
2023	16	大庆油田好大啦！	1	224
2024	17	中国和伊朗石油洽谈圆满成功	5	223
2026	19	中国油田产量高涨	1	223
2027	2	中国和伊朗在北京举行石油洽谈	6	223
2030	22	大庆油田力争成为世界最大的油田	1	224
2031	23	中国石油大国之路很崎岖	2	223
2032	24	第一届石油峰会的时间和地点	2	223
2033	25	石油峰会热烈举行	2	223
2034	26	爱上采油的中国人	1	223
2035	27	中国石油大学校庆热烈举行	3	223
2036	28	大庆油田月产油量过亿	1	224
2037	29	北京石油洽谈成功举行	3	223
2038	3	伊拉克成为世界第一石油大国	1	223
2039	30	石油致富之路	1	223
2040	31	中国油价高涨	1	223
2041	32	数万人参加中国石油大学校庆	2	223
2042	33	中国最大的油田-大庆油田	1	223
2043	34	第一届石油峰会硕果累累	1	223
2044	35	中国有望成为石油大国	2	223
2045	36	油价高涨，节约用油	1	225
2046	37	中外校友参加中国石油大学校庆	2	223
2047	38	油价太高，的哥用不起油	1	227
2048	39	石油洽谈全过程	2	223
2050	40	第一届石油峰会在武汉举行	2	223
2051	41	中国石油大学最成功的校庆	2	223
2052	42	中国石油大学100年校庆	2	223

Fig. 4. The fusion homepage heading message

In Figure 4, the title is the webpage title that we need to fusion, in Figure 5; the subject is our fusion result of relevance website themes, such as "The establishment of Daqing Oilfield" category homepage theme "Daqing Oilfield establishment". The

class_	url_id	title	subject	sum
223	1	中国和伊朗举行石油洽谈	石油 举行	35
224	4	大庆油田成立	大庆油田 成立	6
225	18	采油量高涨	高涨 高涨	1
226	20	油田景象很好	油田 景象	1
227	21	大庆人勤劳致富靠挖油	油 人	3

Fig. 5. The subject fusion result

classid in figures 4 and 5 is the corresponding number, from which we can see which web page is belong to which class, such as "How big of Daqing Oilfield" and "Daqing Oilfield outputs over 100 million tons of oil in a month" were belong to "The establishment of Daqing Oilfield" (id is 224)in the table class. From the result of the two tables, we can see that our clustering is accurate; most relevance web pages are assigned to the right class. Therefore, the web subject fusion algorithm base on evidence reasoning and dynamic clustering we propose and design is feasible, has some practical value.

5 Summary and Outlook

As the web information has inaccuracy, incomplete, inconsistent, and many other defects, we have to take some handle on this information, so back to the network users more accurate and helpful information. Web information fusion can be a better solution to these problems. In this paper, we propose and design the web subject fusion algorithm base on evidence reasoning and dynamic clustering, classification web pages on various themes, to get the theme of the relation homepages. When using the search engine, the user input keywords to find the information, the search engine first to find the class of this information, and then feedback web pages of such topics to the users, which greatly reduce the number of redundant and incorrect pages, so that users can quickly get the most desired information. Practical application of this algorithm achieved relatively good results.

Web information fusion will have a lot of work to do, such as web content, user search habits of the relevant information fusion and so on. There are many sides in web information that need to use information fusion, web information fusion is a long way.

References

1. Yunsheng, L., Jianping, P.: Information fusion research. Computer Engineering and Application (March 2005)
2. Bing, L., Keqing, H.: The research of WEB information fusion system infrastructure. Beijing University of Aeronautics (November 2004)
3. Jie, Z., Zhishe, C.: Information fusion essence and its core techniques. Intelligence Command and Control Systems and Simulation Technology (8) (2003)
4. Limin, C., Li, K.: Information fusion method and its application. Sensor in the Micro Signal 26(3) (2007)

5. Hongying, L., Enhe, X., et al.: Information fusion method and the research of its application. Sichuan Institute of Technology (Natural Science) (October 2007)
6. Dalin, S., Daming, J.: The application of information fusion in Intelligent Traffic System. Journal of Safety Science and Technology (August 2006)
7. Quan, P., Xin, Y.: The basic method and progress of information fusion theory. Automation Technology (April 2003)
8. Chunhua, G.: Information fusion model and its application. Modern Computer (December 2006)
9. Hua, Z.: Information Fusion Research in Electronic Commerce. China's Management of Information (March 2008)
10. Liang, H., Ren, F., Wanli, Z.: The Preliminary Process of Modeling in Deep Web Information Fusion System. In: 2009 International Forum on Information Technology and Applications (2009)
11. Chiwen, W.: Information Fusion Technology Applied Research. Master thesis, Wuhan University (April 2004)
12. Zhengjun, Y.: Intelligent multi-source information fusion algorithm. PhD thesis, Chongqing University (May 2002)

Education-Oriented People-to-People Association Network (E-PAN)

Wenhao Zhu[1], Ben Yang[1,2], Jiaoxiong Xia[1,3], Wu Zhang[1,2], and Minjie Bian[4]

[1] School of Computer Engineering and Science, Shanghai University
[2] High Performance Computing Center, Shanghai University
[3] Information Centre, Shanghai Municipal Education Commission
[4] University of Shanghai for Science and Technology
{Wzhang,Whzhu,leon08720856}@shu.edu.cn,
jshardrom@shec.edu.cn

Abstract. With the analysis on education management in the existing system, we conclude that the resource silo and the lack of resource standards are the major problems faced with the development of e-education. Therefore an education-oriented people to people association network, a short term as "E-PAN", is proposed to enhance education resource management and provide more personalized educational services. On the other hand, the E-PAN shows the main features of user agent and user modeling, which enable the pairing of resource providers and resource receivers to establish the learning activities. The E-PAN layered architecture and basic elements are described in detail, and several application scenarios are presented in the following.

Keywords: resource management, e-education, information silo, learning activity.

1 Introduction

With the researching on the existing framework and architecture of educational resource management, there is the emphasis on resources itself rather than people, which is in fact the primary element of education. This situation will probably influence the quality and efficiency of resource management. It is recently accepted that the administration organization of education management is trying hard to improve the user experiences of both learning and teaching [1]. Rather than keeping focus on building up new e-education facilities, the authorities are now starting to analyze and define the soft problems and issues faced, along with the implementation of infrastructure. At this point, based on the user data and login information [2], which are provided by the Shanghai Municipal Education Commission (SMEC) internal administration, we give a practical analysis and concluded that the resource silo and the lack of resource standards are the major problems faced with the development of e-education.

After figuring out the problems, an Education-oriented People-to-People Association Network (E-PAN) is also proposed to support the current urgent demands of both learning and teaching. Other than manage digital resources, the E-PAN

X. Luo et al. (Eds.): ICWL 2010 Workshops, LNCS 6537, pp. 254–263, 2011.

enables a quality education resource management by setting people as the basic resource element. In E-PAN, people are regarded as resource carrier and divided into two major groups in according to their function in education, say, learning or teaching. And each people have its own agent with the simulation and computing of demands to provide personalized and interactive services, which could be running under the control of Coordinator. Furthermore, the people with similar purpose and demands could be grouped together to analyze the behaviors of specific kinds.

The rest of this paper is structured as follows. First, in Section II, we present a brief view of the existing frameworks and related work, like user modeling, education management, e-education privacy and security. Section III analyzes current solutions running in the wide ranged field and defines those deficiencies. In Section IV we demonstrate the E-PAN and the components of this framework as well as carry out some featured working scenarios. Finally, Section V concludes this paper and shares some fundamental problem and issues.

2 Background and Related Works

All these efforts in the IT industry reflect the rapid development of computer hardware, including computing ability, network connectivity and storage capability. From the point view of authority, the development of infrastructure will also be the task of primary importance in the near future. With this pace, now we can transfer many education related research areas into computing world with the larger capability, which will lead to the introduction of this E-PAN. However, the architecture will cover various research areas, ranging from User modeling, HCI (Human Computer Interaction), social computing, AI, and human-oriented researches, etc. Then, User Modeling will be carried out firstly as for its fundamental influence on the architecture.

User Modeling. Starting from 1994(even earlier), Bruno Errico [5] present a rational reconstruction of user modeling based on first-order logic of their Student Modeling activity to make the interaction more individualized on the basis of needs and characteristics. Till now, the data might be collected from different profiles and from different system. The User Modeling and Personalization Framework (UMP) is introduced to build ubiquitous user models, which are the backbone for understanding the users' interests and demands [4]. The personalization is done through the user model, which collects information about the user. However, the description of user knowledge and feature also involves imprecision and vagueness, a fuzzy user model is proposed to deal with, which uses fuzzy sets for knowledge representation and linguistic rules for model updating [3].

Social Computing. Social computing represents a new computing paradigm and an interdisciplinary research and application field. Wang, Fei-Yue et al [6] believes that the move from social informatics to social intelligence is achieved by modeling and analyzing social behavior. On the other hand, web 2.0 technologies have brought new ways of connecting people in social networks for collaboration in various on-line communities [7]. The papers [8][9][10] give several collaborative applications for the further research and development. All these researches show a tight relation between social computing and social environment which is the major part of education management.

Artificial Intelligence. Early in the 1980s, some scientists predicted that the creation of artificial intelligence would be the product of combined activity of great societies of more specialized cognitive processes [11]. These intelligent agents are described by all kinds of computational resources and storage capability to develop software and hardware which can think like or even beyond human being by means of imitating the cognitive process of human brain. In the E-PAN, the AI agent will be used to provide personalized and interactive service to edu-people with the recommendation system and evolution system.

3 Problems and Challenges

Begun in 1990, the Campus Computing Project (called CCP) is the largest continuing study of the role of information technology in American higher education, which is the first e-education project all around the world. The project's national studies draw on qualitative and quantitative data to help inform faculty, campus administrators, and others interested in the use of information technology. However, over the 20 years development a steady stream of new technologies have given hope to many both inside and outside of academe that some things just might change. Meanwhile, with the trend of intelligent resource management and personalized services, there are still some problems in the researching and application areas of e-education.

In the primary stage of e-education, the computer application is focused throughout the word processing, digital presentation, sheet printing and etc. In the secondary stage, the application system was introduced and developed with the separated services. Without the consideration of data standards and information sharing, the information silo existed among the whole education areas. And then in the higher stage, the priority task could be the integration of the separated system and solve the problem of information silo [12][13].

As mentioned, the one reason for the information silo is the lack of coordination and communication with authority, which should get the responsibility for long term planning and carrying out the standards. In accordance to the data sheets collected from the various departments, all these application system is different from each other such as software version, database, and data standard.

Another reason for the information silo is about management and administration of resources sharing [14]. The resources sharing will accompany the rise of development and maintenance cost as well as raise the possibility for hidden danger. However, without others' sharing, all these costs will come for nothing. Therefore, within the dilemma situation, SMEC as the education authority should promote the development of cooperative and secure resources sharing to enhance the effectiveness and efficiency of the e-education project [15].

4 E-PAN Architecture and Scenarios

At this point, we propose the architecture for education-oriented people to people association network. As the part of the educational planning for the near future, the E-PAN proposes to treat people as the primary factor in the system and not only process the user data alone but also integrate them together into a cluster to analyze the behavior and social relationship. E-PAN represents the existing of individuals (edu-people) in the daily learning education and provides administrative tunnel for authority which means the construction will also follow this discipline.

4.1 Definition and Architecture

E-PAN is an infrastructure framework for the e-education project and its goal is to provide the services to all kinds of education providers and receivers. It's kind of unique and full description to human being in the e-education world. The structure of E-PAN is shown in Fig. 1. It can be divided into two layers: Core Layer and Peripheral Layer.

Firstly, we should give an extended definition of the resources. In the E-PAN, everything involved can be treated as the resource for edu-people, such as learning material, personal information, tutorships and storage & computing capability. The resources are divided into two categories: universal resource and exclusive resource. To be worth mentioning, the exclusive resource can be the time schedule related resources, for example, a teacher might be available for the Friday night and this resource is exclusive for only a small part of edu-people. Therefore, the E-PAN can manage and deliver the extended resources with the request, which means E-PAN could be the counterpart of a coordinator in the system.

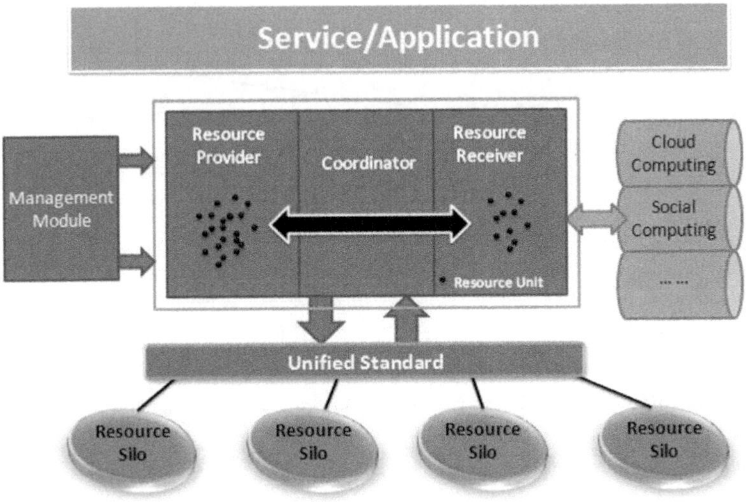

Fig. 1. E-PAN Structure

Core Layer. From the function and structure aspect, the Core-Layer is analog to the resource and information coordinator. Considering the function parts, we divided the Core-Layer into three parts: Resource Provider, Resource Receiver and coordinator, as shown in Fig. 2. The resource provider can manage and provide the resources collecting from various sourcing or the teacher tutorships. It is also in charge of the resource distribution and information transmission. With its own agents, the pairing of resource provider and resource receiver could be made automatically. And then throughout the certain services of coordinator, resource provider reports the specific status and updates related material to coordinator and then will wait for the arrangement of the exact learning/teaching activities such as discussion, correctness, and training. On the other side of the activity, these resource receivers also give the demands and status up to coordinator and then fill in the schedule sheet for the arrangements. After all these steps, the connection is established between the providers and the receivers and the learning/teaching activities will be evaluated for the both sides for the further development.

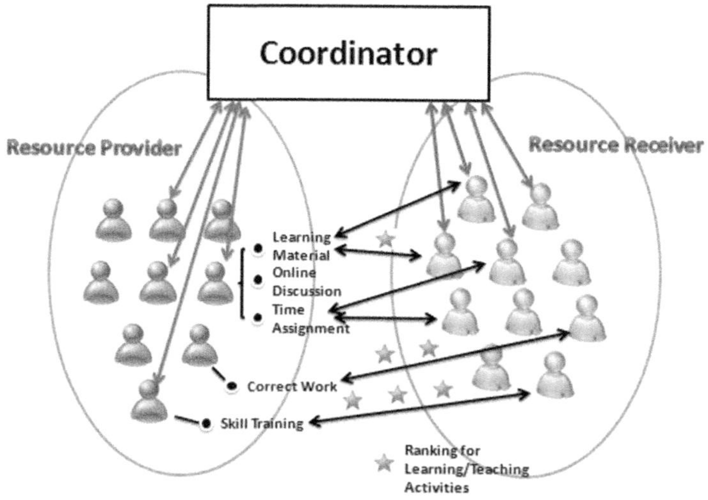

Fig. 2. E-PAN: Core Layer

As the aspect of coordinator, it is composed of four modules listed as below, shown in the Fig. 3.

- People Modeling Module(PMM)
- Cluster Identity Modeling Module(CiMM)
- Policy Trigger Module(PTM)
- Privacy & Security Module(PSM)

People Modeling Module(PMM). Single edu-people can correspond to multiple people modeling, which may be in different working modes simultaneously. Regarding as a completed learning/teaching activity, PMM can provide an integration of user information and status as the basic data. On the other hand, based on the ranking data and detailed learning/teaching information collected in the history, PMM can provide the advanced edu-people information upload to the Cluster Identity Modeling Module as the recommendation.

Cluster Identity Modeling Module(CiMM). As the system developed beyond the Request/Respond mode, it uses the social computing to construct the learning/teaching clusters. In the system, the resource receivers are no longer the passive receivers who get the resources with specific requests. However, the CiMM can provide the recommendation and integrated solution on own initiative according to the same character reflecting in the cluster. Even without including in any cluster, the receiver will be appropriate for the exact cluster based on the behavior and the basic information.

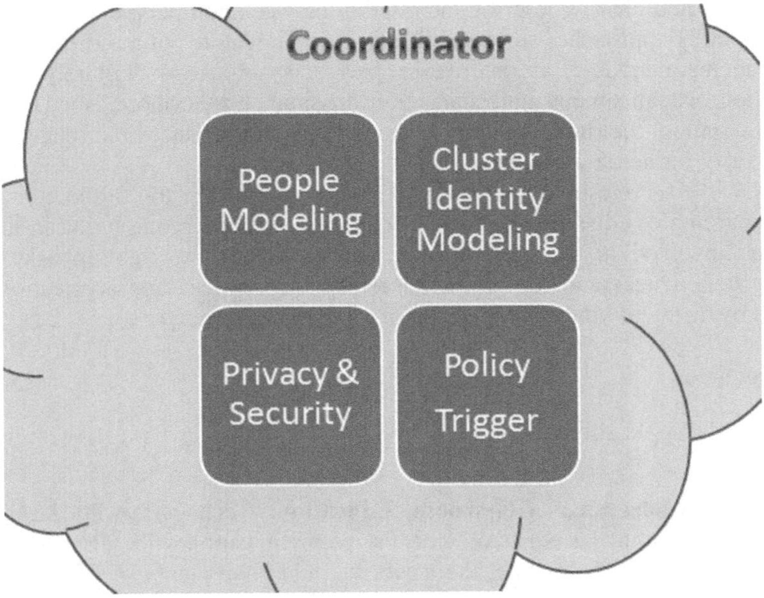

Fig. 3. Coordinator Structure

Policy Trigger Module(PTM). The education in China sometimes is a policy-driven activity in the society. The authority and the administration department play an important role in the specific education activities and project funding. Therefore, in the PTM, the system could make several rectifications in the education plan and activities based on the quantitative analysis of policies.

Privacy & Security Module(PSM). The destruction, fabrication, and clone of the association between edu-people will lead to serious problems. In the E-PAN design aspect, the policy of protection and security need further discussion. Once the edu-people model is falsely designed or constructed using error data, it will bring lots of problems to individual learning/teaching activities. Meanwhile, these sensitive data will be under control of the authority as well.

Peripheral Layer. In Fig. 1, Peripheral Layer is composed of four parts to support the core layer with the different aspects.

From the bottom level, the E-PAN establishes on the resource silo and provides the unified resource standards to realize the universally resource sharing in the system. As the analysis of the current situation and information silo in the above sections, there are lots of resource silos existing in the education fields. As a result, the designed standard is trying to adopt as many as possible existing resource silos rather than closing them for the new ones. This is the basic principle for solving the information silo problems.

On the right side of the core layer, the essential technologies have been considered for the implementation and extending of the system. As mentioned, the cloud computing could provide enormous computing and storage capability which is the infrastructure for the growing demands and better experience. Meanwhile, the social computing could clearly describe the relation between edu-people and cluster. These two computing approaches show elastic and flexible features of the E-PAN.

Management module, as the regular part of system, can definitely manage the connection establishment and data transmission. Furthermore, the management module monitors the running status of the E-PAN and produces the related reports to the authority for better social benefits.

Finally, the services and applications, which build on the top of the core layer, are the outsourcing of education activities. In our opinion, everyone living in the society could be involved in the education activities and has the right to ask for better learning experiences and resources. Therefore, the services and applications can be realized by different kinds of organization for the various purposes.

4.2 Scenarios

The possible applications of E-PAN are given with some typical scenarios in the following.

E-PAN in Adolescence Classroom Education. Teenagers who lack the self discipline and might be negative with the communication will fall into bad habits easily in education. Meanwhile, the teachers could have plenty of learning materials and time, which is not available for all the students. By collecting the achievements and learning schedule, we can build description of teenagers and teachers for different context. Based on the information given by agents, the coordinator makes the pairing of the teenagers and teachers to establish the learning activities. For teenagers, they will be grouped into kinds of resource receiver groups and get derived from specific agent. Through the services provided by agent, the teenagers could get the needed learning resources and will find a certain solution to uncover the interests. For teachers, they could hang the resources in the resource provider pool which is waiting for the pairing in the future. In this scenario, we make use of the pairing capability in the coordinator and try to use E-PAN to affect the learning activity in the real world.

E-PAN in E-learning Education. With the development of the e-learning education, more and more people start to find learning resources in the web. Although treating internet as an important source of knowledge and information, people require more time to search for the needed resources. Gerald E. Smith [16]thinks that the cost of searching resources is much higher than the learning resources itself under certain condition. Therefore in the E-PAN, we enhance the capability of resource providing and receiving by the function of coordinator. You belonging resources could be uploaded into the resource pool waiting for the pairing, while these resources searcher will pair with the existing resources once the needed one appears. In this scenario, we try to change the peoples' mind of searching resources and improve the way of acquiring needed ones.

Besides, E-PAN can also be used in many other applications. E-PAN can be applied in the life-long learning activity which will be involved in more social resources. What's more, being sensitive to the authority policy, the E-PAN can modify the people description to be suitable for the different kinds learning purposes. In a word, the applications of E-PAN have crossed all the area related to resource management and education management. Meanwhile, many problems will occur as well, we will discuss it in the next section.

5 Challenges and Expected Problems

As we discussed in previous sections, the proposed E-PAN shows a great prospect for both enhancing education resource management and providing more personalized educational services. However, the implementation and application of such a architecture brings new challenges that include not only technical issues but also demands for administrative reformation. The technical issues may be simply figured out by enumerating requirement specifications, while, on the other hand, the administration problem is much more complicated with respect to the current situation described in Section 3. In this Section, We briefly summarize the challenges that need to be addressed in the following aspects.

Data standards and association protocols. Technically, the information silo problem can be alleviated by introducing proper standards for every application throughout the whole process of e-education. However, such kind of solution is not likely to be feasible because it is not possible to re-create most of the current systems that are performing well in a limited scope and have already cost significantly. Alternatively, a solution incorporating both data standards and association protocols seems to be more practical.

User modeling. One of the main features of E-PAN is that resources and demands can be discovered by user agent. Thus, user modeling becomes the key problem. The discover performance, including precision and recall, depends on how well people are described in the E-PAN. The most challenging aspect is that the most of data comes from different existing information silos. The fact is that information of the same person in most application systems can be largely different due to his/her development progress. For example, a student's computer skill may be described as "amateur" in his elementary school profile while he may be a professional computer expert in his university record.

Management optimization with new services. The primary objective of E-PAN is that it offers a new solution to manage education resources, which is compatible with the existing e-education systems. Obviously, the implementation of resource coordinator will involve a lot of problems of optimizing pairing efficiency. Although the process scheduling algorithms of operating systems can be good references, there are other issues that should be counted since the purpose of education is not simply maximized the resource utilizing. Besides, the new framework may also bring up some new services such as personalized education, knowledge market and study social network etc.

Administrative reformation and Collaborative issues. Beside the technical problems, administrative and collaborative issues need to be addressed before anything else. E-PAN is a architecture that is proposed as a solution to the current e-education situation of Shanghai. Rather than direct commercial profit, the most benefit of E-PAN in its initial stage is for a better education. Thus, the implementation of E-PAN will expect more political support.

6 Conclusions

In this paper, we discuss the problems faced in the existing system and firstly propose the E-PAN architecture and characteristics as well according to the current education and technology development trends. Then through the implementation and application of such architecture, it brings new challenges that include not only technical issues but also demands for administrative reformation. To solve these problems makes we believe that the most benefit of E-PAN is for a better education.

Acknowledgments. This work is partially supported by the grants from the Ph.D. Programs Fund of Ministry of Education of China (No. 200802800007), Innovation Program of Shanghai Municipal Education Commission (11YZ08), Innovation Fund of Shanghai University (A.10-0108-10-002), Shanghai Leading Academic Discipline Project (No. J50103) and Postgraduate Innovation Fund (No. B16010809026).

References

1. Law, S., Glover, D.: Educational Leadership and Learning: Practice, Policy and Research, 1st edn. Open University Press, Stony Stratford (March 2000)
2. SMEC website, `http://www.shmec.gov.cn/english/index.php`
3. Kavcic, A.: Fuzzy user modeling for adaptation in educational hypermedia. IEEE Transactions on Systems, Man, and Cybernetics, Part C: Applications and Reviews 34(4), 439–449 (2004)
4. Korth, A., Plumbaum, T.: A Framework for Ubiquitous User Modeling. In: IEEE International Conference on Information Reuse and Integration, IRI 2007, pp. 291–297 (August 13-15, 2007)
5. Errico, B., Micarelli, A.: From student modeling to user modeling. In: 1994 IEEE International Conference on Systems, Man, and Cybernetics, 'Humans, Information and Technology', vol. 2, pp. 1885–1890 (October 2-5, 1994)
6. Wang, F.-Y., Carley, K.M., Zeng, D., Mao, W.: Social Computing: From Social Informatics to Social Intelligence. Intelligent Systems, IEEE 22(2), 79–83 (2007)
7. King, I., Jiexing, L., Kam, T.C.: A brief survey of computational approaches in Social Computing. In: International Joint Conference on Neural Networks, IJCNN 2009, pp. 1625–1632 (June 14-19, 2009)

8. Wang, F.-Y.: Social Computing: Fundamentals and applications. In: IEEE International Conference on Intelligence and Security Informatics, ISI 2008, pp. xxxv–xxxviii (June 17-20, 2008)
9. Rashid, A., Metaxiotis, K., Kausar, R.: Role of Social Computing in the Implementation of a Knowledge City Portal. In: 2010 Second International Conference on Computer Engineering and Applications (ICCEA), vol. 2, pp. 379–383 (March 19-21, 2010)
10. Musser, D., Wedman, J., Laffey, J.: Social computing and collaborative learning environments. In: The 3rd IEEE International Conference on Advanced Learning Technologies, Proceedings, pp. 520–521 (July 9-11, 2003)
11. Minsky, M.: The society of mind. Simon & Schuster, New York (1988)
12. Wu, Y.-p., Ding, N.-p.: Exploring to the Forming and Settlement of the Graduate Education Info Island from "The Prisoner's Dilemma". Information Science 2, 35–38 (2005)
13. Lupu, A.-R., Bologa, R., Sabau, G., Muntean, M.: Integrated Information Systems in Higher Education. WSEAS Transactions on Computers 5(7), 473–482 (2008)
14. Picot, A., Reichwald, R., Wigand, R.: Information, organization and management. Springer, Heidelberg (2008)
15. Dede, C.: Theoretical Perspectives Influencing the Use of Information Technology in Teaching and Learning. International Handbook of Information Technology in Primary and Secondary Education 20, 43–62 (2008)
16. Smith, G.E., Venkatraman, M.P., Dholakia, R.R.: Diagnosing the search cost effect: Waiting time and the moderating impact of prior category knowledge. Journal of Economic Psychology 20, 285–314 (1999)

Designing Personalized Learning Difficulty for Online Learners

Guangli Zhu, Wenjuan Liu, and Shunxiang Zhang

College of Computer Science and Engineering,
Anhui University of Science & Technology
232001, Huainan, China
{glzhu,liuwj,sxzhang}@aust.edu.cn

Abstract. With the rapid development of information and education technology, online learning system become more and more important in improving learners' grade. To provide personalized, flexible learning examination and efficiently keep students' confidence, the key problem is how to control the learning difficulty. In this paper, we present personalized learning difficulty-based online learning system (PLD-OLS) which can adaptively provide learning examination with reasonable difficulty for learners. In this method, each exercise is appended a hex string which represents the learners' understanding degree based on exercise difficulty. With the procedure of learning, this string will be automatically changed to represent the current understanding degree of learners. In addition, according to this novel representation, the learning state can be achieved by merging all hex strings to help customize learning examination with personalized learning difficulty for learners' re-learning. Learning results demonstrate that PLD-OLS can efficiently control the learning difficulty and improve learning effect of learners.

Keywords: online learning, learning examination, understanding degree, learning state, personalized learning difficulty.

1 Introduction

With the rapid development of information technology and education technology, the online learning system has been used widely to assistant students' learning. According to [1], E-learning can significantly complement classroom learning and E-learning will keep growing as an indispensable part of academic and professional education. On the past decades, many researchers have contributed on the methods, techniques and tools of online learning system.

In the methods of online learning system, literature [2] proposes real-time interactive virtual classroom. Che Y. et al offers a multimodal human-computer interface by incorporating audio/video presentation, as well as a synchronized whiteboard for collaborative web browsing and annotation [3]. Literature [4] presents automatically or semi-automatically matching the learning contents with the needs and preferences of the learners. Organero, M.M. et al [5] design a service oriented learning-management system. Melia M. et al [6] present adaptive courseware

X. Luo et al. (Eds.): ICWL 2010 Workshops, LNCS 6537, pp. 264–275, 2011.

validation. Literature [7] emphasizes that a teacher can monitor, understand and evaluate the activity of the students in the course. Munoz-Organero, M. et al [8] think that student motivation is an important factor for the successful completion of an e-learning course.

In the techniques and tools of online learning system, Peter B. presents Knowledge Tree for adaptive E-Learning based on distributed reusable intelligent learning activities, attempts to address both the component-based assembly of adaptive systems and teacher-level reusability [9]. To enrich a user's learning experience. Banerjee S. [10] thinks that an E-learning system should have the appropriate security which fosters trust for the student and promote loyalty in the system. Ontologies have become a key technology for enabling semantic-driven resource management [11], defining personalized e-learning experiences [12], predicting the progress of their students by a fuzzy domain ontology extraction algorithm [13]. Literature [14] an interactive E-learning system using pattern recognition and augmented some audio-visual contents on the monitor. In addition, Regueras, L.M.[15] proposes competitive e-learning tools.

In this paper, we propose a personalized learning difficulty-based method for adaptively generating learning examination. This method aims to provide an appropriate level examination for each learner, which can make learner keeping confidence and activity during the procedure of unit/course learning. Fig.1 shows the system framework of personalized learning difficulty-based online learning system.

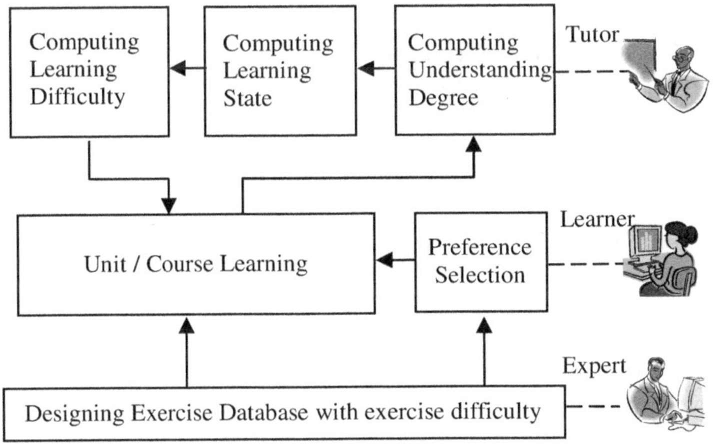

Fig. 1. The system framework of personalized learning difficulty-based online learning system

In Fig. 1, the bottom level is database which contains exercises of some courses or units. All these exercises are classified by the domain experts such as teachers, exercises' developer etc. The second level is unit/course learning which aims to facilitate learners (e.g. students) mastering the knowledge of unit/course. A learner must present his/her preference selection including the favorite course or unit, the types of exercises, and the favorite learning difficulty. After a unit (or course) learning is executed, the understanding degree of each learned exercise is modified, which will be applied to compute the learning state of the given learner. And the personalized learning difficulty is computed, which incorporate accurate learning state to generate more reasonable learning examination. So the proposed system can make learner keeping confidence and activity. The learning state of each learner is also essential reference for teaching in traditional classroom, which make tutor(e.g. teacher) easily trace student's learning and enhance teaching skills.

The major contributions of our work include two aspects: 1) we propose a hex string representation method of understanding degree of an exercise, which can efficiently record learners' learning condition. This representation is used as the essential element data of learning state computing, so it is also basis for generating personalized examination. 2) We present a learning difficulty (LD) function to control the difficulty of generated personalized learning examination. Applying the achieved understanding degree, the learning state of a learner can be computed, which provides the essential parameter for LD function.

The rest of this paper is organized as follows: Section 2 introduces some definitions for PLD-OLS. Section 3 introduces the database designing of PLD-OLS. Section 4 presents the unit/course learning technique which is based on understanding degree, learning state and learning difficulty. Conclusions are given in Section 5.

2 Definition

For the clarity of the proposed online learning system, some basic definitions are defined as follows.

Definition 1. Exercise Difficulty(ED)
Exercise difficulty(ED) is a measurement of content complexity of an exercise. Higher difficulty exercise means that it is difficult to be understood by learners, while lower difficulty exercise means that it is easy to be understood by learners. In our online learning system, the ED is classified into 5 levels and 'no level' by experts such as teachers, exercises' developer etc. The 5 ED levels are named as lower, low, general, high and higher. The representation characters of all EDs are listed in Table. 1.

Table 1. The character representation of ED

ED levels	lower	low	general	high	higher	no level
character	2	5	8	B	E	0

In Table 1, each level ED has a corresponding character which facilitates the automatic process for online learning system. The character '0' means that an exercise has not been classified as one of 5 ED levels.

Definition 2. Understanding Degree (UD)
Understanding degree (UD) is a measurement of cognitive level of a given exercise's content. In our online learning system, the UD is also classified into 5 levels and 'no level' according to learning condition of learners. The representation characters of UD are listed in Table. 2.

In Table 2, each level UD has three characters which respectively represent three possible states of a given exercise related to a learner, namely, 'well done', 'not done' and 'badly done'. The UD is defined on the basis of the ED of an exercise. But there are two differences between them. One is that the lower ED is corresponding to the higher UD. The other is that ED depends on the content of an exercise while UD depends on the cognitive capability of learners. There are two types of UDs:

- **Related to a single learner**, UD is denoted as a character. Let ED_i denotes the *ith* exercise's ED, UD_i^j denotes the *ith* exercise's UD related to the *jth* learner, they should follow the following formula:

$$UD_i^j = \begin{cases} ED_i - 1, & well \quad done \\ ED_i & not \quad done \\ ED_i + 1 & badly \quad done \end{cases}$$

- **Related to mul-learners,** UD is represented as a hex string. Let S_i^m denotes the *ith* exercise's UD related to m learners, its value can be denotes as a hex string $\{UD_i^1, UD_i^2, \cdots, UD_i^m\}$

Table 2. The character representation of UD

UD levels	higher	high	general	low	lower	no level
characters	1,2,3	4,5,6	7,8,9	A,B,C	D,E,F	Y,0,N

Just as 5 levels' UD, the 'no level' of UD has three possible states, namely, 'Y', '0', 'N'. And the 'no level' of ED will be re-assigned as one of 5 levels according to the string of the 'no level' of UD related to multi-learners.

Definition 3. Learning State (LS)
Learning state (LS) describes the total condition of a unit (or course) knowledge understood by learners. Just like the UD, LS depends on a learner himself/herself, which is also defined into two types:

- **Related to mul-learners,** LS is represented as a vector of hex string. Suppose m learners have learned a part of the *ith* unit or course contain n exercises, the LS can be described as follows:

$$LS_i^m = \begin{bmatrix} S_1^m \\ S_2^m \\ \vdots \\ S_{n-1}^m \\ S_n^m \end{bmatrix} = \begin{bmatrix} UD_1^1, UD_1^2, \cdots, UD_1^m \\ UD_2^1, UD_2^2, \cdots, UD_2^m \\ \vdots \\ UD_{n-1}^1, UD_{n-1}^2, \cdots, UD_{n-1}^m \\ UD_n^1, UD_n^2, \cdots, UD_n^m \end{bmatrix}$$

- **Related to a single learner**, LS is represented as a hex string. Suppose the *jth* learner has learned a part of the *ith* unit or course contain n exercises, the LS can be denoted as $LS_i^j = \{UD_1^j, UD_2^j, \cdots, UD_{n-1}^j, UD_n^j\}$.

The learning state related to mul-learners provides data supporting for tutors in making new teaching plan. The learning state related to a single learner is essential to generating examination with personalized learning difficulty.

3 Designing Database of PLD-OLS

As a special tool of data organization and management, database has many powerful, universal functions such as data creation, maintenance, search, security, backup and other access etc. Its technique has been widely applied in various fields including online learning system. In our design, database is used to manage the object of the proposed system such as learners, tutors and exercises.

3.1 Database Table

In this section, we introduce five data tables of PLD-OLS. The structures of these data tables are described as following.

- **Learner Table:** Learner is a generic term that refers to the student or a knowledge seeker who wants to master the content of a course. Whenever a learner registered in PLD-OLS, he/she can begin unit learning or appeared in course learning. As the constitute structure of learner table, the attributes of learner mainly include: ID, name, password, affiliation, major in, class#, and grade etc. The primary key of learner table is ID of a learner.
- **Expert Table:** Expert refers to the teacher or an exercises' developer who can assign an ED level to an exercise. Whenever a person registered in PLD-OLS and get permit of expert identification from manager, he/she can add some exercises or import a batch of exercises. To be an expert, he/she should provide all the necessary attributes: ID, name, password, affiliation, types, academic titles and research interests. The primary key of learner table is ID of expert. The value of types can be teacher, exercise developer.
- **Exercise Table:** Exercise is a generic term that refers to the learning content with an ED level. In our online learning system, the types of exercise only contain multiple choices, true or false, fill in the blank and question & answer. The attributes of exercise table mainly include: ID, course, unit, types, content, answer, ED, UD. Where ID of an exercise (i.e. primary key) is generated automatically by system. ED of an exercise is assigned by an expert, while UD of an exercise will be changed with the processing of learning.
- **Tutor Table:** Tutor refers to the supervisor of learning state of a unit/course. He/she must get the permit of a manager and registered as a tutor. He/she mainly carry out two tasks, one is browsing the learning state of a course or any learner, the other is setting the learning progress and minimal exercise difficulty of his/her students. The attributes of tutor table mainly include: ID, password, name, course1, …, course5. Where ID of a tutor (i.e. primary key) is generated automatically by system.

- **Manager Table:** Manager refers to the maintainer who does data maintenance, security, backup. The attributes of manager table mainly include: ID, password, name, types etc. Where ID of a manager (i.e. primary key) is also generated automatically by the proposed system.

3.2 E-R Diagram

Entity-relationship diagrams (E-R diagrams) are used as an abstract and conceptual representation of data. To explain the objects of the proposed online learning system, we present a conceptual schema applying E-R diagrams (see Fig. 2).

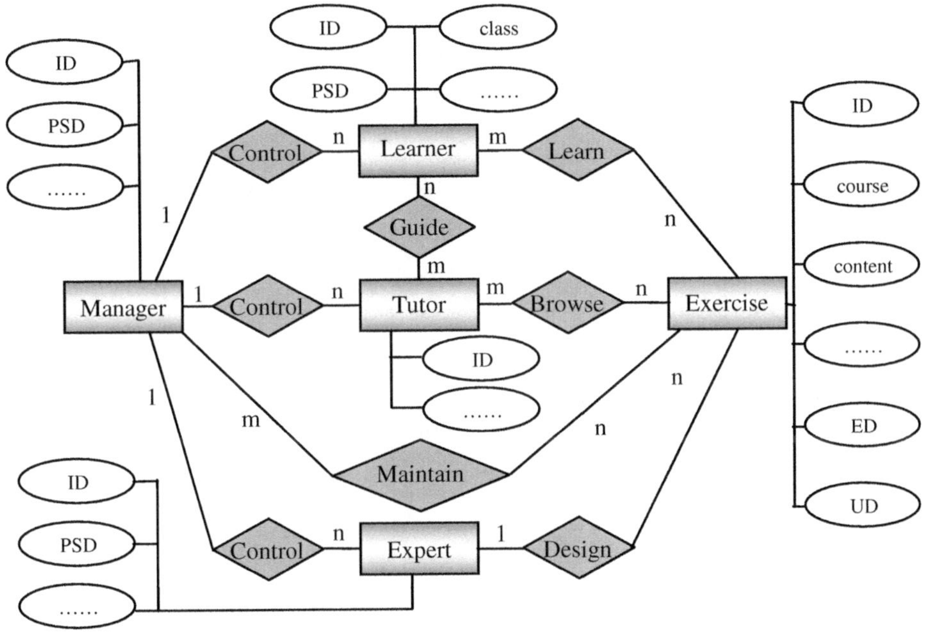

Fig. 2. The E-R diagram of personalized learning difficulty-based online learning system

Fig. 2 describes entities, relationships, and attributes of personalized learning difficulty-based online learning system. The relationships between any two entities mainly include control, maintain, design, browse, learn and guide. Where the relationship 'maintain' means backup exercises and keep the security of all data.

4 The Learning Procedure in PLD-OLS

PLD-OLS aims to provide learning examination with personalized learning difficulty. The learning procedure mainly includes learners' preference selection, unit/course learning, understanding degree computation, learning state computation and re-learning. Learners' preference selection should be executed before unit/course learning to facilitate the computation of learning difficulty.

4.1 Learners' Preference Selection

Learner can select the learning preference such as favorite learning course/unit, the types of exercises and learning difficulty. In these learning preferences, the course and the types of exercises can be directly decided by searching corresponding subset, while learning difficulty (LD) is decided by LD function.

Let r_s denotes basic standard ratio and r_0 denotes the ratio of 'no level' ED, they must follow:

$$5 * r_s + r_0 = 100\%$$

To ensure the generated learning examination only contain lesser exercises of 'no level' ED, usually, the value of r_0 is limited in $0 \le r_0 \le 10\%$.

Let Δ denotes the adaptive adjusting parameter, LD function can be defined as follows:

$$LD1 = LD(r_s + 4\Delta, r_s + 2\Delta, r_s, r_s - 2\Delta, r_s - 4\Delta, r_0)$$
$$LD2 = LD(r_s + 2\Delta, r_s + \Delta, r_s, r_s - \Delta, r_s - 2\Delta, r_0)$$
$$LD3 = LD(r_s, r_s, r_s, r_s, r_s, r_0)$$
$$LD4 = LD(r_s - 2\Delta, r_s - \Delta, r_s, r_s + \Delta, r_s + 2\Delta, r_0)$$
$$LD5 = LD(r_s - 4\Delta, r_s - 2\Delta, r_s, r_s + 2\Delta, r_s + 4\Delta, r_0)$$

Where $LD1$, $LD2$, $LD3$, $LD4$ and $LD5$ respectively denote the learning difficulty from lower to higher.

Set r_s =18%, Δ=3%, the ED ratio distribution of 5 learning difficulty see Fig. 3.

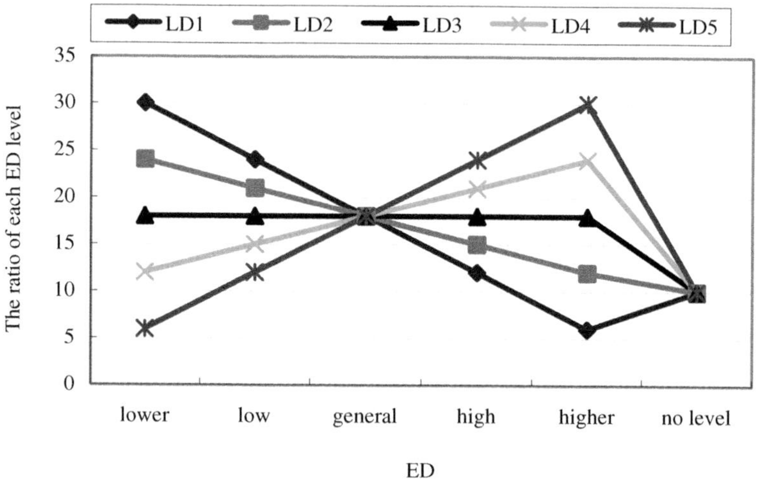

Fig. 3. The ratio of each ED level in different learning difficulty

From Fig. 3, the learning difficulty function is like a teeterboard. It ensures that the lower learning difficulty is decreasing in the ratio of ED and the higher learning difficulty is increasing in the ratio of ED. Therefore, it can efficiently control the learning difficulty of learning examination.

4.2 Unit/Course Learning

As soon as a learner has set his/her preference, he/she can require PLD-OLS generating personalized learning examination. Algorithm 1 describes the procedure of generating a unit/course learning examination:

Algorithm 1. Generating unit learning examination

```
Step1: Building course/unit subset SET1;
Step2: Building the subset of exercise types SET2 according to subset SET1;
Step3: Adaptively computing learning difficulty according to learner's LD function;
Step4:
For (i=1;i<=6;i++)
  {
   Building subset SET3 with given ED according to subset SET2;
   r=0;
   while (r<= the ratio assigned by learning difficulty function)
     {
      Produce random number;
      Select an exercise from subset SET3, add it to learning exercises' subset SET4;
     }
  i=i+1;
  }
Step5: Output the subset SET4 in the forms of learning examination.
```

The time complexity of algorithm 1 is very low. The time complexities of step1 and step2 are all $O(n)$. The time complexities of step3 is $O(1)$. Although the step4 is double circular, the numbers of external and internal circular are usually limited.

4.3 Computing Understanding Degree

Whenever a learner executes unit/course learning at the first time, the UD of an exercise related to him/her is set as the ED. That is, the *ith* exercise related to the *jth* learner UD_i^j is equal to the *ith* exercise difficulty ED_i. After a learner has completed unit/course learning, the UDs of all his/her learned exercise will be modified according to the learning results. The modification procedure see algorithm 2:

The time complexity of algorithm 2 is $O(n)$. It can update the understanding degree related to a learner in time. The updated UDs will facilitate computing the given learner's accurate learning state which is essential for controlling the learning difficulty. The personalized re-learning examination with reasonable learning difficulty can keep the confidence of learners and make them actively participate in re-learning.

Algorithm 2. Computing understanding degree related to a learner

Step1; Let n = Count(*SET4*) and assign the ID of a learner to *j*;
Step2:
For (*k=1; k<=n; k++*)
{
Extracting an exercise from subset *SET4*;
Assigning the ID of the extracted exercise to *i*;
If (the learner's answer is true)
{ $UD_i^j = UD_i^j - 1$; // UD_i^j is the UD of the *ith* exercise related to the *jth* learner.
Else $UD_i^j = UD_i^j + 1$;
}
k=k+1;
}
Step3: end;

4.4 Computing Learning State

The accurate learning state of a learner can be used as the reference of tutors' teaching. More importantly, it can provide supporting for generating the personalized learning examination. The basic idea of computing learning state is find the UD of a learner from the hex string of the corresponding exercise. Therefore, the computation of learning state mainly executes getting sub-string. The detail procedure see algorithm 3:

Algorithm 3. Computing learning state of a learner

Step1; Get the subset *SET5* of a course/unit;
Step2: Let n = Count(*SET5*) and Assign the ID of the learner to *j*;
Step3:
For (*i=1;i<=n; i++*)
Extracting the hex string of the *ith* exercise to *String* ;
Appending Getchar(*String* , *j*) to LS_i^j ;
End for;
Step4: end;

In fact, the time complexity of extracting sub-string is $O(1)$. Therefore, the time complexity of algorithm 3 is also $O(n)$.

4.5 Re-learning and Results Analysis

According to the achieved learning state, we can provide more personalized learning examination for a learner in re-learning. Comparing with the first learning, there are two differences between them.

- The variation of learning difficulty function

From section 4.3, we know that the learning difficulty function contains 6 variables which respectively represent the ratio of 5 level EDs and 'no level' ED. But in re-learning, the learning difficulty function contains 16 variables which respectively represent the ratio of 15 UD level and 'no level' UD. This variation will make generated learning examination more personalized and has more reasonable learning difficulty.

- Adding a controlling variable of new exercises

The adding variable refers to the ratio between the 'done' exercises and 'not done' which aims to ensure that the re-learning examination contain new exercises. The introduction of this variable can efficiently avoid an extra condition, that is, the re-learning examination only contains those learned exercises which probably make a learner lost activity of online learning.

To evaluate the effect of the proposed method, we randomly select 10 learners. Two of them belong to the same learning difficulty. Record their grades in the first learning and re-learning, then plot comparison diagram as Fig. 4.

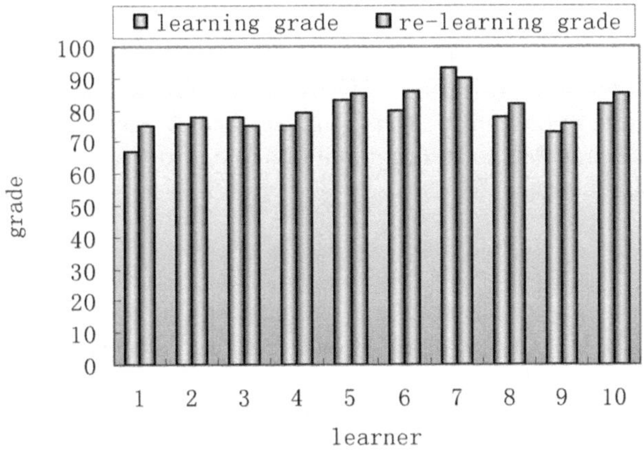

Fig. 4. The grade comparison between learning and re-learning

From Fig.4, we find that 10 learners all get satisfied grades in the first learning and re-learning, although there may be much difference between them in mastering knowledge. More importantly, it can make all learners keep confidence to continue learning new knowledge via PLD-OLS. In addition, most learners have got better grade in re-learning. It shows that the generated learning examination become more personalized after adding the learning state to the computation of learning difficulty.

5 Conclusion

Online learning system plays the key complementary, assistant role in improving students' grade. To keep learners' confidence and activity of online learning, we have proposed a personalized learning difficulty-based method which aims to provide the learning examination with reasonable difficulty. To realize this purpose, our contributions mainly include two indispensable aspects.

(1) The representation method of understanding degree of an exercise has been proposed using a hex string, which can efficiently record learners' learning condition. According to the exercise difficulty customized by experts and the learning results, the understanding degree (UD) of an exercise will be automatically modified. The UD is the essential element data of computing learning state, so it is also basis for generating personality learning examination.

(2) Learning difficulty function has been presented to control the difficulty of personalized learning examination. Based on the achieved UD, the learning state of a learner can be computed, which provides 16 adjustable variables for LD function. The personalized LD function can help customize learning examination with reasonable difficulty for a learner in re-learning. Some learning results have demonstrated the validity of this method.

Acknowledgement

This Research work is supported by the Anhui university province-level natural science research project (project no. KJ2010B327) and the teaching research project (finance no. DG787) of Anhui University of Science & Technology. We thank some students for their contribution in programming. We also thank Professor Jingzhao Li for his precious proposal.

References

1. Zhang, D., Zhao, J.L., Zhou, L.: Can e-learning replace classroom learning? Communications of the ACM 47(5) (2004)
2. Shi, Y., Xie, W., Xu, G.: Smart Remote Classroom: Creating a Revolutionary Real-Time Interactive Distance Learning System. In: Fong, J., Cheung, C.T., Leong, H.V., Li, Q. (eds.) ICWL 2002. LNCS, vol. 2436, pp. 130–141. Springer, Heidelberg (2002)
3. Che, Y., Shi, R., Shi, Y.: SameView: A Large-Scale Real-Time Interactive E-learning System Based on TORM and AMTP. In: Zhou, W., Nicholson, P., Corbitt, B., Fong, J. (eds.) ICWL 2003. LNCS, vol. 2783, pp. 122–133. Springer, Heidelberg (2003)
4. Kim, W.: Starting Directions for Personalized E-Learning. In: Leung, H., et al. (eds.) ICWL 2007. LNCS, vol. 4823, pp. 13–19. Springer, Heidelberg (2008)
5. Organero, M.M., Kloos, C.D., Merino, P.M.: Personalized Service-Oriented E-Learning Environments. IEEE Internet Computing 14(2), 62–67 (2010)
6. Melia, M., Pahl, C.: Constraint-Based Validation of Adaptive e-Learning Courseware. IEEE Transactions on Learning Technologies 2(1), 37–49 (2009)
7. Gaudioso, E., Hernandez-del-Olmo, F., Montero, M.: Enhancing E-Learning Through Teacher Support: Two Experiences. IEEE Trans. on Education 52(1), 109–115 (2009)
8. Munoz-Organero, M., Munoz-Merino, P.J., Kloos, C.D.: Student Behavior and Interaction Patterns With an LMS as Motivation Predictors in E-Learning Settings. IEEE Transactions on Education 53(3), 463–470 (2010)

9. Peter, B.: KnowledgeTree: A Distributed Architecture for Adaptive E-Learning. In: Proceedings of the 13th International World Wide Web Conference on Alternate Track Papers & Posters, pp. 104–113 (2004)
10. Banerjee, S.: Designing a secure model of an e-learning system—A UML-based approach. IEEE Potentials 29(5), 22–27 (2010)
11. Wu, Z.H., Mao, Y.X., Chen, H.J.: Subontology-Based Resource Management for Web-Based e-Learning. IEEE Transactions on Knowledge and Data Engineering 21(6), 867–880 (2009)
12. Acampora, G., Loia, V., Gaeta, M.: Exploring e-Learning Knowledge Through Ontological Memetic Agents. IEEE Computational Intelligence Magazine 21(6), 66–77 (2010)
13. Lau, R.Y.K., Song, D.W., Li, Y.F.: Toward a Fuzzy Domain Ontology Extraction Method for Adaptive e-Learning. IEEE Trans. on Knowledge and Data Engineering 21(6), 109–115 (2009)
14. Lee, S.H., Choi, J., Park, J.: Interactive e-learning system using pattern recognition and augmented reality. IEEE Trans. on Consumer Electronics 55(2), 164–179 (2009)
15. Regueras, L.M., Verdu, E., Munoz, M.F., et al.: Effects of Competitive E-Learning Tools on Higher Education Students: A Case Study. IEEE Transactions on Education 52(2), 279–285 (2009)

Capacity-Building in Nonprofit Organizations: Is There a Blended Learning Paradigm for the Sector?

M.T. Cole[1] and B.J. Garner[2]

[1] Robert Morris University
Moon Township, PA. 15108, U.S.A.
cole@rmu.edu
[2] Deakin University
Burwood, Victoria 3125, Australia
brian.garner@deakin.edu.au

Abstract. Blended learning models are widely-used, successful training vehicles for e-learning and workplace training, in corporate as well as higher education environments. Increasingly, Web 2.0 applications, imbedded within blended learning models, are being recognized for their utility in these settings. Concern for the sustainability and relevance of nonprofit organizations has sharpened the interest in building effective capacity-building models for the sector. Can Web 2.0 technologies enhance capacity-building models in the Third Sector? Because blended learning is a remarkably adaptable and fluid model, its potential for transforming capacity-building models in the nonprofit sector is thought to be significant. This paper introduces the concept of transformational approaches to capacity-building and asks if blended learning paradigms that incorporate interactive next-generation technologies might strike a responsive chord in the sector. The authors present research to date on blended learning and capacity-building to lay the foundation for the introduction of one blended learning model for training and education in the nonprofit sector. While the authors suggest that blended learning, as it is evolving, is the key to driving innovation in capacity-building models, they recognize that tailoring blended learning to the audience is critical in achieving success. It is suggested that for optimal results, capacity-building efforts should be built on holistic approaches to the integration of individual self-actualization goals with mechanisms for organizational and sector empowerment, using the technologies imbedded with blended learning.

Keywords: Blended learning, capacity-building, nonprofit sector, innovation.

1 Introduction

Independent Sector [1] reports that there were approximately 1.9 million nonprofit organizations in the United States in 2008, 1.4 million of which were classified as charities, including hospitals, museums and orchestras, public television and radio stations, private schools and institutions of higher education, soup kitchens, legal services programs, battered women's shelters, religious organizations, and zoos as

X. Luo et al. (Eds.): ICWL 2010 Workshops, LNCS 6537, pp. 276–290, 2011.

well as foundations, among others. There are millions more nongovernmental or voluntary sector organizations in the world providing essential services to people and governments. Many of these depend on support from governmental sources as well as private contributions. As economies falter worldwide and governmental priorities shift, the emphasis on how well an organization can demonstrate effective performance becomes increasingly important to sustainability. Thus, improving performance becomes a linchpin in the work of capacity-building.

Improving performance can be viewed as capacity-building on three levels: the individual, the organizational and the sector. Education and training opportunities for individuals enhance their ability to contribute to their organizations. In addition to the return on investment to the organization from individuals trained, consultants and trainers provide requisite technical assistance and consulting services to organizations to enhance organizational performance. Logically then, it can be said that nonprofit organizations performing effectively (maximum performance for minimum cost while fulfilling mission) strengthen the sector. We argue that what enables this three-tiered capacity-building is the accessibility and adaptability of blended learning - one of the most critical innovations in the delivery of education and training to this audience.

The focus of this paper is the consideration of blended learning paradigms using next-generation technologies to enhance the capacity-building efforts on organizations within the nonprofit sector. Capacity-building in this context refers to e-delivery of education and training to nonprofit organizations and their staffs.

1.1 Blended Learning

Cross [2] asserts that blended learning is a useless concept because he "...could not imagine unblended learning. My first-grade teacher used a blend of storytelling, song, recitation, reading aloud, flash cards, puppetry, and corporal punishment." Granted, the use of a variety of educational tools to facilitate learning is not new. What is new however, is the rich, interactive nature of today's toolbox. By virtue of their utility to users, Web 2.0 applications have enhanced blended learning's potential to reach larger, more diverse and isolated populations.

Garner [3] defines blended learning as a strategy for holistic empowerment and learning. It is an education and training strategy that reinforces learning through a blending of e-learning and face-to-face instruction (in classrooms, workshops, laboratories) using the full range of interactive technologies and media.

What is in a blend? Rossett, Douglis and Frazee tell us that the options are varied. They include formal and informal delivery systems; they can be people- and/or technology-based; independent and collegial; directive and/or discovery-oriented. The type of blend will depend on the stability and urgency of the subject matter, the type and location of the audience, and the teaching and financial resources available to support it. Above all, blended learning objectives must be understood and strategic in order to succeed [4].

Administrators and faculty at the University of Wyoming have employed a blended learning strategy to combat what they experienced as weaknesses in a distance education graduate program. To address the lack of face-to-face interaction and the students' consequent or potential feelings of disconnectedness, the graduate program made use of interactive television (ITV), "arguably the next best thing to a traditional classroom experience" [5]. The advantage of ITV is that it allows for real time discussion, in a visual format, over distances. Use of ITV in the program combined with a two-week, end-of-course format proved to be successful; that is, the students were satisfied. The graduate program's approach to the problem was a blended learning strategy that worked for its audience, a student body that was separated by large distances and made up of working adults.

Researchers at the University of Dayton were interested in whether findings on the effectiveness of online and blended learning programs in graduate and nontraditional student populations would be repeated with a population composed of undergraduates. The undergraduates were teacher candidates who participated in learning modules imbedded in courses that were delivered in online and blended formats.

The study examined student perceptions of competencies developed, comfort level in using those competencies, complexity of course content and the effectiveness of group work in order to determine how blended courses could be used to support diverse learning needs and curricular constraints. Researchers administered a nineteen-item Likert-style survey instrument with a five-point scale (strongly disagree to strongly agree) to students in three courses. One course was fully online (20 students); one was fully blended (33 students); and one was partially blended (27 students). The surveys were administered at the end of the course to students enrolled in the two blended models. For the group in the fully online course, the survey was administered in a subsequent onground course.

Researchers computed correlation coefficients among the delivery models, time spent to complete the curriculum, and students' perceptions of the complexity of the material, of what they learned, of their comfort with their ability to use the material learned, and how effective their teams were. Nine of the fifteen correlations were statistically significant. Interestingly, they found that the delivery method, whether fully online, fully blended or partially blended, made no significant difference in the time students spent on the course or on how difficult they found the material to be. The delivery method did affect how well the students felt they learned the material; how comfortable they were in applying what they learned; and how effective they felt their teams were. Students in the blended models reported higher levels of learning, greater comfort with content, and more satisfaction with their team's effectiveness than did the students in the online-only course [6].

Looking at blended learning from the perspective of the state of educational technology development, Motteram and Sharma in *Blended Learning in a Web 2.0 World* [7], argue that blended learning is the most appropriate solution for classroom instructors wishing to use digital technology. They dispute the claim that novices cannot or will not succeed in a blended learning environment. The authors here are examining the use of blended learning in Second Language Acquisition (SLA). They argue further that mediating artifacts, in addition to the technological artifacts in evidence with the advent of Web 2.0, make SLA instruction well suited for a blend of practices, processes and technologies. The authors were looking at the state of language instruction, noting the ascendency of 2.0 technologies, such as wikis and blogs, internet and mobile phones, and Skype as solutions to barriers that previously had limited access to language learning. On a cautionary note, the authors acknowledge that Web 2.0 may not only be changing the way that knowledge is constructed, but also how knowledge is owned by the learner. Yet, they argue, the most effective uses of technology in the classroom will be focused on blended learning; and, quoting Vaughn and Garrison's 2005 article, *Creating Cognitive Presence in a Blended Faculty Development Community*, the authors state that "Blended learning is on the cusp of transforming higher education." [7].

Blended learning is not a new term, nor as Cross has pointed out, is it a new concept. Cross [2] goes further, predicting:

> Blended is a transitory term. In time it will join programmed instruction and transactional analysis in the dustbin of has-beens. In the meantime, blended is a stepping stone on the way to the future. It reminds us to look at learning challenges from many directions. It makes computer-only training look ridiculous. It drives us to pick up the right tools to get the job done.

1.2 Enhanced Blended Learning

As noted above, online learning is a critical innovation in education and workplace training. However, the very real criticisms of fully online instruction which add to the disconnection reported by students and faculty, such as quality of interaction between student and teacher and among students, delayed communication and timely feedback [5], have led many to consider blended instruction as the key to effective distance learning. Researchers have looked at the role that blended learning can play in shaping the future of e-learning delivery. In *Blended Learning: Uncovering Its Transformative Potential in Higher Education,* Garrison and Kanuka point to the impact that technology - particularly that associated with the Internet - has had on all of us. They ask why we would not expect technology to be "the defining transformative innovation for higher education in the 21st century" [8]. They posit that blended learning is both a low-cost and effective strategy to address (and possibly, integrate) increasingly complex technology. As they define it, blended learning is "the thoughtful integration of classroom face-to-face learning experiences with online learning experiences." Obviously, the integration of the two modes must be effective. As the authors point out, blended learning design represents "a fundamental reconceptualization and reorganization of the teaching and learning dynamic, starting with various specific conceptual needs and contingencies (e.g., discipline, developmental level, and resources)."

Blended learning allows learners to get together and yet remain independent in space and time because the technology exists and is accessible to support it. Garrison and Kanuka argue that blended learning is particularly effective because it can facilitate a community of inquiry, defined as the integration of cognitive, social and teaching presence. A community of inquiry is necessary for students to be able to move through the phases of critical inquiry. In addition, they say, blended learning can provide the learner with the independence and increased control vital for developing critical thinking. The authors conclude with the prediction that higher education could be transformed as blended learning takes hold, becoming a way to mitigate the costs and challenges inherent in classroom teaching.

In response to criticisms that traditional approaches to distance education fail to deliver the holistic and transformational education desired because of the emphasis on quantitative factors rather than qualitative ones, Weigel points to blended learning as a form of "cognitive apprenticeship," stating that collaborative web-based technologies, such as those incorporated in a blended learning model can enrich classroom instruction. Such technologies can add dimensionality by creating virtual spaces for a variety of traditional instructional goals. Weigel argues that there is no categorical dichotomy between physical and virtual space; and, that therefore, there is no rationale for excluding a blended learning model from the instructional palette [9].

With the proliferation of Web 2.0 applications, such as Wikipedia (relied on increasingly by students, if not their instructors to establish context and present data), YouTube and MySpace, among others, the potential for their use in education and training could transform how we approach capacity-building in the nonprofit sector. In their article on using Web 2.0 services to help identify communities of practice, Yang, Zhang and Chen note that one of the essential roles that Web 2.0 technologies can play stems from their ability to enhance communication and interaction among participants [10]. The use of Web 2.0 software, such as blogs and wikis within a blended learning model enables the participant/learner to develop social networks, share information and build communities in ways not as easily done with first-generation technology.

A cautionary note is struck by Grant in her work with staff in the nonprofit sector however. She held a series of semi-structured discussions with participants in a workshop designed to introduce Web 2.0 applications to members of community organizations. She found that despite the enthusiasm and interest generated by learning how social media might improve performance, participants were skeptical that the applications could be implemented and sustained in their own organizations. Grant concludes that, without knowledge of and access to relevant resources, particularly ongoing technological support, nonprofit organizations face significant constraints to successful implementation of Web 2.0 applications. She refers to these constraints as "silos of helplessness" [11].

1.3 Capacity-Building

Describing a multidisciplinary and multilevel framework for social transformation, Maton places capacity-building first among four foundational goals. In his vision, capacity-building possesses a synergistic relationship with the goals of group empowerment, relational community-building, and culture-challenge. "Change in individuals alone, transient changes in setting environments, and interventions that do not ultimately impact community and societal environments cannot in and of themselves make much of a difference" [12]. To address social problems, the author maintains, we must transform the social environment. Capacity-building is the means to influence the instrumental dimension of a social environment. By instrumental, the author means the nature and quality of activities necessary to achieve critical goals. The components of the instrumental environment are core methods, problem-solving capability and leadership. Maton offers capacity-building as an alternative to the external, expert-dominated interventions that have largely failed to solve problems in this domain. Capacity-building is proposed as both a primary transformational process and a goal because of its reliance on community involvement and individual participation in the process of strengthening organizations and communities, and ultimately, affecting social policy.

Maton's is a community development perspective on change. He sees capacity-building as one of the keys to achieving his goal, social transformation. Grindle and Hilderbrand look at capacity-building in the public sector, specifically at improving public sector performance in developing countries [13]. Asking why so many development initiatives have failed, they propose a framework for analyzing capacity-building efforts which takes into account the complex environments in which training activities, organizational performance and administrative structures operate. The hope here is that in using this analytical framework, future efforts at capacity-building (staff training, improving organizational performance and strengthening administrative supports) will succeed. To test this, the authors applied the analytic framework to six case studies – Bolivia, the Central African Republic, Morocco, Sri Lanka, Ghana, and Tanzania. Their framework identified five areas and levels of analysis: action environment, institutional context of the public sector, the task network, organizations and human resources. The studies demonstrated the degree to which performance improvement on the individual and organizational levels are constrained by multiple factors. Conclusions that could be drawn from the studies validated the usefulness of the analytic framework in identifying gaps in capacity. The studies were also useful in that they provided a tool for designing interventions sensitive to the social, political and economic environments in which the people and organizations operated. They found that isolated or individual remedies, such as training or enhanced performance at one organization "may not produce improvements if constraints along other dimensions of capacity are more binding." Arguably, that means that if transformational change is not felt on the broader social, political or economic levels, capacity-building cannot occur in any meaningful fashion.

Capacity-building in the Grindle and Hilderbrand study was defined as performance improvement in public sector organizations. Determination of improved performance included measures of effectiveness, efficiency and sustainability.

For Matachi [14], writing for UNESCO's International Institute for Capacity Building in Africa (IICBA), capacity-building means research, development, training and dissemination. Training is recognized as limited in its reach. Training can build capacity for the individuals involved without any corresponding increase in capacity at the organizational or country level. Addressing the limitations in earlier capacity-building efforts which may have stopped at the level of individuals' capacity- building (training), the author outlined a three-level capacity-building framework for IICBA - individual, organizational and environmental. Individual capacity is defined as the will and ability to set and achieve objectives using the individual's knowledge and skills. Organizational capacity is a much broader notion, referring to "anything that will influence an organization's performance". Capacity at the environmental level means that there is capacity at both the individual and organizational levels that can be supported by the environment. In Matachi's framework, "environment" includes legal, administrative and cultural as well as social, political, and economic variables.

In each of the three discussions of capacity-building the author makes the point that capacity-building is a complex notion that includes individual training and education, knowledge and skill development; organizational supports, technical assistance, human resource development, technological enhancements; and environmental/ societal change. To be successful (and sustainable), capacity-building needs to be long-term, deliberative and participatory.

In 1981, Honadle argued that there was an urgent need for a concept and a purpose in capacity-building [15]. She was addressing the response to federal cutbacks in services and support for public and nonprofit organizations in the United States. Was the test of capacity-building to be merely survivability? Perhaps for the business sector, she argued, but not for public or nonprofit organizations because survivability ignores function. An entity may survive, but without the capacity to perform its mission. Was capacity the ability to provide a service? This, the author maintained, was a nonoperational definition because it failed to define what a capable organization really does. She asked whether capacity-building was a political concept, that is, did it rely on the administration of politics, informal processes and participation or was it a rational one (relationships based on rules that lead to higher levels of rationality)? Was capacity essentially "know how" or was it more the ability to produce more responsive and efficient public goods and services? Was capacity-building the ability to attract inputs or effective functioning of a total system? Was capacity to be measured by activities or results? We would ask, should not capacity-building be concerned with both the how and the what?

Honadle rejected the notion that capacity-building meant increasing the capability of individuals and organizations to do what was required. Instead she proposed a conceptual framework for capacity-building that had as its components the ability to anticipate change (demographic, political, economic); to make policy based on available knowledge; to develop programs to implement policy; to attract resources in support of programs; to absorb and manage those resources; to evaluate activities; and, closing the loop, to use evaluations to increase capacity and improve performance. We suggest that these components may be considered artifacts of the proposed blended learning model for capacity-building described below.

1.4 Capacity-Building and Nonprofit Organizations

In their report on the results of an evaluation of a multi-year effort to influence the nonprofit sector's perception and use of strategic restructuring as a capacity-building technique, Connelly and York [16] point to concerns felt by funders and leaders in the nonprofit sector that have led many to invest in capacity-building efforts. Of particular concern is the need to strengthen management and governance capacity in organizations providing critical public services. How will nonprofits be able to optimize their use of limited resources in constrained circumstances to fulfill their missions? In the United States, questions about accountability to stakeholders–funders, staff, clients, communities–are in the forefront given the increasing attention focused on organizations in the nonprofit sector following the enactment of the Sarbanes-Oxley Act [17]. Stakeholders are asking for transparency and accountability in the organizations in which they have put their trust (see the Independent Sector's Report on the Sarbanes Oxley Act and Implications for Nonprofit Organizations [18]). Concerns about accountability in this sector are not so different from those raised by regulators and taxpayers with regard to the for-profit sector scandals and the more recent "bailouts" of financial institutions.

Capacity-building is a long-term endeavor and one that is complex, because organizational capacity is itself multi-faceted and evolving. Based on their experience in providing consulting and technical assistance services to nonprofit organizations, Connelly and York feel that what may be needed at this point is a means to evaluate capacity-building efforts. However, the authors recognize that the relationship between capacity-building interventions and organizational and program outcomes and ultimate social impact will not be easy to assess. In the qualitative realm, establishing cause and effect is often difficult. With regard to social impact, itself difficult to assess (remember Maton's three challenges to social transformation: the need to move social transformation to the center of our consciousness; the need to articulate a multidisciplinary framework for social transformation work; and, the need to do both with "heart, soul and humility" [12]), evaluation will be challenging. Nonetheless, the authors do propose a framework, a continuum of capacity-building evaluation that relies on a mix of quantitative and qualitative measures to assess the effectiveness of capacity-building activities using a logic model to guide the process.

Cairns, Harris, Hutchinson and Tricker recognize and appreciate the concerns expressed by stakeholders for increased organizational performance in nonprofits and for effective methods to increase capacity [19]. The authors describe the "puzzle", that is, improving organizational performance, as a recurrent theme in the literature and one which is reflected in concepts of capacity, accountability, goal achievement, efficiency and effectiveness, as well as outcome measurement and evaluation. In their article, *Improving Performance? The Adoption and Implementation of Quality Systems in U.K. Nonprofits,* the authors report on the adoption and use of quality systems in the U.K. nonprofit sector (the voluntary and community sector). While not new to the for-profit sector, quality systems, that is, performance improvement approaches which target the quality of management and services, had not been as readily adopted in the public and nonprofit sectors because of the difficulty in assessing "quality" of services (as opposed to the quality of products). The authors report that, due to the pressure from stakeholders to demonstrate organizational effectiveness, more organizations were being encouraged to adopt quality systems. Their research was designed to identify the drivers for the adoption of quality systems in nonprofits. What they found was that the decision to implement a quality system for performance improvement was based on several interrelated factors, both internal and external. As in the Connelly and York report, pressure from funders (the cloud of donor events) was one of the primary drivers as was the perceived need to demonstrate accountability to various stakeholders (stakeholder motivations and priorities). In this instance, the cloud of donor events led to the consideration of how to adapt performance improvement approaches to the nonprofit sector (extraction of innovation drivers), resulting in the adoption of quality systems (knowledge harness for event focused information integration) desired by the stakeholders.

Obstacles to adopting a quality system in the organization reported by participants in the Cairns et al. study included lack of resources, including staff time and organizational capacity as well as lack of staff commitment to the idea of quality systems as an appropriate vehicle for performance improvement. Their study is relevant to the broader issue of capacity-building because performance improvement is used as a measure of organizational capacity to fulfill mission. As might be expected, the study found that the better the alignment of the quality system with the organizational culture and organizational resources, the more successful the adoption and use of quality systems for performance improvement. Also not surprisingly, the more committed the leader to the quality system, the more successful the integration into the organization. As always, change needs champions.

The study was commissioned by the UK's Quality Standards Task Group, created in 1997 to assist organizations in the voluntary and community sector in improving organizational performance through the use of quality systems. In 2004, another government-supported initiative was launched to improve organizational capacity in the sector and to establish the necessary infrastructure to support capacity-building. The authors suggest that for this initiative to be successful, careful attention to developing an integrated approach to quality and to the preferred model of capacity-building (empowerment versus deficit) would be necessary. "How and where infrastructure support is positioned in relation to 'capacity building' is likely to have a significant influence on the future of the 'performance improvement' agenda in the UK nonprofit sector" [20].

Concerns about and interest in capacity-building for organizations in the nonprofit sector are not limited to the United States and the United Kingdom of course. In their report on management practices in Croatian nonprofits, Alfirevic and Gabelica discuss the need for increased professionalism and efficiency in the civil sector. Again, the emphasis on capacity-building stems from funding pressures: " …traditional sources of funding for the non-profit and civil society organizations seem to be vanishing in Central Eastern Europe entirely…"[21]. Published in 2007, the study looks to social entrepreneurship as a means for revitalization of the sector. The authors argue that for social entrepreneurship to compensate for shrinking international donations, the development of professional non-profit management is essential. Here, the focus is on capacity-building in one area, management. The study had found weaknesses in management practices and performance in the organizations reviewed: "… the most significant relates either to inadequate understanding of the managerial position in the Croatian non-profit/social sector, or to the lack of ability of Croatian non-profit managers to perform their jobs in a manner compatible with the theoretical presumptions" [21].

1.5 Measuring Results

In their study of the use of blended learning in the workplace, Kim, Bonk and Oh examined the issue of diverse technologies and delivery methods and questioned how effective blended learning really was. Because of "many unknowns," they state that it is unclear where blended learning is heading and how practitioners will be able to implement it in their organizations. To answer where practitioners might be heading with blended learning, they surveyed human resource managers and personnel directors in government agencies, nonprofit organizations and business entities on their use of blended learning in workplace learning settings [22]. Respondents had moderately positive attitudes towards the use of blended learning in their organizations. Reasons for employing blended learning as a training tool included improving availability and accessibility of learning; improving the quality of the learning experience; reducing costs; and, implementing new strategic directions for the organization. The main benefits to blended learning were richer instructional content, cost-effectiveness and learning appropriateness. The results supported a finding that practitioners considered blended learning to be an effective and efficient mode of training delivery. However, their study also demonstrated several obstacles to adopting blended learning in the workplace, such as the inability to keep up with fast-paced technological advances and insufficient management support and commitment. Several respondents said they were uncertain what blended learning was, although the same respondents said they valued blended learning! Other obstacles noted were: learners' lack of self-regulated learning skills; organizational and cultural resistance; limited bandwidth; boring and low-quality content; limited organizational vision and planning; learner resistance and hesitancy; high costs of delivery; more hype than fact; lack of quality instructors; and, lack of standards. Despite these obstacles, respondents agreed that blended learning was important for their organizations' strategies for training.

What sort of training should be designed for the necessary results? The Kim, Bonk and Oh study respondents said that instructional strategies linking learning and performance using a collaborative and meaningful learning setting would be more useful than the more traditional lecture-based models. The supporting technologies favored included webcasting and video streaming coupled with digital libraries and knowledge management tools for just-in-time training. Wireless and mobile technologies ranked highest for the delivery medium. Respondents said that the evaluation of blended learning would focus on the benefits perceived by the organization (employee performance, cost benefit analyses, and return on investment). The authors conclude that blended learning will be popular in workplace learning in all three sectors, public, for-profit and nonprofit, particularly once practitioners better understand how to integrate the differing instructional methods with the appropriate technologies. We suggest that adoption of blended learning as the instructional method of choice will be made all the easier because of the popularity of Web 2.0 technologies.

2 Innovation in Capacity-Building

The issue of capacity-building in the nonprofit sector is generally acknowledged to be of real concern. Writers most often add to that sentence, "to stakeholders." But, we would ask, who is <u>not</u> a stakeholder in the vitality of the nonprofit sector? Nonprofits, nongovernmental, voluntary organizations are private-sector entities providing public services. They dominate the fields of education and art. They are often the first responders in disasters and the intermediaries for ameliorating social ills. Yet, the question must be asked, how many will fail in the next decade? Economic forces have affected all of them. How can we, also stakeholders, make a difference for these organizations?

2.1 Capacity-Building and Nonprofit Organizations

The conceptual framework offered by Honadle [15] is testament to the holistic vision now emerging for capacity-building through enrichment of the growth model for businesses currently prevalent in thought leadership circles. However, the growth model fails to encompass all stakeholders, particularly in the nonprofit sector. In particular, successful outreach propositions of the nonprofit sector require a capacity to integrate diverse information inputs and to analyze motivational successes of social enterprises, including relevant government agencies. In this regard, the infusion of social network trends and mobile technology directions directly impact the effectiveness of development strategies in nonprofit organizations, as for example, the use of conventional (print) media in soliciting contributions. Fund-raising efforts for disaster relief in Haiti and in Chile successfully relied on web-based technologies to get aid to the stricken regions. Donors and volunteers, particularly Generation Xers and Nexters, reportedly responded well to electronic solicitations for assistance [23].

2.2 Models of Capacity-Building

The private sector has had an ongoing interest in capacity-building, typically using change management processes, to refocus on corporate goal achievement and to create opportunities for leadership and innovation in expanding corporate performance. However, existing corporate models of capacity-building typically have yet to address the holistic requirements mandated by the integration of individual self-actualization goals with mechanisms for organizational and sector empowerment. The current recession, for example, has exposed the lack of institutional processes for capacity-building in adverse economic environments, other than through government stimulus measures.

Our preferred model addresses the requirement for innovation drivers at all three levels - individual, organizational and sector, focusing on scenarios rather than typical growth metrics, and resolution of the complex information fusion requirements using novel paradigms: in effect, a paradigmatic approach in which institutional learning embodies innovation processes and event activation mechanisms driven by blended learning imperatives.

2.3 Evaluation of Innovation Driver Effectiveness

Historically, innovation has been stimulated by hardship and conflict, as exemplified by the medical and scientific advances attained during World War II. During the subsequent decades of growth, innovation models typically have been based on advances in technology, in knowledge management, in lateral thinking and in the diffusion of global 'best practice' techniques. The advent of blended learning support for innovation and institutional effectiveness now offers an unprecedented opportunity for integrated, holistic empowerment in the nonprofit sector through conceptualization of a tiered learning model and the requisite innovation drivers.

The true effectiveness of innovation drivers is assessed not on the basis of the narrow efficiency of learning module delivery, but rather from the rate at which new ideas, whether infused within external material or those stimulated by communities of practice operating within the blended learning framework, are transformed into actionable results at all three tiers. Thus, effective communication and integrative processes within the individual, organizational and sector tiers are essential. While the importance of integrating lateral and vertical communications in knowledge organizations (such as in R&D enterprises) has been known for some time, the development of kindred models based on research and discovery in philanthropic organizations, with rare exceptions (notably the Bill and Melinda Gates Foundation), has not been done.

The proposed blended learning paradigm for capacity-building in nonprofit organizations is adapted from earlier applications in the business sector by Garner and

Chen [24] and by Garner and Song [25].The model is intended to support multiple paradigms in an event-focused information integration scenario. The overarching integration scenario responds dynamically to:

- Event-focused innovation drivers, such as community dislocations/disasters as evidenced by the earthquakes in Haiti and Chile in 2010 and the Gulf Coast oil spill in the United States.
- Learning communities, such as communities of practice, demonstrated by organizational designs for community response in disasters; powerful social networks which have demonstrated an enormous capacity for facilitating e-philanthropy; collaborative knowledge acquisition, such as group support systems used for crisis management in natural and man-made disasters – all of which support the delivery of emergency relief and information services needed in the face of such disasters.
- Advances in visual presentation paradigms (e.g., haptic technologies for disabled persons)
- Results of novel outreach strategies enabled by embedded virtual services such as that described by Lin, Ho, Sadiq and Orlowska for managing business process activities with flexible e-learning that they term "Flex-el" [26].

The following conceptualization of a blended learning paradigm for capacity-building in nonprofit organizations (Figure 1) includes the two requisite inputs for the extraction of innovation drivers and the discovery of event scenario transforms leading to a knowledge harness for the integration of event-focused information for stakeholder attention:

- "Cloud of Donor Events" captured from global sources and institutional intelligence; and
- "Stakeholder Motivations and Priorities", which have been well documented by philanthropic organizations, by governments and by global charities.

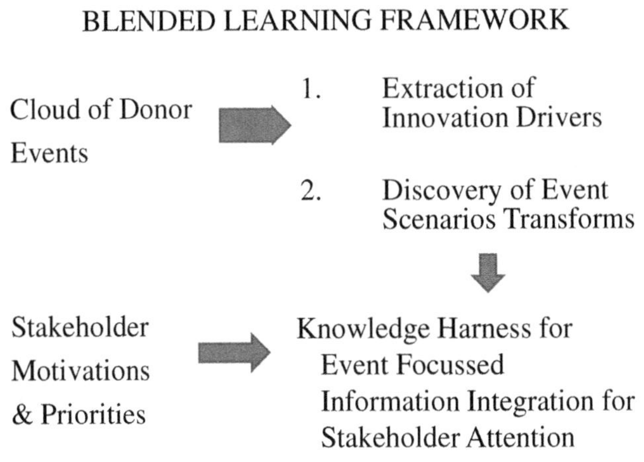

Fig. 1. Blended Learning Paradigm for Capacity-Building in Nonprofit Organizations

The blended learning processes source the requisite innovation drivers for the nonprofit sector and ensure both the discovery of relevant scenario transforms and provision of the information inputs to the knowledge fusion paradigm(s) required for stakeholder action and capacity-building. Additionally, the integration of principles of activity theory with thematic analysis offers a different way of approaching the model using blended learning objectives to extract the innovation drivers.

"Cloud of Donor Events" would normally provide patterns of donor behavior using statistical or other approaches, resulting in classifications of donors appropriate to any specified charity. The driver for donor requests would then require a marketing scenario.

The "Extraction of Innovation Drivers" might use data mining techniques, or be based on in-depth interviews of philanthropic/government institutions to identify new trends and changes to donor expectations.

In "Discovery of Event Scenarios Transforms", "events" relate to such as economic disruptions, natural disasters, and more generally, to the failure of expectations driven by changes in government/corporate priorities. Of course, technological change may also play a big role in transformational change, particularly disruptive technologies.

The novelty of this approach is to refine what is normally a massive data management exercise by focusing on events and the corresponding transformations required of the scenarios currently in use by the charity/donor recipient. This is a dynamic process to ensure that charities can respond rapidly to volatile economic and social requirements.

The proposed blended learning paradigm for capacity-building is designed to be a model for building inclusive partnerships that ensure a capacity to respond dynamically to changes in donor behavior using event-focused knowledge management processes.

3 Conclusion

In the concluding chapter of *The Handbook of Blended Learning: Global perspectives, Local Designs*, Bonk, Kim and Zeng state "...blended learning is more than fashionable; it is the training and educational delivery method of choice" [27]. That said, what does blended learning offer for the future of capacity-building in the nonprofit sector?

Grindle and Hilderbrand suggested that we should ask three questions before deciding on a strategy for capacity- building [13]. First, where should capacity building initiatives be focused? Second, what kinds of incentive structures and interactions contribute to performance? Third, where and when is training an effective means of enhancing performance?

In response to the first question, we propose that we begin with the individual in the workplace, building capacity through training and education delivered through a blended learning model. Kim, Bonk and Zeng in Kim, Bonk and Oh [22] have predicted that eighty to ninety percent of college and corporate training classes will be blended by the end of 2010. They point to blended learning as an innovation in e-learning. To that we would agree, and further, suggest that blended learning enables the discovery of innovation drivers, whether technological in nature or social imperatives, to identify and realize scenarios for holistic empowerment.

To the second question, we point to the blended learning framework as a method to identify and implement incentive structures and performance-related interactions. Lastly, to the third question of where and when is training effective, we suggest that when the audience is known, using blended learning as a driver in capacity-building helps to identify where training should be conducted – whether in the virtual or physical environment- and to design timely training.

The ubiquitous requirement for blended learning to expose and exploit innovation drivers and scenario transforms in capacity-building follows logically from the need to elicit tacit (experiential) knowledge in solving the increasingly complex social problems of the 'Global Village'. The corresponding use of multiple paradigms in knowledge fusion has required a novel approach to blended experiential learning.

If innovation means positive change, new ways to accomplish objectives, blended learning - enhanced by next generation technologies - provides a different way to think about how we provide education and training, particularly within the context of capacity-building in the nonprofit sector. As Grant's research suggests [11], in order to build the successful model, it will be critical to incorporate the realities of the nonprofit sector; that is, the model will need to recognize the constraints and challenges facing those working in the sector and adapt the model to address them. To accomplish that, we need input from leaders of nonprofit organizations, researchers working in the field and from experts now providing capacity-building training.

We began our investigation with a question: can we develop a new model of blended learning that is targeted to the real needs of the nonprofit sector? While we do not yet have an answer, we do have a starting point for additional research that draws on the knowledge of those in the sector.

References

1. Independent Sector, Facts and Figures about Charitable Organizations, `http://www.independentsector.org/programs/.../Charitable_Fact_Sheet.pdf`
2. Cross, J.: Forward. In: Bonk, C.J., Graham, C.R. (eds.) The Handbook of Blended Learning: Global Perspectives Local Designs, John Wiley & Sons, Inc., San Francisco (2006)
3. Garner, B.: Transformational Leadership in Compliance Training. Paper Presented to HK Knowledge Management Association (February 24, 2010)
4. Rossett, A., Douglis, F., Frazee, R.V.: Strategies for Building Blended Learning. Learning Circuits, `http://www.learningcircuits.org/2003/jul2003/rossett.htm`
5. Schuhmann, R.A., Skopek, T.A.: Blurring the Lines: A Blended Learning Model in a Graduate Public Administration Program. The Quarterly Review of Distance Education 10(2), 219–232 (2009)
6. Collopy, R.M.B., Arnold, J.M.: To Blend or Not to Blend: Online and Blended Learning Environments in Undergraduate Teacher Education. Issues in Teacher Education 18(2), 85–101 (2009)
7. Motteram, G., Sharma, P.: Blended Learning in a Web 2.0 World. International Journal of Emerging Technologies & Society 7(2), 8, 3–96 (2009)

8. Garrison, R.D., Kanuka, H.: Blended Learning: Uncovering its Transformative Potential in Higher Education. Internet and Higher Education 7, 95–105 (2004)
9. Weigel, V.B.: Reflection: Place in the Digital Age: Familiar Dichotomies No Longer Apply. Christian Scholar's Review 32(1), 13–18 (2002)
10. Yang, S.J.H., Zhang, J., Chen, I.Y.L.: Web 2.0 Services for Identifying Communities of Practice Through Social Networks. In: 2007 IEEE International Conference on Services Computing (2008)
11. Grant, S.: Silos of Helplessness: A Cautionary Tale about Introducing Social-Media (Web 2.0) Applications in the Community Sector. Third Sector Review 15(2), 89–104 (2009)
12. Maton, K.I.: Making a Difference: The Social Ecology of Social Transformation. American Journal of Community Psychology 28(1), 25–57 (2000)
13. Grindle, M.S., Hilderbrand, M.E.: Building Sustainable Capacity in the Public Sector: What Can Be Done? Public Administration & Development 15, 441–463 (1995)
14. Matachi, A.: Capacity Building Framework: UNESCO-IICBA. United Nations Economic Commission for Africa, Addis Ababa, Ethiopia (2006)
15. Honadle, B.W.: A Capacity-Building Framework: A Search for Concept and Purpose. Public Administration Review 41(5), 575–580 (1981)
16. Connolly, P., York, P.: Evaluating Capacity-Building Efforts for Nonprofit Organizations. OD Practitioner 34(4), 33–39 (2002)
17. Sarbanes-Oxley Act of 2002, PL 107-204, 116 Stat 745
18. Board Source & Independent Sector: The Sarbanes Oxley Act and Implications for Nonprofit Organizations, `http://www.independentsector.org/PDFs/sarbanesoxley.pdf`
19. Cairns, B., Harris, M., Hutchison, R., Tricker, M.: Improving Performance? The Adoption and Implementation of Quality Systems in U.K. Nonprofits. Nonprofit Management & Leadership 16(2), 135–151 (2005)
20. Cairns, B., Harris, M., Hutchison, R., Tricker, M.: Improving Performance? The Adoption and Implementation of Quality Systems in U.K. Nonprofits. In: ARNOVA Conference, Los Angeles, California (November 2004)
21. Alfirevic, N., Gabelica, N.: Management Practices in Croatian Non-Profit Organizations: Results of the Empirical Research. Management: Journal of Contemporary Management Issues 12(1), 25–45 (2007)
22. Kim, K.J., Bonk, C.J., Oh, E.: The Present and Future State of Blended Learning in Workplace Learning Settings in the United States. Performance Improvement 47(8), 5–16 (2008)
23. Reed, R.: Who Gives, Why Do They Give, How Do TheyGivetoNonprofits?, `http://www.prnewswire.com/news-releases/who-gives-why-do-the`
24. Garner, B.J., Chen, F.: Hypothesis Generation Paradigm for Fraud Detection. In: Proceedings of IEEE Region 10's Ninth Annual International Conference on Frontiers and Computer Technology, Singapore (1994)
25. Garner, B.J., Song, D.: Financial Planning Scenarios (1999)
26. Lin, J., Ho, C., Sadiq, W., Orlowska, M.E.: On Workflow Enabled E-learning Services. In: Second IEEE International Conference on Advanced Learning Technologies, ICALT, p. 0349 (2001)
27. Bonk, C.J., Kim, K.J., Zeng, T.: Future Directions in Blended Learning in Higher Education and Workplace Learning Settings. In: Bonk, C.J., Graham, C.R. (eds.) The Handbook of Blended Learning: Global Perspectives Local Designs, John Wiley & Sons, Inc., San Francisco (2006)

Formal and Informal Lifelong Learning in a Virtual Communities Platform

Luigi Colazzo[1], Andrea Molinari[1], and Nicola Villa[2]

[1] Department of Computer and Management Sciences
[2] Laboratory of Maieutics, University of Trento
Via Inama, 5 – 38122 Trento (Italy)
Tel.: +39 0461 28{2144, 2344, 2339}
{luigi.colazzo,andrea.molinari,nicola.villa}@unitn.it

Abstract. The paper presents our experience as designers, developers and administrators of an e-learning system used by the Faculty of Economics of the University of Trento and from the Autonomous province of Trento (Italy). We recently managed the evolution of the system towards the provision of a new Personal Learning Space to the users. In this moment the platform is in a phase of complete redevelopment and the final objective will be the adaption of the typical approaches of the web 2.0 and social networks into an e-learning formal platform. In particular one of the objectives will be to integrate an informal learning metaphor into a classic formal one. The term informal learning has been used in education field, in particular in the adult education, for several reasons; one of them is providing to the learners a greater flexibility in the learning process. This approach highlights that the lessons from the others could have a great social significance, but implies that the education agencies (e.g. the universities or the training institutions) have the capability to increase the socialisation level into the learning environment. Following the informal learning approach is necessary to focus the attention to the learning that takes place in the spaces surrounding the activities that take place in a much wider variety of settings than the formal education and training. This approach is not a substitute of the formal learning but could be complementary, integrating the personal experiences and the learning exchanges with the other participants. We will introduce the problems related to the integration of these two different logics into a single e-learning platform (learning spaces and social networks), and how to connect these two worlds into one single architecture. The system that we have developed, named On Line Communities, provides the idea of virtual communities as pillars of the interaction mechanisms provided by the platform to the users.

Keywords: e-learning, Personal Learning Environments, learning virtual communities, web 2.0, social networks.

1 Introduction

The Learning Management Systems (LMSs) are normally used by educational institutions to manage their training activities [1]. These systems use the network to

X. Luo et al. (Eds.): ICWL 2010 Workshops, LNCS 6537, pp. 291–300, 2011.

create different learning environments related to the learner needs (distance learning, blended training, back-end activities management relate to training processes, etc.) [2]. As any other type of management system, these applications are also connected to the management model that is represented in the software [4]. In the case of e-learning applications, the represented model is the way by which the institution conceives its learning / teaching processes [3][5]. The simplest model is the one used in distance learning, when the system becomes a container of learning objects, designed to be effective in the students self-learning processes, the remote control of the current level of learning, the certification of the results achieved and the management of the organizational / financial relations with the training institution.

Much more complex are the systems oriented towards a blended approach. In this case, the LMS offers a virtual space corresponding to what is carried out in the real didactical institution. In this way, the student learns not only in the traditional courses (in the classroom) but also using the virtual space as reinforcement to face-to-face lectures. This model is the most widely used by the academic institutions. More complex are the systems that tend to support innovative forms of learning such as learning by project, learning by problem and cooperative learning. In this case, the LMS must provide not just a virtual space associated with a course but also special virtual spaces able to work with other similar environments. The section 2 of this paper shows, referring to two systems that are designed, implemented and managed by us, such as the shift from an LMS based on metaphor of the Course to one based on the metaphor of the Virtual Community can produce significant changes in the architecture of a LMS.

The LMS evolution from simply content containers to real cooperation spaces is now in a new phase of transition. The spread of Web 2.0 applications provides the possibility for these systems to evolve and support all those forms of learning excluded from the classical formal and institutional learning methodologies. It is banal to note that the interrelationship between formal and informal learning includes new challenges to the educational institutions and also to the change of the LMSs' architectures. In this paper we present the solution that we are studying in this moment, and the object of a technological integration between the e-learning processes and the current aspects of social networking.

The paper is organised as follows: in the first part we will describe the LMS developed for the University of Trento, named On Line Communities, and its evolution from an e-learning system based on the metaphor of course to a more complex virtual environment based on the metaphor of virtual community. In the second part we will introduce the current study of our research group directed to the integration of the social networking aspect into our environment. In particular we want to underline the risk of a direct adoption of social network logic into an academic environment, and what could be the correct strategy for the integration of the two types of approaches into a "bridge" platform.

2 On Line Communities

In the academic year 1999/2000 the Faculty of Economics of the University of Trento decided to have a software system able to enrich its traditional teaching as an extension on the Web. The first aim was to settle the increasing number of teachers' personal web pages into a single platform. To pursue this result it was necessary to have a Learning Management System (LMS), capable of supplying a virtual environment able to support the educational courses of the Faculty. The resulting system started to function from the second half of 1999 and during this period, the system counted approximately 1,500,000 accesses. Being a quite traditional LMS, in 2002 some observation convinced us to redesign the software:

- The needs for cooperation within the academic environments is extending to all the activities that constitute the context in which didactic takes place, not just to the specific "lecture";
- models of teaching / learning (such as learning by problems, learning by projects, cooperative learning and their combinations) can hardly be connected to the e-Course, especially when the software directly represents the metaphor of traditional courses;
- the organizational didactic scenario changed with new regulations made by academic institutions, and these changes inevitably reflected on the LMS functionalities. It is important to note that these types of changes are usually the result of a debate process in which both elements of cooperation and negotiation interact;
- the didactics of an university are not built only as a set of studies and tests, but these activities are inevitably intertwined with the university's organization and its information system;
- in an academic context, not everything concerning teaching: for example, the entire faculty is more than a container of degree courses and a degree course is more than a container of lessons.

To answer these (and other) needs, another founding paradigm was need, with at least three basic characteristics:

1. generalization respect to educational settings;
2. suitability to support cooperation processes;
3. capability of modelling and preserving organizational structure and roles of the educational institution.

This new way of conceiving the collaboration platform was found in the concept of virtual community. The system that arose, called *On Line Communities* [6], was born in 2003 and runs in February 2005. The collaborative approach [7] [8] is a very strong incentive for us to develop On Line Communities; the philosophy that led us to rebuild the system is to allow the exchange of users' experiences within a virtual environment, and within well-defined areas known as "communities". This approach is very different, for example, from the traditional ones available in other LMSs. Our work started before the boom of web 2.0 [9], that has now invaded and changed the way people think and build services on the net. The main characteristics of a community could be summed up as follows:

- Each Community offers many services to registered users that have different roles/permissions inside the community
- The services are general applications that enable the users to communicate in

synchronous and asynchronous way, to publish contents, to exchange files, to coordinate events, etc.

- Services offered by a community are activated by a manager of the community according to the needs, and the users of a community can use them with different rights and duties.
- Rights/duties in the community are different from rights/duties for the services
- Communities can be aggregated into larger communities with hierarchic mechanisms and infinite nesting levels. Communities can also be aggregated in an arbitrary way into larger communities disregarding the possible position of a hierarchical structure, in a sort of "transversal" link that overcomes the concept of "hierarchy" and follows the idea of "mesh". Thanks to these features, a complex but powerful mechanism of propagation of services/roles/permissions/ rights/duties can be set among communities of the same branch or of different branches.
- All users are recognized by the system and by the community: people external to the system can see public part of the community (services, material, contents etc.) only if managers allow this (ex. a blog of one community could be opened to external contributions)
- Services can take advantage of the "mesh" structure of Online Communities to provide some interesting though non-existing features, like "transversal wikis", or "merged blogs". One blog, in fact, can be the "fusion" of all the blogs of children communities, or a wiki can take the definition transversally from all wikis in related communities.
- Last but not least, a VC is the container for collaboration processes not limited to educational activities, but for any collaboration activity needed in an organization. Research teams, recreation groups, friends, meetings, conferences, secretariats, board of directors, colleagues, next social dinner, anything could be an aggregation of people around a scope that can take advantage of the virtual spaces offered by the Virtual community.

The core of the application is composed by some abstract entities, i.e., VCs as aggregation of people to which some communication services are available in order to obtain certain objectives. With this approach, it could be possible to represent all the hierarchical relationships between different types of educational communities (such as Faculties, Didactic Paths, Master Degrees, Courses, etc.), as any other relationship among communities inside organizations.

3 The Architectural Influences of LifeLong Learning in the Architecture of on Line Communities

In 2007 On Line Communities has been chosen as the official technological platform for LifeLong Learning projects of our Province's public administration. In particular the name of the project is *L3* (LifeLong Learning) [14]. The project has been commissioned by the Autonomous Province of Trento (PAT) and it will be the technological environment for training projects within the PAT itself and connected offices.

The aim of our work is mainly technological. That is to say that our task is to supply the province with an instrument enabling it to implement internal training processes.

The evolution that Online Communities is going through implies not easy implementation complexities, considering that the differences between the two approaches according at least four dimensions:

a) *Temporal*: the concept is amplified on larger spectrum, that is to say, the life of the subject, not necessarily dependent on schooling or university studies.
b) *social*: the platform could be used in social contexts of totally diverse life-long learning, even in conflict with each other. Let us take as example subjects who, while interested in continuous learning, change the country of their residence, company where they work, training needs, etc.
c) *spatial*: the place where the learner is conditions the modality of the supply of training iter and situated learning. Let us think, for instance, at the various learning needs of a person responsible for maintenance, or a medical doctor when facing an emergency case, or a tourist in front of a work of art in a museum.
d) *anthropological:* the subject uses the platform in completely different life periods; starting with pre-school age until the end of working activity and, not to be excluded, even beyond. The problems linked to these aspects represent something extremely stimulating and as yet unexplored.

Considering these observations linked to the approach of lifelong learning, meaning that, if the prospect of e-Learning offered by continuous training is extended on the temporal horizon, the architectural choices and the services supplied by the new platform are in need of complete re-engineering, in quantitative terms (dimension of personal space) as well as in organizational terms (services supplied, utility of management, updating and erasing, historical change of context, etc.); the changes must follow a careful analysis that takes into consideration various aspects:

- The system will operate on a territorial basis and in a context characterised by solid co-operation among the citizens.
- The system should be able to guarantee temporal continuity of the training experience which goes beyond the single case of training and ideally is extended to at least many years.

There is also another delicate problem be taken care of, that could be called "persistence of digital data"; reasoning along very long temporal scales, the moment a user utilizes several platforms in the course of his/her life, starting with compulsory school up to the last training activity in a working environment, a series of digital information will be stored inside very different systems:

-the registry system of the various institutes where the user passed,
-the accounting system concerning the various taxes, enrolments, etc.,
-the system of making public diploma or degree assignees, fairly widely spread in Italy too.

Information concerning not only learning in the strictest sense, but intrinsically correlated to the learning environments consulted by the user during his/her career, that are a wide source of information.

This context of application has brought up a number of questions, crucial in a life-long learning environment.

Indeed, while in an academic institution the learning communities for the bigger part coincide with the training experience (one course, one study line, etc.) in case of lifelong learning the communities are more permanent. In a certain sense they pre-exist virtual communities and survive the training experience itself.

4 Learning and Social Networks: Two Architectural Strategies

If we look at the whole range of application fields where we are using On Line Communities, the platform clearly evidences its nature of a collaborative environment that wants to stimulate the participation and put to value users' cooperative work. Today, with the advent of new communication and collaboration paradigms, On Line Communities has become an example of a Computer Support Cooperative Work system (CSCW) dedicated to teaching/learning. In recent years, we extended our system to functionalities and services typical of Web 2.0. However, some relevant differences exist between the approaches used by web 2.0 applications and the ones used in On Line Communities. To overcome these differences, a changing of the rules used in the virtual space is required, and these changes have a direct influence on the entire architecture of the system.

The cooperative virtual space of On Line Communities is actually a closed environment. The users participate to the activities inside the system directly with their real identity. In fact, a person who enters a virtual community of our system is authorized firstly by the platform administrator (for certifying user's credentials), and after by each community administrator for each community the user wants to enrol with. Once the user is accepted inside the community, from that moment he/she is automatically in contact with all the people inside the community. This is the pillar of the virtual community: I'm in the community because I share its scope, and all the people of the community have more or less the same interests / objectives / tasks. Following this logic, the user is not obliged to declare, accept, or manage his/her contacts inside that community: s/he will never have to face the "domino" effect of most social networks, where you will be connected to a friend of a friend of a friend. On Line Communities allows each user to manage friends' lists but this is different from managing community members. The differences between "friends" and "community members" are very precise and marked, and the user is allowed by the platform to manage these two different concepts.

Given that the increase of social interactions is not a negative aspect in principle, the risks deriving from the direct use of the most used social network approach (like for example the approach used by Facebook [10]) into an environment with different aims are very high. According to some statistics [11], the majority of users who use the so called "social networks services" are concentrating on the well-known *"people surfing"*: navigating into the friends' profiles, look at pictures, personal information, etc. We are aware of the clear phenomenon that is emerging from friends' social networks [12]; it is true that the action of adding a person to the friends' list requires an approval, but it is also true that a user can see at any moment the people connected to his/her friends; a critical consequence is to become implicitly a friend of my contacts' friends, thus starting a sort of recursion in the friends' list of friends.

The circumstances that we consider favourable in our system (lack of anonymity and control of the external accesses) have origin in two explicit requirements of our Faculty of Economics. The exclusion of anonymity is the result of a belief that normally indicates that the anonymity into virtual learning environments should be banned, so that the actors cannot shirk from their responsibilities. The second circumstance (access control) stems from the will of a substantial number of teachers to block the publication on the network of their own courses' Learning Objects. These choices made the system impermeable to the users' social dynamics, or to the communities existing in the social networks.

To overcome these limits without affecting our constraints requires a radical change of the system architecture that sees the person as a member of one or many communities. On the other hand, in the web 2.0 applications, the participants exist as individuals who, for example, can create themselves a specific community. The rethinking of the system with these ideas could change our community system to a sort of "community 2.0" system: we like to define it as a "*Private community Environment*" (PCE). The difference between the two approaches is that the communities in our systems are created as an extension in the virtual space of real didactics. On the contrary, in web 2.0 social networks, virtual communities emerge from the interaction among users' own networks.

Following this line, we studied how to modify the architecture of our system, as we wanted to implement the good part (from our perspective) of the incredible revolution introduced by social networks. We wanted to transform our virtual communities platform into a sort of bridge system between the classical methodology followed into the most famous LMSs (like for example Moodle [13]) and the new web 2.0 and social networks applications (like for example Facebook, MySpace and Flickr), without losing the focus on the learning processes.

The architecture that we developed has two fundamental goals:

- As we have said, to make our system more permeable to all experiences that take place inside the web, including applications for social networking and Web 2.0;
- Keep control, up to a certain level, of the actions taken by users of our system. In fact, our context is connected to learning environments / academic settings, and not directly to leisure time.

Following these approaches, many drastic changes have been introduced into the platform, moving the focus from "community" to "user". As an example, when the user connects to the system, the user' personal home page and its services are presented, creating a real Personal Learning Space (PLS).

We are imagining the new users' Personal Learning Space as an aggregation of two distinct environments. The user will be free to decide what part of his/her relations and contents to import (into On Line Communities) or export (to social networks applications). This solution required a strong review of many parts of On Line Communities, and in particular the management of users' roles and permissions.

This approach has different values, in particular regarding the teaching strategies; in fact exporting the contents outside an e-learning platform could accentuate the social role of the educational institution as a source of knowledge and of better didactic practices.

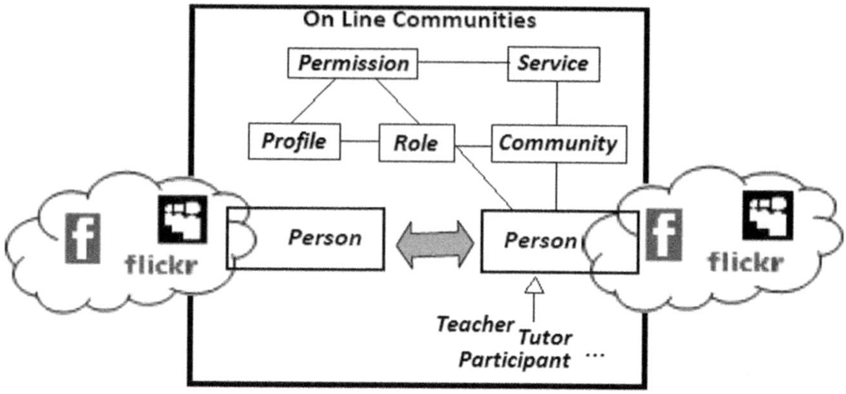

Fig. 1. The representation of the new On Line Communities architecture

On one side, this solution gives to the user more freedom than into a classic LMS, but on the other side, it is more difficult for didactic institutions to be implemented. In fact, while the institutions are becoming a knowledge centre through the participation of its members, at the same time they are being exposed to the risk of the complexity and the personal relationships of its members.

According to this solution, it is important also to develop a new interface of the Personal Learning Space of each user; the metaphor of community makes possible to implement some interesting features, directly connected to the user and his/her list of contacts. In other words, this gives the possibility to the users to manage their own learning spaces: in some way to enable the users to create a "*Personal Learning Space*" for their needs. Each user has the opportunity to access to his/her personal page, which will contain personalized services. As a result, some interesting new services can be provided, for example:

1. access to communities where the user was registered;
2. view the most used services by each user;
3. access to contextual services for each community;
4. access to the personalized services;
5. add some services into the personal learning area.

The user can access to the list of communities where s/he is enrolled in, because this is the primary scope of connecting to this system. But together with this, the user finds a set of services that are typically connected to his/her own person, a sort of personal space within the system. The services are "general", so in this condition the user will see services that are at "personal" level. This can be repeated and nested when the user enters inside a community: he will find (more or less) the same services, but this time these will be the services of *that* community, with different permissions, roles, list of contacts etc. A typical example is the Blog service: when I'm inside my PLS, the Blog is *my blog*, when I'm inside the community "workgroup XWZ", the service *Blog* refers to the blog of *that community*: same service, totally different context and contents, totally different the role of the user could be. Finally, thanks to the inheritance mechanism among communities provided by the platform, the blog of that community can be merged with the blogs of parent community/ies, or with the child communities, or with sister communities (children of the same parent community).

5 Conclusions

One of the thoughts that arises from the discussion presented is that the extension of a learning management system towards a Web 2.0 approach is not simply a matter of adding some services (blog, wiki, friends etc.) to a LMS. We experimented the "long and winding road" of architectural choices, needed for taking full advantages from these tools. Moreover, coupling this web 2.0 tools with a virtual communities approach, rather than the traditional "course" metaphor, we obtained many advantages in the possible services provided to end users. In particular, it was evident that social applications are profoundly different from what is provided by traditional e-learning applications. Our system, originally followed a logic of blended learning, was also focused on the metaphor of the course. The evolution to a different metaphor (the community), has opened new perspectives, different from anything that can be seen as formal learning. Our new focus on the development of web 2.0 and social network services, increasingly common in the worldwide web, seemed to be quite naturally.

References

1. Coates, H., James, R., Baldwin, G.: A critical examination of the effects of learning management systems on university teaching and learning. Tertiary Education and Management 11, 19–36 (2005)
2. Adelsberger, H.H., Collis, B., Pawlowski, J.M. (eds.): Handbook on Information Technologies for Education and Training. Springer, Berlin (2002)
3. Schakelman, J.L.: The changing role of on-line pedagogy: how many istructional management systems, metadata, and problem-based learning combine to facilitate learner-centered instruction. In: SIGUCCS 2001 (2001)
4. Sharpe, R., Benfield, G., Francis, R.: Implementing a university e-learning strategy: levers for change within academic schools. Research and e-Learning Technology, ALT-J 14(2), 135–151 (2006)
5. Derntl, M., Motschnig-Pitrik, R.: The role of structure, patterns, and people in blended learning. The Internet and Higher Education 8(2), 111–130 (2005)
6. Colazzo, L., Conte, F., Molinari, A., Villa, N.: Real communities vs. Virtual communities: structural adaptation of a Learning Management System. In: World Conference on E-Learning in Corporate, Government, Healthcare, and Higher Education 2007, pp. 2416–2423. AACE, Chesapeake (2007); E-Learn 2007 Conference, Quebec City (October 2007)
7. Anderson, C.: The long Tail: how endless choice is creating unlimited demand. Random House Business Books, N.Y. (2006)
8. Chambers, S.A.: Working on the democratic imagination and the limits of deliberative democracy. Pol. Res. Q 58(4), 619–623 (2005)

9. O'Reilly, T.: Web 2.0: Compact Definition? (2005), http://radar.oreilly.com/archives/2005/10/web_20_compact_definition.html (retrieved)
10. Facebook (2009), http://www.facebook.com/
11. Compete.com (2007), Facebook Activity Breakdown (August 2007), http://blog.compete.com/2007/09/14/facebook-activity-breakdown-application/ (October 2008)
12. Boyd, D.: Friends, friendsters and mySpace Top 8: writing community into being on social network sites. First Monday 11(2) (December 2006), http://www.firstmonday.org/issues/issue11_12/boyd (accessed October 2008)
13. Moodle (2009), http://www.moodle.org
14. Colazzo, L., Molinari, A., Villa, N.: Lifelong Learning and Virtual Communities in the Public Administration: a case study in Italy. International Journal: Advanced Corporate Learning 2(3), 5–11 (2009), http://www.i-JAC.org, doi:10.3991/ijac.v2i3.1025

Groupized Learning Path Discovery Based on Member Profile

Xiuzhen Feng[1], Haoran Xie[2], Yang Peng[3], Wei Chen[4], and Huamei Sun[5]

[1] Economics & Management School, Beijing University of Technology, Beijing, China
[2] Department of Computer Science, City University of Hong Kong, Hong Kong
[3] Department of Computing, The Hong Kong Polytechnic University, Hong Kong
[4] School of Computer Science & Technology, Beijing Institute of Technology Beijing, China
[5] School of Management, Harbin Institute of Technology, Harbin, China
xfeng@bjut.edu.cn, hrxie2@student.cityu.edu.hk,
peterpeng204@gmail.com, wchen@bit.edu.cn, shuamei@hit.edu.cn

Abstract. With the explosion of knowledge nowadays, it is urgent for people to learn new things quickly and effectively. To meet such a requirement, how we can find a suitable path for learning has become a crucial issue. Meanwhile, in our daily life, it is important and necessary for people from various backgrounds to achieve a certain task (eg. survey, report, business plan, etc.) collaboratively in the form of the group. For these group-based task, it often requires members to learn new knowledge by using e-learning system. In this paper, we focus on addressing the problem on discovering an appropriate study path to facilitate a group of people rather than a single person for effective learning under e-learning environment. Furthermore, we propose a group model to capture the expertise of each member. Based on this model, a groupized[1] learning path discovering (GLPD) algorithm is proposed in order to help a group of learners to grasp new knowledge effectively and efficiently. Finally, we conduct a practical experiment whose result verifies the soundness of our approach.

1 Introduction

With the explosion of knowledge nowadays, it is urgent for people to learn new things quickly and effectively. To meet such a requirement, how we can find a suitable path for learning has become a crucial issue. Meanwhile, in our daily life, it is important and necessary for people from various backgrounds to achieve a certain task (eg. survey, report, business plan, etc.) collaboratively in the form of the group. For the group-based task, it often requires the whole group to learn a particular topic of knowledge effectively through e-learning. Hence, in this paper, we focus on addressing the problem on discovering an appropriate study path to facilitate a group of people rather than a single person for effective learning under e-learning environment. Compared with a single person, some characteristics of the group should be mapped in the group learning task.

[1] We use the term "groupized" to versus "personalized".

X. Luo et al. (Eds.): ICWL 2010 Workshops, LNCS 6537, pp. 301–310, 2011.

- Knowledge Diversity. A group in the real life or virtual environment often gets its members with various knowledge backgrounds and personal characteristics. For the group learning task in the e-learning system, diversity indicates that members might have different pre-knowledge and levels.
- Preference Variety. Members in a learning group may have different learning preferences when they are learning a particular new topic of knowledge. So that they would have the particular preference in different parts of a new topic.

Therefore, it is inadequate and unsuitable to use conventional shortest learning path selection [4] and personalized path generation [5] to solve this problem. To best of our knowledge, this is the first piece of work on group learning path discovery. The contributions of this paper are listed as follows.

- We propose a group model to capture the characteristic of group members.
- Based on the group model, a groupized learning path discovering (GLPD) algorithm is proposed to help a group of learners to grasp new knowledge effectively and efficiently.
- We conduct an experiment in two classes, which consist of learning groups, and the result verifies the soundness of our approach.

The rest of paper is structured as follows. In Section 2, a survey on related works is given. Subsequently, in Section 3 and 4, we introduce the proposed group model and groupized learning path discovering (GLPD) algorithm correspondingly. The process of how the experiment is conducted and its result are discussed in the Section 5. Finally, we conclude this work and discuss the possible future directions in the Section 6.

2 Related Works

For the past few years, many researchers have focused on developing the learning management system. Meanwhile, for the learning path discovering, the related researches could be divided into two areas; one is explicit, which means providing the learning method (eg., learning path, learning plan, etc.) to users directly, the other is implicit, which means offering the learning method through the learning materials (eg., courseware recommendation, courseware delivery, etc.). Before we introduce our GLPD approach, some related researches which focused on learning path delivery and courseware personalization for LMS are discussed as below:

Learning Path Delivery. Researches on learning path delivery are mainly focused on providing an appropriate learning path individually in order to improve the learning performance. In [1], Chen et al proposed a genetic-based personalized learning path generation scheme for individual learners and proved that it can promote learner's learning effectiveness during learning processes. An approach [2] on the use of concept maps for deriving prerequisite relations and structures based on CbKST has been generated by Steiner and Albert, with the purpose to achieve personalization in web-based learning. Madhour and Forte [3] presented the Lausanne Model and introduced the ACO algorithm which is based on the User model and other user's experience so as to provide the best-possible personalized learning path to users. Another recent work done by Zhao and Wan [4], in which an algorithm for selecting the shortest learning path to learn the target knowledge was proposed to save the time and efforts. Elvis and Li [5] established a dynamic conceptual network mechanism for personalized study plan generation, which can formulate different study plans for different students to meet their personalized needs.

Courseware Recommendation. Courseware recommendation have been widely adopted in current e-learning system to provide users with an implicity learning path. A personalized CAI courseware system [6] was introduced by Wei et al., and it can provide the same courseware tree to the students within the same group to improve the performance. Ge et al. [7] presented an algorithm in the courseware recommendation module, which combines content filtering (recommend from a single user information) and collaborative filtering (recommend from other users perspectives) to reflect the users full interests in courseware selection. Moreover, in the research done by Li et al. [8], a three-tier profiling framework has been proposed, in which course content is modeled by using concept nodes, and it could offer a unified way for modeling and handling a variety of student learning needs and the different factors that affect course material relevance.

3 Group Modeling

3.1 Topic Graph

For group-based learning, it usually needs members to learn a new topic of knowledge, which may contain several knowledge units. We formally define the **topic graph** to represent a new topic of knowledge as shown in Fig. 1, which is in the form of two elements tuple as follows.

Definition 1. A **topic graph** for a new topic of knowledge , denoted by TG, which is a two elements tuple as follows:

$$TG = < U, R >$$

where U is a set of weighted knowledge unit nodes in the graph and the weight t_{u_i} is the time to learn this unit and $R \subseteq U \times U$ is a relation set which represent the edges between the knowledge units. The relation indicates the learning sequence for the topic graph. R also can be represented as a matrix whose row and column representing all knowledge unit nodes and entries by using binary value to indicate whether there is a sequential relationship between two units or not(if there is a relationship, 1 is given. Otherwise, 0 is given).

People usually have different knowledge backgrounds and learning preferences when they are learning a new topic of knowledge. To acquire a learners' pre-knowledge and levels, there are mainly two kinds of strategies.

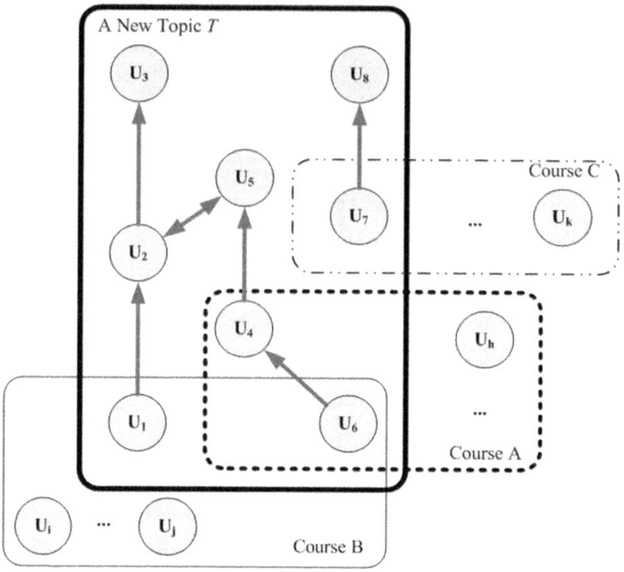

Fig. 1. The relationships among a new topics, past courses and knowledge units

3.2 Objective Pre-knowledge Level Acquisition

To some extend, a learner's objective data such as past course grades, pre-test scores may reflect his/her per-knowledge and levels for a new topic. A higher course grade may indicate the learner is in a higher level in related pre-knowledge. We use an **objective pre-knowledge level vector** to represent a learner's pre-knowledge levels, which are acquired by objective data.

Definition 2. An **objective pre-knowledge level vector** for a learner i, denoted by $\overrightarrow{L_i}$, which is a vector of pre-knowledge unit-value pairs as follows:

$$\overrightarrow{L_i} = (u_1 : v_{i,1}, u_2 : v_{i,2}, ..., u_n : v_{i,n})$$

where u_x is a pre-knowledge units[2] and n is the total number of pre-knowledge units for a new topic, $v_{i,x}$ denotes the level value of u_x of learner i. The higher value of $v_{i,x}$ is, the more knowledge of the learner has for this pre-knowledge unit.

To convert past course grades to the level value of $v_{i,x}$, we observe the relationships among a new topic, past courses and knowledge units as illustrated in Fig. 1. Some past courses may overlap with some knowledge units, which may reflect the level of a learner in these knowledge units. In Fig. 1, course A overlaps to a new topic T by unit 4 and 6, noted that a knowledge unit in topic TG might overlap with multiple courses (e.g. unit 6 overlaps with course B and A).

[2] We use terms "pre-knowledge units" for learner and it can be regarded "knowledge units" as well.

The level value $v_{i,x}$ for pre-knowledge units u_x can be obtained by a formula as follows:

$$v_{i,x} = \frac{\sum_{u_x \in K}^{\forall K} S_K}{\varepsilon \cdot N}$$

where K denotes the course containing knowledge unit u_x and S_K represents the course grade, N denotes the total number of courses and ε is normalized parameter to represent the length of course grade value range to normalized the value degree to $[0, 1]$ (e.g. $\varepsilon = 100$ for hundred mark system).

3.3 Subjective Pre-knowledge Level Acquisition

A learner's past grade may not reflect all his/her pre-knowledge completely, because a learner may be interested in some knowledge units that are not appeared in the course. Therefore, it is necessary for learners to specify their pre-knowledge and corresponding levels explicitly based on their own understanding. Similarly, we use a **subjective pre-knowledge level vector** to denote a leaner's pre-knowledge levels, which is acquired by his/her subjective feeling.

Definition 3. A **subjective pre-knowledge level vector** for a learner i, denoted by $\overrightarrow{L_i'}$, which is a vector of pre-knowledge unit-value pairs as follows:

$$\overrightarrow{L_i'} = (u_1 : v'_{i,1}, u_2 : v'_{i,2}, ..., u_n : v'_{i,n})$$

where u_x is a pre-knowledge units and n is the total number of pre-knowledge units for a new topic, $v'_{i,x}$ denotes the level value of u_x of learner i. The higher value of $v'_{i,x}$ is, the more knowledge of the learner has for this pre-knowledge unit.

3.4 Learning Preference Acquisition

For acquiring learning preferences from a learner, two possible ways are provided. The first one is letting the learner to specify a value [0,1] to indicate how much he/she is interested in past courses that overlap with this new topic of knowledge. The other is selecting the interested knowledge units explicitly by the learner himself. We use an **learning preference vector** to represent a learner's preferences for a new topic of knowledge.

Definition 4. A **learning preference vector** for a learner i, denoted by $\overrightarrow{P_i}$, which is a vector of pre-knowledge unit-value pairs as follows:

$$\overrightarrow{P_i} = (u_1 : w_{i,1}, u_2 : w_{i,2}, ..., u_n : w_{i,n})$$

where u_x is a pre-knowledge units and n is the total number of pre-knowledge units for a new topic, $w_{i,x}$ denotes the preference degree of u_x of learner i. The higher value of $w_{i,x}$ is, the more preference of the learner has for this knowledge unit. The $w_{i,x}$ can be obtained as follows.

$$w_{i,x} = \begin{cases} 1, & \text{once } u_x \text{ is selected explicitly} \\ \frac{\sum_{u_x \in K}^{\forall K} D_K}{N}, & \text{if } u_x \text{ is contained by some courses} \\ 0, & \text{otherwise} \end{cases}$$

where u_x is a knowledge units and n is the total number of knowledge units for a new topic, K denotes the course containing knowledge unit u_x and D_K represents the learner specify value of interesting degree for this course, N denotes the total number of courses. Note that the $w_{i,x}$ will be given as "1" once it is selected by the learner explicitly. Because it is quite sure that the learner has high preference on this units instead of other methods.

3.5 Member Profile

We aggregate subjective, objective pre-knowledge level vectors into **unified pre-knowledge level vector**. Then we defined **member profile** to represent the complete pre-knowledge and levels for a member (learner) and his/her learning preference in a group.

Definition 5. A **member profile** for a member (learner) i, denoted by $\overrightarrow{M_i}$, which is a tuple containing two vectors as follows:

$$\overrightarrow{M_i} = (\overrightarrow{L''_i}, \overrightarrow{P_i})$$

$$\overrightarrow{L''_i} = (u_1 : v''_{i,1}, w_{i,1}; u_2 : v''_{i,2}, w_{i,2}; ..., u_n : v''_{i,n}, w_{i,n})$$

where $v''_{i,x}$ denotes the level value of u_x of member i, $\overrightarrow{P_i}$ is the learning preference vector. The $v''_{i,x}$ is obtained by the aggregating subjective and objective pre-knowledge level values as follows.

$$v''_{i,x} = \begin{cases} v'_{i,x}, & \text{if } v_{i,x} = 0 \text{ and } v'_{i,x} \neq 0 \\ v_{i,x}, & \text{if } v'_{i,x} = 0 \text{ and } v_{i,x} \neq 0 \\ \alpha \cdot v_{i,x} + (1-\alpha) \cdot v'_{i,x}, & \text{otherwise} \end{cases}$$

where α is a parameter to adjust the effect of the level values from subjective and objective pre-knowledge vectors, $v''_{i,x}$ is the linear combination of level values from subjective and objectives pre-knowledge vectors except one of them is zero.

A learning group is consisted of some group members and we defined the **learning group** based on its members.

Definition 6. A **learning group**, denoted by G, which are two $i \times n$ matrix of member profiles as follows:

$$G = A_{i \times n}, B_{i \times n} = \begin{pmatrix} 0.5 & 0 & \ldots & 0.2 \\ 0.3 & 0.1 & \ldots & 0.7 \\ \vdots & \vdots & \vdots & \vdots \\ 0.9 & 0.4 & \ldots & 0 \end{pmatrix}, \begin{pmatrix} 0.2 & 0 & \ldots & 0.2 \\ 0.3 & 0 & \ldots & 1 \\ \vdots & \vdots & \vdots & \vdots \\ 0.4 & 1 & \ldots & 0 \end{pmatrix}$$

where $A_{i \times n}$ denotes all group members pre-knowledge level matrix and $B_{i \times n}$ denotes their learning preference matrix correspondingly.

4 Groupized Learning Path Discovery

In this section, we devise the groupized learning path discovery (GLPD) algorithm to find the suitable path for a group. GLDP approach mainly considers two levels of aims. The first one is the **group-based aim**, which requires that the whole group rather than a single member can grasp the new topic efficiently. In other words, it means the union of the grasped knowledge units for all group members should be as many as possible. The other one is the **member-based aim**, which is to select a suitable learning path by taking his/her preferences as more as possible.

For example, given a group containing two members Tom and Kate, Tom is a programmer and Kate is a business school graduate. If they need to learn a new topic "business information system", the most efficient way may be let Tom to learn technical units and Kate to learn business units. However, Tom might have more preference to learn units related to management and Kate is more interested in units on the decision-making support system. The group-based aim is focused on the efficiency aspect for the whole group while the member-based aim is focused on the interest aspect for the individual member. In addition, we observe these two aims associated with the learning time. Back to our example, if the group is given limited time to learn, efficiency needs to be considered, firstly; but if enough learning time is provided, preferences could be taken into account, since no matter how their path is selected, the group-based aim can be achieved.

Input: Matrix $A_{i\times n}$, and vector C
Output: T_{Lower}, $InitialPath_i$ for member i, and cost Matrix $CM_{i\times n}$
for $j = 1;\ j \leq C.length;\ j++$ **do**
  for $k = 1;\ k \leq n;\ k++$ **do**
    for $s = 1;\ s \leq i;\ s++$ **do**
      $a[s,k] = a[s,k] \times t_{u_j}$;
      $CM[i,n] = a[s,k]$;
    end
  end
end
for $k = 1;\ k \leq n;\ k++$ **do**
  for $s = 1;\ s \leq i;\ s++$ **do**
    $Value_s = a[s,k] + RowValue_s$;
  end
  if $Value_s == Min(Value_1\ to\ Value_i)$ **then**
    $RowValue_s = a[s,k] + RowValue_s$;
    Add u_k to $InitialPath_s$;
  end
end
T_{Lower} = Max($RowValue_1$ to $RowValue_s$) $InitialPath_i$ is a sequence of knowledge units. $CM_{i\times n}$ is initialized.

Algorithm 1. Lower Time Boundary Discovery

Therefore, our GLDP approach includes two major steps. Firstly, we discover two temporal boundaries for a learning group. Then, according to learning time for the group, a corresponding strategy is to select to find the suitable learning path.

Input: T,T_{Lower}, T_{Upper},$InitialPath_i$ for member i, cost Matrix $CM_{i \times n}$, $B_{i \times n}$, Relations Matrix $R_{n \times n}$ in topic graph
Output: $FinalPath_i$ for member i
if $T \leq T_{Lower}$ **then**
  for $j = 1; j \leq InitialPath_i.length; j++$ **do**
    for *Each two adjacent nodes* u_a *and* u_{a+1} *in* $InitialPath_i$ **do**
      if *entry* $R[a+1, a] == 1$ *and* $R[a, a+1] == 0$ **then**
        $u_a \leftrightarrow u_{a+1}$ in $InitialPath_i$;
      end
    end
  end
end
if $T_{Lower} < T < T_{Upper}$ **then**
  for $j = 1; j \leq InitialPath_i.length; j++$ **do**
    while $T_{Lower} + T_{Cost} < T$ **do**
      for *Each node in* u_a *in* $InitialPath_j$ **do**
        Compare u_a with u_1 to u_n;
        if $r[a, b] == 1$ **then**
          Find Max u_b in j-th row in $B_{i \times n}$;
          Add u_b to $InitialPath_j$;
          $T_{Cost} = cm[i, b] + T_{Cost}$;
        end
      end
    end
  end
end
if $T \geq T_{Upper}$ **then**
  for *Each knowledge unit* u_a *to Memberi* **do**
    if $b[a, i]$ *is maximal value in row i in* $B_{a,i}$ *and* $b[a, i] == 1$ **then**
      Add u_a to $InitialPath_i$;
    end
  end
end
$FinalPath_i = InitialPath_i$

Algorithm 2. Learning Path Discovery

4.1 Temporal Boundaries Discovery

For the first step, we need to discover two temporal boundaries for different groups. We name the maximum time for every member to learn all knowledge units as "upper boundary time" (denoted by T_{Upper}), and we name the minimum time for the whole group to grasp all knowledge units as "lower boundary time" (denoted by T_{Lower}). To find out T_{Upper} and T_{Lower}, the time cost for each knowledge units is needed, and we name the **time cost vector** to represent the time cost for each unit in a topic graph. We use $C = (t_{u_1}, t_{u_2}, ...t_{u_n})$ to denote time cost vector, where t_{u_x} is defined in **Definition 1** to represent time cost for learning unit u_x. T_{Lower} can be obtained by Algorithm 1 and T_{Upper} is calculated by the following formula.

$$T_{Upper} = max((J_{i \times n} - A_{i \times n}) \times C^T)$$

where $J_{i \times n}$ is a matrix of ones, $max()$ denotes the maximum value in a vector, C^T is the transpose of C.

4.2 Learning Path Discovery

Given a learning time T, we compare it with T_{Lower} and T_{Lower} to determine which strategy is to use. There are three cases as follows and their algorithms are unified in Algorithm 2.

1. $T \leq T_{Lower}$. With limited time, we mainly consider pre-knowledge level and relations in the knowledge units to achieve the group-based aim firstly.
2. $T \geq T_{Upper}$.If the time is adequate to finish both two aims, the member preference is most important aspect for learning path discovery.
3. $T_{Lower} < T < T_{Upper}$. If the time is enough to finish the group-based aim, the member preference can be also considered partially.

5 Experiment

We conduct two experiments on students in two classes. The number of students is 32 (Class I) and 29 (Class II). Since it is an elective course that is open for all year 2 to year 4 undergraduate students in the university from different majors, it is suitable for illustrating our problem. Then we let 3 or 4 students to form a group so that we get 8 groups in Class I and 7 groups in Class II. Afterward, we give a topic of "business decision support system" which includes about 6 knowledge units, and it would take about 5 hours to digest them normally. We give them 1 hour to learn and then give a test that includes 20 multiple choice questions across all the points in 5 units to each group. For Class I, we generate the learning path for them according to each group member profile. For Class II, they learn by their own decision. The second test is that we provide another topic, which is consisted of 7 units and required 8 hours to learn, and we give 4 hours for each group. The setting is the same with the previous one. In addition, we test each group member separately and collect the right answers to regard as the group mark. The experiment results are shown in Table I. From results, the Class I in the three tests have always outperformed Class II. These results have verified the soundness of our approach.

Table 1. Average grade results in Test 1 and 2

	Test 1	Test 2 (Group)	Test 2 (Member)
Class I	67.3	80.6	72.3
Class II	58.4	74.2	63.0

6 Conclusion

In this paper, we have proposed the groupized learning path discovery (GLPD) algorithm, which is based on the group model. It offers a shortcut for a group of people to learn new knowledge under the e-learning environment as well as meets the different preference of each group member in his learning process. Different with conventional learning path discovery approaches, what we offered is a suite of learning paths for group learning according to different learning time limits. Through the experiments, the soundness of our approach is also verified. For future works, one of the possible directions is that identifying some learning style patterns for group to explore how to discover learning path in different learning styles.

Acknowledgement

The research described in this paper has been supported primarily by National Natural Science Foundation of China (Project 70971032).

References

1. Chen, C.-M.: Intelligent web-based learning system with personalized learning path guidance. Computer & Education 51, 787–814 (2008)
2. Steiner, C.M., Albert, D.: Personalising learning through prerequisite structures derived from concept maps. In: Leung, H., Li, F., Lau, R., Li, Q. (eds.) ICWL 2007. LNCS, vol. 4823, pp. 43–54. Springer, Heidelberg (2008)
3. Madhour, H., Forte, M.W.: Personalized learning path delivery: Models and example of application. In: Woolf, B.P., Aïmeur, E., Nkambou, R., Lajoie, S. (eds.) ITS 2008. LNCS, vol. 5091, pp. 725–727. Springer, Heidelberg (2008)
4. Zhao, C., Wan, L.: A shortest learning path selection algorithm in e-learning. In: ICALT 2006 (2006)
5. Leung, E.W.C., Li, Q.: A Dynamic Conceptual Network Mechanism for Personalized Study Plan Generation. In: Zhou, W., Nicholson, P., Corbitt, B., Fong, J. (eds.) ICWL 2003. LNCS, vol. 2783, pp. 69–80. Springer, Heidelberg (2003)
6. Wei, C., Fang, Z., Zhang, Y., Jin, Y.: A personalized CAI courseware system. In: CISE 2009 (2009)
7. Liang, G., Weining, K., Junzhou, L.: Courseware Recommendation in E-Learning System. In: Liu, W., Li, Q., Lau, R. (eds.) ICWL 2006. LNCS, vol. 4181, pp. 10–24. Springer, Heidelberg (2006)
8. Li, F.W.B., Lau, R.W.H., Dharmendran, P.: A Three-Tier Profiling Framework for Adaptive e-Learning. In: Spaniol, M., Li, Q., Klamma, R., Lau, R.W.H. (eds.) ICWL 2009. LNCS, vol. 5686, pp. 235–244. Springer, Heidelberg (2009)

Semantic Annotation of Educational Resources through Linked Data*

Estefanía Otero-García[1], Juan C. Vidal[1], Manuel Lama[1], Alberto Bugarín[1], and José E. Domenech[2]

[1] Depto. de Electrónica e Computación, Universidade de Santiago de Compostela
15782 Santiago de Compostela, Spain
{estefanianatalia.otero,juan.vidal,manuel.lama,alberto.bugarin.diz}@usc.es
[2] Netex Knowledge Factory, 15172 Oleiros, A Coruña
jose.domenech@netex.es

Abstract. In this paper a context-based algorithm to semantically annotate e-learning contents is presented. This algorithm explores the DBpedia graph and uses both syntactic and semantic analysis techniques to identify the RDF triples which annotate the relevant terms that characterize the educational content. This algorithm has been applied to annotate learning fruits which are learning pills presented as web books that provide links to access to complementary and relevant information about the course.

1 Introduction

Learning process is immersed in a transition from the use of conventional paper textbooks to digital books. This transition, however, should not only consist in a content translation between both kind of books, but digital books should be adapted from both a technological and educational point of view. One of the new proposals to facilitate this transition are the learning fruits[1].

Learning Fruits (LFs) are knowledge pills [1] and interactive activities centered on topics of the school curriculum. From a technical point of view, LFs are web books that provide a friendly and interactive interface to facilitate *the access and the navigation* through the course contents. An important feature of LFs is that they provide links to other content that complement and extend the information to students and teachers. This step is expensive when implementing a course: *(i)* it involves identifying which parts need to be complemented with external information, that is, it is necessary to determine the important topics of the LF; and *(ii)* it involves selecting and analyzing the external links in order to determine if they contain accurate information.

In this paper we propose a semantic and context-based approach to minimize the cost of enriching and annotating LFs with external contents. Our solution is

* This work was supported by the Ministerio de Educación y Ciencia and the Xunta de Galicia under the projects TSI2007-65677C02-02 and 09SIN065E respectively.

[1] `http://www.netex.es/santillana/eng/index.html`

X. Luo et al. (Eds.): ICWL 2010 Workshops, LNCS 6537, pp. 311–320, 2011.

based on the application of semantic technologies *(i)* to identify and annotate the relevant concepts of the LF; and *(ii)* to retrieve the corresponding contents from the web, in our case from Linked Data [2]. With this approach we deal with the drawbacks of other approaches for annotating learning contents. Most of these approaches [3–6] use their own ontology to annotate educational contents. Instead, our solution uses standard, accepted and available ontologies to semantically annotate and enrich the LF content. These ontologies are obtained from Linked Data repositories, in our case the DBpedia [7], where data are modeled through standard and well-known ontologies which are interlinked to provide a better and more reliable semantic descriptions of the information.

However, since we want to enrich and annotate the LF with relevant data, we need to discriminate important information from which is not. In this work we called *context of a LF* to the set of terms that determine the topics of the course. In the annotation process, this context will establish the degree of relevance of the concepts and relations filtered from the DBpedia, and therefore will influence the creation of the the most appropriate graph to annotate the LF terms. In other words, we will use the context of the LF to filter the RDF triples that describe its content.

The paper is structured as follows: in section 2 we explain what a LF is. In section 3 processing tasks to obtain the LF context are described, and in section 4 the context-based algorithm we have implemented to annotate the LF with the DBpedia semantic data is presented. Finally, in section 5 we summarize the main achievements of the paper.

2 Learning Fruits

LFs are digital books with clear texts that are adapted to the students age, providing a simple and user-friendly access to the audiovisual and interactive resources. LFs are described in XML files and created to make more dynamic and flexible the learning process. Thus, LFs have *(i)* identical content than textbooks, but with links to other websites or contents in order to enable both students and teachers to *access to complementary and relevant information* about the LF content; *(ii)* an XML format that facilitates both the work in the classroom through whiteboards or personal computers and the individual student work at home; *(iii)* Internet-like hyperlinks to navigate through the educational contents of the LF; and finally *(iv)* availability of interactive glossaries, photo gallery, videos and animations, interactive activities, relevant links, and so on.

Figure 1 depicts a Learning Fruit about the *Ancient Egypt.* Boxes emphasize the different sections identified as *fields* that shape the document. Relevance of a word changes depending on the field in which it appears or its decoration. For example, in Figure 1 bold text (box 3) are more important than words in normal text in the same section (box 2). Likewise, section title (box 1) is more important than the rest of the content, because it synthesize that content.

Fig. 1. Screenshot of a LF about the *Ancient Egypt*, where some relevant fields of the document structure are highlighted

3 Learning Fruit Context

Figure 2 depicts the sequence of processing that must be executed to obtain the LF context. The first step is to parse the LF XML document in order to get its most representative *fields*, such as title, sections, paragraphs, etc. Once identified, we weight the content according to the field where it has been found, because the relevance of a term vary depending on the field in which it appears. Specific values of these weights are listed in Table 1 as they are obtained from the pedagogues that create the LF. The result of this step is a document made up of fields whose content is classified and weighted according to where it has been located.

Table 1. Fields that compose the structure of a LF

Field	Description	Weight
Objectives	What you learn in the course.	1
Knowledge	Prior knowledge that the student has about the subject.	1
Page Content Title	Title of the content pages that summarizes the content of the course.	3
Page Content HTML	Paragraph that explains the content of the page.	1
Pop-up Title	Title of the pop-ups. Pop-ups are suggested contents which are related with the content of the page.	4
Pop-up HTML	Pop-up content.	2
Image Title	LF are not very large, so title of images is very representative of the content.	5
Footnote	Footnotes make extra contributions in the content, so they are relevant.	5
Section Title	They contain information about a specific topic of the course.	4
Section HTML	Information content found in the section.	3
Activity Title	Title of the proposed activities of the learning unit.	2
Bold	Terms or phrases marked in bold. They are usually considered candidate terms to belong to the keywords of the course.	7
Link	Links to other contents that provide extra information about the term they are linked, so a link increase the relevance of the term.	7

From this document, we analyze the *morphology*, *similarity*, and *frequency* of the terms in order to determine the most relevant ones, and so characterize the context of the LF:

- *Morphological analysis.* The morphological analysis is carried out with the GATE tool [8], and it is used to determine the grammatical category of each word in the document. This analysis affects the LF context creation in two points:
    - Terms that are not representative to characterize the document content or are not included in the DBpedia will be ruled out. For example verbs, conjunctions, prepositions or determiners are never included in the context.

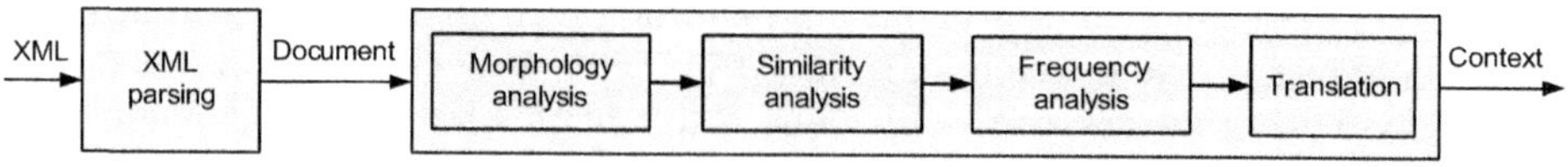

Fig. 2. Sequence of tasks to obtain the context of a LF

```
Macro: COMPOSITE_NOUN
(
 (UPPERCASE_NOUN|UPPERCASE_ADJ) (UPPERCASE_NOUN)+ |
 (UPPERCASE_NOUN) ({Token.string=~"[Dd]e"}|
 {Token.string=~"[Dd]el"})(UPPERCASE_NOUN|UPPERCASE_ADJ)|
 (UPPERCASE_NOUN) {Token.string=~"[Dd]e"}
 {Token.string=~"[Ll][oa]s"}(UPPERCASE_NOUN|UPPERCASE_ADJ)|
 {Token.category==ADJ} (UPPERCASE_NOUN)
)

Macro: ROMAN_NOUN
(
 {Token.length > 1} ({Token.orth == allCaps} |
 {Token.length == 1, Token.orth == upperInitial})
)

Rule: Entity
(
 (COMPOSITE_NOUN) | (ROMAN_NOUN)
):entity
-->
 :entity.Entity = {rule = "Entity"}
```

Fig. 3. JAPE rule that identifies composite Spanish nouns and nouns with a Roman number

- Identification of composite terms. Thus, terms like *Ancient Egypt* or *Ramesses II* cannot be considered separately, and they are detected as regular expressions through the JAPE rules of the GATE tool. For example, the *Entity* rule defined in Figure 3 identify these expressions through macros. On the one hand, the macro `COMPOSITE_NOUN` detects Spanish composite nouns like *Antiguo Egipto* or *Valle de los Reyes*. On the other hand, the macro `ROMAN_NOUN` recognizes nouns with roman numbers like *Cleopatra IV* or *Ramesses II*.

– *Similarity analysis.* Since a term may appear in different forms, we create clusters of terminological similarity in order to increase the frequency of occurrence of a word, and also to avoid words that share the same meaning or arise from the same word. In our approach, we use the metrics Monge-Elkan [9] and Jaro-Winkler [10] to calculate the similarity among the document words, because both measures return adequate values for words with a common root. Given strings s and t, divided into substrings $s = a_1 \dots a_K$ and $t = b_1 \dots b_L$, the similarity between those words is calculated as:

$$sim(s,t) = \frac{1}{K}\sum_{i=1}^{K} \max_{j=1}^{L} sim'(A_i, B_j) \qquad (1)$$

where sim' is a secondary distance function, in our case two metrics mentioned above.

– *Frequency analysis.* The frequency is a quantitative measure which provides the number of occurrences of a term in the LF document. It indicates the relevance of a term within the document and, therefore, it must be combined with the field weights to obtain a relative weighted frequency for each document term:

$$f_i = \frac{\sum_{j=0}^{K}(n_{ij} * p_j) + s}{N} \tag{2}$$

where n_{ij} is the number of occurrences of the term i in the field j of the document; p_j is the weight of the field; N is the sample size; and s is the number of similar terms of the term under analysis. It is important to remark that the similarity analysis is used to calculate the relative frequency of each document term.

As a first approximation, we consider terms whose relative weighted frequency is between 4% and 15%: terms are discarded if this frecuency is less than 4%, because they are not representatives, or greater than 15%, because we consider them too general.

The last step for obtaining the LF context is the translation of terms to the English language. Although some of the properties of concepts in the DBpedia are multi-language, most of them are only in English. Thus, if the LF is in a different language, a translation should be performed to obtain better results. Table 2 shows the context of a LF written in Spanish, whose subject is the *Ancient Egypt.* Note that although all the terms of the Table 2 are included in the context, some of them are too general. For example, the term *land* is not relevant in the domain of the Ancient Egypt.

4 Semantic Filtering of Linked Data

The objective of the semantic filtering is to select the DBpedia nodes that are relevant to annotate the terms of the context that characterizes the LF document. As it is depicted in Figure 4, to get this objective the first step is to identify the DBpedia URI (resource) that match each context term. Once this step is executed through the DBpedia lookup service we need to deal with two issues: *(i)* the lookup service may retrieve many URIs for a given keyword, but a term can only be paired with a single URI; and *(ii)* not all the relationships that describe the URI are relevant to annotate the LF context term. For example, if the LF is about the *Ancient Egypt*, we are not interested in relationships with URIs that describe contemporary facts or persons.

To solve these two issues each URI is expanded to asses whether the node deserves to be considered. This expansion process is an *iterative deepening depth-first algorithm* [11], which carries out a detailed search through the semantic DBpedia graph until a depth limit. Figure 5 depicts a (sub)graph related with the context of the LF showed in Table 2. The context is generated as result of filtering nodes obtained from the search with a depth limit of 4. Circle nodes are

Table 2. Context of the LF about the *Ancient Egypt*

Term	Translation	Relevance
Osiris	Osiris	0.054814816
Horus	Horus	0.057777777
templo	temple	0.05925926
tumba	tomb	0.062222224
Cleopatra VII	Cleopatra VII	0.06518518
Ra	Ra	0.06962963
sacerdote	priest	0.07111111
dios	god	0.072592594
tierras	**lands**	**0.07703704**
faraón	Pharaoh	0.07851852
Ramsés II	Ramses II	0.08592593
Pirámides de Gizeh	Pyramids of Giza	0.08888889
Nilo	Nile	0.093333334
Egipto	Egypt	0.11111111
Antiguo Egipto	Ancient Egypt	0.14222223

DBpedia resources (URI) and rectangles are literals. Arrows are the semantic relations between nodes. Numbered arcs represent the exploration order of the DBpedia graph through relationships. These relations were obtained analyzing the context with the content of literals of a URI. If the search do not reach the limit depth, the algorithm get into the URI to explore its relations. For each URI we perform a SPARQL query and retrieve all its relationships; that is, all its related RDF triples. Considering Figure 5, the algorithm starts with root node *Pharaoh* (*http://dbpedia.org/resource/Pharaoh* URI) and then retrieves all its relations. According to the type of the object of those RDF triples, we take the following actions:

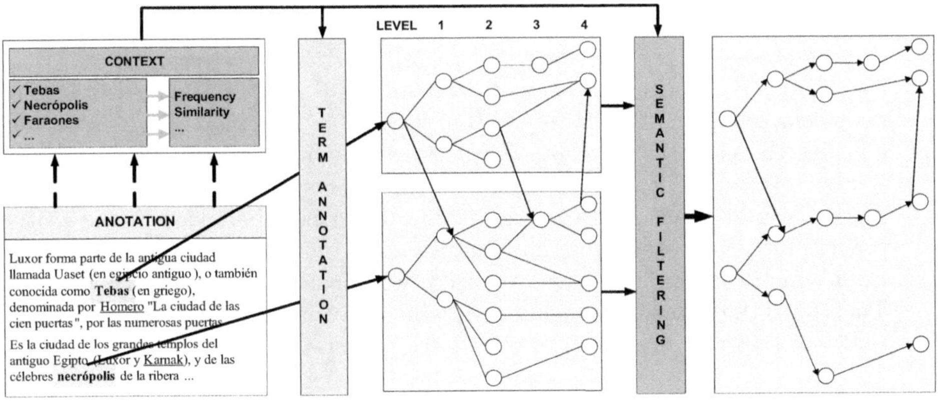

Fig. 4. Filtering process to annotate LF documents

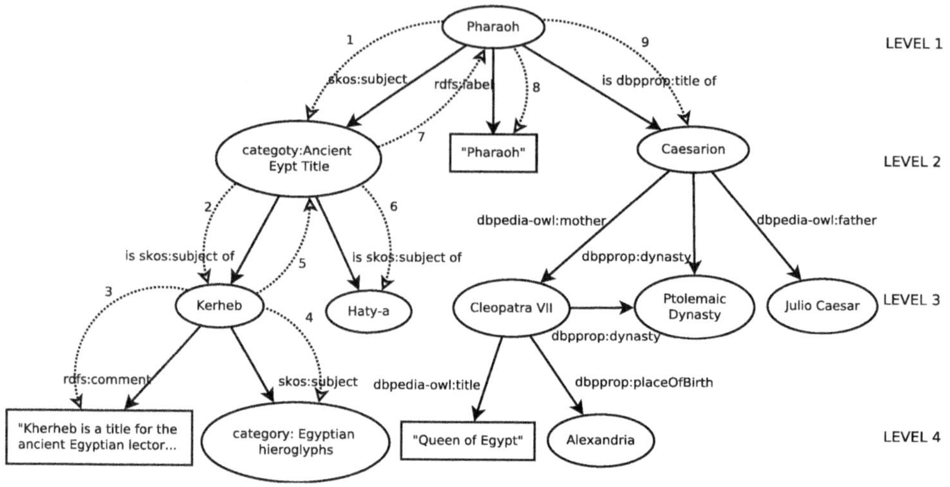

Fig. 5. Application of the algorithm to explore the *Pharao* term in the DBpedia

- *If the object is a literal*, we analyze the literal to check the relevance of the relationship. We consider that a literal is related to the LF if it contains any of the context terms, and its relevance is assessed with the similarity measures described in section 3. This analysis also takes into account the relative frequency of the terms of the context and uses a threshold to consider which relations are relevant or not. For example, the relation *dbpedia-owl:title* between the node *Cleopatra VII* and *Queen of Egypt* is considered relevant since the Term *Egypt* is included in the context of the LF with a relevance of 0.111.
- *If the object is an URI* and we have not reached the depth limit, we continue the exploration through this URI. At this point we have distinguished between two types of URIs:
  - Those that describe a concept. For example, the term *Caesarion* is represented with the URI *http://dbpedia.org/resource/Caesarion.*
  - Those that defines a category that allows to classify the resource. For example, *http://dbpedia.org/resource/Category:Ancient_Egypt_titles* specifies the category *Ancient Egypt titles* in which the resource identified by *http://dbpedia.org/resource/Pharaoh* is classified.

  In the case of categories, the algorithm adds a new behavior: if the search process retrieves a resource that shares one of the categories of the resource from which the expansion was realized, we consider this category relevant. Therefore, the category is expanded, which means that URIs with this category will also be processed in our filtering process.

Figure 6 shows the result obtained when this algorithm is applied to the LF about the *Ancient Egypt*. In this example, we have retrieved 1579 RDF triples for the 15 terms that compose the LF context.

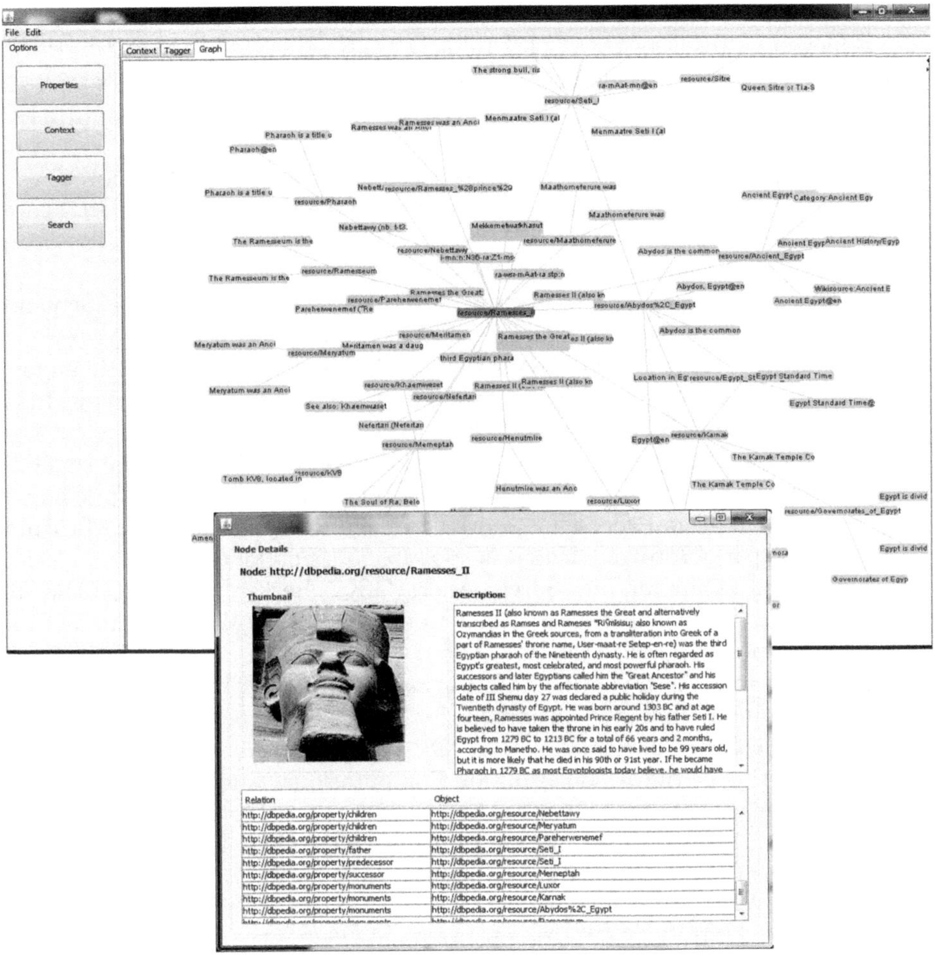

Fig. 6. Screenshot of the application for semantic annotation of LF documents

5 Conclusions

In this paper we described two of the key processes for enriching the contents of LFs with information extracted from the DBPedia. The first process identifies the main topics of the LF, by means of the combination of frequency, similarity and morphology analysis. From the result of this first process, a filtering process retrieves from the DBpedia the most suitable (sub)graphs to annotate the terms of the LF.

References

1. Rosen, A.: e-Learning 2.0: Proven practices and emerging technologies to achieve real results. AMACOM Books (2009)
2. Bizer, C., Heath, T., Berners-Lee, T.: Linked Data: The story so far. International Journal on Semantic Web and Information Systems 5(3), 1–22 (2009)
3. Mukherjee, S., Yang, G., Ramakrishnan, I.: Automatic annotation of content-rich HTML documents: Structural and semantic analysis. In: Fensel, D., Sycara, K.P., Mylopoulos, J. (eds.) ISWC 2003. LNCS, vol. 2870, pp. 533–549. Springer, Heidelberg (2003)
4. Handschuh, S., Staab, S.: Cream: CREAting Metadata for the Semantic Web. Computer Networks 42(5), 579–598 (2003)
5. Jovanovic, J., Gasevic, D., Devedzic, V.: Ontology-based automatic annotation of learning content. International Journal on Semantic Web and Information Systems 2(2), 91–119 (2006)
6. Simov, K., Osenova, P.: Applying ontology-based lexicons to the semantic annotation of learning objects. In: Proceedings of the RANLP-Workshop on Natural Language Processing and Knowledge Representation for eLearning Environments, Borovets, Bulgaria, pp. 49–55 (September 2006)
7. Bizer, C., Lehmann, J., Sören Auer, G.K., Becker, C., Cyganiak, R., Hellmann, S.: DBpedia: A crystallization point for the Web of Data. Journal of Web Semantics 7(3), 154–165 (2009)
8. Cunningham, H., Maynard, D., Bontcheva, K., Tablan, V.: A framework and graphical development environment for robust NLP tools and applications. In: Isabelle, P., Charniak, E., Lin, D. (eds.) Proceedings of the 40th Annual Meeting of the Association for Computational Linguistic (ACL 2002), Philadephia, USA, pp. 168–175 (July 2002)
9. Monge, A., Elkan, C.: An efficient domain-independent algorithm for detecting approximately duplicate database records. In: Proceedings of the ACM SIGMOD-Workshop on Research Issues on Data Mining and Knowledge Discovery (DMKD 1997), Tucson, Arizona, USA (May 2003)
10. Cohen, W.W., Ravikumar, P.D., Fienberg, S.E.: A comparison of string distance metrics for name-matching tasks. In: Kambhampati, S., Knoblock, C.A. (eds.) Proceedings of the IJCAI-Workshop on Information Integration on the Web (IIWeb 2003), Acapulco, Mexico, pp. 73–78 (August 2003)
11. Russell, S.J., Norvig, P.: Artificial Intelligence: A modern approach, 3rd edn. Prentice Hall, Englewood Cliffs (2009)

Mining Association Rules of Optional Courses for Course Coordinator

Youngseok Lee[1], Jungwon Cho[2,*], Seungdo Jeong[3], Sungjae Han[1], and Byung-Uk Choi[1]

[1] Department of Electronics Computer Engineering, Hanyang University, 17 Haengdang-dong, Sungdong-gu, Seoul, 133-791 Korea
{yslee38,sjhans,buchoi}@hanyang.ac.kr

[2] Department of Computer Education, Jeju National University, 66 Jejudaehakno, Jeju-si, Jeju-do, 690-756 Korea
jwcho@jejunu.ac.kr

[3] Department of Information & Communication Engineering, Hanyang Cyber University, 17 Haengdang-dong, Sungdong-gu, Seoul, 133-791 Korea
sdjeong@hycu.ac.kr

Abstract. In the aspect of the faculty, a course coordinator plays a significant role in managing the curriculum and counseling students on academic matters and fostering their progress in the course. However, the course coordinator cannot afford to advise students on which fields of their faculty fit them and which courses they have to take. We searched for relationships between subjects, using association rules, by mining data about the courses already taken by students, and compared these to existing course trees. And we wish to do so that can utilize to taking a course tree enactment or when revise reference data using subject information that association rule through this research. This information could be used for updating course trees.

1 Introduction

The faculty offers an opportunity of wide selection of courses to students and does to study over various fields. However, the faculty system generated various kinds problem unlike the meaning. Students taking a course rather than other courses always involves many issues, including teachers (who teaches), time (when), easy or difficulty (easy to pass?), and so on. Students' credit acquisition easy subjects apply mainly and studies. As a result, professionalism that college graduate must equip is lacking point[1].

To solve these problems, in Korea, a guidance professor check the students' graduation important matter, and recommends suitable subject. However, it is not easy that students receive actual help. Academic administration system started in form that use intranet, developed to wire internet base. Furthermore, according to the rapid progress of administration system, the system works in wireless network to heighten the convenience.

* Corresponding author.

X. Luo et al. (Eds.): ICWL 2010 Workshops, LNCS 6537, pp. 321–327, 2011.

Association rules have been used to discover patterns in other databases. For example, university course enrollment data were analyzed to identify combinations of courses taken by groups of students [2, 3]. After analyzing a considerable volume of course attendance data, we applied an association rule to understand the link between subjects chosen with those proposed by faculty guidance advisors. We applied a minimum support and minimum confidence variable, variously, and found an association rule. As the result of examining the validity of this rule, we wish to apply to a revision enactment, or reference data, to the attending lecture tree.

2 Background

2.1 Course Coordinators

Course coordinators create and manage course curricula. They are appointed from the group of senior lecturers, associate professors, and professors belonging to the faculty. Coordination of a registered degree course is the responsibility of one particular course coordinator who is responsible to the head of the academic unit offering the course [4]. The appointment of course coordinators enhances inter- and intra-faculty course coordination. A course coordinator's role includes the following [4]:

- developing and monitoring efforts for continuous course improvement, and reporting on course improvement projects to the faculty advisory committee through the department head;
- determining appropriate course plans (in consultation with department heads, study center directors, and other coordinators) for students transferring to the course from another course or institution, once exemptions and credits have been determined;
- ensuring that student enrollments conform with the course structure and prerequisites, and that students have met all course requirements before being certified eligible for graduation;

2.2 Association Rules

The determination of association rules is an interesting subfield of database mining. Association rules describe how often items(e.g. supermarket shopping data) are purchased together. For example, the association rule "beer -> diaper (80%)" means that 80% of customers who purchased beer, bought diapers. Such rules can be useful for decisions concerning [2].

A mathematical model was proposed to address the problem of mining association rules [2, 5]. Let be a set of items. Let D be a set of transactions, where each transaction T is a set of items such that T. Associated with each transaction is a unique identifier, called TID. Let X be a set of items. A transaction T is said to contain X, if X T. An association rule is an implication of the form X -> Y, where X, Y and $X \cap Y = \emptyset$. The rule X -> Y holds in the transaction set D with confidence c if c percent of transactions in D that contain X also contain Y. The rule X -> Y has support s in the transaction set D if s percent of transactions in D contain $X \cup Y$ [5, 6]. Given a set of transactions D, the problem of mining association rules lies in finding all rules that have support and confidence greater than the user-specified thresholds. That is to say, given a database of transactions, a minimal confidence threshold, and a minimal support threshold, the problem consists of finding all association rules whose confidence and support are greater than the corresponding thresholds [5].

2.3 Related Works

Intelligent Online Academic Management System (IOAMS) consists of functionality such as automated enrollment and enrolment variations, providing academic advice based on the student's personal profile and interests, creating a study plan for the student according to his/her current stage, calculating credits and final signing off [7]. The system contains a powerful inference engine which is based on PT resolution (Resolution with Partial Intersection and Truncation) [8]. There is 'COURSE FINDER' that recommends a suitable studying course selecting student's interest field and military merit and profession information that want that wish to apply in the college [9].

3 Inquiry into the Association Rule in Relation to Lectures

This paper investigates the association rule for 214 senior students registered in Hanyang University's Department of Electrical and Computer Engineering in 2008 [10]. MCCS recommended major options from a course tree. The target of the association rule is 40 major optional subjects. Enterprise Miner Release 4.1 within SAS System ver.8 was used for data mining.

studentNum	lecNum
1994111101	COM307
1994111101	ELE201
1994111101	PHY213
1994111101	ELE207
1994111101	PHY208
1994111101	COE351

...

1994111101	ECE458
1994111101	ENE439
1994111101	ELE417
1994111101	GEN358
1994111102	COM307
1994111102	ELE201

Fig. 1. Taking a Lecture Record – Relation DB

Table 1. Taking a Lecture Record – Transactions DB

Transaction-id	Courses
1994111101	COM307, ELE201, ...
1994111102	...
...	...
1994111214	...

The data required to find the association rule are the student number (studentNum) and the course number (lecNum) as shown in Figure 1. The relational database form was changed to a transactional form, as shown in Table 1, so that all courses that a student has taken can be found in one transaction.

4 Analysis Results in Relation to Taking Lectures

4.1 Data Visualization

This is the analysis of course enrollment data before we obtain the association rule [10, 11]. Table 2 shows the number of subjects students took for each term. Support means the percentage of student enrollment for each subject. The set up subject shows the number of courses that are basic level courses, which can branch out into more specific majors.

Table 2. The Number of Subjects students took for each term

Term	Minimum Support Subject			Set up Subject
	Over 50%	Over 40%	Over 30%	
2-1	3	4	5	6
2-2	2	2	2	3
3-1	2	2	5	7
3-2	0	2	2	7
4-1	1	1	1	10
4-2	1	2	2	7
Total	9	13	17	40

Table 3 shows the number of subjects that satisfy the minimum support of 50% and 40% of core subjects and recommended subjects in each field. The courses Communication and Digital Signal Processing had the highest enrollment of students.

Table 3. Subject Numbers of courses taken in each field

Support / Fields	Core Subjects			Recommended Subjects		
	Over 50%	Over 40%	Set up Subject	Over 50%	Over 40%	Set up Subject
Communication	5	7	8	2	2	4
Semiconductor & VLSI	1	2	6	3	4	6
Digital Signal Processing	4	4	7	5	8	17
Energy & Control	2	3	11	3	3	3
High Frequency	1	2	7	2	2	4
Computer	0	1	8	0	0	1

Figure 2 shows the ratio of courses taken in a Signal processing field and Figure 3 shows the ratio of courses taken in a computer field. The computer field is different from other fields because it has high ratio of enrollment of courses throughout all terms. Electronic circuit has a very high ratio of course taken at 91%, in spite of subject importance being 3 points. Computer network is low by the ratio of courses taken at 42%, but subject importance is 10 points. Such courses could become target for change at the next course tree revision.

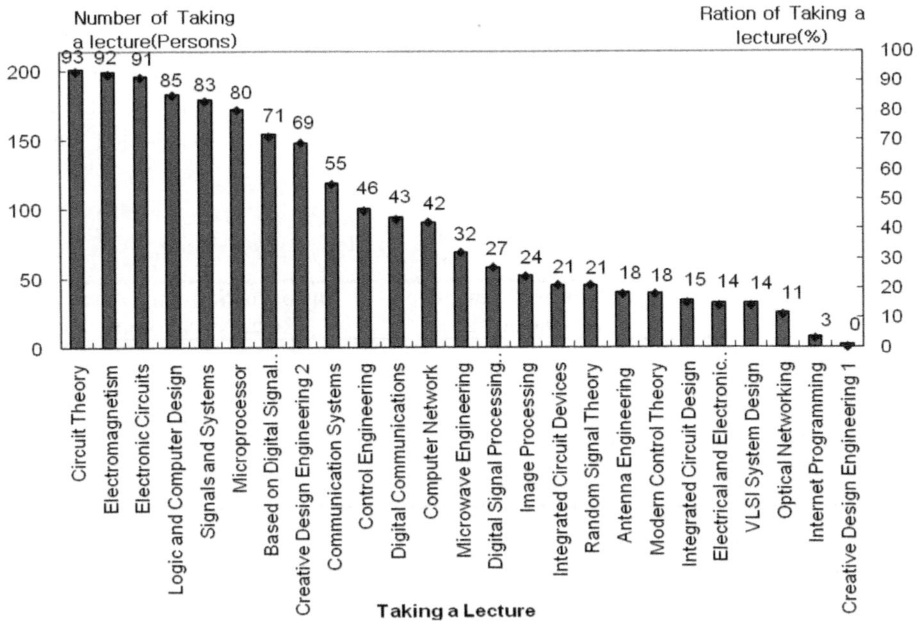

Fig. 2. Ratios of Taking Lectures in the Signal Processing Field

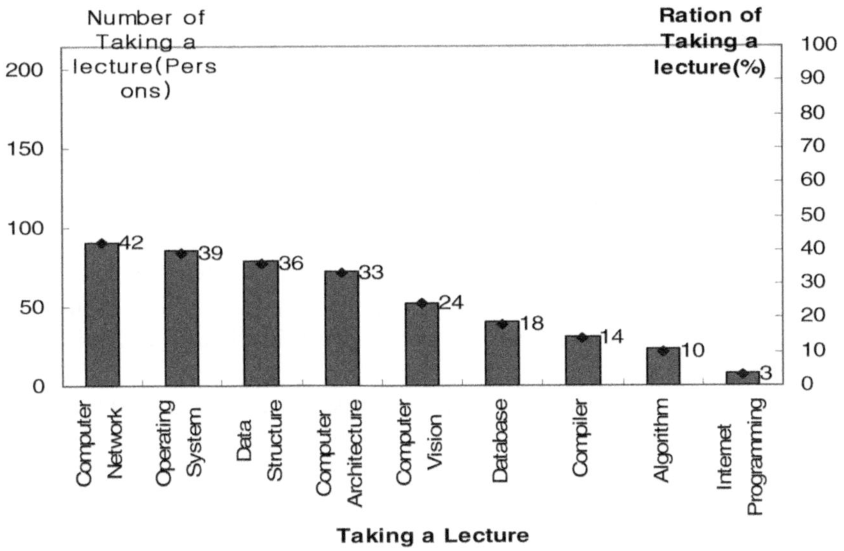

Fig. 3. Ratios of Taking Lectures in the Computer Field

4.2 Analysis Results of the Association Rule in Relation to Taking Lectures

This paper sets a minimum confidence level of 80%, and uses minimum support levels of 50%, 40%, and 35% to search for other types of pattern by Table 4. This constitutes a very high numerical value, and is unlike the general association rules for pattern analysis.

Table 4. Association Rules about Optional Subjects

	Number of Searching Association Rules	Number of Searching Association Rules get out course tree
min_sup : 50% min_conf : 80%	1004	0
min_sup : 40% min_conf : 80%	1652	13
min_sup : 35% min_conf : 80%	1787	78

For a support level of 35%, we found 1787 association rules and confirmed in the 20 association rules that 'Operating System' is included as following of association rule 78 between subjects that do not belong in same field in taking a course tree. Because 'Circuit theory', 'Electromagnetism', 'Electronic circuit' are included mainly to these rule, these subject may include 'Operating System' subject in new good handle field.

5 Conclusion and Discussion

The faculty system provided great opportunities that students could select and study courses of broad fields. As a result of it, however, a student had a lack of expert knowledge that a graduate should have had.

In the aspect of the faculty system, the course coordinator plays a significant role in building and managing curricula and finally counseling students with regard to them. However, the course coordinator cannot afford to advise students on which fields of their faculty fit them and which courses they have to take. Some previous academic administration management systems have a function which advises students for personal curricula.

We searched for relationships between subjects, using association rules, by mining data about the courses already taken by students, and comparing these to existing course trees. After analyzing a considerable volume of course attendance data, we applied an association rule to understand the link between subjects chosen with those proposed by faculty guidance advisors. As the result of examining the validity of this rule, we wish to apply to a revision enactment, or reference data, to the attending lecture tree.

References

1. Chu, K., et al.: Designing a Course Recommendation System on Web based on the Students' Course Selection Records. In: Kommers, P., Richards, G. (eds.) Proceedings of World Conference on Educational Multimedia, Hypermedia and Telecommunications, pp. 14–21 (2003)
2. Agrawal, R., Srikant, R.: Fast Algorithms for Mining Association Rules in Large Databases. In: Proceedings of the 20th International Conference on Very Large DataBases, pp. 478–499 (1994)
3. Chen, J.-S.M.-S., Yu, P.S.: An Effective Hash Based Algorithm for Mining Association Rules. In: Proceedings of ACM SIGMOD, pp. 175–186 (1995)
4. Queensland University of Technology, Manual of Policies and Procedures, Chapter B - Human resources, `http://www.mopp.qut.edu.au/B/B_03_05.html`
5. Mehmed, K.: Data Mining: Concepts, Models, Methods, and Algorithms. IEEE Computer Society, IEEE Press (2003)
6. Piatetsky-Shapiro, G.: Discover, Analysis, and presentation of strong rules. In: Piatetsky-Shapiro, G., Frawley, W.J. (eds.) Knowledge Discovery in Databases, pp. 229–238. AAAI/MIT press (1991)
7. Ivanto, I.J., et al.: Intelligent Online Academic Management System. In: Zhou, W., Nicholson, P., Corbitt, B., Fong, J. (eds.) ICWL 2003. LNCS, vol. 2783, pp. 320–326. Springer, Heidelberg (2003)
8. Liu, F., Moore, D.H.: GOPT-Resolution and Its Applications. In: Proceedings of the Eighth International Conference on Artificial Intelligence Applications, pp. 9–14 (1996)
9. La Trobe University., Course Finder, `http://www.latrobe.edu.au/courseDB/courseFinder/courseFilter.jsp`
10. Hanyang University. EzHub, `http://ezhub.hanyang.ac.kr`
11. Kopanakis, L., Theodoulidis, B.: Visual data mining modeling techniques for the visualization of mining outcomes. Journal of Visual Language and Computing, 543–589 (2003)

Agile Team Learning Model Based on Fast Task Mining

Xiaobo Yin[1], Guangli Zhu[1], and Li Feng[2]

[1] College of Computer Science and Engineering
Anhui University of Science and Technology, 232001, Huainan, China
[2] Propaganda Department
Huainan First People's Hospital, 232007, China
{xbyin,glzhu}@aust.edu.cn,
fl.hnfph@gmail.com

Abstract. Team learning needs explicit shared task and certain environment. In this paper, we presents an agile team learning model based on fast task mining (ATLM) that can be used with network environment and without more guidance. This model can improve the precision of knowledge acquisition and shorten the learning period. The learning process presented in ATLM can be applied in school education, corporate training, and spontaneous learning.

Keywords: team learning, agile team learning, task mining.

1 Introduction

Team learning is the process of working collectively to achieve a shared learning objective in a group [1]. Currently, team learning has been more popular by learning organizations, many researchers have contributed on the methods, model and environment of team learning. Kasl, E. et al [2] proposes a research-based model of team learning. Van Der Haar, S. et al [3] presents a shared mental models of the task and team. Marija Cubric [4] and Xie Kefan [5] describe the special team learning based on agile development principles. Peter M. Jansson et al [6] emphasizes that the learning environment could be created through engineering clinics.

However, team learning needs shared task and certain environment. Without explicit shared learning task or more guidance, the effort of team may be in vain. In this paper, we presents an agile team learning model based on fast task mining (ATLM) that can be used with network environment and without more guidance. This model can improve the precision of knowledge acquisition and shorten the learning period. The learning process presented in ATLM can be applied in school education, corporate training, and spontaneous learning.

The outline of this paper is as follows. In section 2, we propose an agile team learning model based on fast task mining. In section 3, we introduce the fast task mining method. In section 4, we describe an experimental application of team learning. Conclusions are given in section 5.

X. Luo et al. (Eds.): ICWL 2010 Workshops, LNCS 6537, pp. 328–335, 2011.

2 Agile Team Learning Model

Learning teams, for the most part, could not obtain the valuable and shared learning task until the learning objectives were obvious or instructors appeared. In this situation the team learning is passivity, lacking organization, planning or method. Therefore, we build the agile team learning model based on fast task mining (ATLM), in order to develop the learning method, shorten the learning period and improve the precision of knowledge acquisition.

As shown in Fig. 1, ATLM divides the whole process of team learning into three phases: (1) Information Acquisition, (2) Fast Task Mining, (3) Team Learning. The designs of each phase are listed as follows.

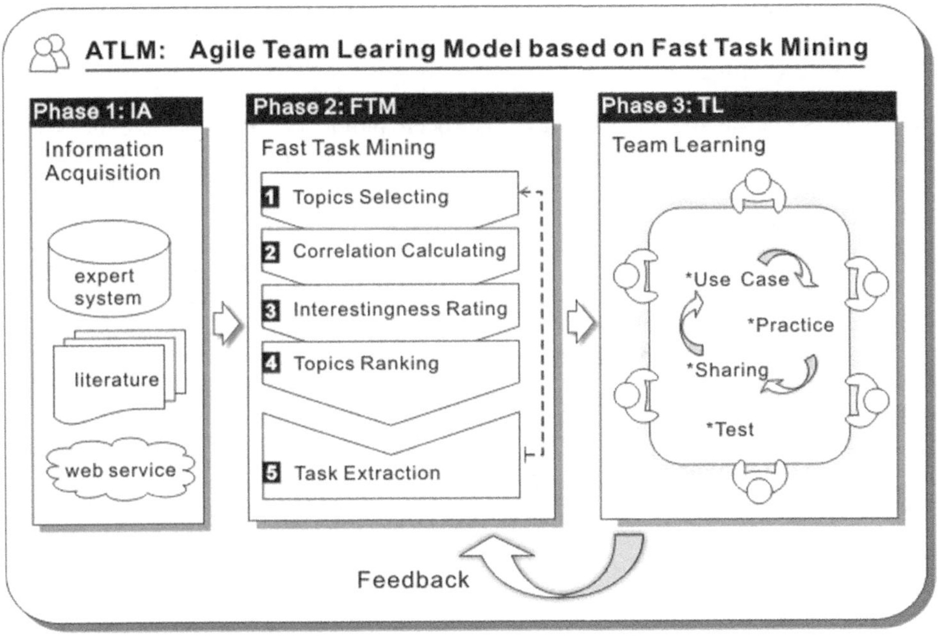

Fig. 1. Agile team learning model based on fast task mining (ATLM)

2.1 Information Acquisition (IA)

The preparation phase of team learning is IA. The goal of this phase is to acquire as much as possible the most relevant information. We recommend that all team members should collect initial information from current information platform, such as expert system, literature, and network services, etc., according to the learning courses (see Fig. 1). The work of this phase can be finished by members separately or together

2.2 Fast Task Mining (FTM)

Building shared vision is the third discipline of learning organizations [7]. If the team has the shared interesting learning task, in order to achieve this shared vision, members will self-conscious expression excellence, and constantly progress, active rather than passive dedication, and follow up.

Considering the importance and the interestingness of shared learning task, we built a FTM method to extract the shared task without any instructors. As shown in Fig. 1, the FTM method includes five steps as follow:

1) Topics Selecting
2) Correlation Calculating
3) Interestingness Rating
4) Topics Ranking
5) Task Extraction

The details of above steps will be described in section 3. The work of this phase requires teamwork.

2.3 Team Learning (TL)

As soon as the shared learning task has been build, TL phase should be started immediately. In order to accomplish the learning task quickly and accurately, four crucial steps (Use Case, Practice, Sharing, Test), which are shown in Fig. 1, are proposed as follows:

1) **Use Case.** Create according to the real projects or members' interests. Each use case focuses on describing how to achieve the knowledge points in learning task.
2) **Practice.** Team members should play different roles in each use case, and try to practice use case through teamwork. After that, they may exchange roles and practice again.
3) **Sharing.** Knowledge sharing is the important factor that can strives to increase learner engagement [8]. Team members should share achievements and complement skills for each other.
4) **Test.** Test is the final step of team learning, which can check learning effect and provide feedback.

Use Case, Practice and Sharing can make a cycle process until all use cases have been finished. Then, the team performance could be checked by the final test. If the learning effect had not been achieved, a quick decision should be made that whether to relearn again or go back to FTM phase.

3 FTM Method

After the initial information has been selected, the final shared learning task will be extracted by FTM method according to both importance and interestingness. The process of FTM method includes five steps, which are described as follows:

3.1 Topics Selecting

Each team member should give several topics obtained form all kind of information platforms. The topic that all members think it important and interesting should be selected. Then, a set of selected topics *SET1* will be built. *SET1* can be defined as

$$SET\ 1 = \{t_1, t_2, \cdots t_i, \cdots t_n\} \tag{1}$$

In equation (1), t_i is the selected topic and n is the number of selected topics.

3.2 Correlation Calculating

The importance degree of the selected topic can be represented by the correlation between the course subject and the selected topic. First, we extract the keyword of course subject (*Ws*) and the keyword of selected topic (*Wt*). Next, we use web searching engine to search *Ws* and *Wt* in curriculum related knowledge field such as wikis [4]. Then, the correlation between the course subject and the selected topic (CR_t) can be measured as follows:

$$CR_t = \log_2 \frac{P(Ws, Wt)}{P(Ws) \cdot P(Wt)} \tag{2}$$

In formula (2), *P(Ws)* is the total number of searched pages for *Ws*, *P(Wt)* is the total number of searched pages for *Wt*, *P(Ws,Wt)* is the total number of searched pages for both *Ws* and *Wt*.

3.3 Interestingness Rating

The interestingness of selected topic (I_t) can be calculated through team vote. First, each team member should vote for selected topics according to the personal interest. And then, I_t can be figure out as follows:

$$I_t = \sum_{i=1}^{m} V_i \tag{3}$$

In formula (3), m is the number of team members, Vi is a vote score of topic t from member i.

3.4 Topics Ranking

Which topic will be confirmed as key topic? Considering the importance and the interestingness of selected topics, first, the weight of topics should be measured aaccording to these two factors, then, topics need to be ranked according to the weight, next, the key topics could be confirmed by team members form the ranked topics. The process of this step is described as follows:

1) Calculate the weight of the selected topic (WT_t), which is defined as

$$WT_t = \frac{(\alpha^2 + 1) \cdot CR_t \cdot I_t}{\alpha^2 \cdot (CR_t + I_t)} \tag{4}$$

In formula (4), CR_t is the correlation between the course subject and the selected topic which can be obtained from formula (2), I_t is the interestingness rating of selected topic which can be obtained from formula (3), α is the weighting coefficient which can adjust the weight of CR_t and I_t.

2) Rank all selected topics according to topic's weight WT_t, and re-build a set of selected topics *SET2*, which is defined as

$$SET\ 2 = Rank\ (SET\ 1) = \{T_1, T_2, \cdots T_i, \cdots T_n\} \tag{5}$$

In equation (5), *SET1* is a set of selected topics from equation (1), n is the number of selected topics, T_i is the selected topic ordered by the topic's weight WT_t.
3) Build a set of key topics *SET3* which is a subset of selected topics *SET2*. According to topic's weight WT_t, *SET3* can be defined as

$$SET\ 3 = Key\ (SET\ 2) = \{K_1, K_2, \cdots K_i, \cdots K_m\} \tag{6}$$

In equation (6), *SET2* is a set of selected topics which is obtained from equation (5), K_i is the key topic selected from *SET2*, m is the number of key topics, m is less than the number of selected topics.

3.5 Task Extraction

Task extraction is the final step of FTK. The shared team learning task (*TASK*) should be build according to the combination of key topics. *TASK* can be expressed as

$$TASK\ = Extraction\ (SET\ 3) = \{TK_1, \cdots TK_j\} \tag{7}$$

In equation (7), *SET3* is the set of key topics which can be obtained form equation (6); TK_j is the optimization combination of key topics which is extracted by team members.

If the shared team learning task could not be confirmed by this step, we should return to the first step of FTM quickly to get a new set of selected topics.

4 Experiment

As a new team learning model, its feasibility and result need to be tested in practice. In this experiment, we focus on whether ATLM model can be used in corporation training programs.

Participants
Twenty-one new employees from maintenance department of Anhui GMP (Good Manufacturing Practices) enterprise completed the experiment.

Training Design
Participants were asked to learn the same course in 30 days. The course, which named as "GMP factory energy supply systems", is related to the professional knowledge which will be directly applied to their real works. But, no explicit learning task was given to them, and they must be examined by a skill test at the end of learning period.

Learning Conditions
Study area, environment, curriculum related data and information were provided as follows:

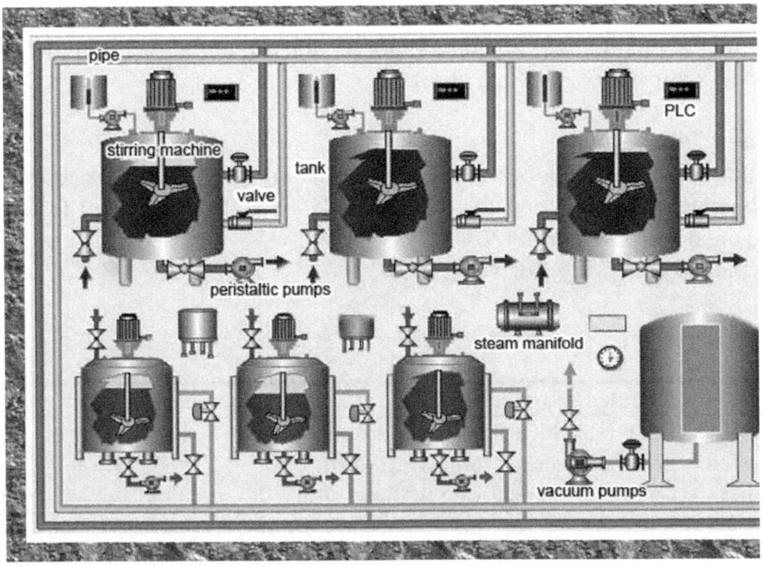

Fig. 2. The sketch map of energy supply workshop

✓ Meeting rooms having projector and network environment
✓ Energy supply workshop
The energy supply system composed by different equipments (e.g., vacuum pumps, stirring machine, tanks, peristaltic pumps, air compressor, steam manifold, PLC, valves, pipes), which can be seen in Fig. 2.
✓ Equipment SOP (standard operating procedure)
✓ SFC (shop floor control) manuals

Learning Process

Participants were divided into three learning teams, which have different learning process as follows:

✓ ***Team1.*** Seven participants volunteered to join Team1, which used ATLM-based learning method. ATLM is Agile Team Learning Model based on Fast Task Mining. First, team members spent 1 day to acquired primary information of energy supply system. Next, team spent 1 day to executive FTM process and built the shared learning tasks (e.g., process management, accident treatment, equipment maintenance, etc.). Then, use cases (e.g., steam supply, machine maintenance, power outages emergency, etc.) were created for team members to practice and share.
✓ ***Team2.*** Seven participants volunteered to join Team2, which used Project-based team learning method [9]. A professional instructor was assigned to train this team. The team learning was organized in meeting room and job site according to real projects in workshop.

- ✓ ***Team3.*** Seven participants volunteered to join Team3, which used collaborative learning method [10]. Team members organized the learning by dialogue, discussion, practice, sharing, etc.

Results and Discussion

The learning effects of three teams were examined by final test. As is shown in Table 1. The average score (76) and the pass rate (71%) of Team1 closed to the average score (85) and the pass rate (86%) of Team2, and were well above the average score (53) and the pass rate (43%) of Team3.

Table 1. The results of team test

team No.	team learning method	average score	pass rate
Team1	ALT-based learning without tutor	76	71%
Team2	project-based learning with tutor	85	86%
Team3	collaborative learning without tutor	53	43%

Comparing three groups of data, we find the instructor is very important for team learning. The reason is very simple, because the instructor could clear learning goals and provide direct guidance However, Team1 could also achieve good learning effect without any instructors. The reason is that Team1 could self-design learning tasks by using ATLM model under the network environment. Therefore, in the situation that no explicit learning task could be provided, ATLM is a good choice.

5 Conclusions

Team learning needs explicit shared learning task and certain environment. In this paper, we presents an agile team learning model based on fast task mining (ATLM) that can be used with network environment and without any instructors. The major contributions of our work include two aspects: 1) We build an agile team learning model, which can develop team members' teamwork ability and provoke their interest in learning process. 2) We propose a fast task mining method, which can improve the precision of knowledge acquisition and shorten the learning period. The learning process presented in ATLM can be applied in school education, corporate training, and spontaneous learning.

Acknowledgement

This Research work is supported by the Anhui university province-level natural science research project (project no. KJ2010B327) and the youth foundation of Anhui University of Science & Technology (finance no. QN200719). We thank some students for their contribution in programming. We also thank Professor Jingzhao Li for his precious proposal.

References

1. Decuyper, S., Dochy, F., Van Den Bossche, P.: Grasping the dynamic complexity of team learning: An integrative model for effective team learning in organizations. Educational Research Review 5(2), 111–133 (2010)
2. Kasl, E., Marsick, V., Dechant, K.: Teams as Learners: A Research-Based Model of Team Learning. The Journal of Applied Behavioral Science 33(2), 227–246 (1997)
3. Van Der Haar, S., Jehn, K., Segers, M.: Towards a model for team learning in multidisciplinary crisis management teams. International Journal of Emergency Management 5(3/4), 195–208, Inderscience (2008)
4. Cubric, M.: Agile learning & teaching with wikis: building a pattern. In: WikiSym 2008. ACM, New York (2008)
5. Kefan, X., Qian, W.: The Agile Team Learning in Unconventional Emergency Decision-making. In: Proceedings of the International Conference on E-Business and E-Government, pp. 1579–1583. IEEE, Los Alamitos (2010)
6. Jansson, P.M., Ramachandran, R.P., Schmalzel, J.L., Mandayam, S.A.: Creating an Agile ECE Learning Environment through Engineering Clinics. IEEE Transactions on Education 53(3), 455–462 (2010)
7. Senge, P.M.: The Fifth Discipline: The Art and Practice of the Learning Organization. Doubleday, New York (1990)
8. Chau, T., Maurer, F., Melnik, G.: Knowledge Sharing: Agile Methods vs. Tayloristic Methods. In: Proceedings of the Twelfth IEEE International, pp. 1080–1383. IEEE, Los Alamitos (2003)
9. Boss, S., Krauss, J.: Reinventing project-based learning: Your field guide to real-world projects in the digital age. International Society for Technology in Education, Eugene (2007)
10. Knapp, R.: Collective (Team) Learning Process Models: A Conceptual Review. Human Resource Development Review, 285–299 (2010)

Author Index

GPSR Compliance

The European Union's (EU) General Product Safety Regulation (GPSR) is a set of rules that requires consumer products to be safe and our obligations to ensure this.

If you have any concerns about our products, you can contact us on ProductSafety@springernature.com

In case Publisher is established outside the EU, the EU authorized representative is:

Springer Nature Customer Service Center GmbH
Europaplatz 3
69115 Heidelberg, Germany

Batch number: 10844619

Printed by Printforce, the Netherlands